PICTURED KNOWLEDGE

Copyright, 1916, by F. E. Compton & Company
Copyright, 1917, by F. E. Compton & Company
Copyright, 1919, by F. E. Compton & Company
Copyright, 1920, by F. E. Compton & Company

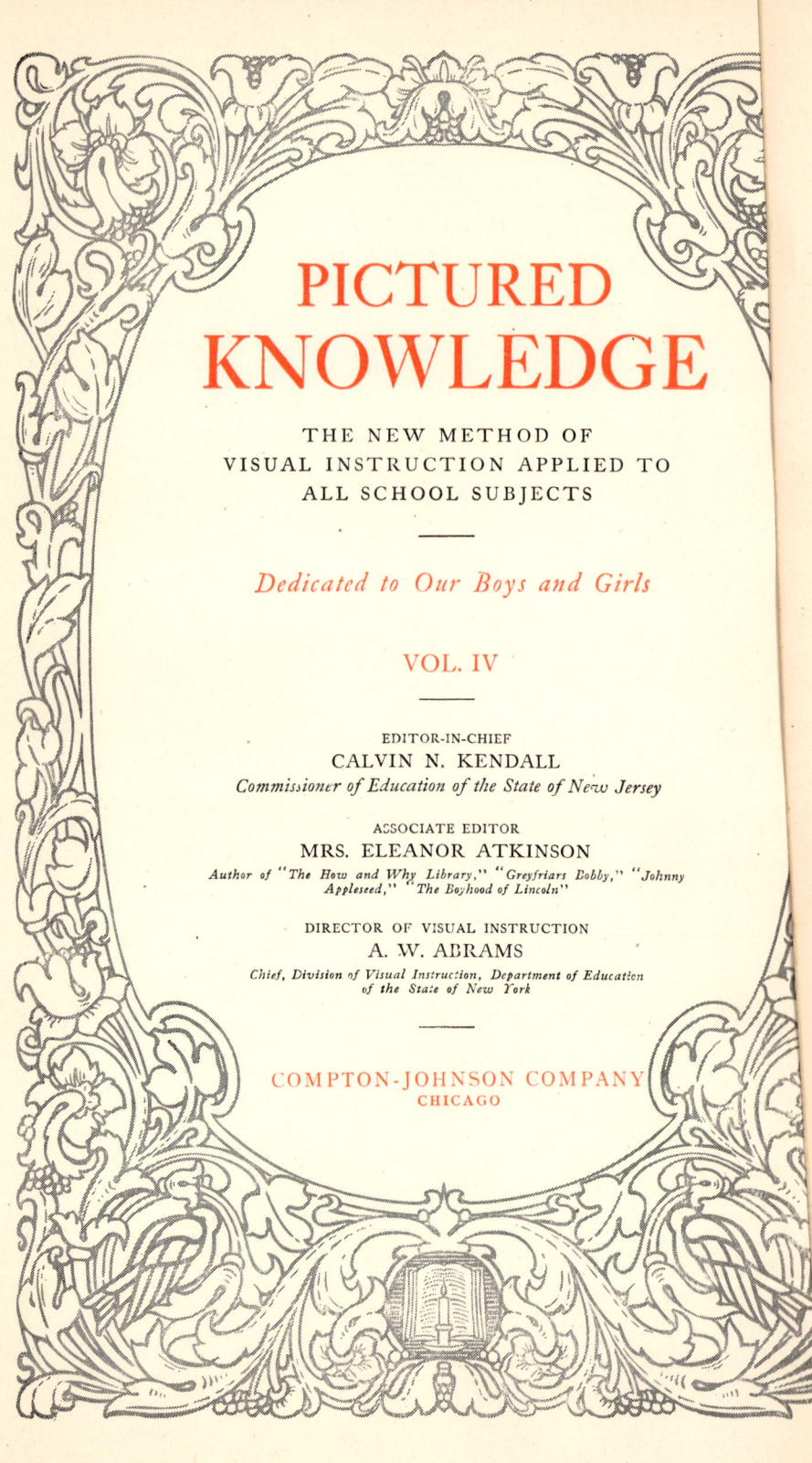

PICTURED KNOWLEDGE

THE NEW METHOD OF
VISUAL INSTRUCTION APPLIED TO
ALL SCHOOL SUBJECTS

Dedicated to Our Boys and Girls

VOL. IV

EDITOR-IN-CHIEF
CALVIN N. KENDALL
Commissioner of Education of the State of New Jersey

ASSOCIATE EDITOR
MRS. ELEANOR ATKINSON
Author of "The How and Why Library," "Greyfriars Bobby," "Johnny Appleseed," "The Boyhood of Lincoln"

DIRECTOR OF VISUAL INSTRUCTION
A. W. ABRAMS
Chief, Division of Visual Instruction, Department of Education of the State of New York

COMPTON-JOHNSON COMPANY
CHICAGO

LESSONS AT HOME AND AT SCHOOL
STORIES FOR CHILDREN

The Children's Home Library

"WHAT books should I buy for the children?"

That question is asked anxiously every day, by countless fathers and mothers. Kindergartners, teachers, librarians and city and state school superintendents have spent years in seeking the answer. Upon a few things they are all agreed. The books read in earliest childhood have a deep and lasting influence upon the character and should be as carefully chosen as the food a child eats. Second, the true, the good, and the beautiful can be made as interesting to the child as the weak and vicious.

Here's an Alice in Wonderland of a different sort than the one in the story—a little girl in the wonderland of books. If you have ever journeyed far into that wonderland, you know how truly thrilling it can be, what strange, interesting, jolly people you meet there and what pleasant surprises there are on every side.

The Best Books Not Expensive

It is impossible to give here a list of all the good books for children, for there are young people's reading rooms in the big city libraries, that have ten thousand titles on the shelves. But, in buying even a few, one will learn of others of the same character. City book stores and publishers will send catalogues on request by mail, and submit lists. The larger text-book publishers should not be overlooked, for many of the very best books for young children are the supplementary readers used in schools. But no school has them all, and they are not on sale in the book and department stores. From thirty to fifty cents brings many a careful selection of world-famous short stories, or reprint of a longer classic, within reach of people of small means. And they are better printed, illustrated and bound than most of the new

1143

"juveniles" that are offered for sale.

Very little folks must be amused in ways that will awaken the mind and stimulate self-activity. They have eager curiosity about this "brave new world." They love color, movement, adventure, fun. Mother Goose is baby's first book. It should be boldly illustrated with pictures of few details, and in the primary colors. A three-year-old child will soon learn the jingling rhymes and the pictures that go with them. Then come Aesop's Fables, the class fairy stories such as Red Riding Hood and The Three Bears, and the linen picture books of animals, birds, flowers, children, trains, ships and housekeeping.

Avoid the Cheap and Crude in Illustrations

Care should be taken to get the best pictures. All of these baby books are issued in many editions, most of them crude and in violent colors. And many mothers do not know that famous artists and clever minor ones have given their best talents to illustrating the classics of childhood. Walter Crane has made pictures for "Baby's Own Aesop" and for "The Best Nursery Tales and Rhymes." Kate Greenaway has given us her quaint alphabet book "A—Apple Pie," "The Pied Piper" and a number of other books. Helen Stratton has illustrated "Grimm's

Artists Who Draw for Children

If you have not read Oliver Goldsmith's "Vicar of Wakefield" you should do so at once. Here is a scene from it. The two pretty daughters of the old Vicar liked fine clothes as well as any girls, but their father thought their new gowns were too full in the skirt for modest, minister's daughters. To prove to him that they were not vain, they cut down the skirts and made clothes for their younger brothers out of the extra cloth. Here you see them cutting up the stylish, full skirts of which they were so proud and fitting a waistcoat made of one of them on their youngest brother. Don't you think they look a little sorrowful?

Fairy Tales"; Sir John Tenniel and Arthur Rackham, "Alice in Wonderland." "La Fontaine's Fables" inspired the best efforts of Boutet de Monvel. L. Leslie Brooke draws wonderful talking animals; Reginald Birch and Jessie Willcox Smith, graphic reproductions from old and modern masters are used to illustrate legend and biography. Bound volumes of the best magazines will make children familiar with the really good illustrators of the day. If brought up on such charming,

Shakespeare at Court

Here is Shakespeare as a young man, reciting a selection from his plays before Queen Elizabeth and her court. See how wrapped up in his subject he seems, forgetful of his surroundings. And notice the expression on the faces of his hearers—how moved they are, and how astonished at the things this wonderful young man is saying.

charming children; Howard Pyle the heroes of old romance. The best comic artists are Peter Newell, Gelett Burgess and Palmer Cox. Burgess' "Goops," Cox's "Brownies," Grover's "Sunbonnet Babies," Newell's "Topsys and Turvys" and Rose O'Neill's "Kewpies" are a delight to little folks and big. For older children nothing can surpass the delight of the "really, truly" Indians and cowboys of Frederick Remington, and the delicate nature drawings of A. B. Frost. Photo- delicate, truthful pictures, children will be indifferent to the vulgar scrawls of the Sunday supplement.

Little folks like "Peter Rabbit," "The Pinafore Palace" and "Posy Ring," by Kate Douglas Wiggin; "The Nursery Rhyme Book," of Andrew Lang; "The Hiawatha Primer," by Florence Holbrook. The first book of poetry is Stevenson's "Child's Garden of Verses," illustrated by Jessie Willcox Smith.

Many people are of the opinion that a child should not be given

PICTURED KNOWLEDGE

The Canterbury

Before Shakespeare wrote his great dramas, Chaucer gave us valuable pictures of the manners and customs of the times when he lived, in his "Canterbury Tales." The Tales are a series of stories told by a big party of people journeying together on a pilgrimage to the shrine of a saint. They are written in queer, old-fashioned English that is a little hard for us to understand today. You will read

linen books. They think the smallest child should be taught to be careful of books, to handle them only with clean hands, and never to mark, tear or cut them.

The First Four Years in School

It should be kept in mind that, until the fourth or fifth year in school, children's vocabularies are too limited for them to read many books readily. These are the years that the text-book publishers make special effort to supply a great variety of educative and interesting reading matter, in type suitable to little folks' eyes. The character of these books follows closely along the lines of the school courses, so parents should know just what interests are being awakened in a child as he passes through the grades.

In the very first year in school the child begins to get a background of biography and history and to observe nature with interest and intel-

Enlarging the Child's World

ligence. He hears about Indian and Puritan life; about Columbus, Washington and Lincoln; about Thanksgiving and Memorial Day; about animals and plants. Some day he will come home bursting with the news that "Eskimos live in snow houses! Did you know that, mama?" He is ready, then, for Mrs. Peary's story of her own "Snow Baby" and Lieut. Schwatka's "Children of the Cold."

He is soon ready for Andrew's "Seven Little Sisters" and "Children of Our Own and Other Lands" in this book; for stories of Hiawatha's childhood, for Kipling's "Just So" stories and the "Jungle Book"; for Uncle Remus; Scudder's Stories from the Arabian Nights; Brown's "Book of Saints and Friendly Beasts"; Baldwin's "Fifty Famous Stories."

Before a child is ten years old he should know all of the best fairy

STORIES FOR CHILDREN

Pilgrims

some of it when you study English literature in High School. These two pictures show us the pilgrims as they are riding along, laughing at each other's jokes, listening to stories and altogether having a very jolly time.

tales of Andersen, Grimm, Lang, Jacob's Celtic collections, Mabie's and Dasent's Norse tales, the Arabian Nights and Gulliver's Travels. The stories of Ulysses, King Arthur and other legendary heroes have been written by such distinguished people as William Morris, Howard Pyle, Hamilton Mabie and Sidney Lanier, and by such tried and true text-book authors as Baldwin. Every sort of heroes—of invention, exploration and discovery have been put into brief form and simple language. Hiawatha, Miles Standish and many short poems of Longfellow, Whittier and Tennyson can be read to children under ten. And in their libraries should be some good volume of selected verse such as "Poems Every Child Should Know," or "The Book of Famous Verse," by Miss Repplier.

Children's Heroes in Poetry

The Fascination of Fiction

Children *will* have stories—pure fiction. "Robinson Crusoe" is the boy's own book. That interest should be followed up by Dan Beard's books on things a boy can do. Girls adore Miss Alcott's wholesome story of home life, "Little Women." That can be followed by Lin Beard's books for girls, and little cook books. If you catch a boy reading a "yellow back" or cheap blood-and-thunder story give him Stevenson's "Treasure Island." That is as exciting as any dime novel, and it is such good literature that he will have a distaste for the cheap and vulgar. Read Stevenson's "Kidnapped" to him, Cooper's Indian tales and Howard Pyle's "Merry Adventure of Robin Hood." Cooper will lead naturally to Thompson Seton's animal books, Kipling, Uncle Remus, Olive Thorne Miller's bird books, and all the delightful out of doors. For pure romance children of ten will listen to Miss Mulock's "Little Lame Prince," Kingsley's "Water Babies," Carroll's "Alice in Wonderland,"

Famous Books for Young People

1147

Mrs. Wiggin's "Bird's Christmas Carol," Ouida's "Dog of Flanders," Eggleston's "Hoosier School Boy." Among the most wholesome of modern stories are "Mrs. O'Callaghan's Boys" and Mrs. Wiggin's "Rebecca of Sunnybrook Farm."

For Children from Ten to Twelve

Some children are more mature in mind than others. But before twelve most children will be doing a good deal of independent reading. *St. Nicholas* or *The Youth's Companion* should be subscribed for. The child should have, and know how to use, an unabridged dictionary and an encyclopedia adapted to his interests and needs. No one can know everything. More important is the ability to find what one wants to know, and teaching the use of reference works is now a part of the school curriculum.

At the age of ten or twelve, boys and girls begin to differ widely in their choice of reading. The boy's interests are adventurous and industrial, the girl's romantic and domestic. Boys are hero-worshippers. From Ulysses and King Arthur they should be led to brief lives of Columbus, Washington, Franklin, Paul Jones, Daniel Boone, Fulton. They should read Tappan's "American Hero Stories" and Roosevelt's

At the Adolescent Period

Milton, the Boy

In this picture you see the poet Milton as a boy of twelve. Such a beautiful, serious young face! As though he were already dreaming of the lofty poems he would write when he became a man!

"Heroes of American History." Girls will read Miss Alcott, Mrs. Burnett and Mrs. Wiggin.

As a boy passes through a dime novel stage, so a girl, a little later, usually has a sentimental period of reading silly romances. Then give her "Romeo and Juliet." Read it with her; read "Jane Eyre" and other really great love stories. "Evangeline" and "Enoch Arden" are examples.

How the School Introduces Children to Great Writers

The best authors are usually the simplest. It took Whitman to write

STORIES FOR CHILDREN

"O Captain! My Captain"; Browning, "The Pied Piper"; Barrie, "Peter and Wendy"; Hawthorne, "The Snow Image." By the end of the seventh year in school, or at thirteen years of age, children have Burroughs, Dickens, Scott, Lamb and many others. At home these new interests should be fed. Most fourteen-year-old boys and girls will enjoy Hawthorne's "House of Seven Gables," Eliot's "Silas Marner,"

John Milton was a serious Puritan poet who lived in the time of Cromwell's Revolution in England. His "Paradise Lost" is the most majestic composition in the English language. He has also written some beautiful shorter poems. L'Allegro for example, which is about
"Quips, and cranks, and wanton wiles,
Nods, and becks, and wreathed smiles"
is one of them.
When Milton was old he went blind and all his work had to be dictated to one of his three daughters.

learned something of fully fifty great writers. Careful selections have been made for them from all the American and English poets and story-tellers, essayists, books of travel, biography and the natural sciences. Before sixteen, literary taste has been formed, and an incredible amount of reading done. It is important, then, that children should have the best.

The Upper Grades and High School

In the upper grammar grades children get bits of Hawthorne, Dickens' "Chimes," "Christmas Carol" and "Cricket on the Hearth." They will read Scott's "Tales of a Grandfather," Bennett's "Master Skylark," Kipling's "Captains Courageous," Hughes' "Tom Brown's Schooldays," Barrie's "Peter and Wendy" and "A Window in Thrums," Cooper's "Spy" and "Last of the Mohicans," Van Dyke's "Story of the Other Wise Man," Mark Twain's "Tom Sawyer" and such novels of times and manners as "The Vicar of Wakefield" and

"Uncle Tom's Cabin."

A good introduction to Shakespeare is through "Lamb's Tales." Historical romances such as "Ben Hur," "The Last Days of Pompeii" and "A Tale of Two Cities" should lead to the boy's own historian, Francis Parkman. In nature books Kipling, Thompson Seton, Long, Sharp and Mrs. Miller should lead to Burroughs, John Muir and Thoreau.

Good Books for Little Citizens

There are certain books that every American boy and girl should read, to learn what a privilege it is to be a citizen of the United States, and living in this great age of discovery, invention and freedom. These are Hale's "Man Without a Country," Myra Kelly's "Little Citizens" and "Little Aliens," Booker T. Washington's "Up From Slavery," Helen Keller's "Story of My Life," Mary Antin's "Promised Land," Jacob Riis' "The Making of an American" and Jane Addams' tender social studies of the lives of the poor in great cities.

Parents will have to take some pains to discover new books that are worth while. The advertisements of publishers and advice of friends are not reliable guides. A literary review, such as *Review of Reviews, Current Opinion, The Nation, The Dial,* or daily papers that give special expert attention to books, should be taken. There always are a few living writers for children from whom a new book is an event; and now and then an unknown writer appears with a book that the world is unwilling to lose. The best books, as a rule, make their way slowly. A "best seller" is apt to disappear quickly. A new book, one that is unknown and that has not been approved by educators, should be read by the parent or teacher before it is given to a child. Remember, all old books are new to children.

Portia

Perhaps you have read Portia's speech in "The Merchant of Venice"—how she defended her husband's friend against the revengeful Shylock. Here is one artist's idea of her (Shakespeare tells us she was fair-haired and blue-eyed). She is sweet and serious, thoughtful and noble; her fine character is revealed in her face.

LESSONS AT HOME AND AT SCHOOL
PAGEANTRY

How to Give a Pageant
Inspiring Feature of School and Community Life

The Minuet of Our Forefathers

This picture shows a pageant given at Bennington, Vermont, in which the young people danced the minuet on the green just as they used to do in Colonial days. Notice how the gallant young gentlemen make an archway with their swords above the gracefully moving figures of the ladies.

WHEN we see what children can do in various forms of dramatization in the ordinary life of the school, it becomes evident that all that is needed in any community to introduce the delight and inspiration of pageantry is the will to do it. Never before have there been such opportunities to study the principles of pageantry. The movies are a continual pageant—not always artistic, but full of good suggestions as to acting and playing a whole story by movement and gesture. If the wide ambition for the stage were directed into local pageantry, it would add greatly to the joy and profit of community life and save many disappointments.

Festivals and holidays offer some of the best opportunities for either indoor or outdoor pageantry—May Day, Harvest Home, Hallowe'en, Christmas, Washington's Birthday, Fourth of July, Thanksgiving.

Nearly every town has one or

Pageantry and the Movies

more heroes in its history, whose story would furnish the foundation for a pageant; and there are Indian legends in the history of nearly every community if you will go back far enough in local records or in the memories of old residents. Our story of the Indians in the History series is full of suggestion for similar pageantry.

Rich Material Near at Hand

The service of the local librarian will be invaluable. The librarian not only knows the material in the public library—local histories and documents—but will be helpful in the location of other public records, and nearly every town has one or more old settlers who know the traditions and who have probably collected relics that will be of service.

The educational value of a pageant—and its educational value is great—depends, of course, upon historical accuracy. Accurate information is to be found in these town records, acts of legislation, court decisions, newspapers of the time dealt with, county histories, etc.

The pageant is pre-eminently fitted for welcoming home a hero, opening a fair, celebrating a victory, inaugurating a public enterprise, observing an anniversary. Uncle Sam's birthday is an especially appropriate season for Americanizing the foreign-born element by teaching the meaning of liberty, equality, fraternity, through a reproduction of the struggles of those who fought for the faith. Any city in the United States may give a patriotic pageant if a local area at least two hundred feet square can be found adjoining a lake or ample river. Take a few of the most salient events in American history—the coming of Columbus, arrival of the Pilgrims, signing of the Declaration; introduce one or two local scenes bearing on national affairs; find an Indian legend connected with the locality; call out a detail from the Grand Army; enlist representatives from various nationalities which colonize in every city for a suite of folk dances; give a sumptuous court scene in one of the countries from which America was peopled, introducing Henry the Fourth of France, Queen Elizabeth or George III; as a finale let Uncle Sam review the players and The Goddess of Liberty lead the entire gathering in singing the "Star Spangled Banner."

Good Subjects for Pageants

First Steps in Preparing a Pageant

As soon as the project of giving a pageant is decided, the best thing to do is to call a joint mass-meeting and announce that some prominent pageant author or director will speak, to point out the possibilities of that particular locality. From this assembly, committees may be chosen, for attendance of those present indicates an active interest in the project. Several committees are necessary if the pageant is a large one—an executive committee, a committee of finance, of publicity, (including the programs) of costumes, of music and dancing.

The Writing of the Play

In every community there are people who, while they are not poets, have imagination which can be applied to shaping an episode in the life of the community into a pageant. The writing of the pageant may be done by one person or several collaborating, or a committee working under the direction of a

PAGEANTRY

chairman; but the chairman must have proved himself or herself capable of directing, and should make a careful study of pageantry.

Let the plot be simple, with as few scenes and with as little dialogue as possible. Remember that the actors in a pageant are to be seen rather than heard. There is little opportunity for effective dialogue.

The Site, the Scenery, and the Stage

In selecting a site for a pageant, its adaptation to the character of the scene in the pageant should be carefully considered. If the background is a far-off vista, one of the entrances should be up this vista. A steep hill or a rocky cliff is the ideal background for action of a pictorial character. Rocks and shrubbery in the middle ground should be related, both to the action and to the grouping. All the fore stage should be made level and cleared of things that will shut out the view. Dancing is an important feature of pageantry, and you cannot dance on rough ground. Do not make the mistake —as many do—of building a wooden platform in the foreground. The element of the picturesque is fundamental in pageantry; and a platform is not picturesque. The green fields, the rocks, the woods, are the stage, and there should be as little suggestion of the indoor theater as possible.

Pageants have been given in a clearing in the deep woods, as at Peterboro, N. H.; on the fair grounds, as at Oxford, Mass.; on the military parade ground, as at St. Augustine; on the college campus, as at Charlottesville, Va.; on the town common, as at Warwick, Mass. An open field bordered by woods is desirable. Hemlock or cedar trees may be effectively set up by way of landscape gardening.

The Selection of a Site

And here is a "don't" for indoor pageantry which needs emphasizing. Don't hang a large flag in the center of the background. This is misdirected patriotism. The red, white, and blue of the flag are too belligerent, too conspicuous, to blend with anything else. Unless the story requires a flag, confine this form of decoration to the walls of the room.

Unwise Use of the Flag

Put your scenes as close to the audience as possible and let the space in which the performance takes place be approximately that of an assembly hall at school. Use your supernumeraries as spectators who form an enclosing wall on three sides. Such properties as you have to have—tables, chairs, etc.—may be brought on and carried off again at the end of each scene.

The Costumes of the Pageant

In costuming the pageant there are certain standard types of dress for each period. The Norsemen, Indians, explorers, Puritans, Quakers, Cavaliers, Revolutionary patriots, 1812 soldiers, frontiersmen, Jesuits, Civil War veterans—all easily identified. Good books about costumes, are "Two Centuries of Costume in America," by Alice Morse Earle; "Historic Dress in America," by Elizabeth McLellan; "Costumes for Dramatic Festivals," by C. D. Mackay; "Chats on Costumes," by G. N. Read; "Dress Design," by Talbot Hughes. Local artists should advise on the color schemes which may be very beauti-

Standard Types of Dress

ful either by striking contrasts or subtle harmonies. Delicate shadings of browns, yellows, grays, and greens for fairies are charming. Groups of industrious and willing townswomen velvets you do not require either silk or velvet. For velvets and other heavy cloths use cambric or canton flannel. The cheapest grades of cheese cloth are soft, and hang well.

The Pageant of the Year

A beautiful Pageant of the Year was given by the Brookline, Massachusetts, High School. The picture shows the members of the cast on the stage of the Assembly Room. In the center of the group, at the back, is Father Time. You can tell what month each girl represented by the sign of the Zodiac. The first on your left as you look at the picture is May, represented by the sign of the Twins. Next comes June, represented by the sign of the Cancer. Then in order, the Lion, July (represented by his tail); the Virgin, August; the Balance, September; the Scorpion, October; the Archer (two arrows), November; the Goat, December; the Water Bearer (represented by the wave-like lines), January; Pisces (two fish joined together), February; the Ram (represented by his face and horns), March; the Bull, April.

should gather for social sewing bees. Home-made costumes are best. Elaborate suits may be hired for two dollars per day.

For costumes of different periods consult also reproductions of paintings, statuary and pictures of historic relics relating to the period to be shown in the pageant. The penny reproductions of paintings are of great value. Histories to be found in the local library are full of valuable illustrations, such as those in our Stories of History.

To get the effect of rich silks and

For lace use ordinary netting. For costumes of stiff material use burlap. Stencil or paint this burlap to imitate brocades and embroideries. Chintzes are useful for 18th Century dresses; canton crepe for soft and clinging gowns. *Rich Effects With Cheap Materials* For armor use burlap. Coarse knitted or crocheted goods serve excellently for chain mail. A derby hat with the rim cut off can easily be converted into a knight's helmet of the simpler sort. Make the more picturesque shapes of cardboard. Paint

PAGEANTRY
Pageants as Teachers of History

Float in Historic Pageant, Showing Building of First Church in 1701

Raising the First Flag on an American School House
(From a pageant given at Colerain, Massachusetts.)

PICTURED KNOWLEDGE

The Pageant of

This pageant was given at Richmond, Virginia. Compare these figures with those in Sargent's Frieze of the young women have reproduced the artist's great work. In the center is Moses with the tablets of the law. (seated), Hosea, Amos, Nahum, Ezekiel, Daniel (with the scroll), Elijah, Joshua (drawing his sword), Jeremiah,

armor, mail and helmet with aluminum powder mixed with glue. The glue must be thin and hot. The Indian's buckskin suit can be made with either wool or cotton "ratteen," and the bead work and other trimmings painted on with oil colors.

In all costumes avoid unnecessary detail. Remember that these details are lost on a distant audience.

Properties of all kinds, except furniture, can be made in the carpenter shop or in the manual training department—spears, swords, bows and arrows, shields, guns. Paint with gold, silver or aluminum. Borrow historic relics, such as spinning wheels and musical instruments, from people in the community.

The Color Question

A word more on the color question. In deciding upon colors and color combinations, remember that these are to be seen in the open, under sunlight and with masses of green all around. Ruby red, red orange, are good colors—and so on through the scale. Never use black. For dark colors use blue or dark brown. Pure white is also very effective from a pageantry standpoint,

1156

PAGEANTRY

the Prophets

Prophets, a picture of which you no doubt have in your High School room. You will see how remarkably the The first figure on the extreme left, as you look at the picture, is Zephaniah. Next in order are Joel, Obadiah Jonah, Isaiah (with both arms raised), Habakkuk, Micah (hand at brow), Malachi, Zechariah.

as you can see from watching the players in a tennis game.

In Indian costumes use warm brown. For head dresses, wine red; and remember that the Indian's sense of color was barbaric and he liked color contrasts of vivid hues for "full dress" occasions.

For mountain spirits that will "look the part" use deep blues or purples and a few greys. The "styles" in wood nymphs run to greens and browns, with touches of autumn colors. In dressing flower spirits be careful; do not make them

The Indians and the Spirits

too bright or you will interfere with your general color plan. In the use of two or more tints in the same costume let these tints gradually fade into one another—no sharp contrasts.

In the costumes of the men of the 17th Century the distinctive colors were brown and silver. The women dressed in grey and neutral colors, with an occasional sharp contrast in apron or petticoat.

Music and Dancing

Music is an important part of community expression because it is

1157

The Mother Goose Procession

This is a Mother Goose procession in a pageant given at Greensboro, N. C. Do you notice in the procession the figure of the little man who went to London to get him a wife? You remember, he was a bachelor and lived by himself, but the rats and mice led him such a life that he resolved on matrimony, because a wife is supposed to know how to get rid of rats and mice, as well as everything else about housekeeping. He found the London streets so broad and the lanes so narrow, that he brought his wife home in a wheelbarrow.

the most readily appreciated, without training or education, of all the fine arts. Orchestral music should be, in part at least, composed for the occasion by working out special motifs, as the forest motif in the Redwood pageants of California; the mountain motif at Thetford, Vt.; the life-saver motif at Cape Cod. The orchestra should be screened by shrubbery or placed in a sunken pit. There must be a leader of vocal music, as old favorite songs and hymns are always happily introduced and may be sung by the entire company.

Character of the Music

The lyric side of pageantry appears in the dance. The language of action is most readily understood by all classes. The rhythmic dance makes an elemental appeal, developing elasticity of body and spontaneity of movement. In the pageant are the folk dances, collective social dances, descriptive dances, symbolic dances and solo dances. The folk dances include Italian Tarantella, Portuguese chamarita, Irish reel, Scotch fling, Spanish fandango, Polish mazurka and so on. Books on dancing are "The Folk Dances for Schools," by Elizabeth Burchenal; "The Folk Dance Book," by C. Ward Crampton; "Dramatic Games and Dances," by Caroline Crawford; "The Festival Book," by Jeanette E. C. Lincoln; "Play Songs," by Alys E. Bentley. The interludes of the pageant are often used for symbolic dancing to bridge over the different episodes.

Place of the Rhythmic Dance

Getting the People Out

Publicity consists of newspaper

The Old Woman Who Lived in a Shoe

PAGEANTRY

Greek Dancers in Pageant of the Tree, Boston

"The language of action is most readily understood by all classes. The rhythmic dance makes an elemental appeal, developing elasticity of body and spontaneity of movement."

Advertising the Pageant — advertising, posters, and post cards. Descriptive circulars should be sent out, about a month before the production, to prominent citizens within the automobile radius. Special artistic stationery should be designed for the occasion. Watch fobs, buttons, banners, are sometimes used. An old stage coach full of colonial dames is good advertising on the day of the "show." Uncle Sam striding through the streets has been tried successfully.

The Day of Presentation

The day of presentation is a busy one for the master. He must be at a point of vantage. A conning tower is sometimes erected from which to direct the performance. *Necessity of Rehearsals* — Several rehearsals should be held, and one, at least, on the pageant grounds so that the players may become familiar with the environment. A decrepit piano may be kept under a temporary shed. Some pageants have been whipped together in two weeks. Two months is short enough time. Clock-work precision comes from repeated rehearsals.

A Word to the Players

Just a word about the acting. The actors are, of course, amateurs, and it is a very common fault of amateur actors to be interested only in their parts. You can see that each is waiting until his cue comes and is not particularly interested in what the others are saying. In real life this is bad manners. On the stage it is bad acting, but particularly in a pageant, because in the pageant there are no "star" parts. The size of the pageant stage makes group acting a necessity.

Shades of facial expression and

1159

slight gestures are lost on a distant audience.

In reproducing the life of any period, careful study should be made of details of the manners of the time. Good historic novels, to which the librarian can direct you, will give a graceful upward movement of the fingers. The gentleman extending and the gentleman receiving the courtesy bowed, the latter taking a small pinch between his thumb and finger. The owner of the snuff box then transferred it to his left hand,

Greek Pageant Given at Nashville, Tenn.

you what you want. Taking snuff, for example, sounds like a very simple operation—but not so. Among the aristocrats of colonial times taking a pinch of snuff was almost as elaborate as a state ceremonial. It was always offered in the right hand. The lid was struck open by took a pinch himself, and again they bowed. The lid was then snapped to, the snuff inhaled by both simultaneously, with grace and delicacy of movement. Then each flicked his shirt frills and waistcoat with his lace handkerchief—and the thing was done! A great deal of ceremony, but therein lies the beauty.

Only a Pinch of Snuff But—!

LESSONS AT HOME AND AT SCHOOL
TRAINING IN ENGLISH

Home Training in the Mother Tongue

You see they are all alike—children all over the world. It's easy to talk—their little tongues are going most of the time—but when it comes to writing—particularly when it comes to writing "compositions" and things like that, it's different.

These are little French children in a French school, and the picture, which was painted by Jean Geoffroy, as you already know from your picture study in school, is called "Composition Day."

"SHE'S little, but she's sweet, and absolutely without guile. I think we ought to have her."

"Is 'guile' the same as guilt?" inquired Emma Jane Perkins.

"Yes," the president answered, "exactly the same, except one is written and the other spoken language. Written language is for poems and graduations and occasions like this—kind of like a best Sunday-go-to-meeting dress that you wouldn't like to go blueberrying in, for fear of getting it spotted."

So spoke Rebecca, one of the delightful children written about by Kate Douglas Wiggin.

"Her pencil moved as easily as her tongue, and no more striking simile could possibly be used. Her handwriting was not Spencerian; she had neither time, nor patience, it is to be feared, for copy book methods, and her unformed characters were frequently the

Learning to Write by Writing

1161

despair of her teachers, but write she could, write she would, write she must, and did, in season and out; from the time she made pot hooks at six, till now, writing was the easiest of all possible tasks—."

In these quotations we have the leading ideas set forth in hundreds of books about the use of English, and, if properly interpreted, more sound sense than some of the books exhibit.

Five Principles of Training in English

Broadly speaking, these ideas may be summarized thus:

1. The use of English involves speaking and writing.
2. Ordinarily, written English is more formal than spoken English.
3. Speaking and writing are easy when one has a motive or purpose in expressing his thoughts.
4. Ease in writing comes by use and habit.
5. Attention to penmanship is of secondary importance.

The child learns to speak English by imitation. He imitates what he hears in the home, and at play with other children. If he hears a large vocabulary, accurate pronunciation and enunciation, and correct grammatical construction, his speech reflects all these good qualities as a *habit*. If he hears their opposites he gradually builds up habits that may never be broken. Stilted language *Habit Governed by Example* is far from being desirable in children or anybody else, but there is no need of avoiding it by going to the opposite extreme of slovenliness; children can remain child-like and form good habits of speech. The formation of good habits cannot be begun too early, and there is small danger of too much insistence on reasonable standards of English speech. Until the child goes to school the home is responsible for what he learns. The responsibility is largely one of giving him an opportunity to imitate good models.

Home training can be more useful than most school training; first, because in the home the training can be directed to one child at a time, while in school the large class is the unit nearly always; second, because in most schools there is *Why Home Training is Necessary* far too little conscious attempt to train children in correct habits of speech. True, many teachers, more or less insistently, correct errors as the children make them, but in most schools the children in grade eight are making the errors made in grade four. In school we have long attempted to teach children to write and spell, frequently with gratifying results, but it has been done at the expense of oral expression. Considering that most adults write only to write letters and that seldom does one spell orally, while talking is the one thing everybody does, we have put the emphasis of our instruction in the wrong place. The ears are not tuned up to hearing their own errors.

The child's earliest training, then, is to hear good English. As early as he can be interested, read aloud to him. Begin with Mother Goose and *Reading Aloud, Story Telling* keep right on, every night for years. No parent will have difficulty in finding suitable material, as scores of good reading lists have been published and hundreds of good volumes edited for just this purpose.

Acquire the art of story-telling, if you do not possess it. It is valuable training for both parent and child. As early as possible have the child tell the stories read and told to him. Repeat until they are his permanent possessions.

Encourage him to play his stories. This is best done when there are two or more children habitually playing together. My little girl and her playmate have played at being everything from "a wild hop-toad." to colonists in Plymouth.

Memorizing selections from good literature adapted to children's taste, interest and capacity is a valuable aid in fixing habits of correct diction. Most children take to such exercise readily, and as they grow in ability get more and more pleasure from it.

Memorizing Good Selections It was suggested above that many good stories should be retold until the child knows them; let us add, until he can repeat them. "To endear by repetition; to accumulate a stock of old familiar songs that graft themselves deep in the affections and reveal gradually, as the child grows, their music and meaning"—this is a worthy and attainable aim in every home.

Select for memorizing only prose and poetry that are good and worth remembering. Reject the puerile and "jingly." Such selections are found in too many school readers, although there has been a marked improvement in recent years. In nearly every public library can be found excellent compilations of verse and prose for home use with children.

Every parent wishing to train children in English will do well to study these books: *Self-Cultivation in English,* George H. Palmer; *How to Tell Stories to Children and Stories to Tell to Children,* Sara Cone Bryant; *Graded Poetry Readers,* Blake-Alexander; *The Teaching of English,* Chubb. (First eight chapters.)

The child's free self-expression is developed best by drawing upon his own personal experience. That is what the youngest child knows best and can talk about best. Imagination follows experience directly. Reproduction has to do largely with what lies outside of the personal experience of children, to things that they really do not know. Memory is the principal factor in reproduction. Experience and imagination have little to do with it. It is, therefore, the least profitable field for children's free expression, and should be sparingly used.

Oral composition, as the term is here used, means a great deal more than ordinary talking or conversation, which as often as not is fragmentary and disconnected. By oral composition is meant a body of connected speech, large enough in scope *Oral and Written Composition* to demand attention to its structure and form. Development will, of course, be gradual. But there will be no improvement at all, unless children are habituated from the first to be critical of their spoken English, in so far, at least, as the more flagrant mistakes in syntax are concerned, and the more fundamental matters of sentence structure and use of connectives.

When the child has learned to read and write, some time every day should be given to drill in speaking. For want of a better term we can call this oral composition. The aims *Drill in Speaking* of such work are stated in the preceding section. Just as soon as possible connect this with written expression. (See "Writing English," following.)

Remember that the vital thing to work for is correct habits of speech;

be watchful of errors, and pleasantly persistent in correcting them. When a child's ears are tuned up to hearing his own errors the battle for good speech is half won.

Mistakes Commonly Made

It may be worth while to note here a few common errors to be avoided. The parent who eradicates these from children's speech will be able to correct others as they appear.

1. In use of verbs:

sit and *set*
lie and *lay*
is and *are*
there is and *there are*
was and *were*
see, saw, and *seen*
do, did, done
draw, drew, drawn
throw, threw, thrown
show, showed, shown
eat, ate, eaten
grow, grew, grown
blow, blew, blown
freeze, froze, frozen
teach and *learn*
may and *can*
Use of *hadn't ought*

2. Pronouns:
(a) Nominative forms after *is, are,* etc., as *It is me,* for *It is I. It was her,* for *It was she.*
(b) Relative *who* instead of *whom* when used as an object.
(c) *Them* for *those.*
(d) Use of *yourn, hisn,* etc.
(e) When the personal pronoun is unnecessary in expressions such as "John, he went."

3. Use of double negatives, as:
I didn't do nothing.
I haven't hardly any.
I hain't got no knife.

4. Miscellaneous mistakes:
to home for *at home.*
yep or *yeh,* for *yes.*
what, as in "The pencil what I brought."
good for *well.*
don't for *doesn't.*
Improper or superfluous use of *got,* as "I haven't got the book."
Use of *ain't, hain't,* etc.
Use of *like* for *as.*
talkin', writin'

It may not be easy to train children in writing English in the home, but in many instances the difficulties are due more to a lack of plan and definite object than to inherent difficulties.

The child's thoughts often run ahead of his fingers, because he has to remember so many things. His attention is divided between what he wishes to write and the manner of writing, so that he attempts less than he can, and frequently would like to perform. Gradually he forms the habit of being satisfied with low standards of thought content, and manner of expression.

The mechanics of writing include: (a) Penmanship. (b) Spelling. (c) Punctuation. (d) Certain formalities regarding capitals, indentation of paragraphs, and the like.

Written expression should, during the early years, be based on oral expression. Seldom, if ever, should a child attempt to write anything he has not thought out and expressed orally. By training a child to talk *First Oral,* in clear-cut sentences and *Then Written* then to write what he *Expression* has spoken, his ear is trained, his power to express increases, his habit of thinking before speaking or writing is cultivated. Both in speaking and in writing, children frequently begin a sentence without knowing how it will end, or what is to come between the beginning and the end. This mistake should certainly be avoided during the time allotted for training in English. Granted that certain technicalities must be mastered and require constant drill, never lose sight of the fact that the most important aim in writing is to have something to say, and to say it in a way that will interest the reader.

Things that happen in the home, in the school, on the playground;

the life of his pets and his life with his pets; things the child observes about plants and insects in Nature Study, in school or home gardening; the books he reads, the books his mother reads to him and the things read aloud to the class in school, the lessons in History and Geography—all these furnish subjects for expression, oral and written, and the inspiration to express.

The study of pictures, now so common in the schools, is another rich source for composition material. Let the child tell in words what the pictures say to him. Select pictures where the interest centers around two to five individuals. They should be pictures of action, showing people doing things which the child can readily understand, and should be large enough so that all the members of the class can see it. One picture may be used for an entire class, or there may be a number of pictures. Vary the method. Where all express what they see in one picture, there are valuable opportunities for comparison in observation and expression. The use of several pictures gives variety.

The best way to teach children penmanship in the home is to provide wall space for a blackboard and charts, supply chalk, paper and pencils, encourage them to imitate models, and answer their questions. A blackboard with script alphabet at the top can be purchased at small cost. Two charts, one with capital letters in script, about four inches tall, the other with small letters of proportionate size, can be bought of any school supply house. Keep these before the child daily, let him refer to them constantly, encourage him to write, and he will soon memorize the letter forms and acquire reasonable skill in using them.

Unfortunately great numbers, possibly a majority, of children taught in public schools have come to regard writing English as an irksome task, because of too great insistence on penmanship of particular quality or style. *Aim Only at a Good Plain Hand* Legible handwriting is desirable for everybody; "copy-book" standards are of small value to anybody except those few people who earn a living as clerks and copyists. If such standards are needed in one's daily work, they can be attained by concentrated, specific training for that purpose, but to demand them of all children, knowing full well that little folks cannot attain them except at a sacrifice of vastly more important ends, is absurd.

Handwriting is largely a matter of muscular control. The degree of control necessary to approximate copy-book standards can be obtained in children between six and twelve years of age, except in rare instances, only by extraordinary care and patience. Every parent knows the awkward age between twelve and sixteen; often a period of rapid growth, the muscles lengthen rapidly, the child cannot co-ordinate his movements, and painfully acquired accuracy in handwriting is frequently lost. Don't try to force adult standards on immature children.

Learning to Spell Well

Most of the standard reading systems have a teachers' manual giving sufficiently plain directions for teaching to read, and for work and sentence building, by using cut letters and words. Such material is inexpensive. Assuming that the child can read, he will, from his reading, automatically memorize the sequence of letters in many simple words.

Bearing in mind the fundamental principle that the child should form the habit of writing only what he has thought out and expressed orally, good spelling habits can be formed by adhering to this simple rule:

Drill on words the child uses naturally and spontaneously in his oral preparation for writing.

Coincident with learning to read, the child should learn to write script letters, and write them in words from copy on the blackboard. A little time—not too much—can well be spent in copying short sentences. Soon the child will learn that every sentence begins with a capital letter and has some sort of mark at the end.

With these preliminaries mastered, the child is ready to learn to spell, and express his thoughts in writing. Oral spelling is of little value; we need to spell in order to write. Memorizing word lists is of questionable value, for the child may be wasting time on words he does not need in writing.

Writing words in lists has only one thing in its favor. It is said to save time, but this claim is open to question, and, in any event, a wise use of time is the sensible consideration. Try this method. Have the *How Color Aids Memory* child dictate three sentences. Write them on the board. Point out difficult words, and the difficult syllables in them; underline these with colored chalk. Remembering the advertising principle of keeping things constantly before the eye, let the sentences remain on the board until the next lesson. Then cover the board with a cloth, and redictate the sentences to the child for writing. Have him compare his results with the original sentences, finding his errors, if any. Help him to memorize the correct form of any words on which he has failed at the first writing.

Have a package of blank cards on which to write every day the misspelled words. Hang these beside the blackboard. These are the "ogres" that our young "Jack the Giant-Killer" must conquer. He will do it, and in a year's time, given six minutes of drill a day, will have built up a right *habit* of attacking a new word.

Gradually introduce the method of testing his knowledge by dictating a sentence or two, using words on which he has previously failed; if he fails again, hang up this card for another "fight."

If the cards are arranged in a box alphabetically, the child will soon learn to refer to them, if he needs to use a word in writing, and is not quite sure of the spelling. This search for "lost treasure" will be the beginning of the dictionary habit.

Principles Summed Up in "Don'ts"

A few "Don'ts" may help in mastering a reasonable writing vocabulary. Don't expect a child to spell every word he can recognize in reading. Don't attempt to drill on words he seldom uses in writing; it is better to tell him how to spell an unusual word if he wants it. Don't select spelling words from his reading vocabulary; wait until he uses them in speaking. Don't refuse to tell him how to spell any new word he wants.

In a recent study of children's spelling, these conclusions were reached:

1. Students in the highest grade

of our common schools have, on the average, less than 2,500 words in their writing or spelling vocabularies. We are giving children words they do not use, and we are not teaching them to spell the words they do use.

2. The words which give most trouble in spelling are found, almost without exception, in the writing vocabularies of the lower grades; and since these troublesome but useful words are not pointed out and effectively dealt with in these early grades, our handling of the most dangerous spelling material is not efficient, and students go on misspelling, year after year, words that should be mastered in the early school years.

Catch the Errors While Young

Since grade students commonly use from 500 to 2,500 words in writing, yet on the average misspell about fifty words, *not one child out of a thousand misspelling as many as one hundred words,* our spelling problem is not so gigantic as it is commonly believed to be, for the reason that a handful of words misspelled over and over by each student has misled us in our judgment.

How to Master Punctuation

By imitation of sentences in his reading book, and from blackboard copy, the child soon learns that at the end of every sentence is a mark. During the first year of home study he can learn to use the period and interrogation point without error. After that the teaching of punctuation should be governed by the need of it in written work.

Discuss the punctuation marks he finds in his reading. Let him answer this question: "What does that mark tell you to do?"

The child can learn early to sense the need for punctuation by this simple rule: *Some mark of punctuation is needed when one naturally makes a pause in reading aloud what is written.* This "sense" can be readily transferred to his writing, for before he writes anything, he composes it orally, and always he should have in mind that what he writes, somebody is going to read.

Simple Guide to Punctuation

During the early years, punctuation is largely a matter of developing this sense. When the child is old enough to need a variety of punctuation, one of the most useful devices is to dictate several sentences from a standard author, carefully phrasing according to the marks given. Have the child compare his writing of this dictation exercise with the original, and discuss with him any differences he finds in his punctuation.

"Why did the author punctuate in his way? Why did you punctuate in your way?"

A book on composition should be at hand for constant reference.

Fixing the Paragraphing Habit

When a child writes more than one sentence, he should become conscious of the paragraph. Study the reading book. When he writes, have him use a *margin paper* prepared as follows:

Fold a sheet of drawing paper one and one-half inches from the left hand edge. Fold again so that the left hand edge meets the crease. Let the child place his paper in the fold, so that the left hand edge meets the crease of the long fold. This gives the correct margin for the first word of a paragraph; similarly the short fold gives the margin for the following lines.

After using this device a year the habit of indentation will be fixed.

An Outline of Work

The following suggestions should be varied as need appears in written work. In listing, the writer has had in mind that while many of these things are to be mastered in usage and habit, at some time the child should learn the reasons for the usage.

First Stage. Capitals: Beginning of sentence. Pronoun *I.*
Punctuation: Period, interrogation point.
Verbs: Correct use of *is* and *are; was* and *were.*

Second Stage. Capitals: Names of persons, places, days of week. Word *O.*
Punctuation: Period in abbreviations given below. Interrogation point.
Abbreviations: Mr., Mrs., St.
Plurals: Ordinary formation by adding *s* and *es.*
Verbs: Correct use of *see, saw, seen.*

Third Stage. Capitals: First line of poetry. Names of months.
Punctuation: Apostrophe in possessive singular. Period in abbreviations. Hyphen at end of lines where a word is left unfinished and only at the end of syllables. Comma and periods in dates.
Abbreviations: Names of months. Doz., lb., qt., in., ft., yd., ct. or c., $. Certain states—begin with native state.
Address: Pupil's own address with correct punctuation.
Plurals: Few irregular plurals, such as *mouse, mice; loaf, loaves.* Avoid special difficulties.
Possessives: Possessive singular. In the best usage, the possessive singular of such words as James and Dickens is formed regularly as James's and Dickens's, unless the word following begins with *s*: *James's book,* but *James' sister.*
Verbs: The correct use of the following irregular verbs: *draw, throw, show, ring, sing, blow, grow, break;* also the use of *you were, there is, there are, there was,* and *there were.*
Pronouns: Nominative form of personal pronoun after verb *to be.* Emphasize this particularly. Have the children repeat the correct forms, as "It is I," "It was she who told me," etc., until the correct forms become a habit.

Fourth Stage. Capitals: Names of the Deity, the words *Bible,* etc.
Punctuation: Comma after word *O.* Comma in address. Comma before short, direct quotations. Quotation marks in simple, unbroken quotations. Period in abbreviations. Exclamation point.
Abbreviations: No., sq., ft., yd., pk., bu., bbl., A.M., P.M., M., U. S., Co., Rev., Dr., R. R., E., W., N., S. (for points of compass), etc.
Addresses: Of other people.
Possessives: Possessive plurals.
Plurals: Boy, and the rule for such words; lady, and the rule for such words, together with all plurals.
Contractions: Explain how contractions are formed. *I'll, isn't, aren't, wasn't, didn't.* Emphasize distinction between *don't* and *doesn't.*
Verbs: The correct use of *sit* and *set, run, wear, drown, tear, come, buy, do, give, write, freeze, has* and *have.*
Use of words: *Their* and *there, may* and *can, got* and *have, in* and *into.*
Pronouns: Correct use of the order of personal pronouns.
Syllabication and Accent: Division of words into syllables; accent marks.

Fifth Stage. Capitals: Words *North, South,* etc., used as a part of the country and not simply as points of the compass.
Punctuation: Comma in series. Comma after *yes* or *no* in an answer. Hyphen in compound words.
Abbreviations: Acct., G. A. R., Gen., Col., Capt., Supt., Jr.
Plurals: Nouns like *hero, potato, negro,* etc. Compound words such as *son-in-law.* Words ending in *f* or *fe* changing to *ves.* Other irregulars, as *mouse, man, woman,* etc. Avoid special difficulties.
Contractions: Use of *couldn't, wouldn't, shouldn't, mustn't, we've, 'tis, I'm, they're, they'll, mustn't, hasn't, haven't, hadn't* and *isn't.*
Verbs: The correct use of *drink, sink, swim, go, lie, lay, come, think, take, shine, hurt, lose, shake, teach, show, rise, raise, beat, eat, bring* and *swing.*
In such verbs as *drink, sink, sing, swim,* the best usage confines the forms in *a* to past tense and those in *u* to the perfect.
Correct use of the subjunctive forms: *If I were, if it be.*
Correction of the expression: *I didn't get to go.* Correction of such expressions as: *He didn't work like I did. Like* should be followed by a noun or pronoun only, never by a clause; *as* should precede a statement. Emphasize this distinction.
Possessives: Possessives, as in *Mason and Dixon's Line, Webster's* or *Worcester's Dictionary.* Synonyms.
Quotations: Quotations within a quotation. Make use of readers and other books.
Pronouns: Review carefully: Personal and relative after common prepositions; after transitive verbs. Emphasize the use of *between you and me,* etc. Correct use of *those* for *them.*

Dictionary Study: Begin use of dictionary and teach: (a) Pronounciation of words by means of diacritical marks and use of pronouncing key. (b) Division of words into syllables; accent marks. (c) Definitions. Show that many words have more than one meaning. Have pupils illustrate the meanings of words in interesting original sentences. In each spelling lesson mark one word diacritically.

Names: Teach distinction between Christian names and surnames.

Keep the Child Interested

At the outset I said: "Speaking and writing are easy when one has a motive or purpose in expressing his thoughts." This is equivalent to saying that the child must be interested if the best results are to be attained. The method of getting interest must be adapted to the nature of the child; some are susceptible to praise; some want to emulate an older brother or sister; some can be reached by introducing the game element; and one child I know well works hard from a variety of motives, not the least of which is that she wants to postpone the day of school confinement as long as possible. Whatever motive you can find, use it. My children have learned to write correct notes of invitation by giving Christmas and Hallowe'en parties to the other members of the family. You may be sure that they require equally correct acceptance. When I am traveling, they write interesting letters. "Having something to say" produces vastly different results from "Having to say something."

A six-year-old child can, by following the oral and written drill methods suggested, learn to write three or four sentences that are correct in structure, and have some interesting quality. By the time he is nine years old, he can tell a connected story of several sentences, and arrange them for writing in an order that will best command the interest of the reader. He can be trained to be self-critical. A compact, well-constructed paragraph, showing due attention to sentence structure, choice of words, and the technical details above mentioned, is a reasonable assignment for a child of twelve. When a child appreciates that good writing is not "how much" but "how well," and knows the qualities that make up the "well," he has advanced beyond many graduates of elementary schools.

The Rapid

All peacefully gliding,
The waters dividing,
The indolent batteau moved slowly along;
The rowers light-hearted,
From sorrow long parted,
Beguiled the dull moments with laughter and song:
"Hurrah for the Rapid! that merrily, merrily
Gambols and leaps on its tortuous way;
Soon we will enter it, cheerily, cheerily,
Pleased with its freshness, and wet with its spray."

More swiftly careering,
The wild Rapid nearing,
They dash down the stream like a terrified steed;
The surges delight them,
No terrors affright them,
Their voices keep pace with their quickening speed:
"Hurrah for the Rapid! that merrily, merrily
Shivers its arrows against us in play;
Now we have entered it, cheerily, cheerily,
Our spirits as light as its feathery spray."

Fast downwards they're dashing,
Each fearless eye flashing,
Though danger awaits them on every side;
Yon rock—see it frowning!
They strike—they are drowning!
But downward they speed with the merciless tide:
No voice cheers the Rapid, that angrily, angrily
Shivers their bark in its maddening play;
Gaily they entered it—heedlessly, recklessly
Mingling their lives with its treacherous spray!

CHARLES SANGSTER

LESSONS AT HOME AND AT SCHOOL
HANDWORK

Handwork for the Little Folks

This is a chariot race between Teddy Bears. Isn't it exciting? The bears, the chariots and the horses are all the work of children of the Second Grade in the schools of Pasadena, California. The race was originally run on a table in the schoolroom, but our artist, with a few deft touches, has transformed the table into a field, and that makes it look still more real. But just imagine how vivid the chariot races, in their stories of ancient days, must be to the children themselves after they have worked out a scene like this.

"EDUCATION is that which changes our behavior," says Dr. Thorndike. If we are to succeed in directing a child's education upward along good lines, we must accept him as he *is,* and to the best of our ability make the influences for good more attractive to him than the influences for evil, that his behavior may improve.

Meaning of the Child's Busyness

When we accept him *as he is,* how do we find him? His most striking characteristic is his activity. He must always be doing something. He calls it play, but he puts forth tremendous energy, and works harder at it than many of his elders work at their daily tasks.

What sort of things does he do when left to play freely and naturally? To a very large extent, he is imitating what he sees done by his elders. He is riding a horse or running a locomotive or street car. He is building a house or making a store.

His great business is getting acquainted with this big, wonderful world, and he is full of curiosity about the things he finds in it. What are they? What will they do? What can he do with them? He examines and experiments. He likes to see what will happen if he drops a stone or a stick into the pond. He likes to test his own power. How fast can he run? How far can he throw? How large a nail can he drive and how straight can he drive it? These are all natural and legitimate occupations and desires. Rightly directed, they help him grow in the right direction. Undirected or misguided, they may turn into mischief. In a desire to be like father, he may carry his best cane

Mischief or Mental Growth

practical, help shall be given by way of suggestion, just as when he is learning to walk we help him to his feet when he falls, but we do not carry him. It is just as needful for him to *go alone* in his thinking and doing as on his feet.

In the Sugar Camp

Here's another fine example of how well children can make their own "pictured knowledge"—this scene illustrating the work of the sugar camp. And how nicely it will fit into our story of sugar. This work was done by Third Graders in Columbia, Mo. The grass is real; transplanted into the sand. And that is a cake of real maple sugar on the table. The kettles and the horses are made of clay. The kettles are held up by tripods of matches. The buckets are of paper and they are catching imaginary sap from maple trees of twigs. The houses are of wood with a paper roof. That cute little ax is made with cardboard and is fastened in a log made from a piece of wood which was split at the end to make it easy for the little ax to pretend it did it!

and lose it; or he may drive tacks in mother's choicest chair.

Experimentation with all sorts of tools, materials and processes is essential if a child is to find himself, to know what he can do, and discover his niche in the world. Experimentation implies freedom, but freedom in the educative process does not mean unguided, unrestricted liberty in purposeless activity. It means, rather, that when his ideas and purposes are worthy, he shall be allowed to go as far as he is able in executing them, that he may feel the intense satisfaction and sense of power that goes with saying: "I did it all by myself." It means, that when his ideas fail or are unworthy or im-

Relation of Toys to Education

Many parents, in the desire to keep children employed, provide them with quantities of expensive toys and are surprised and grieved when the toys are abused and broken, or when the children soon tire of them and ask for new things. Others, wishing to avoid the selfishness and carelessness that often develops when desires are too easily gratified, go the other extreme, and provide little or nothing in the way of playthings. Of the two, the child, who has too little, is probably better off than the one who has too much; but an intelligent use of the common materials easily obtained in any home, and above all, a sympathetic inter-

HANDWORK

Making vs. Breaking of Playthings est in, and encouragement of, the child's crude efforts will, in most instances, strike the desired happy medium between the two extremes. If we will take the trouble to study the child's tendencies and interests and provide a legitimate field for and offers a big field for imagination and ingenuity. Homemade toys have a double value. The process of making is as much fun as playing with them later.

Picture Making and Paper Cutting

Every child loves pictures and pic-

Work and Days

A long time ago there was a Greek farmer named Hesiod who wrote a poem called "Work and Days," in which he told of a farmer's life, by days and seasons. Here we see how some little artist poets in the Third Grade told of work and days at home: Monday, washday; Tuesday, for ironing; Wednesday, sewing; Thursday, callers' day; Friday, sweeping; Saturday, for baking the cookies and things. On Sunday, of course, everybody goes to church. All the figures are cut out of paper and neatly mounted on a card.

them, many mischief-making habits may be avoided and useful habits developed in their stead. Children can be taught to make pictures in their own scratch tablets, and not on the walls or in valuable books. They can be taught to drive nails and saw boards that are provided for the purpose, and not cut cherry trees, or hack furniture. The *teaching* is quite as necessary as the supply of materials to work upon, but will be easier and more effective because of them.

Paper and scissors, paints, crayons and paste, may be made to produce wonderful pictures and satisfy several childish needs at the same time. Empty boxes may be turned into fine houses and attractively furnished through the use of odds and ends of paper and cloth, which usually find their way into the waste basket. The sandbox, whether indoors or out, has infinite possibilities

ture books. The desire for them is seldom fully satisfied. Good pictures play an important part in the educative process. The story is more easily understood and becomes more educative through the use of pictures. The child's attempt to make illustrations for stories of all sorts still further deepens impressions, and thought is clarified through the attempt to express. The gain in this particular cannot be measured by the quality of the result, according to our adult standards. Often a very poor picture may represent a real triumph in thought and expression on the part of the maker, a deepening of impression, a growth of imaginative power.

Paper cutting is less used and less understood than either drawing or painting, and yet has many points of advantage over either of these. Free hand cutting means cutting out objects directly without the use of a pattern, outline drawing, or other help. Its value lies in the necessity for the worker to see with his mind's eye what he wishes to make, which is what the psychologist calls "to visualize," a very important factor in clear thinking. Repeated attempts to express the mental picture in form and material which the child can understand will help to strengthen power, both in thought and expression, especially if some one is sympathetic, and while admiring the crude result, drops a suggestion for its improvement. For example, the child brings, in triumph, a bit of paper, and says, "See the man I have cut." The cutting may show nothing but an abnormally large head and appendages that suggest legs, but it indicates that the "big, blooming, buzzing, confusion" of his impressions of the world is beginning to take on some system and order. If instead of laughing at his crude attempt, we say, "Your man has fine legs, but where are his arms?" his next attempt will show the additional members. By continuing the process of encouragement and suggestion, the little one is led happily on to better and better results.

Advantages of Paper Cutting

How Much a Few Words Will Do

If, on the other hand, in our anxiety for more rapid progress and apparent results we *help* by doing the work for him, by cutting a good man for him to use as a pattern, we *hinder* in so far as we make him lose his feeling of independence and begin to lean upon us. Continued, this method blights the bud of his originality and inventive genius, and makes him afraid to think any thought for himself, until he finds some one else who has expressed it first. We hinder his development also by substituting *our* paper pattern for *his* mental picture of man. The paper cutting in itself is of small importance. The mental picture is all-important.

This Kind of Help Does Harm

Some mothers object to paper cutting because it sometimes litters the floor, but this is not a necessary accompaniment to the work. Cleaning up is almost as much fun as any other part, if it is just a part of the game, and there is no reason why it should not be treated as a game. Children coax to be allowed to do many things we call disagreeable tasks until they find how we regard them, and then, very naturally, they imitate our opinions as well as our actions. Making play of disagreeable jobs helps a great deal with little folks and big ones, too. Emerson points out that we all do our best "easily and in sport."

Making Duty Attractive

Paper cutting, brush work and colored crayons may be used to make posters and scrap books illustrating the stories the children read, the flowers, birds and animals they learn about and the things people do at home and elsewhere.

Use of the Sand Box

Sand box projects are an extension of the same principles underlying picture making. They have been called "pictures in three dimensions." All sorts of ideas may be worked out in the sand; illustrations for stories read, scenes showing foreign peoples, as well as interesting subjects nearer home. The sand pile offers equal, if not greater opportunity, for developing the fundamental instincts outlined above in connection with picture-making. It

HANDWORK

Homes of the Pueblo People

Some Second Grade children learned and then told each other a story of a little girl named White Cloud who lived in a pueblo. A pueblo, most of us know by name, was an Indian village made of sun-dried bricks, where the houses are grouped together on the side of a hill in terraces like this. But no matter how old we are, we don't know a pueblo as did the children who built this one with their own hands and made the bricks and the ladders and all. "Learning by doing" is one of the greatest principles in the modern method of teaching.

amuses, perhaps, but does not especially benefit a child, to look on while some one builds castles and forts for him. Playing *with* him is helpful, provided the adult playfellow does not take the lead too much and relieve the child of the need for thought, or cheat him out of his chance to grow through the effort to overcome difficulties.

The crude thing he does all alone may be worth more than an elaborate thing he helps some one else to build. This is not to put a premium on crudeness, but rather upon independence and resourcefulness, and the children should always be encouraged to do their best and discouraged in wilful carelessness.

It is almost invariably true that the child, who works freely on the level of his own development and appreciation, is conscious to a great extent of the weakness of his work. He will tell what it lacks, and how much better he could have made it had proper time and material been available. Knowing what is wrong is a long step toward getting a thing right. Under more closely directed work, a child often obeys directions and corrects mistakes without knowing why they are mistakes.

Building a Playhouse

Building a playhouse is an excellent project in the winter months, for either home or school. A house project may take on as many varieties as real home life presents. It may be a playhouse pure and simple, or it may represent some special

PICTURED KNOWLEDGE

Little Architects and Their Playhouses

All over the world and as far back as history goes, we find children have delighted in house building, house furnishing and house keeping. Only in recent years, however, have our educators seen the wisdom of allowing this instinct to have free play in school. But to be truly educated the children must do the work themselves. This picture shows a child-built house. The rooms are made of boxes with connecting doors carefully cut so the openings match; wall paper (scraps donated by a local dealer) carefully selected and much discussed as to color combinations and border designs; floors covered with rugs or matting made by the children, or linoleum, according to the purpose of the room.

phase of home life, as the homes of foreign children, or of story-book friends. It may consist of one or more small boxes set on table, shelf or floor in the play room; or in the summer, big boxes that the children can play in may be used. In any case it will furnish much profitable employment, and in school may serve

The Schooling in a Playhouse as a means through which many valuable facts and some otherwise dry information may be connected with the real life of the child and taught in a vital way. The character of the house may be suited to the age and interests of the children, varying from a playhouse for the Three Bears to a model in house furnishing, planned by the larger girls.

Use clean, empty boxes of wood or corrugated paper. Arrange these in convenient form on table, shelf or floor.

Plan and saw out windows and doors. In wooden boxes bore holes at the corners of windows and saw out with a keyhole saw. In paper boxes the openings can be cut with a sharp knife.

How to Do the Building and Furnishing In school this part of the work forms an excellent reason for learning to measure.

After the doors and windows are cut, the walls may be papered. Plain papers are best, as any patterned paper is likely to have figures much too large for the small rooms. Borders may be planned from paper cuttings or crayon designs.

Rugs may be woven for the floor on home-made weaving frames, as shown in the illustration. Carpet rags are in many respects more satisfactory than the weaving materials sold for school use, and cost practically nothing.

The most satisfactory furniture is made from scraps of wood. A square block with a thin strip nailed on makes an excellent chair. A larger block and a taller strip will make a fine dresser if a bit of tinfoil

HANDWORK

The Work of the Loom

You see now where the "imported" rugs used in that dear little playhouse came from, don't you? The children made the looms, too. For the more complicated loom on the left, to be sure, they had the help of boys in the Manual Training classes, but the other one was "easy" and the little folks did every bit of it. They drove nails a quarter of an inch apart at the end of a shallow box and stretched the warp threads across the open top. That's all. And do you know what those smallest rugs were woven on? A little loom made of just a piece of cardboard, by punching holes on opposite sides and stringing the warp through them.

is used for a mirror, and drawers indicated with pencil lines. Tables, beds, piano, stove and all necessary furniture may be worked out by this means, giving ample scope for a child's inventive genius, and free play for his imagination, while meeting his need for activity in a way that appeals to his interest.

The making of bedding and draperies calls for some sewing. Simple stitches may be learned on small pieces that do not tire little fingers.

Clay may be used to model bathroom and kitchen furniture. Clay-modeling has so much value, and is so fascinating to children, while its cost is practically nothing, that it is surprising so little use is made of it, in either home or school. Plasticine and similar preparations are a little more convenient to use in some ways, but are more or less expensive. Clay should be kept in a covered earthen jar or enameled can. If a wet cloth is kept on top of the clay, it will remain at a workable consistency indefinitely.

Supplying a Family for the House

After the house is finished, dressing a family of small dolls to live in it will add greatly to its interest and to interest in learning to sew as well.

Throughout the house-building process, the choices made by the builder will give a hint as to the level

Life on the Sand Table Farms

This modest little farm house with its out-buildings, fences, animals, and all, was planned and built by children in the Second Grade in Columbia, Missouri. And they grow real crops on these sand table farms. The sand must be very wet before the seed is put in and sprinkled twice a day; for these little farms are as thirsty as the Sahara. After the roots once get started, however, they find enough moisture down in the sand. In this way you can keep your farm green for several weeks and have corn, wheat, oats, barley, timothy, blue grass, and clover all growing.

of development in appreciation of color and ideas of form, and will indicate the point at which teaching is needed. Suggestions at the right moment have great influence, and the incidental development possible is limited only to the wisdom of the mother or teacher who supervises the work.

Rich Stores in the Little Stores

Play stores may be built on the same general plan as the playhouse, using empty boxes and stocking them with make-believe merchandise or with real samples. Playing store will help to familiarize the children with weights, measures, money, and business customs. Any activity, in which children take a keen interest, may serve as the starting point for pictures, playhouses or sand box projects. Sympathetic encouragement in working out their ideas, and helpful suggestions at the right moment will often bring results that surprise us by their ingenuity.

Valuable Guides for Teaching

LESSONS AT HOME AND AT SCHOOL
KNITTING AND CROCHETING

How to Knit

YOUR two little friends in the photographs are both knitting the plain, common knitting stitch. One is making an afghan and the other a neck scarf to match the pretty brown knitted sweater she is wearing.

You can soon master this stitch and be able to use it for knitting all kinds of attractive, practical articles.

The first step in learning to knit is to make a loop with the yarn like Fig. 1 and slide the loop on a knitting needle Fig. 1. Hold this needle in your right hand and bring the short end of yarn over the first finger, holding it in place with the second and little finger Fig. 2. Now carry the long end of yarn to the far side of the first finger of your left hand, pass the yarn around the finger, then across over and around to the far side of the needle in front of the loop. Next bring the yarn down and hold it with thumb and first finger of left hand Fig. 2.

Slip the yarn which is on the first finger of your right hand up over the needle Fig. 3, with your needle bring

1179

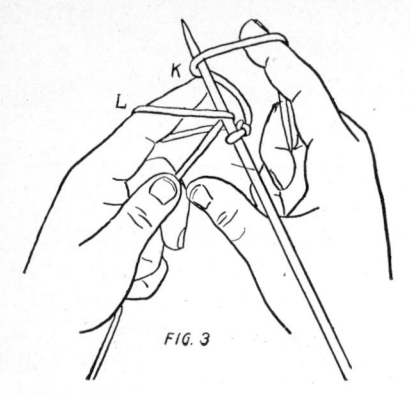

FIG. 3

FIG. H
LONG END
SHORT END

the loop K, Fig. 3, down through the loop L, held by the left hand Fig. 3. Draw this stitch entirely off the left hand onto the needle, leaving the left hand free.

Make the second stitch by carrying the long end of yarn around the first finger of left hand exactly as you did when making the first stitch and slipping the needle through as in Fig. 2; then bring the yarn on first finger of right hand up over the needle Fig. 3, and through the loop on first finger of left hand Fig. 4; pull the stitch through while sliding the yarn off the left finger. Cast the third stitch in the same way and continue to cast stitches until you have the requisite number.

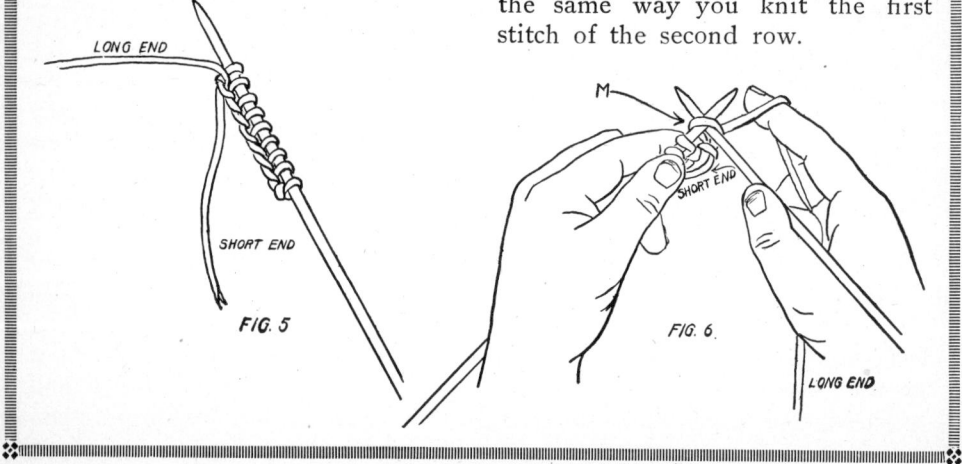

Fig. 5 shows the first nine stitches cast on knitting needle. For the next row of stitches, take the needle in your left hand and in the right hand hold the empty needle.

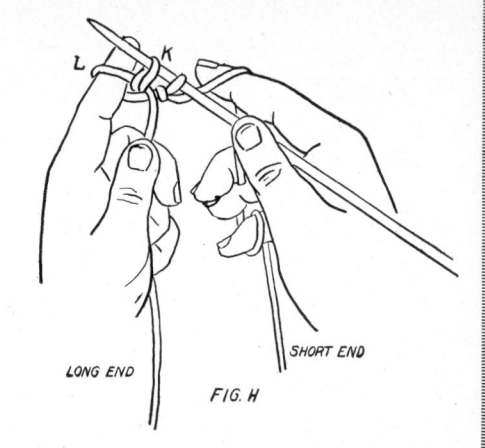

Slip the right-hand empty needle into the first stitch M Fig. 6, and with the first finger of your right hand pass the yarn over between the points of the two needles; then pull it down through the stitch M Fig. 6, with the right-hand needle. Doing this gives the first stitch of the second row, and the stitch will be on the right-hand needle. Again slide the right-hand needle into a stitch on the left-hand needle and knit it over on the right-hand needle in the same way you knit the first stitch of the second row.

LONG END
SHORT END
FIG. 5

FIG. 6
SHORT END
LONG END

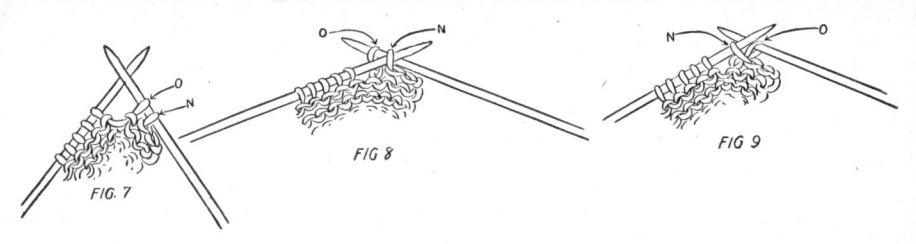

Repeat this process until all the stitches are on the right-hand needle, then take the needle containing the stitches in your left hand, the empty needle in your right hand and knit the third row of stitches. Continue in this way until the strip is finished.

How to Bind Off

Knit two stitches from the left-hand needle to the right-hand needle N O Fig. 7. With the left-hand needle take up the stitch N Fig. 7, and Fig. 8, and while N still remains on the right-hand needle and is also on the left-hand needle, pull the stitch O through the stitch N with the right-hand needle, at the same time slide the stitch N off the left-hand needle; this will leave one stitch on the right-hand needle.

Again insert the right-hand needle into the top stitch on the left-hand needle and knit a stitch over on the right-hand needle, which gives you a second stitch on the right-hand needle. Now bind off the second stitch precisely as you bound off the other one. Knit a stitch and bind a stitch, knit a stitch and bind a stitch. Do this over and over again, always remembering that only two stitches must be on the right-hand needle and when one is bound off you knit on another making the necessary two. Proceed in this way until all stitches are bound off. When only one stitch remains draw your yarn through and break it off.

Purling or Seaming

To purl or seam means to make ridges as in the top of mittens, stockings, etc., and this is the way to do it. With all stitches on the left-hand needle, begin purling by first slipping the first stitch off the left-hand needle onto the right-hand needle without knitting. Knit the second stitch and you will then have two stitches on the right-hand needle. The third stitch you must purl. Bring the yarn in front of the right-hand needle P, Fig. 10; then slide the right-hand needle in front of the left-hand needle and through the stitch Fig. 11. Carry the yarn in front of and up over the right-hand needle, bringing the yarn P, Fig. 12 entirely around the right-hand needle. Hold it in place with the right hand as you held the yarn in Fig. 3, while with the right-hand needle you bring the yarn up through the stitch held open by the two needles and carry it over on the right-hand needle, which will give three stitches on that needle. Now bring the yarn back of the needle and plain knit one stitch; then carry the yarn in front again and purl a stitch, bring the yarn back and knit a stitch, keep on purling a stitch and knitting a stitch, never forgetting the yarn must be *in front* of the needle for the purl stitch and *back* again before making the plain

FIG. 10. FIG. 11 FIG. 12

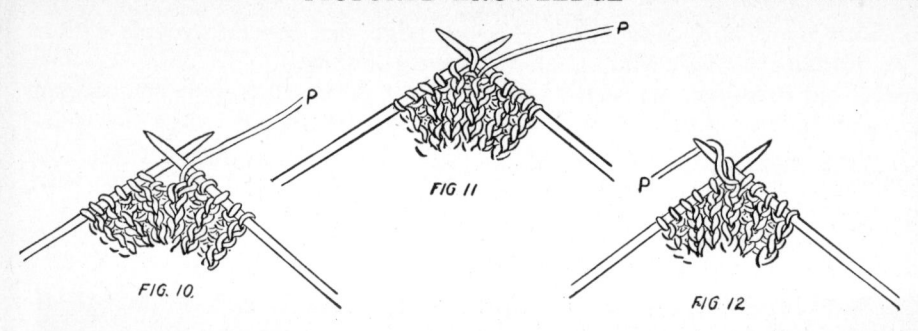

knit stitch shown in Figs. 7, 8 and 9.

To Narrow

Knit two stitches together as one stitch.

To Slip Stitch

Slide the stitch from one needle to the other needle without knitting.

To Increase Stitches

Knit the front of the stitch and leaving the stitch on the left-hand needle, knit the back stitch; this gives you two stitches in place of one.

Using merely the plain knitting stitch and two knitting needles, you can make for your mother a long-sleeved sweater, kimono shape, sewing up the sleeves and sides after you have finished the knitting.

Commence by casting about 70 stitches for back of sweater, knit 74 rows; then cast on 40 stitches for the sleeve, knit across and on the opposite end cast on 40 stitches for the other sleeve. You now have 150 stitches; knit across these 44 times, then knit 65 stitches and bind off 20 stitches for the neck; again knit 65 stitches. Thread a string through the first 65 stitches until you need them.

Knit two rows for the shoulder, after which increase 1 stitch at the front on every other row for six rows and you will have added three stitches. Now cast on 8 stitches at the front and knit 44 rows; then bind off 40 stitches for sleeve. Knit the remainder until this half front equals the length of the back; then bind off, and knit the other half front to match. With over-and-over stitch sew up the sleeves and sides of the sweater.

Knit a border of contrasting colored yarn, shaping the border to fit the edge of the sweater, and sew it

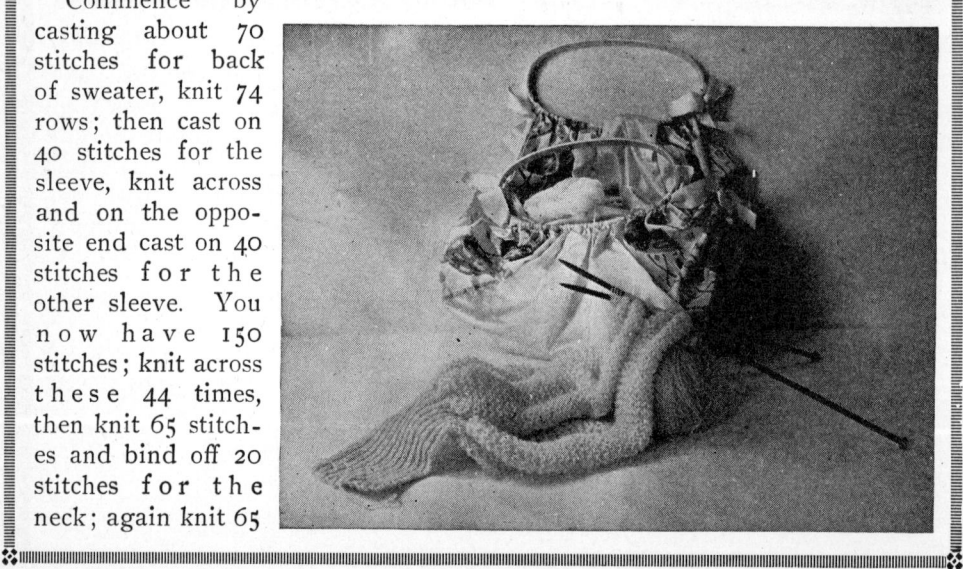

KNITTING AND CROCHETING

on with over and over stitch.

A turban is made like a short scarf; fold this scarf across the center, sew the two edges together and it forms a bag. Turn up the bottom; then bring down the corners of the top, fasten each corner on the turned up edge and cover the spots with a yarn pompon.

Knit the scarf as wide and as long as you wish it and fringe the ends.

Knit some toy horse reins 1½ inches wide and trim them with sleigh bells.

How to Crochet

WHEN you know the simple crochet stitches, you can make shawls, jackets, scarfs, doilies, and also slippers and lace as the two busy little workers you see in the picture are doing.

We start crocheting with a loop like Fig. 13; the next step is to place the crochet needle over the loop and under the long end of yarn which lies across under the loop Fig. 14, then holding the loop in the left hand, with the right hand you catch the long underlying yarn with the hook on the crochet needle and pull the yarn through the loop Fig. 15.

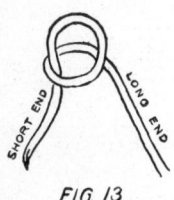

FIG. 13

FIG. 14

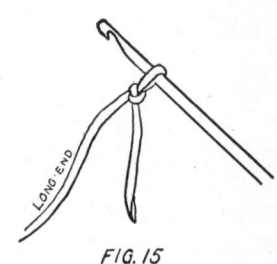

FIG. 15

FIG. 16 FIG. 17 FIG. 18

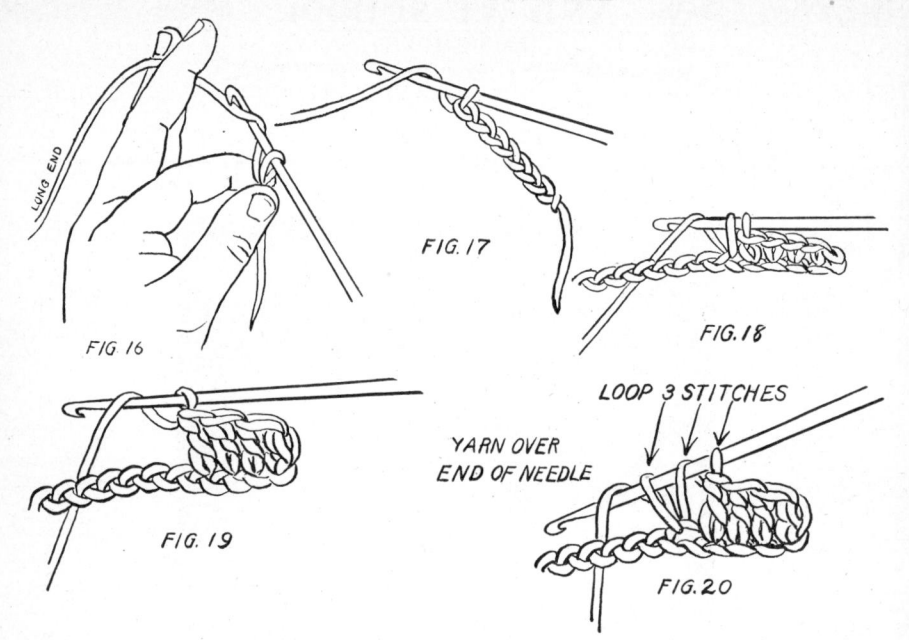

FIG. 19

YARN OVER END OF NEEDLE

LOOP 3 STITCHES

FIG. 20

Having the first loop, it is easy to pass the yarn under and back of, then over the needle Fig. 16, and pull the yarn through the first loop. This makes another loop.

Repeat many times, crocheting a series of loops which form the chain stitch. The chain stitches are the foundation for crocheting Fig. 17.

With the last loop of the chain on your needle, begin to crochet the single stitch Fig. 18. Turn back and pass the needle through the next chain stitch, then bring the yarn over the needle as in Fig. 16 and pull it through the chain stitch, which makes two loops on the needle Fig. 18. Carry the yarn over the needle Fig. 18 and pull it through the two loops. With the one loop now on the needle, again pass the needle through the next chain stitch and crochet another stitch as before.

Long Stitch

With the end loop of the chain stitch on your needle, pass the yarn around the needle as in Fig. 16; then while the needle still has the yarn around it Fig. 19, slide the hook through the next chain stitch, pass the yarn over the end of the needle and with the hook bring the yarn through the chain stitch. This gives you 3 loops on the needle. Now carry the yarn over the end of the needle Fig. 20 and draw it through the first two loops, making only two loops now on the needle; carry yarn over needle and bring it through these two loops, then do it all over again to make your second long stitch, as shown in Figs. 19 and 20.

LESSONS AT HOME AND AT SCHOOL
EMBROIDERY

How to Do Embroidery

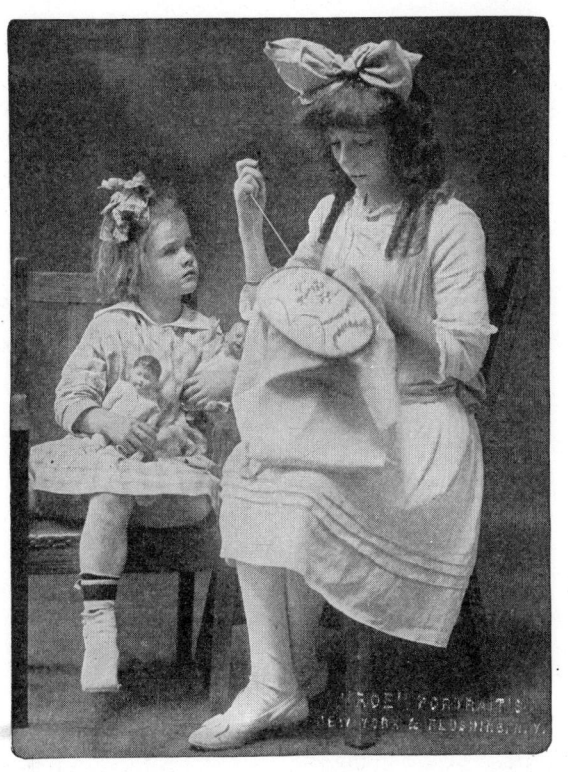

"I love to embroider, and when I must stay indoors I would rather embroider than do almost anything," said the little curly-haired girl as she busily sewed on the cross-stitch design you see in her hands. Little Sister watches eagerly, for she, too, wants to work the cross-stitch.

You can readily do this embroidery, and like our little friend in the picture, you will enjoy every stitch taken.

Have a stamped pattern, or copy some design by working over coarse scrim basted on the material to be embroidered. When finished, the canvas can be pulled out thread by thread from under the stitches. Fig. 1 gives the first stitch, after drawing thread from wrong to right side of goods. Fig. 2 shows second stitch. Fig. 3, third stitch; Fig. 4, a row of stitches.

Quick work can be accom-

FIG. 1   FIG. 2   FIG. 3   FIG. 4

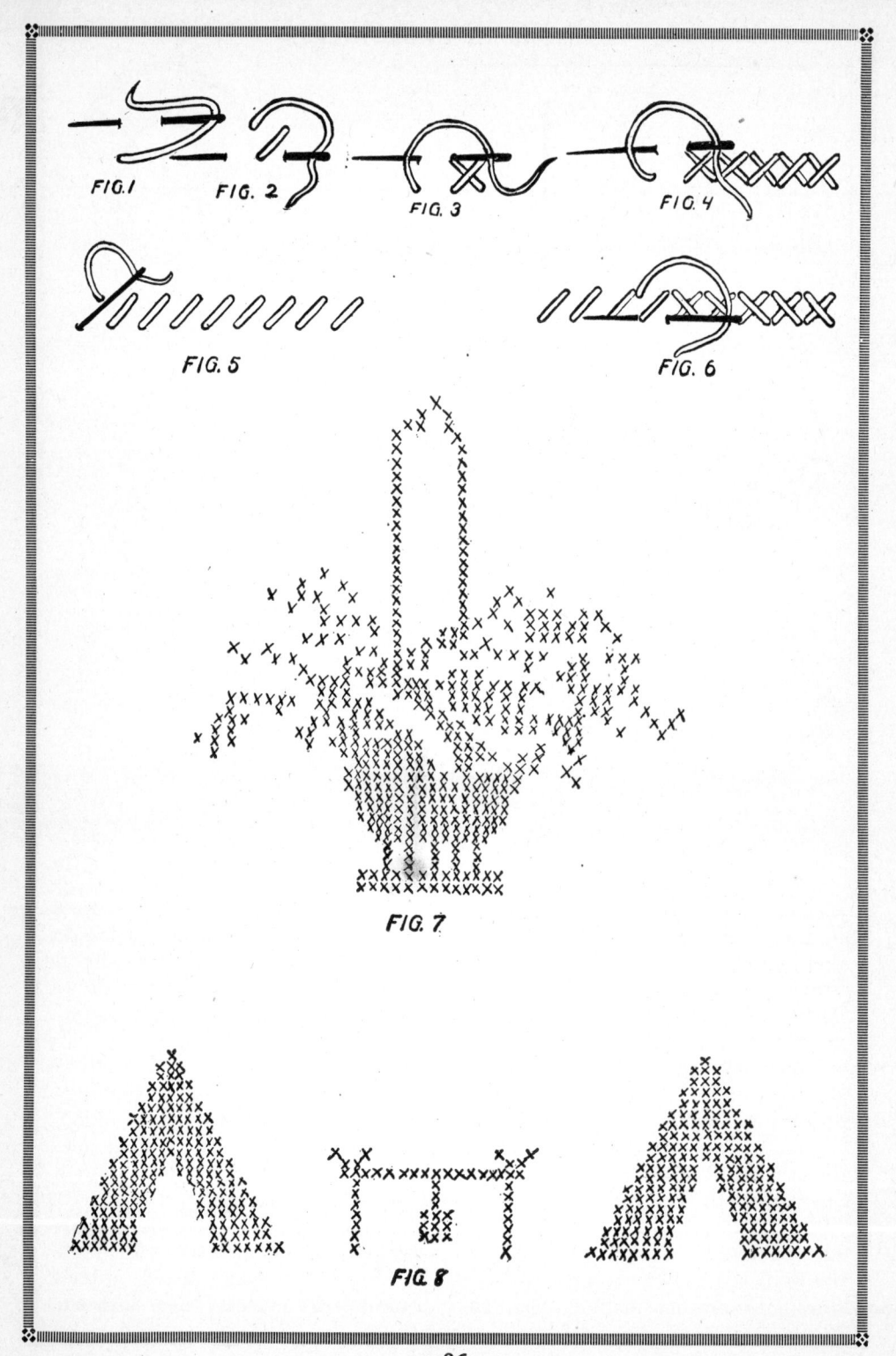

FIG. 5   FIG. 6

FIG. 7

FIG. 8

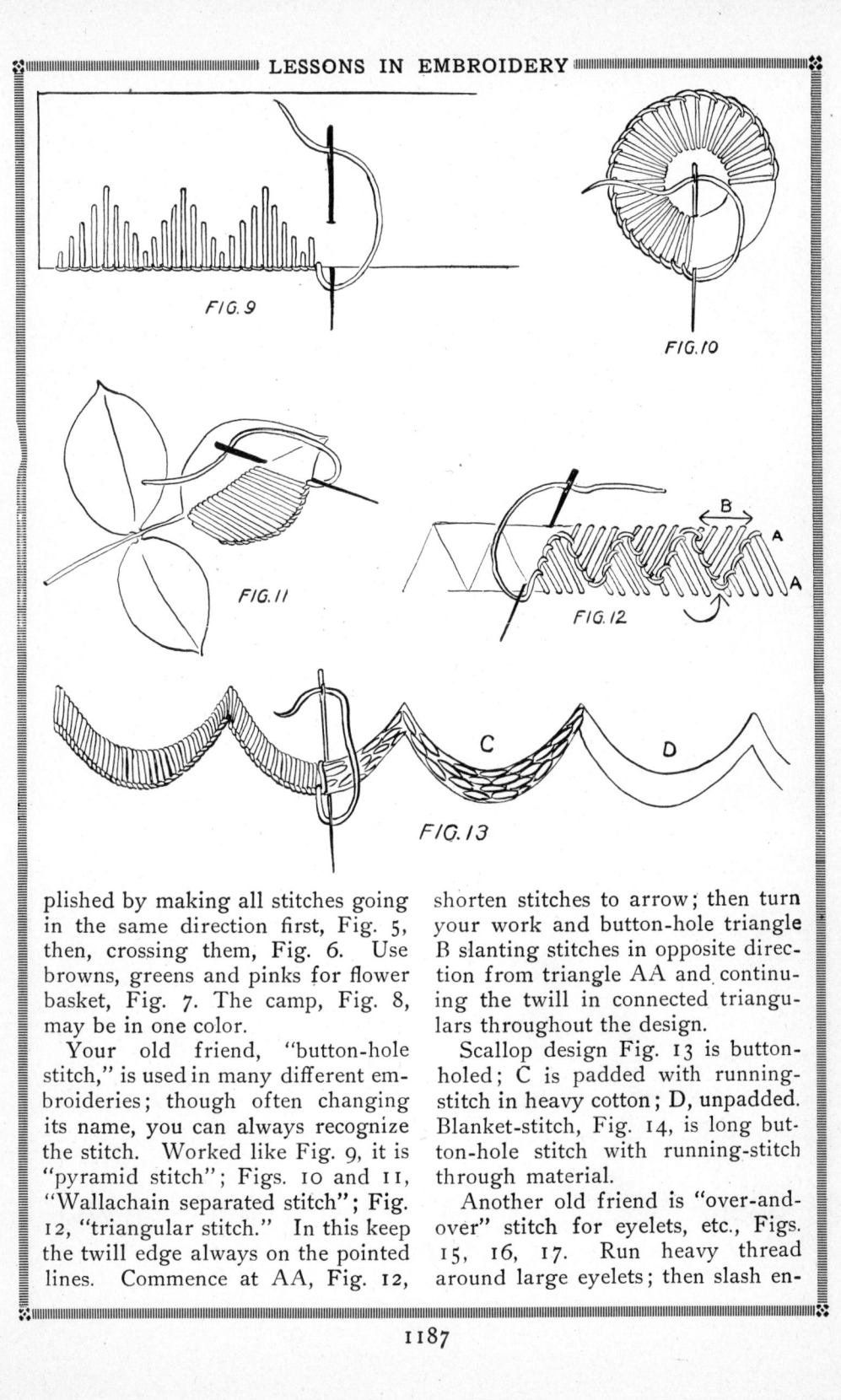

LESSONS IN EMBROIDERY

FIG. 9

FIG. 10

FIG. 11

FIG. 12

FIG. 13

plished by making all stitches going in the same direction first, Fig. 5, then, crossing them, Fig. 6. Use browns, greens and pinks for flower basket, Fig. 7. The camp, Fig. 8, may be in one color.

Your old friend, "button-hole stitch," is used in many different embroideries; though often changing its name, you can always recognize the stitch. Worked like Fig. 9, it is "pyramid stitch"; Figs. 10 and 11, "Wallachain separated stitch"; Fig. 12, "triangular stitch." In this keep the twill edge always on the pointed lines. Commence at AA, Fig. 12, shorten stitches to arrow; then turn your work and button-hole triangle B slanting stitches in opposite direction from triangle AA and continuing the twill in connected triangulars throughout the design.

Scallop design Fig. 13 is button-holed; C is padded with running-stitch in heavy cotton; D, unpadded. Blanket-stitch, Fig. 14, is long button-hole stitch with running-stitch through material.

Another old friend is "over-and-over" stitch for eyelets, etc., Figs. 15, 16, 17. Run heavy thread around large eyelets; then slash en-

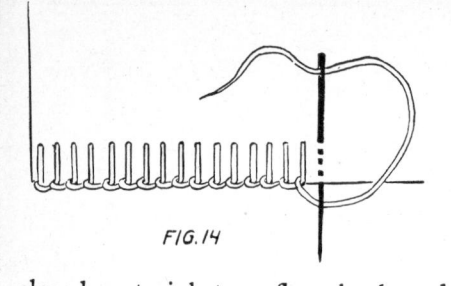

FIG. 14
FIG. 15 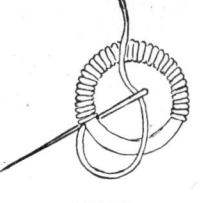
FIG. 16 

closed material, turn flaps back and embroider. Punch the small eyelet holes with a stiletto.

Long-and-short stitch is "over-

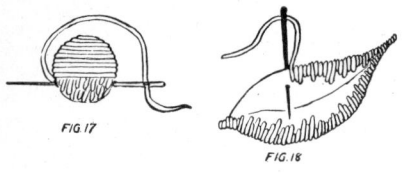

above it, with lower edge of row uneven. Kensington stitches should be taken away from you with needle pointing toward you, which requires

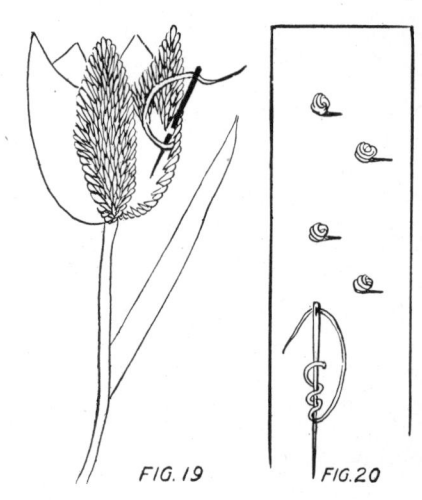

FIG. 17
FIG. 18

and-over" stitch worked in long, short and shorter stitches, Fig. 18.

Satin-stitch is "over-and-over" stitch, but this is worked with even edges.

Fig. 19 gives kensington stitch which is better adapted to unwashable goods. Begin with long-and-

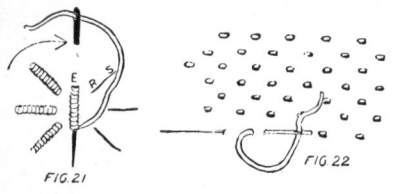

FIG. 19
FIG. 20

FIG. 21
FIG. 22

constant turning of the work. Take short stitches on wrong side, long ones on right.

French knots, Fig. 20, are effec-

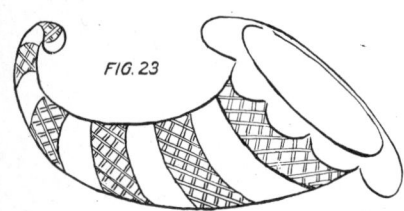

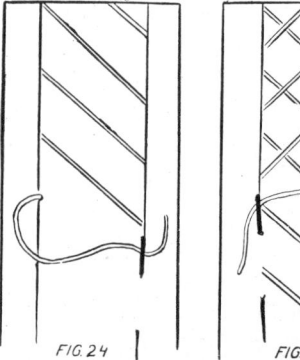

FIG. 23

short stitch around leaf edge, slanting stitches toward base of leaf, Fig. 19; then cover inner space with uneven rows of long and short stitches, each stitch dovetailing between two

FIG. 24
FIG. 25

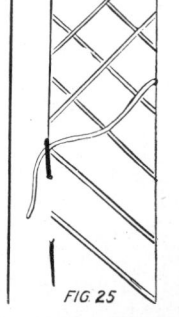

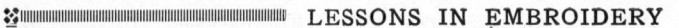

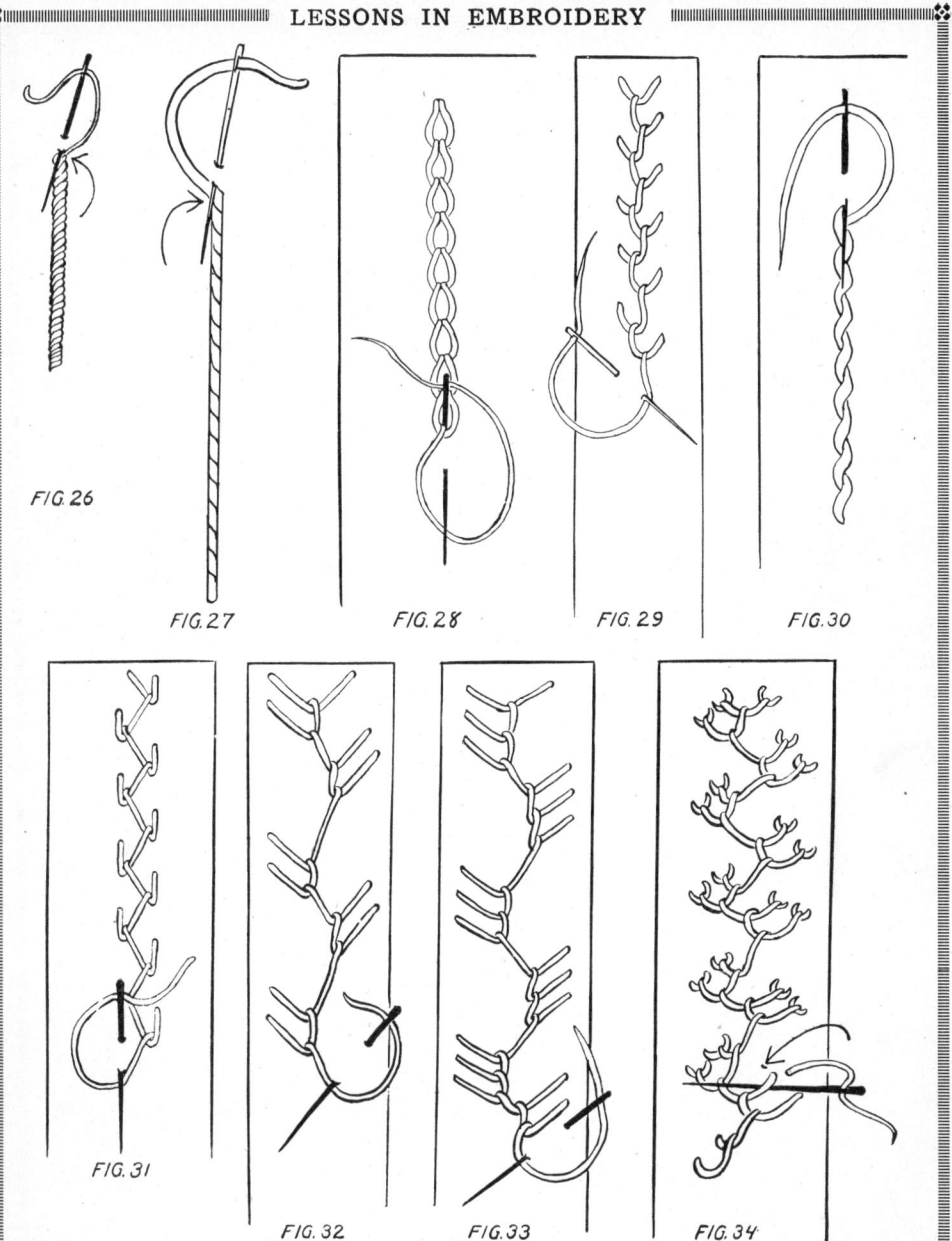

LESSONS IN EMBROIDERY

FIG. 26
FIG. 27
FIG. 28
FIG. 29
FIG. 30
FIG. 31
FIG. 32
FIG. 33
FIG. 34

tive; bring needle from wrong side of material to right, wind thread three times around needle while holding thread taut with left thumb and twisting needle; then run needle through to wrong side of goods in almost the same spot where it came out. Bring needle out again where you wish next knot.

Bullion stitch, Fig. 21, is like the French knot only more thread is around needle; it must be wound the same number of times for each stitch. For a star-like design, Fig. 21,

1189

bring needlepoint from wrong to right side of goods at E, wind and turn it back through where the arrow points at outside end of ray. Take a long stitch, bring the point again out at R, wind and turn back to S. Again insert needle, bringing it out at base of next ray. Repeat process.

Seed-stitch is the "back-stitch" taken short on right and long on wrong side of material. The stitches must be evenly spaced in rows and stitches in each row made midway in space below two stitches above, Fig. 22.

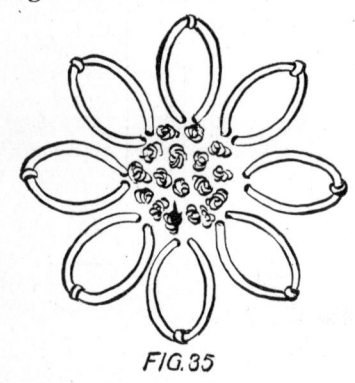

FIG. 35

Fig. 23 is lattice embroidery much enlarged, used only on small spaces. Fig. 24 shows how to make the slanting stitches, inserting needle with straight stitch along edge of band, first on one side, then on the other. Fig. 25 explains the slanting stitch across first stitches.

Fig. 26 is rough outline-stitch. Fig. 27 shows the outline-stitch.

When making chain-stitch, Fig. 28, hold the thread down with left thumb while the needle is pulled through, and take next stitch close to where the first one came out.

To embroider the feather-stitch, Fig. 29, attach thread at top of line and work toward you, taking a short diagonal stitch on one side; then another lower down on the other side. Hold thread under needle for each stitch.

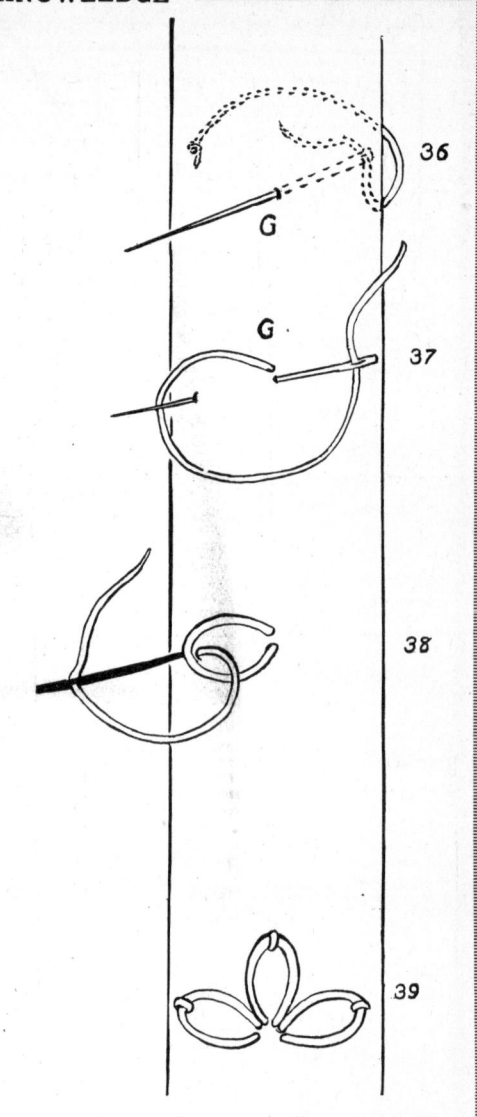

Fig. 30 is a variety of outlining-stitch. For Fig. 31 make straight instead of slanting feather-stitch.

Fig. 32 gives double feather-stitch, and Fig. 33 shows the same with three stitches. Seaweed-stitch, Fig. 34, is like Fig. 29, only with two instead of one feather-stitch.

LESSONS IN EMBROIDERY

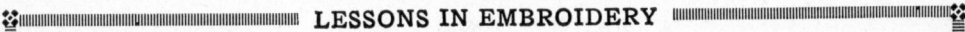

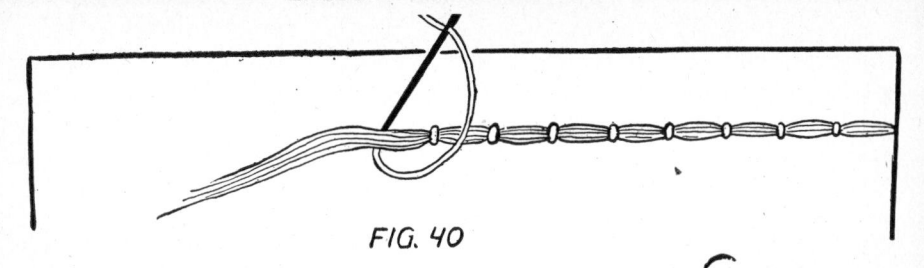

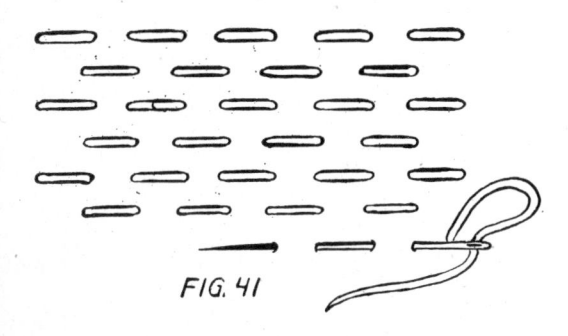

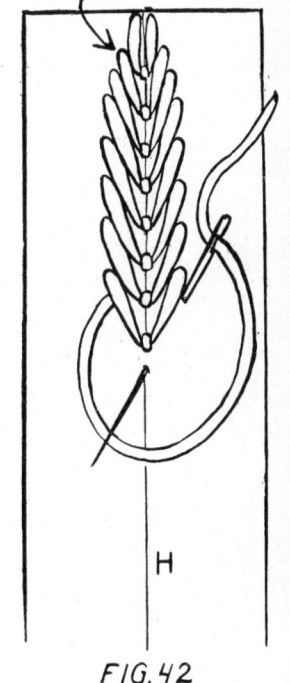

FIG. 40

FIG. 41

FIG. 42

Arrow indicates spot where needle passes through, finishing the stitch.

Lazy-daisy stitch, Fig. 35, is a flower. Dotted line, Fig. 36, shows thread and portion of needle under the material to be pulled through at point G for first lazy-daisy stitch. Fig. 37 shows thread through at point G and needle taking first stitch with loop of thread under needle point. Fig. 38 gives needle taking second stitch at base of loop, binding it to the material.

Fig. 39 is a clover-leaf in lazy-daisy stitch. Couching is fastening strands of floss or a cord to the material in ornamental lines by means of separated over-and-over stitches taken at equal intervals with heavy floss, Fig. 40.

Darning embroidery, Fig. 41, is for backgrounds and large spaces. It is the running-stitch made in rows, all stitches of same length and evenly spaced. Every stitch is made under center of space between two stitches in row above.

Van Dyke stitch, Fig. 42, is much the same as lazy-daisy stitch—a loop fastened with a short stitch. Start at top, left hand, take stitch to center, like H; bind with small stitch. Bring needle through close to outer left edge of first stitch (see arrow), make second stitch. Continue these stitches until design is finished.

The smocking-stitch, Fig. 47, can be embroidered on a stamped pattern, or you can mark the goods yourself. Fig. 43 is an evenly spaced and lined cardboard, made by measuring ½-inch distance be-

1191

FIG. 43

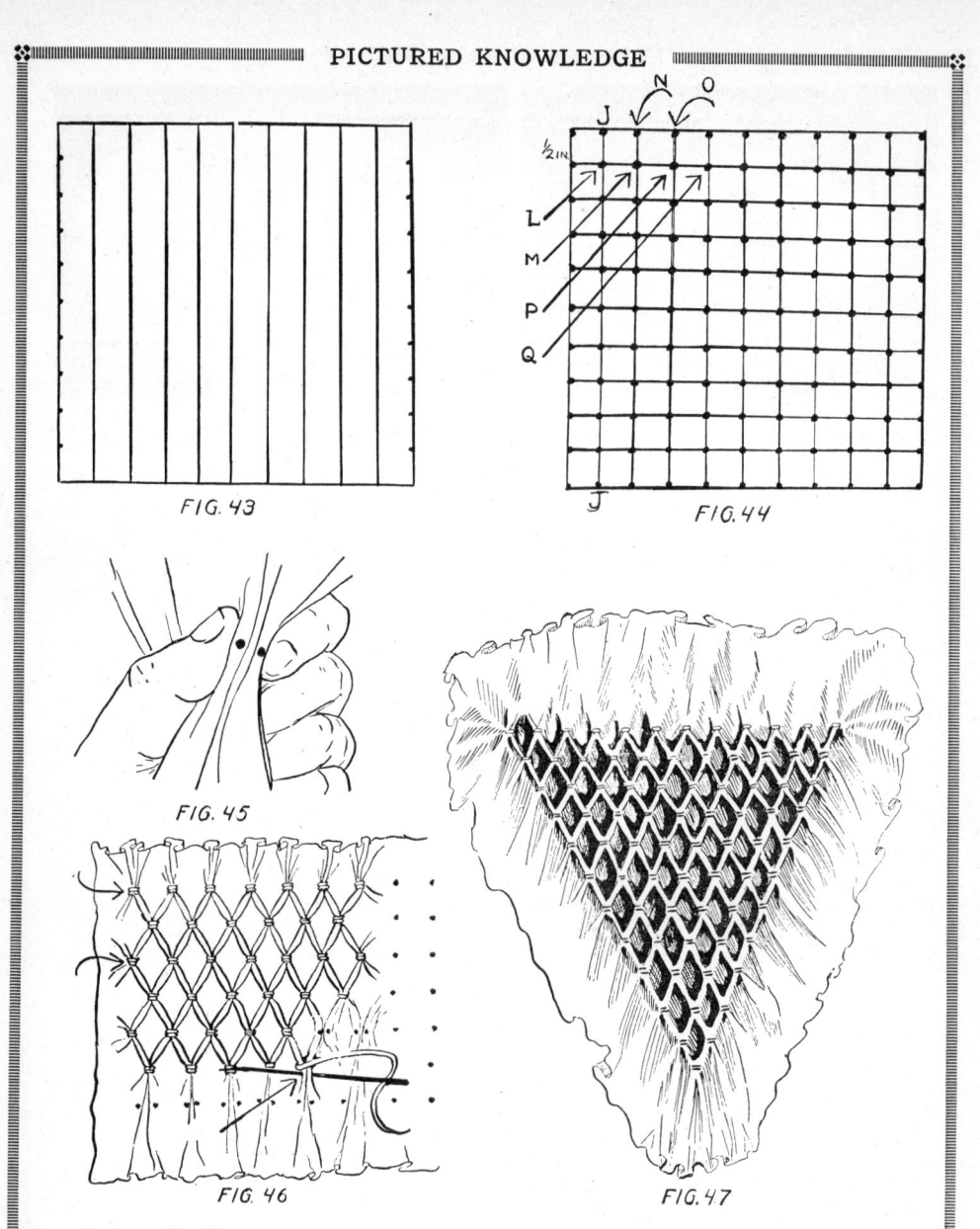

FIG. 44

FIG. 45

FIG. 46

FIG. 47

tween each line with dots, on sides. With a ruler as guide, draw lines across from each of the two opposite dots; then cross the lines, Fig. 44. Dot corners of squares and puncture each dot with coarse darning needle. Have your cloth perfectly smooth, lay the card over it and with soft leadpencil mark through each perforation of the card. Slide the card along for making more dots, being careful to have the row of dots, JJ, Fig. 44, exactly over the last dots on material, for success in this work lies in exactness of detail in marking the goods.

When ready to sew, start at top left hand dot, bring your needle

LESSONS IN EMBROIDERY

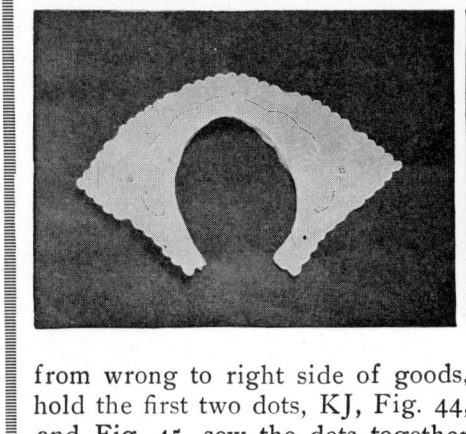

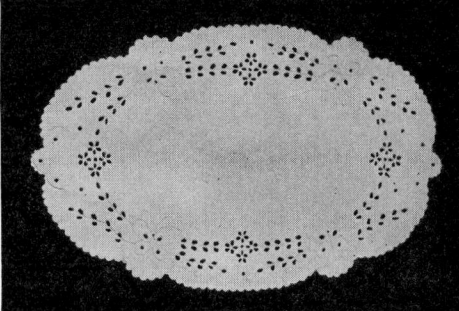

from wrong to right side of goods, hold the first two dots, KJ, Fig. 44, and Fig. 45, sew the dots together with three over-and-over stitches; then slip needle through to wrong side of goods, slide it down to dot on second line, L. Sew L and M (arrows indicate) together and pass needle up to dot N; sew this to O and bring the needle down, fastening P and Q together. Fig. 46 gives method, and Fig. 47 shows honeycomb diamond smocking finished.

A Child's Laughter

All the bells of heaven may ring,
    All the birds of heaven may sing,
All the wells on earth may spring,
All the winds on earth may bring
    All sweet sounds together;
Sweeter far than all things heard,
Hand of harper, tone of bird,
Sound of woods at sun-dawn stirred,
Welling water's winsome word,
    Wind in warm wan weather.

One thing yet there is, that none
Hearing ere its chime be done
Knows not well the sweetest one
Heard of man beneath the sun,
    Hoped in heaven hereafter,
Soft and strong and loud and light,
Very sound of very light
Heard from morning's rosiest height
When the soul of all delight
    Fills a child's clear laughter.

Golden bells of welcome rolled
Never forth such notes, nor told
Hours so blithe in tones so bold,
As the radiant mouth of gold
    Here that rings forth heaven.
If the golden-crested wren
Were a nightingale—why, then,
Something seen and heard of men
Might be half as sweet as when
    Laughs a child of seven.

                ALGERNON CHARLES SWINBURNE

The Way for Billy and Me

Where the pools are bright and deep,
Where the grey trout lies asleep,
Up the river and o'er the lea,
That's the way for Billy and me.

Where the blackbird sings the latest,
Where the hawthorn blooms the sweetest,
Where the nestlings chirp and flee,
That's the way for Billy and me.

Where the mowers mow the cleanest,
Where the hay lies thick and greenest,
There to track the homeward bee,
That's the way for Billy and me.

Where the hazel bank is steepest,
Where the shadow falls the deepest,
Where the clustering nuts fall free,
That's the way for Billy and me.

Why the boys should drive away
Little sweet maidens from the play,
Or love to banter and fight so well,
That's the thing I never could tell.

But this I know, I love to play,
Through the meadow, among the hay;
Up the water and o'er the lea,
That's the way for Billy and me.

— JAMES HOGG

LESSONS AT HOME AND AT SCHOOL
YOUNG PEOPLE'S CLUBS

Learning to Work Together

"LET'S have a Club."

Doesn't that sound familiar? Did you ever know a boy or girl who did not, at some time, belong to a club? It is fun, and a group of children working and playing together can do a great many interesting things that none of them could do alone. Very little boys and girls can have a Robinson Crusoe Saturday play, or a Jenny Wren doll's dressmaking club, and they can join the Humane Society and the Audubon Society and take part in the world-wide work of protecting animals and birds. With grammar and high school pupils, literary and debating societies for self-improvement and social pleasure are the favorites. In many places, now, there are Junior Citizens' Leagues, to help make towns cleaner, safer, and more beautiful places to live in. They do a lot of good, too. You know what "team work" is, don't you? All these group activities prepare young people for the team work of grown-up social, civic, and industrial life.

Learning How to Work Together

But grown people often find themselves unable to take a full part or to find as much pleasure as they might in social clubs and political work, because they are puzzled by the formal way in which meetings are conducted. Everything is done quickly, quietly and exactly; many questions are taken up and settled in the shortest time and without confusion and dissatisfaction, by a system of rules known as Parliamentary Law. Unless one knows these rules, he can do little as a delegate to a convention, as a member of a city council or in a business meeting of a club. He cannot properly call or conduct a meeting or get a chance to be heard. This seems unfair, but it is not. It is fair to the greatest number. The rules are simple and can easily be mastered. Not to know them interferes with other people. They can be learned and practiced in the smallest children's clubs. Don't you think it would be useful to know them? Well, then: Let's have a real club, conducted by Parliamentary Law.

Value of Parliamentary Law

First Steps in Forming a Club

Who shall be in it, how many, and what shall be its purpose? In the first place, a club is not a fraternity or a sorority—those small, exclusive, social groups to which many school authorities object. It is much better, for it is formed on the American plan of equality. It should admit all the pupils of a room or of several classes—everyone who will enjoy it, who will make a useful member and who behaves well. From forty to one hundred is a good working number, for

Make it a Club for All

1195

they can all get into one room for business meetings, and take part in the club activities.

To start a club, leaders are needed. There are, in every school, a few natural leaders—boys and girls with original ideas, energy to carry them out, and popularity, so that others follow them. From three to five pupils, with the consent of teacher and principal, should write out, sign and post a notice in the room, hall or office, something like this:

The Posting of the Notice

All pupils in the (name the class or classes), who are interested in having a good time and of being of larger use in the school and town, are invited to meet in Room — after school, on Friday, September 20th, to form a club.
(Signed) John Norwood,
Rosamond Dean,
Mary Alice Brown,
Otto Klein,
Robert Alcott.

Everybody remains! It is like an old-fashioned New England town meeting. When the teacher is gone there is a buzz of excitement for a moment, then John Norwood, whose name headed the call, should rise on the platform, rap for silence, if necessary, and say: "The meeting will please come to order and nominate some one for temporary chairman."

Calling the Meeting to Order

Anyone in the room may get up and say whom he would like for chairman, but only one should do so at a time, and he should say: "I nominate A—— for chairman." If someone else wants the same person, he should rise and say: "I second the nomination of A—— for chairman." There should be other nominations for the office, made in the same way, as there should always be more than one candidate, so there will be a chance to express choice on the part of members. When the nominations are all made, the voting begins.

Nomination of the Chairman

Voting may be done in three ways: By taking the vote on each candidate separately, in order of nominations, and calling for the "ayes" and "noes"; then: "All those in favor of A—— for chairman say 'Aye.' All of those not in favor say 'No.'" If there are more "ayes" than "noes," the acting chairman announces: "It is a vote, and A—— is elected our chairman." When the number present is large, so it is hard to judge the votes fairly, it is better to call upon those in favor of the candidate to stand and be counted, or raise the right hand. A third way is to pass slips of paper, announce the names of candidates and have each voter write the name of his choice. The ballots are then collected, sorted and counted, and the result announced.

The Voting and the Counting

Rules Governing Elections

A majority elects, and that is one over half of all the votes, or if there are three or more candidates, a plurality elects, that is the largest number of votes received by one candidate. After counting, the acting chairman announces: "There are sixty-five votes. Thirty-three elects. A—— has thirty-nine votes, B—— twenty-six. A—— is elected our chairman." These are the ways in which all elections are conducted. When there is previous notice of an election to be held at some future date, a committee is usually appointed to prepare a list of candidates, and to write or have printed, ballots with the names of all candidates for all offices on them. This is the way it is done in political elections.

Nominations are not made in the meeting, and the voting is all done at once. It saves time. Of course the committee should find out who are wanted for officers by the members. On a prepared ballot, choice is expressed by putting a cross after one candidate for each office to be filled.

Completion of the Organization

In this imaginary meeting, John Norwood steps down, and, amid handclapping, the elected chairman takes his place. The chairman should then call for nominations for the office of temporary secretary. With the election of these two officers, the temporary organization of the club is completed. The secretary sits at a desk and writes a report of what has been done, something like this:

"September 20, 1910. On the part of the signers to the call to form a club, John Norwood called the meeting to order. Otto Klein was elected temporary chairman, and Mary Alice Brown temporary secretary." *Secretary's Record of the First Meeting*

She merely records what was done, not what was said. Then she waits until something else is done. The next thing is for the temporary chairman to announce the purpose of the meeting:

"This meeting was called to form a club for useful work and social enjoyment. The ideas of those present are invited."

A dozen are apt to jump up and begin to talk all at once, so no one can be heard. In that case, the chairman raps for order, and he recognizes the one who stands quietly, and addresses him properly.

"Mr. Chairman."

"Miss Dean."

Rosamond Dean has "addressed the chair," been recognized and "has the floor." She states a fact and makes a "motion."

"We will have to form a club, but haven't done it yet. I move that a club be formed at this meeting."

The temporary chairman may wait to see if this is to be seconded, or he may restate the motion, saying: "It is moved that," etc., and put it to the vote at once. The motion being carried, a boy rises. *How the Chair Manages a Meeting*

"Mr. Chairman."

"Mr. Howard." (You see everyone is very polite and respectful to each other.)

"I move that a committee be appointed to frame a Constitution and By-Laws for the club."

When this is voted upon, a motion should be made, stating the time and place of next meeting, and then a resolution to adjourn, although the temporary chairman may announce that the meeting is adjourned, if no motion for it is made.

The Making of a Constitution

The next meeting is called to order by the temporary chairman, who calls upon the temporary secretary for a report of the previous meeting. The chairman asks if anyone notices errors or omissions in the report. If not, he announces that the report stands approved. A secretary's report, once approved, is taken as proof of what actually happened, and not what anyone present remembers. This alone makes club members have respect for accuracy and less for hearsay in all other matters. Next, the report of the committee on Constitution and By-Laws is called for. The members of this committee have elected a chairman of their own, to preside over their meetings and to be their spokesman. He rises and reads:

Article I. This club shall be known as the Canton High School Social Club.

He should be allowed to read the report through without interruptions. Article II may state the object of the club. Article III states the officers it shall have, the time of their election and the length of service. Other articles should deal with the time and place of the annual and business meetings and *What the Constitution Should Be* provide for special meetings; fix the number of members who must be present at any meeting to transact business (this is called a quorum); fix the amount of the club dues, define the conditions of membership and the duties of officers. There should always be a provision for adding amendments. You know the Constitution of the United States has had to be amended a number of times because of new questions that come up and that were unprovided for originally.

By-Laws should follow, also divided into articles. By-Laws are special rules that a society makes to fit its own needs. Good models for Constitution and By-Laws can be found in any manual of Parliamentary Law. A small public library should *The Debate on the Articles* have several. When the reading is finished the voting begins, and that is great fun. Each article is read again separately, debated upon and voted. Changes and amendments may be offered. Thus a club can, in the second meeting, learn many things about amending, sending back to committee, laying on the table, voting the previous question, being out of order, and other things. For instance, Article I proposes a name for the club. Some one jumps up.

"Mr. Chairman."

"Miss Arnold."

"I don't think the name proposed expresses all the purposes of the club. I move the words 'and Civics' be inserted between the words 'Social' and 'Club.'"

A Caution About Discussions

This has to be voted upon, and if carried, the name must be changed in the committee report, and then the changed name restated and voted. Speakers should learn to be brief and to the point. Debate should never be allowed to become tiresome or to result in nothing. A debate may be stopped in several ways—by a motion to commit, that is *Discussions Should Be to the Point* send it back to the committee for reconsideration; by a motion to lay it on the table, where it remains until another motion takes it off; or by "moving the previous question." This means that the maker of the motion wishes to vote at once on the question that is being discussed. Sometimes, in a club or council meeting, you may hear sitting members say, "question," "question," "question," like popping corn. These are impatient reminders that the debate is too prolonged. The chairman may call the objectors to order, and he does not recognize that the previous question is wanted until some one rises and makes the formal motion.

Election of Permanent Officers

After the Constitution and By-Laws are adopted, the club next proceeds to elect its permanent president, secretary and treasurer and to install them in office. The club is then organized and ready for work. The hard work of the club, the place *Advantage of Committee Work* where one can learn the most and discover his talents, is in a committee, so the members should take turns in serving. It is not fair to ask the ablest and most energetic members to do all the work, nor fair to the less able to give them no opportunity to learn. Besides, some of the quiet ones are apt to surprise you with fine, practical ideas and the common-sense way in which they present them.

The proper committees for such a club would be one on Social Entertainment, one on School Improvements, and one on Civic Betterment. A committee of three or five is large enough. It may be elected, but a club usually prefers to have the president appoint the members, as this saves time. If the president appoints, he should keep a list of the members of the club and check off names as they are appointed, so as not to put one person on two committees, and not to overlook those who have not served at all. Committees would better be temporary, serving for a very short time, or only for some definite, immediate purpose.

At this meeting the entrance fee, of say five cents, should be assessed, for a little money will be needed to buy record and account books for the secretary and treasurer, and to purchase two copies of some good manual of Parliamentary Law. Mo- *Other Features of the First Session* tions have to be made for these expenses and voted upon, for the treasurer can make no expenditures without the authority of the club. The manuals should be on the table at every business meeting, so that the secretary can look up disputed points—and there will be a good many of these while the club is learning. Between meetings the manuals should circulate, a member being allowed to take one for twenty-four hours, or over Sunday. The object of this is to educate members in the rules as rapidly as possible. Another and very interesting way to learn Parliamentary Law is to see it in action in the City Council.

Reports of the Committees

Before the next meeting the committees have met in each other's houses, elected their chairmen, exchanged ideas and finally decided upon some course of action to recommend. After the meeting is called to order, and the reports of the secretary and treasurer are heard and approved, the reports of the committees are called for. The chairman of the committee on social entertainment may report:

"Mr. President, as there is very little money in the treasury, we recommend an entertainment that will cost nothing, or that should pay for itself. As the old gentlemen and ladies of this town think that the young people of today are not taught to spell, we move that this club challenge an equal number of adults to an old-fashioned 'spelling match.'"

Wild applause and a unanimous vote! To carry out the plan, a number of committees are necessary—one to ask permission of the school board to use the assembly hall on a certain evening; another on publicity, to post notices and secure pub- *Work for Several Committees* lication in local newspapers; others on decoration of the hall, music, ushering, and drumming up of contestants. It is decided to charge a small admission to non-contestants, to pay for the heat and light, as is required. Before they are aware of it, from eighteen to twenty-four of the members are on committees, and each one knows exactly what he is to do to make the affair a success.

The committee on school improvement may recommend that a certain teacher whom all admire for her uniform courtesy, be asked to give a lecture on manners before the club.

When this is voted in the affirmative, there is a lively debate about the manner of extending the invitation. Some are in favor of a committee, but it is finally decided that the secretary be instructed to write a letter, making the request formally in the name of the club.

A Benefit to the Whole Community

The chairman on civic betterment may recommend that the club members use their united influence to stop the smaller children's bad habit of marking buildings, fences and sidewalks with chalk and charcoal, and *A Little Work in Social Reform* that they pledge themselves to remove any such marks that they may see, and thus improve the appearance of the streets. It is further suggested that a committee be appointed by the president to attend the next meeting of the City Council and to report anything of interest they observe.

Everyone leaves that meeting feeling that they have "started something." And they have. In small towns where there are few public places of amusement, and in city neighborhoods where there is little money to spare for theaters, concerts and lectures, the people must provide their own fun. Young people can do a good many things to get their tired parents out of their rocking-chairs in the evenings. A spelling match will wake up a town or a *Putting Life into the Community* neighborhood. An afternoon lecture on manners should bring out a good many mothers. The report on the council meeting sends a good many boys to their fathers with questions about the practical work of law-making. Thus the whole community is interested, informed and amused by the activities of the young people's club.

Some of the Benefits to Members

When the committee that attended the council meeting brings in its report, the club finds that it needs a plat of the town to find out where lot 35, block 7, of Hubbard's Extension to Smith's Subdivision of East Canton is. A new sidewalk is ordered there. By the plat, hanging in the club room, the members are soon able to locate every new lamp post, catch basin, sewer extension and every sort of improvement, before it is put in. Besides, they learn Parliamentary Law in action. They learn what it is to be "out of order," to "divide a motion," "to appeal from the decision of the chair," when one may properly rise to "a question of privilege." And they learn that a president is not the master of a club, but the servant. It is his duty to direct the proceedings so that everything runs along smoothly and quickly, but he must be impartial and just, give everyone an equal chance to be heard, and keep the meeting from running away with itself.

Such a club trains members for future work in clubs, conventions and legislative bodies, sets them to work for the good of the school and the town, and increases their social opportunities. Specifically, it could study the water supply, lighting, sewer, and telephone systems, fire and police protection, municipal law-making, tax assessments and what is done with the money, the comparative cost and durability of pavings. It would clean up alleys and vacant lots and arouse public sentiment to keep them clean; get up campaigns against conditions that breed flies and mosquitoes. By planting trees, vines and flowers on school grounds, protecting against bill-posting and chalk marking, it could start a movement for the Town Beautiful.

Best Training for Citizenship

Things to Be Done for the School

For school betterment, such a club could raise the standard of manners, morals, and scholarship. It could get the use of vacant grounds for ball games, gardens and play; put in sand piles and swings for the little ones and buy seeds and tools, and superintend, by committees, the work and play. It could find out people who knew things of importance and interest and get them to come out and talk about it—the doctor about health, the dentist about teeth, the banker about savings and investments, the engineer about steam, the telephone manager about electricity. They would find the people with fads for local geology and start a natural science museum of native specimens.

Improvements and Educative Entertainment

Of social affairs, there could be a variety that would cost nothing, or whose cost would be covered by a small admission fee. One public debate should be held and an oratorical contest, also a school exhibit of manual training and domestic science. A stereopticon travel or nature lecture could be arranged for, and a historical lecture. A musical and literary evening is not difficult to manage. There could be a spelling bee, a taffy pulling in a church kitchen, with chaperons to be responsible for propriety and property; snow ball and coasting frolics; an ice carnival by bonfire and torchlight, if there is a lake or river for skating; an old-fashioned evening party with charades, games and simple refreshments. A May pole dance was given for the children in the neighborhood, in the court yard of Hull House, in the most crowded district of Chicago.

At the end of the school year there should always be class-day exercises out of doors and a reception for the graduating class. A club picnic in a park or the country is always popular. And every year such a club should make some gift to the school —a picture or plaster cast for the hall or assembly room, a case for the museum, an encyclopedia or other reference work for the library. A club of one hundred members, with dues of only ten cents a month, collects one hundred dollars in a year, and should have a fourth of that for a gift of permanent value.

At the End of the School Year

With what enthusiasm such a club could come together at the beginning of the next year. The incoming class should be admitted automatically, the outgoing class should be kept as honorary members—a sort of alumni. So organized, it would be kept up and would have the active sympathy and co-operation of the grown-up people of the place.

The Woman's Manual of Parliamentary law, by Harriet R. Shattuck, is the best text-book for such a club. It is small, compact, simple, and costs only seventy-five

Manuals of Parliamentary Law

cents. Warrington's Manual, at fifty cents, is also good. Fish's Guide to the Conduct of Meetings, Cushing's Manual, and Crocker's Parliamentary Procedure are recommended. Authorities differ on minor points.

The Fairies

Up the airy mountain,
  Down the rushy glen,
We daren't go a-hunting,
  For fear of little men;
Wee folk, good folk,
  Trooping all together;
Green jacket, red cap,
  And white owl's feather!

Down along the rocky shore
  Some make their home,
They live on crispy pancakes
  Of yellow tide-foam;
Some in the reeds
  Of the black mountain-lake,
With frogs for their watch-dogs,
  All night awake.

They stole little Bridget
  For seven years long;
When she came down again,
  Her friends were all gone.
They took her lightly back,
  Between the night and morrow,
They thought that she was fast asleep,
  But she was dead with sorrow.
They have kept her ever since
  Deep within the lake,
On a bed of flag-leaves,
  Watching till she wake.

High on the hill-top
  The old King sits;
He is now so old and gray
  He's nigh lost his wits;
With a bridge of white mist
  Columbkill he crosses,
On his stately journeys
  From Slieveleague to Rosses;
Or going up with music
  On cold starry nights,

To sup with the Queen
  Of the gay Northern Lights.
By the craggy hill-side,
  Through the mosses bare,
They have planted thorn-trees
  For pleasure here and there.
Is any man so daring
  As dig them up in spite,
He shall find their sharpest thorns
  In his bed at night.

Up the airy mountain,
  Down the rushy glen,
We daren't go a-hunting,
  For fear of little men;
Wee folk, good folk,
  Trooping all together;
Green jacket, red cap,
  And white owl's feather!

—WILLIAM ALLINGHAM

CHILD TRAINING IN HOME AND SCHOOL
THE COUNTRY SCHOOL

Beautifying Life in the Country School

The Beauty of the Trees
Nature often favors the country school by giving it beautiful surroundings which all the work of the landscape gardener can't improve upon. Such oaks as these lining the road past this little wooden schoolhouse would make almost any school grounds beautiful.

THIS is a big subject, and a very important one when the relation of the country school to the development of a more attractive country life is considered. Life on the farm, too often, is barren and unsatisfactory, because the country school and the country home do not give it social and educational significance. The human or social side of American agriculture has been neglected and we have been endeavoring to increase crop yields at the expense of man yields. It is entirely possible for the school to assume the leadership in creating a sentiment for a more beautiful environment to change the outlook to nature; to build up in the child the appreciative side of trees, flowers, shrubs, vines, etc.; to catch the spirit of forest and prairie; in

Crop Yields vs. Man Yields

short, to spiritualize agriculture. This can not be accomplished in a day, a year, or a generation, perhaps. But so powerful is the force of an ideal, that one hesitates to say what days have passed and new conditions face American agriculture. The country school should be improved in its course of study so that the youth of the fields may be educated

Where the Children and the Flowers Grow Up Together

Cozy and warm in the winter, this little country school with its grassy yard, the flowers, the fine old trees, the vines climbing the stone walls, the wide fields stretching away on every hand, becomes a most beautiful and happy place in the growing season and one of the best places in the world for growing the right kind of boys and girls.

might be accomplished in country school improvement with an army of ten million country boys and girls, led by two hundred and seventy-five thousand country school teachers.

The Country School and the Republic

The country school should be improved because, traditionally it is the most significant and democratic of all American institutions. It is important because the great majority of the children of the country are getting their only education, so far as books are concerned, in this roadside school. Pioneer in terms of his environment. It should be improved as to the character of the building, its architecture,

Education of Country Guard

its fitness as a workshop in country life education, with due regard to artistic and sanitary values. And no one has ever asserted that the treeless, cheerless country school ground of itself has any power to charm and enthuse childhood. The daily routine work at home is much harder to bear if at school the child gets no fine ideals, or standards of what an attractive country life is. The country school at present may be said to be giving the country children only half an education. This institution is showing to farm youth the attractive side of city life, but it is not seriously trying to show the attractive side of country life, nor is it trying to train boys and girls how to live the attractive farm life.

best country home. This will help to spiritualize country life and agriculture. Are we dreamers if we contend that the glory and beauty of country life may help the youth to decide for the farm, as well as the vision of larger yields of corn?

How the Children Help

And one of the best things about these lovely country school grounds is that the children themselves help make the grounds attractive; raking up rubbish, stirring the soil, planting and watering the flowers. All of which, to quote from Mr. Stevenson's Garden of Verses, is "One of the pleasantest things ever a child can do."

A Place for High Ideals

The country school grounds should set forth the highest ideals and influences of all the country side. They should be as attractive as the best farm home in the community. This does not imply that the school building must be as expensive as the farm dwelling, or the school grounds as extensive as the farm. It does mean that the educational plant, the school premises, should exert an influence as wholesome as that of the

In a really large sense, the country teacher is assuming that leadership in a program of community betterment through the co-operation of school and home. Through the children the parents are reached. The children in school will quickly respond in an organization to improve the school grounds. If boys and girls are the farm's best crop, then their early years should be filled with impressions of the best pictures "that can be thrown upon Nature's great canvas—the earth." Help the children to create these pictures.

The Teacher and Community Leadership

PICTURED KNOWLEDGE

First Step in School Improvement

It must never be forgotten that the children themselves should take part in making both the school room and the school grounds attractive. Encourage them to use their initiative, and to do as much of the work as possible. Discuss plans with them, and encourage them to make suggestions.

home flower gardens in the village, and learn to make cuttings from plants, root them in sand, pot and care for them during the winter. In the autumn give a flower show. Hold a May Party exhibition of work done by the children during the winter in manual training and sewing, and devote the proceeds to paying the expenses of the flower and vegetable garden the following summer.

The Tools that Work the Magic

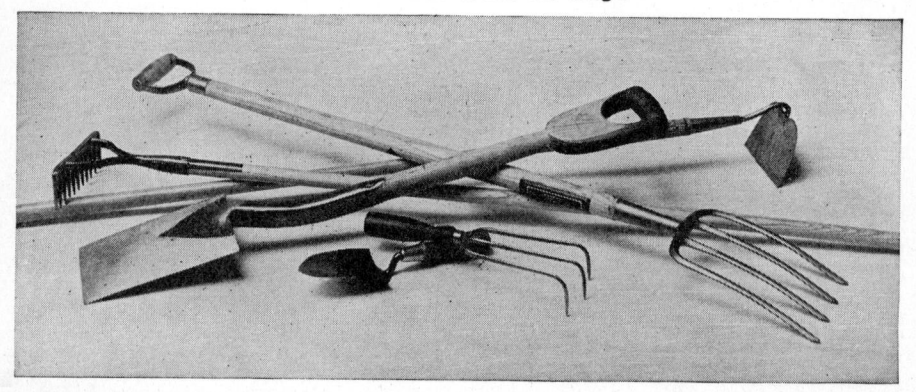

These are the garden tools which, combined with a little "know how" and enthusiasm, and plenty of good wholesome work by the boys and girls, are transforming hundreds and hundreds of cheerless country school grounds into the attractive places they should be.

The Children and the School Gardens

In making the school grounds attractive, plenty of work will be found for the children. Ground that can be made to "blossom as the rose" may be at first full of weeds, witch grass and boulders. Remember, also, that the typical schoolyard soil must frequently be replaced by good, light, sandy loam.

The interest of the community in beautifying school grounds and making gardens, both for flowers and vegetables, will increase the interest of the pupils. The use of a small outbuilding for storing the tools is frequently given by the sympathetic farmer, and the community will help to offer prizes for good results. Boys are invited to beautiful

Kind of Tools to Be Used

It is not generally wise to use mere toy tools. The triangular hoe, which strawberry growers use, is very easy to handle and does excellent work. Any child, large enough to work in a garden at all, can handle a 10 or 12-foot rake. If small crops are gardened, a hand weeder will be found useful. Spades smaller than the ordinary garden spades for the children to spade up their own gardens can be secured from local hardware merchants.

Laying Out the Gardens

A good size for individual gardens is 10x20. This will keep even the most energetic boys busy. If it

1206

proves too much for some of them—and it often does—others will take their places. And if a teacher is wise, the interest will grow. In many schools boys come twice a week after school and work two hours, and two days a week during summer.

The plans should be carefully drawn to scale and exactly followed. Mark the handles of the hoes so that the boys can measure by them. Always use a line and have it long enough to go around the entire garden. Four-strand braided twine is excellent for this purpose.

Before going into the gardens to stake them out, explain what is to be done, illustrate it on the blackboard, and talk it over together. For their individual gardens give children seeds in packages with just enough seeds, and teach them not to waste. This is one of the most important lessons of gardening, as it is of life.

And no subject offers a richer field for correlation with other studies. The measurements and other phases of mathematics involved in school gardening are of great importance in vitalizing this subject. It is a fact that few children are able to apply mathematics outdoors, although they may be bright in the mathematics of the school-room—mere book arithmetic.

Teach the children to study the construction of insects—what wonderful little machines they are!—to tell the harmless from the harmful, and how to get rid of the latter. In one summer, children can learn to recognize over fifty insects. Lead them to see how the beautiful colors, markings, and forms of flowers are made to attract insects, and the purpose of this in the fertilization of the flowers. What a striking thought it is that bees and butterflies have the delicate taste of artists with regard to color and form; otherwise why should Nature go to the trouble of producing these beautiful colors and infinite forms? Nature is always practical; she never wastes any effort.

One special word about the wild flowers. It is true, and it is a pity, that so many children—even those who live in the country in the midst of them—are ignorant of the beauty of the native wild flowers. These should be given a prominent place in the school gardens, and children taught to appreciate and care for the rare and fast-disappearing species.

Things will grow without a plan

Use and Beauty Side by Side

The school garden serves two purposes—it is a thing of beauty and has a very definite value in the education of the child. The children in the picture have just planted a bed of poppies and next to it they are putting in lettuce seed. The poppies will improve the appearance of the school yard and the lettuce will do duty in summer salads. From both of them the children learn about growing things and their care.

if proper planting directions are observed. It is not the lack of a plan that causes so many things to die on country school grounds when once planted. Improper planting and neglect tell the story of most failures. But if trees, shrubs, and vines, perennial material, are so planted and cared for that permanent growth results, the effect is so much more

The Alphabet of Beauty

border effect and open spaces for the playground and lawn. Mass effect has been secured by the artistic groupings of shrubs and trees.

One standing in the middle of the playground, or along the side, would see graceful curves made in outline by irregular lines of shrubs, trees and border planting of flowers. And it is Ruskin's contention that "all

Curve Effect in School Grounds

Country School Grounds on City Lots

The larger communities, as well as the country schools, have learned the advantages of school gardens. These children are at work in a thriving school garden at Mt. Vernon, N. Y. School gardening has proved to be so important and attractive a part of the life of the school that in many small towns as well as cities they have a superintendent of school gardens. Groton, Mass., is one of these places. The boys who are marking out the beds in the preceding picture are from the Groton schools.

pleasing if a simple artistic plan has been followed, instead of scattering things over the grounds. There is what is called the ABC of planting; the fundamental principles of the best landscape art along natural lines. This is the alphabet of beauty that should be taught to children in the school. For the letter "A" read "Leave open spaces"; for the letter "B" read "Plant in Masses" and for the letter "C" read "Curved Line Effect" or "Avoid Straight Lines." A careful study of the planting plan for a country school yard will show how the artist has secured the curved

forms of acknowledged beauty are composed exclusively of curves."

By "curve" is not meant the circular flower bed in the center of the lawn. Nothing could be more out of place, so far as landscape art along natural lines is concerned. The circular flower bed is out of harmony with the naturalness of the open country. The same number of plants arranged in a bed along the fence (straight edge next to the fence) with a long, graceful curve bordering the lawn, gives that beautiful undulating effect one sees when

Avoid the Circular Bed

An Exhibit of School Garden Products

As you can see by this interesting exhibit in a country school, the school gardens are not devoted wholly to pretty things to look at, but also to things that are good to eat. Here are beets and corn and tomatoes and several other vegetables. The interest in growing things is also made the means of teaching other subjects; for example, the fine arts as related to country life. On the wall you see prints which include illustrations from famous landscape painters; and, as related to industry, you see on the right, specimens of different kinds of wood and a cross section of a small tree showing how a tree tells its age by its rings.

the wind billows the wheat field. And since we are planting trees and shrubs for permanency, why not arrange them along the borders to secure the most satisfying effect? Woodbine, or Virginia Creeper, or American five-leaf Ivy (all names for the same vine); and Fig. 18, Bitter Sweet or Woodbine, at each fence post.

As to the material to plant. It is

Plan for School Grounds and Garden

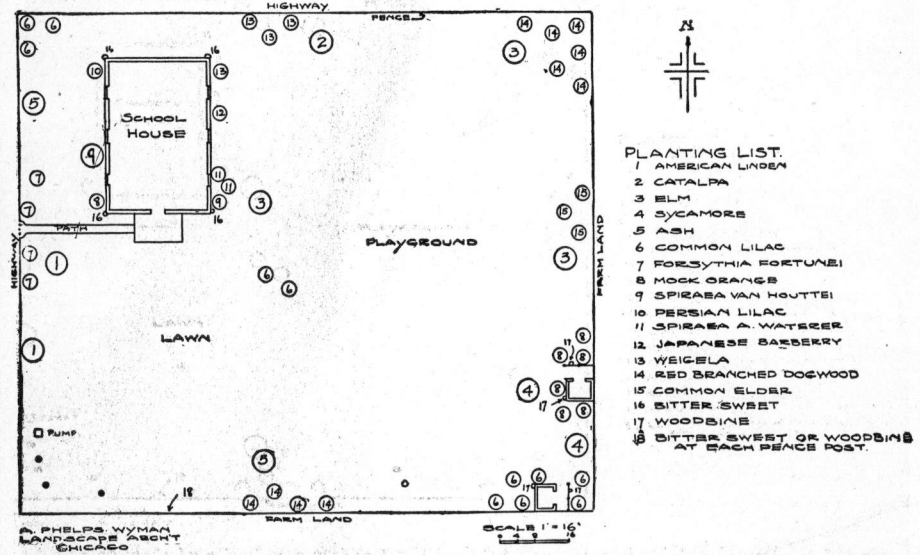

This plan made by a landscape architect will be found a very useful guide in beautifying country school grounds. It may be modified both as to the planting list and the location of flowers, shrubs and trees. Before any work in this line is due, it should be carefully planned, and talked over with the children. The blackboard will be very useful in this connection.

Analysis of the Model Garden Plan

It is absolutely impossible to suggest in one planting plan what is best for the three hundred t h o u s a n d country school grounds in the United States. In the plan for trees, Fig. 1, the American Linden; Fig. 2, Catalpa; Fig. 3, Elm; Fig. 4, Sycamore; Fig. 5, Ash. For shrubs, Fig. 6, Common Lilac; Fig. 7, Forsythia Fortunei; Fig. 8, Mock Orange; Fig. 9, Spiræa Van Houtte; Fig. 10, Persian Lilac; Fig. 11, Spiræa Anthony Waterer; Fig. 12, Japanese Barberry; Fig. 13, Weigela; Fig. 14, Red Branched Dogwood; Fig. 15, Common Elder. For the vines, Fig. 16, Bitter Sweet; Fig. 17,

Patronizing "Home Talent" in Trees

not necessary to send off for foreign trees, shrubs and flowers. These should not be entirely ignored, of course. But each locality has something worthy of place around the home or in the school yard. Why not transplant some of the wild flowers and shrubs found along country roads and brooks? The golden-rod, brown-eyed Susans, blue-bells, violets, sweet-briar, purple asters rival many of the cultivated flowers, and the country roadside surpasses in beauty the drives in city parks. The sumac is a hardy perennial and is easily transplanted. It is good material to use in large

The "Tree" of the Castor Bean

Though originally a tropical plant, the castor bean can be made to grow in temperate regions, and its wide, shiny leaves and good height make it very satisfactory for the school grounds. This one was planted by the children of a country school in Winnebago County, Ill., and has produced some beautiful blossoms which the little girl in front of it is admiring.

masses for a screen to outbuildings, or in clumps scattered in a curved border effect along the playground. by country school teachers for names of good trees to plant on school grounds. This is always answered

Use of the Climbing Vines for Screen Fences

In the summer when they are green, the trees and climbing vines form effective screens on schoolhouse grounds. And even in the winter time the dead vines, still clinging thickly to the lattice work, help to serve the same purpose.

Transplanted Roadside Charms

The color effect in autumn is beautiful, and the blaze of glory it then gives repays all the trouble of spring-time planting. The common elderberry has beautiful foliage, blossom, and berry. The dogwood and the wild crab-apple are not to be despised because they are common and found in the country. These go unnoticed ofttimes, while the committee on selection of material to plant on school grounds pay large prices for shrubs far less beautiful.

The writer has often been asked

The Nobles of the Woods

by asking "What trees seem to thrive best in your locality, on the farm along the fences or by streams?" If the teacher knows these, then plant them. The white oak, the rock and the Norway maples, American elm, linden, black walnut, hackberry, sycamore, are varieties that in time make noble trees. But they all will not grow equally well in every state. The American elm is well-nigh universal and makes a most graceful tree where allowed plenty of room to develop. The almost universal fault in planting trees on school

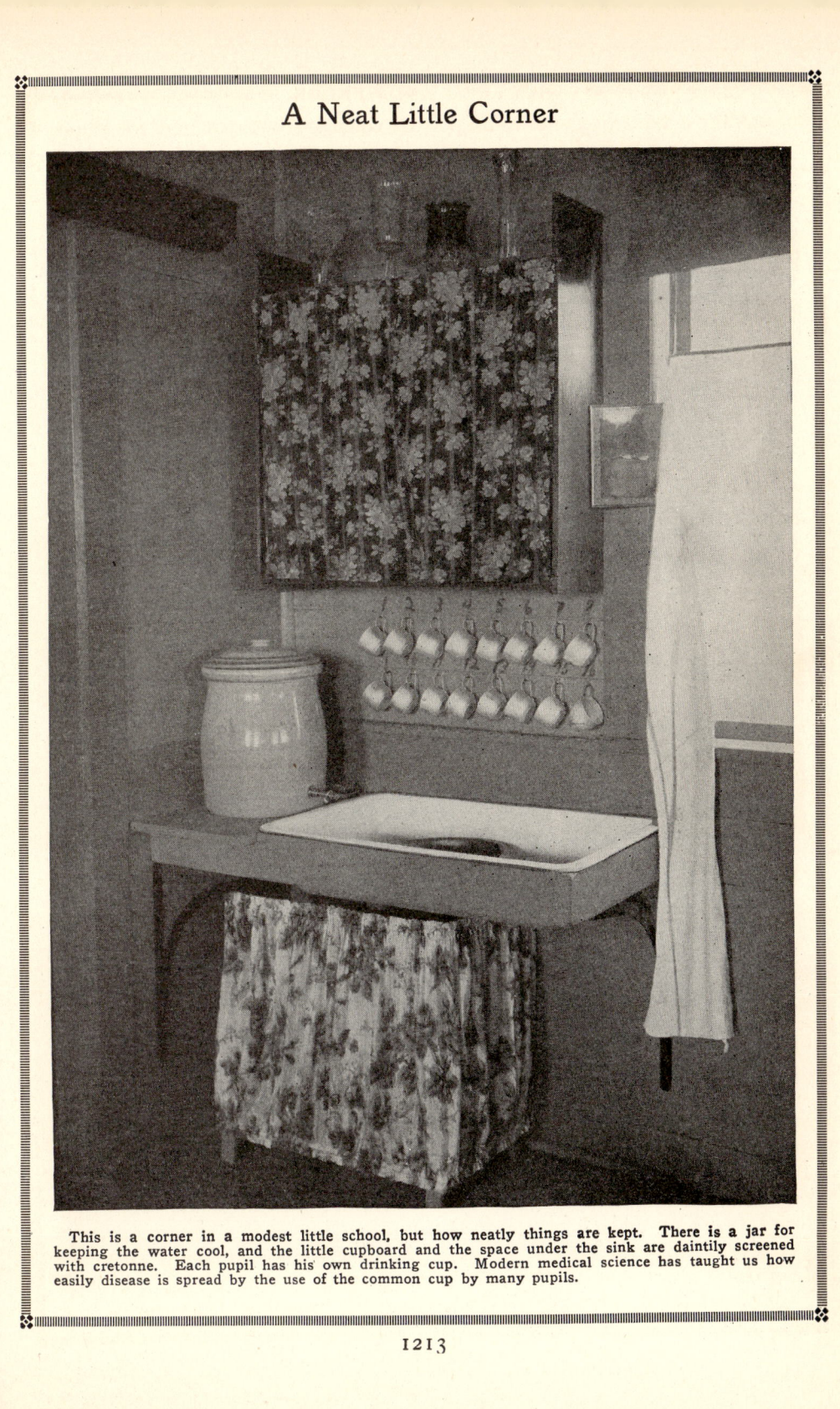

A Neat Little Corner

This is a corner in a modest little school, but how neatly things are kept. There is a jar for keeping the water cool, and the little cupboard and the space under the sink are daintily screened with cretonne. Each pupil has his own drinking cup. Modern medical science has taught us how easily disease is spread by the use of the common cup by many pupils.

grounds—on home grounds too for that matter—is that they are placed too close together. Forty feet should be the minimum distance between elm trees planted around the outer edge of a school ground. This dis-

The following list of shrubs, vines, and flowers is recommended to schools for planting. From this list the reader will doubtless find something suitable for his particular situation. Some shrubs are more

Different Types of School Houses

Here is a series of models showing the different types of school houses to be found in Colorado. The crudest form is the little sod hut. Next come somewhat more ambitious structures, one of which is built of stone and the other of logs. Beyond this is a neat little frame building with a belfry, and next comes a beautiful little school of the most modern design containing several rooms. Beyond is a handsome high school building. All of this illustrates how much money and thought are being given to our schools to make them good to look at as well as places in which to learn.

tance may seem too great when the trees are young but when the trees are forty years old it is none too great. We should encourage the planting of hardwood trees, the nut bearing trees for permanent effects. The poplar and silver maple are better than no trees when conditions are such that no other tree will grow. The main thing is to plant the tree and *plant it so that it will live.* In every school district there must be at least one man who has been successful in growing trees. Get his advice as to how to plant a tree properly.

Avoid Too Close Planting

suitable for planting along the base of a building, while others are more suitable for border planting around the school yard.

1. *Tall Shrubs:* Lilacs, Giant Flowered Mock Orange, Althea or Rose of Sharon, Hydrangea Grandiflora, Smoke Tree, Hamamelis or Witch Hazel, Viburnum Lentago, Wayfaring Tree, Russian Olive, Wild Plum, Strawberry Tree, Bush Honeysuckle, Nina Bark, Elderberry, Sumac.

2. *Medium Shrubs:* Tall Bush Cranberry, Spiræa Van Houtte, Diervilla, or Weigela, Mock Orange, Dentzia Snowballs, Forsythea,

Library on the Teacher's Desk

Sweet Shrub, Flowering Currant, Japanese Spiræa, Japan Quince, Rosa Rugosa, Privet.

3. *Small Shrubs:* Japanese Barberry, Coral Berry, Mahonia Acquifolia, Spiræa Anthony Waterer.

4. *Vines Needing Support:* Matrimony, Trumpet, Wistaria, Woodbine, Bitter Sweet, Rambler Roses, Hall's Honeysuckle.

5. *Self-Supporting Vines:* English Ivy, Boston Ivy and Engelmann's Ivy.

6. *Annual Flowers:* Scarlet Sage, Phlox, Drummondi, Asters, Pansy, Nasturtium, (both climbing and dwarf) Verbena, Petunia, Lobelia Ageratum, Sweet Alyssum, Snap Dragon, Balsam, Bachelor's Button, Helianthus Cumerifolius Stella, Pink, Castor-Oil Bean, Sunflower, Marigolds, Sweet Peas, Geranium, Portulaca.

7. *Annual Vines:* Japanese Morning Glory, Gourds, Cucumber, Cobaea and Kudzu Vine (Peniraria). These will give quick and effective results if sowed at the right time, in properly prepared seed beds and cared for while growing. This applies to plantings of all kinds.

8. *Bulbs for Spring Months:* Tulips in variety, Iris Ranunculus, Yuccas, Scotch Pinks, Campanulas, Sweet William, Spring Beauties, Trillium and Violets.

9. *Perennials:* Phlox, Golden Glow, Columbine, Bluebell, Coreopsis, Larkspur, Foxglove, Hollyhock, Golden-rod, Wild Asters, and Brown-eyed Susans.

In reading of the lives of great men—Lincoln is only one example,—you must have noticed that their success was often in indirect proportion to the number of books they had to read to begin with. Having so few books they valued them the more highly. While city children have great public libraries to draw from, children in the country often have few books, but on this very account they make the most of them and the country is the place where they raise some of our best men.

School Grounds and the Co-operative Spirit

Children can be led to co-operate in social activity to make the school garden a means of beautifying the school grounds. There are beds of

PICTURED KNOWLEDGE

A Clean, Cheery School Room

A clean, cheery country schoolroom, with the light coming from the left and back of the children, is what every country teacher should strive for. This is a good example of what can be done in a country school where carefulness and tidy habits prevail.

wild flowers—the hardy perennials—that know how to survive during the long vacation and contribute the autumn welcome when school days return, or make the closing days of the spring term more enjoyable. This does not mean that the hardy annual—the tame flower—is to be banished from the general flower scheme. And there are beds of hardy native shrubs which know how to survive. These with vines along the fences, with some low growing shrubs, not necessarily native, but hardy and acclimated, along the foundation of the school building, furnish the opportunity for country school garden work. As the writer said several years ago, "The best way to have a school garden is to have it." So with shrubs, vines, trees, etc. Just have them. Much excellent literature is now available for the help of the teacher.

The School Should Have Its Share — There are situations, of course, where under present conditions nothing can be grown on the school grounds. This is true in the arid or semi-arid regions. But in such regions, wherever water can be secured for irrigation so that trees, etc., grow around country homes, sentiment ought to be created that water be turned on to the school grounds and vegetation grown there as well. The appearance of the school grounds even in an irrigated region, should bear comparison with that of the most attractive home in the district.

Within the School Room Walls

No less important than the planting and the growing of native trees, flowers, shrubs, and vines on the

1216

THE COUNTRY SCHOOL
Some Things This Picture Teaches

The specimens of leaves at the back and the good pictures in this schoolroom, as well as the general air of neatness and order which prevails, show that a careful, interested teacher is in charge. The schoolroom is not as well arranged as it might be, but this is not the teacher's fault. Several of the desks are too high for the children who sit at them. And the stove makes the seats in the back of the room uncomfortably hot. A much better arrangement is to have the stove in the center of the room.

school grounds is the improvement of the interior of the school house.

The first consideration in making a school-room attractive is cleanliness and neatness. Charts and maps are apt to get torn, and should be mended. They should also be hung properly and kept free from dust. Good housekeeping in the schoolroom requires that the old bell, the water pails, and all the cups should be properly scoured. Have the boys paint the water bucket to match the woodwork, and see that the coloring of the woodwork, either through the use of paint or stains, is made worth matching.

Cleanliness Comes First of All

Often, where the school funds will not supply the means for employing a painter, the older boys will be glad to "pitch in" and do it. Avoid glaring colors. See that both the woodwork and the ceilings are kept clean.

In short, lead the children to feel that it is their school, and to assume their share of responsibility for the care of both room and premises, including the keeping of the closets neat. Have them bring individual drinking cups and individual towels. This is now required in some states.

Wall pictures are not only decorative, but are a most valuable means of education in good taste and the appreciation of art in their relation to various school studies. Moreover, bare walls are depressing. Let the children help in the selection of pictures. Do not overdo the matter of "old masters" and other paintings that appeal especially to adults. Remember that the appreciation of art, as art, is a matter of development and does not exist in the minds of children in the middle and grammar grades.

Pictures on the Walls

Pictures of animals and of children—particularly pictures that tell a story—appeal to children. Lead the children to select pictures that will give them something to think about. Children never tire of pictures that have something to say to them and that set them thinking. Select pictures of simple outlines and little detail. Children will also show a preference for colored pictures. See that those are selected that are true works of art.

Art dealers will send loan exhibits of their pictures to schools desiring to raise funds for the buying of pictures. At these exhibits a small admission fee is charged, which the school can use for the purchase of pictures in the exhibit.

Keep growing plants in the windows. Both boys and girls can help supply these plants from home and take turns in caring for them.

School room sanitation and decoration do not depend upon irrigation, natural or artificial. Money—some money—is needed, of course. Fifteen dollars will go a long way toward purchasing a porcelain lined sink, a sanitary earthen water jar and aluminum drinking cups, one for each child. Good pictures and books can be secured through the co-operation of school and home by means of a school social. Heating *Transforming* and ventilating systems *the School* are being installed, al-*Room* though not so rapidly as they should be. The demand for all these things has to be created. And the creation of this sentiment, from the very nature of the situation, is a slow process. There are those who hold that the school social should not be for the purpose of making money. It might be more convenient, perhaps, if the money for books, pictures, playground apparatus, and so on, was appropriated by the school board. But since the average country school board does not see its way to purchase these things by taxation, then some other legitimate means will have to be employed. In fact, it may be fairly questioned whether it is best for the community to have everything done for it by the powers that be, and a properly conducted school social is certainly an unobjectionable means of raising a few dollars for school improvement. Of course, the monetary object should not be the only or chief motive in bringing the people together at the school house.

In the Old Buildings

In the old building which has stood for forty years or more, there is not much choice when it comes to the improvement of walls and woodwork. While not strictly sanitary, in many cases all that can be done for the side walls and ceiling is to repaper every two or three years. In *Brightening* the pattern and tint of *Up Old* the paper, however, *Walls* there is an opportunity to exercise good taste in selection. With proper colored window shades and neat, white muslin sash curtains or colored drapery for windows, very pleasing effects may be secured at no great expense. All that can be done in such cases with the old woodwork of the interior is to paint it a color that will be in pleasing contrast to the dominant tone of the paper on the side walls.

The new building when erected should represent the best taste in a style of architecture that is suited to the open country. There should be plenty of space for all the activities necessary in the new country life education, manual training, agriculture, domestic science and the social participation of the community life. The heating, lighting, and ventilation should be as good as that in the best city school. The interior should be simple, artistic, and consequently beautiful. The interior woodwork should be stained to harmonize with the color scheme of walls and ceiling. So shall the best of art go to enrich lives of country boys and girls.

In the Modern Country Schools

The Crocus

Out of the frozen earth below,
Out of the melting of the snow,
  No flower, but a film, I push to light;
No stem, no bud—yet I have burst
The bars of winter. I am the first,
  O sun, to greet thee out of the night!

Bare are the branches, cold is the air,
Yet it is fire at the heart I bear,
  I come, a flame that is fed by none;
The summer hath blossoms for her delight,
Thick and dewy and waxen-white.
  Thou seest me golden, O golden sun!

Deep in the warm sleep underground
Life is still, and the peace profound;
  Yet a beam that pierced, and a thrill that smote,
Call'd me and drew me from far away—
I rose, I came, to the open day.
  I have won, unshelter'd, alone, remote.

No bee strays out to greet me at morn,
I shall die ere the butterfly is born,
  I shall hear no note of the nightingale;
The swallow will come at the break of green,
He will never know that I have been
  Before him here when the world was pale.

HARRIET E. KING

CHILD TRAINING IN HOME AND SCHOOL
SCHOOL AND HOME DISCIPLINE

Training for Good Behavior

PLATO compared the human body, with its animal appetites, to a team of unruly horses, and the soul to its driver. The moral problem is how to "hold your horses!"

The vulgar idea of freedom is "doing as one pleases"; that is, as *the horses please,* and not as the driver pleases. To do as the driver pleases is different from doing as the horses please. The latter leads to moral runaways; the former to the goal that is set. True freedom is control of self and mastery of outward lures. Success and happiness in life depend upon skill in moral horsemanship.

The Gymnastics of the Will

The driver, in the foregoing simile, is the will; the horses (a multiple team) are the sensual desires. The desires are meant to be the servants, not the masters of life. Uncontrolled and free of rein, the desires drain life and sap character. Hunger becomes gluttony; thirst, drunkenness; thrift, parsimony; strength, tyranny; and so with the rest. To curb harmful desire is the office of the will.

The will can be trained and cultivated for this control as easily as the muscles of the body. But as with the muscles, so with the will, daily practice in small things must be the rule; "here a little and there a little," as Isaiah says. For moral health we must work daily in the gymnasium of the will, as for physical health we must work daily in the gymnasium of the body.

Habit is the friend as well as the enemy of character. Little by little we are undermined; so, little by little we are built up. Say "No" daily to this little temptation, refuse daily that sweetmeat, decline weekly this invitation that interferes with some duty, and the strength and facility of control you acquire in the field of little and inconsequential things will follow you automatically in the field of big things. Fasting is as important for the hygiene of the will as it is for the hygiene of the body. It is the primary school for education in self-control. Extend this training into all domains. Let every one take daily practice in the calisthenics of the will.

The Family and the School as Ethical Workshops

Be not cast down. Your child, your pupil is not worse than those that have gone before. The correction-process must be repeated with every individual of every generation. The moral problem remains eternally the same.

Rather rejoice that you have repeated opportunities to begin over again, and to re-apply your hard-won skill. Did you ever reflect, you the parent, or you the teacher, that your own improvement in manners, morals, and knowledge is the result of the reaction of your conduct on you? Your reward, therefore, in this labor, is two-fold.

Look upon every misdemeanor, not as a disaster betokening incurable moral depravity, but as a glorious opportunity afforded by nature for effecting early a moral cure that otherwise might have been missed. Delve into your own hearts, uncover the deep, dark shafts of your own moral history; you will find there rich material for educational use. At least once upon a time you told a "fib"; perchance pilfered; perchance bore false witness against your neighbor; perchance cheated in some ancient examination. Let not your moral indignation, therefore, wax too hot. Rather examine and weigh. Analyze and explain. Take the child or pupil into your confidence. You will be startled by his intense interest in moral problems, by his thirst for guidance in the bewildering maze of temptations that beset life. Consider your home or your school as an ethical workshop in which both parent and child, teacher and pupil, are privileged to labor in common, charitable accord on the greatest masterpiece constructible by man—his own character.

On Moral Economics, and the Kicking of One's Self

The majority of children grow to manhood in the tacit belief that it is the business of some one else to shape and correct their conduct. So, too, many adults remain in this respect children all their lives. The clerk expects correction from the shop-keeper; the subordinate officer from the head of the department; the teacher from the superintendent; and so in all other walks of life. The office of the admonisher and the corrector is conceived to be lodged in a different person from that of the admonished and the corrected. A large part of moral education consists in combining the two offices in one person, in imprisoning the two functions within the same skin. The free moral man is he who embraces both master and servant, both scolder and scolded, both corrector and corrected within himself. The more we can exercise, ourselves, the function of changing our own conduct, the freer we shall be from controlling personalities and from pressures from without.

Think of the outlook this view affords us all for relief. Think of the economy of it and its wondrous saving of moral friction. Do you, both man and boy, woman and girl, do your own "nagging," your own chiding? If the teacher "has a pick on you," discharge her and get a "pick on yourself." Put scolder and scolded within the same skin and your life will be happy.

I once had to deal with a boy who was the acme of moral obtuseness. He was morally deaf; he did not understand the language of correction or reproof. He was, also, as such children frequently are, morally dumb: he disdained to reply either to sympathetic questions or to scathing rebuke. Suddenly I simulated anger and announced that I was going to administer corporal punishment until he consented to talk to me on the subject in hand, and would show some sensitiveness to what I was trying to drive home. Then I abruptly stopped and said, "No, I have another idea. What do you think of my letting *you* do it yourself? You have heard, haven't you, of people kicking themselves? Will you promise me, if I let you off, to go home tonight and go out in the woodshed and kick yourself?" For the first time in a year's acquaintance a smile illumined his face. He had never smiled before, but the humor of the suggested correction appeared to appeal to him, and I also extracted from him the first articulate word that in such interviews I had heard him utter. He went home and probably did administer to himself some moral buffets that otherwise might not have been applied. In any event, he never afterwards met me without a smile, and there doubtless was left sticking in his moral consciousness an idea even we adults may well ponder.

On Being Late; and the Typical School Excuse

Tardiness is the besetting sin of childhood. Condoning of it by teachers and parents leads to fixed habits of unpunctuality and to a chronic inability to keep appointments. These are serious handicaps to business or social success, and here is the point—future business and social success—at which we must attack this vice.

Unpunctuality is an infallible symbol of weakness of character. The tardy, the unpunctual child must be shown that he is the plaything of accident and circumstance, never master of his own fate, and the defeated victim of every chance-happening of his environment. A certain percentage of the pupils of every school are chronically tardy. The reasons for the tardiness must be analyzed and shown to be trivial and in a great majority of cases *avoidable*. The following are common excuses:

"There was sickness at our house and I had to go to the drug store this morning." To this the answer might well be: "Did you not know there was sickness? And if you knew, could you not have foreseen you would have had to go on this errand? Could you not have got up earlier and so have gained time on this errand, which you knew would be very likely to be demanded of you? Would your father, who works in a switch tower, have allowed such an errand to prevent him from being on time? It is such forethought about one's business in life that makes successful men. You would like to be a successful man, wouldn't you?"

"I was interrupted on my way to school by a friend of the family who gave me a message to deliver." Answer: "Why do you not do one of two things; either always start for school early enough to make allowance for such trivial interruptions; or, politely, but firmly, inform your friend that you couldn't stop to talk or you would be late to business, your business being going to school. Or, ask him if it would not interfere with *his* business to walk toward the school with you and talk on the way. He would admire you all the more for your strict attention to business and your thoughtfulness. You will have to acquire this habit for your later business life. Why allow every chance passer-by, or every chance-happening in your environment to interfere with your business now?"

The same arguments may be fruitfully applied to the other typical school excuses, such as appointments with dentists, doctors, dressmakers, going to church on holy day (where there is a late and an early service the same morning), being kept home for work, and the rest.

Pupils who have the habit of allowing themselves barely enough time to reach school before roll-call, should be shown that an increase of five or ten minutes through earlier rising will forestall all accidents and bring the pupils immeasurably more happiness and freedom than the few stolen moments of indulgence or rest their tardiness has gained them, and that they will avoid thus the continual scoldings and "naggings" their unpunctuality brings them.

But the children are not altogether at fault on this score. Very few parents are themselves clear on these subjects, many are even coadjutors of their children in seeking flimsy excuses, and the majority will do well to analyze also their side of these situations and take heed of the suggestions here offered. It should be remembered, too, what psychologists have clearly established, that the sense of the lapse of time is lacking in most children and must be carefully cultivated through training and direction. What we need is not punishment, but careful explanation and correction of these faults. The correction frequently has to take the form of punishment, but the end, which is the establishment of character, must always be kept in view.

Playing Hookey with the Collusion of Mama

"Hookey" is an ancient school sin. It is our old friend "the lie" in a submersible form—the making parent or teacher believe one is where one is not. Conniving at deception to explain unjustified absences is not alone a weakness of the child. Parents, by facilitating school absences on trivial pretexts (for homework, errands, engagements with dentists, doctors and dress-makers, for hang-over days at vacation and week-ends, for "educational movies" and for feigned or imagined illnesses), directly contribute to practices of evasion and self-deception that ultimately become fixed and ruinous habits. Outright hookey is easy to handle; but hookey obscured by subtle collusion with mama (and all the more subtle because usually it is unconscious in the parent), is insidious to the utmost; it corrupts insensibly the child, and foils all but the most practiced disciplinarians. Untold are the cases where pupils are first absent from their own free and errant wills and for purposes of self-indulgence, yet afterwards bring to the teachers written excuses for these wrongful acts, originally unknown to the parents, yet subsequently condoned by them.

The teacher has a double duty here; first, to break up by firm but kind procedure the self-deceptive habit in the child, and secondly, to intimate tactfully to the parent the insidious results of this practice. Parents' Associations could accomplish much in this field; and generally their co-operation for moral ends is one of their greatest opportunities for good.

The Appeal of "The Job"

Directly in line with this thought —the vital relation between school "business" and the "get there" ambition so near to the human heart—

is the question of getting and holding a job.

Discuss the question. You will find in such talks that the minds of the pupils will be raised to so white a heat of interest in their business and industrial future, that you will be able to divert your discussion of the question of how to get a job to the obverse of the question, namely, the most effective methods of losing a job. You will be able to develop in the minds of the young people, by their own participating efforts, the reasons for the rules and regulations of your school or family; to show that the habits of body and mind, which the infraction of these regulations brings with it, will slowly but surely sow the seeds of failure in their subsequent business life and social career, and you will be enabled in this way to strike effectively at the roots of certain minor evil practices in the school, ranting against which is usually of little avail. Hookey, cheating, pilfering, unpunctuality, time-wasting, gadding, gossip, gum-chewing, and the rest, now take their natural places as insuperable obstacles to the business and social success of each individual, and the corresponding virtues will no longer figure as the adornments of spineless weaklings.

Gossips Not Wanted

Always use concrete cases. For example, I have often told pupils that once when I had asked an employer seeking an office girl whether he wished one more proficient in bookkeeping or in stenography, he had replied that he preferred above all, one "who could keep her mouth shut." This remark naturally led to a very interesting discussion of the pernicious habits acquired by indulging in petty school gossip. I cited for the boys dozens of other cases, definite and concrete, with the names of prominent local employers —cases where unpunctuality, "soldiering," pool-playing and other forms of extravagance on small salaries, led to disaster. The fact also that the business men of the community were in the habit of actually watching the boys with regard to manners and habits was also very effectively applied.

We see from this that the "trick" invariably is so to shape a given situation that *the interest in the problem springs from the student* and not from the teacher. Ethical instruction in this view is incidental rather than systematic, and ordinarily requires only constant watchfulness on the part of the teacher in the selection of situations, and appropriate tact in the exploitation of them. Every teacher and every parent is richly surrounded by these situations; they occur in multitudes daily. The problem is correctly to select and develop them, for the student and with the assistance of the student, in all their moral implications. The most effective time for teaching the evil of dishonesty is when the student is dishonest; the evil of cheating, when the cheating is done. In other words, these great moral crises in child and adolescent life *should not be used solely as occasions for punishment, but as magnificent opportunities offered by nature for effective ethical instruction.* Not that we should wait until a person steals before condemning and forbidding stealing and the rest, but simply that when these derelictions do occur, we should take advantage of the psychological and ethical white heat of the situation to exploit them to the fullest. Every one will admit that the best tale with which a moral can be adorned is a lively chapter out of the boy's own life.

On Cheating in Examinations

An investigation made in a prominent High School in Illinois disclosed the fact that 40 percent of the students were—they confessed it—addicted to cheating in examinations. The disclosure was not necessarily a reflection upon the moral tone of the school investigated; it is possibly a reflection simply of the traditional attitude of public opinion that in school life dishonesty, trickery, pilfering, destruction of property, and the various other school and college pranks constitute a class of misdemeanors that stand apart from similar practices in life outside the school. Until public opinion, and especially the opinion of individual parents, on this subject changes, there is little hope of a decided improvement in the school world. *What we need here is a corrective pedagogy of parents.* Both parent and child must see that the school is a moral gymnasium, that all the exercises and all the work and business of the school are actually pieces of life itself. The school in a miniature way presents as many temptations and as many moral crises as life itself; and, whereas the punishments and corrections should always take into account the ignorance and lack of experience of the culprits, it should never slur the seriousness and importance of the end to be attained.

The full correction of the practice of cheating in examinations and of certain other forms of school dishonesty, depends primarily upon the correction of public and parental opinion in this regard, and on the establishment of a pronounced tone of high public moral feeling in the school itself. True correction should proceed from within and seek to remove the impulse and the motive. Honor-systems are helpful, but do not go to the root of the situation.

Parable of the Lost Umbrella

"I forgot," "I forgot." A dozen times daily these words fall from childish lips. Their mere utterance implies immunity from responsibility at home. "Father, father," exclaimed a boy, once, on returning from an outing with his parent and holding triumphantly aloft the article referred to, "we forgot to lose our umbrella today!"

The trail of every child is dotted with the shadows of forgotten duties and articles. But the articles or duties forgotten are not so significant as the fact that the practice is considered normal and pardonable in childhood. What moral antiseptic may we apply to counteract this habit, hardening with age?

I once had several pupils time the emptying of the class-rooms on the ringing of the dinner-bell, and afterwards called the attention of the school to the fact that the time for clearing the building at this winsome signal was shorter than that required for emptying it on a fire-alarm. I said that thereafter I would interchange the signals. The comparison created laughter, but incidentally stimulated thought. How can we give the call of duty the speed of carnal desire, how trick out the summons of character with the lure of sense?

Partly again by appealing to the selfish motive of future business and social success, partly by holding the victim of the habit up to good-natured raillery, partly by indicating the humiliating embarrassments the practice leads to, and partly by re-enforcing these negative methods by a practical and vigorous positive technique of memory.

Show that forgetfulness betokens a lamentable weakness of will, and makes its victim the sport of every chance diversion. Show that distraction or absent-mindedness fastens on its victim the reputation of unreliability and, unless corrected, makes failure in any service or calling a foregone conclusion. Picture the losses connected with it as disloyalty to self-sacrificing parents. Show that *the will to remember* can be trained. Instruct the child to forget the thousand and one distracting trivialities of the day, and to fasten his attention with cannibal zeal for weeks at a time on a few necessary duties or objects—as rubbers, hats, sweaters, and books. The training of increased attention to a few things will then extend to larger things. Plan intensively for the small, and the large will follow automatically.

On Taking Bread from a Teacher's Mouth

Juvenile pranks sometimes assume an organized impersonal form that is difficult to reach. Mischief making in school is as contagious as disease, and frequently attains concert heights of annoyance, before which the hardiest pedagogues quail. The classical battle grounds for the badgering of sensitive teachers are the study-hall, the chorus, the orchestra, dramatic organizations and group-work generally. The new and the substitute-teacher alike are historic targets for these assaults. Such subtle and impersonal group-attacks may sometimes be disposed of by appeals like the following:

"Did it ever occur to you that the troubles you are creating render the work of this school ineffective; that the authorities hold this teacher, whom you are treacherously and cruelly badgering, responsible for a state of order such that the school work may be properly done; and that if she fails she will lose her position? Did it ever occur to you that the selfish sport in which you are indulging not only injures yourself, is robbing you and your comrades of the most valuable time and opportunity of your lives, and so constitutes the highest disloyalty to yourselves and your self-sacrificing parents, *but also may be taking the bread out of a poor woman's mouth,* or out of that of a mother dependent upon her, and may be the means of blighting a career that has cost money and self-sacrifice for its preparation? Would you like to have your sister or brother treated so? And would you care to have the example of fair play that you are here exhibiting toward a defenseless woman cited in the recommendation which I may soon be called upon to give to your future employer?"

Such an appeal to the chivalry of pupils seldom fails of its effects.

Meddlesome Matty

Oh, how one ugly trick has spoiled
    The sweetest and the best:
Matilda, though a pleasant child,
    One ugly trick possessed,
Which, like a cloud before the skies
    Hid all her better qualities.

Her grandmamma went out one **day**,
    And by mistake she laid
Her spectacles and snuff-box gay
    Too near the little maid;
"Ah, well!" thought she, "I'll try them on
    As soon as grandmamma is gone."

Forthwith she placed upon her nose
    The glasses large and wide,
And looking round, as I suppose,
    The snuff-box too she spied.
"Oh, what a pretty box is this!
    I'll open it," said little miss.

"I know that grandmamma would **say**,
    'Don't meddle with it, dear!'
But then she's far enough away,
    And no one else is near;
Besides, what can there be amiss
    In opening such a box as this?"

So thumb and finger went to work
    To move the stubborn lid,
And presently a mighty jerk
    The mighty mischief did;
For all at once—ah woeful case!—
    The snuff came puffing in her face.

Poor eyes and nose and mouth and chin
    A dismal sight presented;
And, as the snuff got further in,
    Sincerely she repented—
In vain she ran about for ease;
    She could do nothing else but **sneeze**.

She dashed the spectacles away
    To wipe her tingling eyes,
And as in twenty bits they lay,
    Her grandmamma she spies.
"Hey-day! and what's the matter **now?**"
    Cried grandmamma, with lifted brow.

Matilda, smarting with the pain,
    And tingling still and sore,
Made many a promise to refrain
    From meddling evermore.
And 'tis a fact, as I have heard,
    She ever since has kept her word.

                                            JANE TAYLOR

My Mind to Me a Kingdom Is

My mind to me a kingdom is,
  Such present joys therein I find,
That it excels all other bliss
  That earth affords or grows by kind:
Though much I want which most would have,
Yet still my mind forbids to crave.

I see how plenty (surfeits) oft,
  And hasty climbers soon do fall;
I see that those which are aloft
  Mishap doth threaten most of all;
They get with toil, they keep with fear;
Such cares my mind could never bear.

Content to live, this is my stay;
  I seek no more than may suffice;
I press to bear no haughty sway;
  Look, what I lack my mind supplies:
Lo, thus I triumph like a king,
Content with that my mind doth bring.

Some have too much, yet still do crave;
  I little have, and seek no more.
They are but poor, though much they have,
  And I am rich with little store;
They poor, I rich; they beg, I give;
They lack, I leave; they pine, I live.

I laugh not at another's loss;
  I grudge not at another's pain;
No worldly waves my mind can toss;
  My state at one doth still remain:
I fear no foe, I fawn no friend;
I loathe not life, nor dread my end.

My wealth is health and perfect ease:
  My conscience clear my chief defence;
I neither seek by bribes to please,
  Nor by deceit to breed offence:
Thus do I live; thus will I die;
Would all did so well as I.

                        Sir Edward Dyer

LESSONS AT HOME AND AT SCHOOL
CHOOSING A VOCATION

How to Choose a Vocation and How to Make a Success of It

© C. Klackner

This boy is leaving the old home for the first time, to make his way in the world. His success and happiness will depend upon how wisely he chooses his vocation and how much of the life of the home—its loving thoughtfulness, its devotion to duty—he carries into his relations with the world at large.

The Right Job the Road to Success

TAKING his first job is the biggest event in the life of a young man. Nearly all the poverty in this country, where opportunity awaits whoever cares to grasp it, can be traced to taking the wrong job as a boy. We see failures everywhere about us —square men in round jobs, and round men in square jobs. The labor experts trace the drift of men, from place to place, and eventually to the workhouse, to the unfitness of the men for the positions which they try to fill.

A Dangerous Kind of Guessing

Life Work Chosen on Whim

Although the selection of a vocation means so much to a youth, the process is often attended with no more care than is used in picking out the first pair of long trousers. The result is a tremendous annual waste of human material. The boy who is temperamentally suited for a civil

1229

engineer may choose medicine, because he has a fancy for dosing cats and dogs; thousands without analytical minds go into law, thinking of the great fees of a few corporation counsels; the salesman by nature frets and fumes as a jeweler's apprentice. It is all a hit or miss game, with more misses than hits. Hence the number of men who mark time on small salaries—the men who are in "blind alleys," and who see nothing ahead excepting discharge when they have outlived their usefulness.

Leaving one's vocation to chance expresses great confidence in destiny or luck, but most captains of industry or finance declare that they have made their own luck, have shaped their own destinies by finding what they could do best, and then sticking so everlastingly to it that they became better than anyone else, and won the big prizes.

How to Climb the Stairs

The president of one of the largest industrial corporations in the world began work as a youth in a steel-wire mill in New Haven, Connecticut; he had no education and no pull, but he liked steel-making. He studied his work, and he studied his books—he made himself a workman with knowledge. He went a step higher each year, until he reached the top. The president of another large concern has spent his life in the one company—but not in the one job.

Educational Opportunities in a Job He deliberately started out for the presidency, although that start was made pushing trucks at a few dollars a week. Whenever he felt that he knew a department, he asked to be transferred to another department, regardless of salary; he became an expert mechanic, but he was not content to be a mechanic, and had himself transferred to the draughting department at half the wage—he learned designing. So, on he went, from department to department. Finally the heads of the business learned that they had in their employ, in a subordinate position, a young man who knew more about the business than any other man in the place. Then they took him into the executive offices, and he moved along, step by step, to the presidency.

Another man set out to be a banker. He knew the best way was to begin as a bank clerk. He entered a Boston bank and worked along for six years. Then he decided that he needed a higher view of banking. The place of bank examiner being open for competitive examination, he entered the contest and won the appointment. The duties of bank examiner enabled him to gain a knowledge of methods throughout a wide section—he gained a broad outlook on banking. Because of these qualifications he had a chance to enter a Boston bank as assistant cashier. Later—you can see why—he stepped up to the vice-presidency. Then he saw the advantages which would result from the consolidation of several banks, and he led such a consolidation. The New York financiers, ever alert for ability, had their eyes on the young man; they made him an offer, and now he heads one of the biggest banks in the country, and his salary is larger than that of the president of the nation.

Studying the lives of our leading business men, we discover that few of them started life with either wealth or education, but having found the work which held their interest, they educated themselves. They always made ready for the place ahead, or having reached the top, started a new concern of their own.

Don't Leave This to Chance

It is now generally recognized that the choosing of a vocation is far too important to be left to chance or circumstance. The boy who gets into the right job at the beginning has a lead *Consider Well* over the boy who scat-*What You* ters three or four years *Are Fitted For* in an endeavor to discover something he can do. The odds are always on the job which requires skill and training; the truly skilled man is seldom unemployed—and is never unemployed for long periods. Skill is attained in years, not in months; the chances for employment for the man under forty are much greater than for the man over forty. Therefore, the person who has attained high skill when he is about thirty is in a far better position than the one who does not acquire this skill until some years later. Every profession and every trade is better learned in youth than in maturity; the mind is quick, and both hand and mind are easily trained.

But Don't Start Too Early

Starting early is a comparative term. If a profession is decided upon, the early start will not be in the actual practice of the profession, but in studies which will mould you for the work which is to come. And among the professions themselves the time differs, for in a profession, as well as in a trade, the best mental equipment possible should be attained in advance of seeking to earn money. The engineering professions may be learned in an ordinary four years' course at college, but law is best taken up in a law school after *Relation of* three or four years of the *School Work* ordinary academic col-*to Success* legiate course. Most of the best law schools now require a college degree as a preliminary to admission, and the highest medical schools also have requirements for a degree. It has been found that only the trained mind will get the most out of the law and medicine. After graduation in law, the best plan is to gain knowledge of actual practice by two or three years in the office of a busy lawyer; during this period the student will receive either a very small salary or no salary at all. The doctors get on fastest who spend one or two years after graduation as interns in a hospital. Few boys are ready to enter college before eighteen, they can then be ready to engage in the engineering profession at about twenty-two, but three years must be added to this for the lawyer, and six years, counting the hospital training, for the doctor. The long period of education for medicine and law makes it inadvisable for any young man to engage in them, unless he is prepared to finance himself, or to be financed, until he is nearly thirty years old.

Learning the Trades

A boy entering a trade should begin as soon as he has left the high school; a mechanic with a high school training, has in him the makings of a better mechanic than one who has been forced to abandon school early. But the second boy, if he has the right stuff, will gain the high school education after hours.

The importance of education cannot be too greatly emphasized—but it must be the right kind of education. The idea prevails that specialized education, an education which becomes technical at once, is the best. The experience of practical men teaches otherwise. The important quality in a worker is brains, and brains are developed in their fullest capacity only by hard thought. The courses in school which compel thought are the most valuable; a man whose mind is filled with facts is not necessarily an educated man—he must be able to use the facts. The use of facts come only through mind training, and mind training is achieved by hard thought, such as is required in all good school work and useful reading. When a boy's mind has once been trained to think, he can quickly grasp and use every fact that comes to him, but if the mind be untrained, these facts are only a confusing jumble to him. Most boys, and many fathers, protest that practical subjects are not taught in school, but the boy who is at once plunged into technical study without preliminary mind training will become a mere unthinking machine.

Knowing and Knowing How

Kind of Brains That Are Wanted

Brains and executive ability are the qualities which the business men are looking for; ordinary skill can be bought—it has a definite market value, but brains, coupled with executive ability, make their own values. John Wanamaker said: "I am looking for men who will compel me to make them partners. I like the employes who cannot be kept down." The president of a great American exporting company says: "The man with ideas and executive ability, the biggest type of man, is hard to get, and yet harder to keep, he will not work for wages—it is necessary to share the business with him." Another big business man has a rule which he puts this way: "Make every man organize himself out of his job." By this he means that every man in the company should be qualified for the place ahead. Another big concern has a monthly report in which the heads of departments are required to classify their clerks into four divisions. One division is for the clerk with good ability, and likely to become increasingly useful, the second is for the exceptional man, who should be especially encouraged, the third is for the ordinary clerk of moderate ability, and the fourth class takes in those of less than moderate ability. The men in the last two classes are weeded out. That firm does not want a man in its employ who is not able to advance.

A Business "Elevator" System

All have read of the great ironmaster, famous for his "boys," as he called the young men who were associated with him, all of whom became millionaires. While in business he said: "I am always searching for the man who can teach me something about running my business—who can find a way of doing something which is better than the way I know."

On Merely Being Steady

The day of the mere "steady" man has passed. Of course every boy must have good habits—that goes without saying; very few large corporations will employ anyone who drinks, either in or out of hours. The Pennsylvania Railroad led this reform. To be sure, employers appreciate the type of faithful soul who proudly says: "I have had the same job twenty years," but they want most the man that cannot be kept in the same job for many years, the man who has the brains and the initiative to become too big for his job. They promote him and give beginners a chance in the lower positions.

But what job ought to be selected? There are 9,326 gainful occupations, but they are not all equally gainful, and every boy or girl is not equally suited for each of the 9,326 places. However, there are enough different kinds of places to give an opportunity to every kind of disposition.

The Important Thing in Choosing a Vocation

The important thing in choosing a vocation is to use care and common sense in the selection. Benjamin Franklin's father took him about Boston to see the workings of every trade, then young Benjamin selected printing, and he became a very good printer. Franklin's fame does not rest on his printing, but it was through printing that he came first into authorship, and then into public life. The Franklin way probably remains the best way, but it is now easier to investigate the different lines of work than it used to be, for many books have been published which tell all about the opportunities and conditions in the various trades. Most public libraries contain these books.

Good Books Are Good Guides

The occupations to be avoided are those which promise a fair wage at the beginning, and which do not call for skill and hard work. The unskilled places always pay better at the start than the skilled, for the new employe is of little use in skilled work at the beginning. The boy who starts at sixteen in some job where the work is easy and clean will probably get $5 a week; when twenty years old, the boy will have $10—and he can never expect to get higher wages in that place. These places are not for boys, they are for the men who have demonstrated that they are not worth more money. These places are called the "blind alleys," because they lead nowhere. Among these places may be mentioned those of messenger boys, errand boys, stock boys, elevator boys, cash boys, packers. Many boys have risen by using the job only as a means for getting forward to some other job; they have not wasted years in the easy tasks.

The right job for a boy or girl depends upon the boy or the girl. A college education will always help, but it is not so important as to warrant great sacrifices, unless the young person has an exceptional mind. And the young person with an exceptional mind will get on anyhow. The thinking power acquired through a college education is valuable, and a degree is necessary for the engineering professions, but many of our big men of business are without college training.

Place of the College Education

And, after all, the work of a college is like the work of a school—it doesn't get you anywhere unless it leads you to read, to study, and to think—through your own voluntary effort—outside of school and college, and beyond school and college days.

Every job which requires skill must be given a preference over the unskilled. For places in offices and stores the supply is far beyond the demand. It is the mechanical arts that need more men and women. The professions, especially law and medicine, offer little except to the "stars," and even then the wait is a long one. All the trades give openings to the boy who is willing to work and to learn. Using the same ability, he can make more money in them than he can in a profession.

A Sure Way to Find Your Place

The sure way to find the right place is: (1) Study many kinds of endeavor; find out all about the line which you think you like. (2) Talk with people who are in that line. (3) When you find what you think will suit, try it. (4) Be guided by future prospects rather than immediate returns. (5) If you find that you have made the wrong choice, go into something else at once. And remember, these are the qualities which employers are after.

Five Points in Choosing

Intelligence with which to analyze problems.

The power to organize.

The stamina to press on amid difficulties and discouragements.

Right ideals and courage.

Good health and vitality.

Once you have found your job—know all about it. Read the technical papers and magazines relative to that line; study your subject, find out what other people are doing—in short, get a big, outside view of your work. Then apply your knowledge to doing your work better. James J. Hill put it this way: "Give me the man who will do things which he could not be blamed for not having done." That is—improve your work.

Vocational Training in Colleges

Most of the larger colleges and universities, especially those located in the large cities, have now special courses which are designed to fit the student for business. In most cases the courses may also be taken in the summer schools alone, or in connection with other studies. The design of the collegiate studies is to equip the student with a thorough knowledge of business practice, and thus to enable him to grasp the actual problems of business with understanding. They teach the methods of bookkeeping, of finance and of banking, they teach the movements of money, the foundation of cost systems, business and political economy. The idea behind all of these courses is different from that of the ordinary business school or college, which teaches only how to do certain lines of work—as bookkeeping and stenography. The courses in the colleges tell the "why" of things, and do not go into detail; they leave the detail to actual experience. The Wharton School of the University of Pennsylvania has an excellent course; so has Columbia University, New York University (which also has classes in practical business conducted in the business districts of New York), the Amos Tuck School of Dartmouth College, Harvard University, Chicago University, Northwestern University, University of Michigan, University of Minnesota, the University of Colorado, Indiana University, the University of California, Boston University and the College of the City of New York.

Character of Subjects Studied

In addition to these purely business courses, which fit boys for business life, are the technical universities, such as the Massachusetts Institute of Technology, the Case School of Applied Science, Stevens Institute, and the engineering departments of the large universities, such as Cornell, the University of Pennsylvania, Harvard, Yale, and practically all of the state universities of the country. Vocational study for women reaches its highest development in Simmons College, Boston.

Value of Correspondence Schools

To the young man who is unable to take a course of vocational training at any of these institutions, the Correspondence School offers an excellent substitute. Education by correspondence has developed to such an extent that courses are obtainable in almost every line offered by the technical and professional schools, and in many not covered in these schools.

In the large Correspondence Schools the texts used are prepared by the professors in those subjects in the best technical schools, so that the student may rest assured that the presentation is thorough and reliable.

While the Correspondence School lacks the stimulus of personal contact with professors and fellow students, it has, on the other hand, some distinct advantages over the residence school. One of these advantages is that, through his correspondence in connection with his work, the student learns to think straight, and to express himself briefly and clearly, as he frequently does not do in oral recitation. There are no opportunities for overindulgence in college athletics, and the student is removed from other temptations peculiar to the student body. The young man is thrown on his own resources of industry and determination. There is no "log-rolling" between students in a recitation period. He is receiving his training under conditions that correspond more nearly to real life—to actual employment in his chosen field. We have only to consider how large a majority of the most eminent men, which the world has so far produced, have been what we call "self-made" men, to appreciate the importance of these facts. Such men have made themselves with but little help from schools—often with no help from colleges—but with a great deal of help from good books.

"Learning to Earn" Through Books

Any public library will give a list of books which may be read with profit by the boy or girl who is seeking a career. The lives of leading men offer much inspiration. Among the books of value are:

Good Books on Vocations

"Learning to Earn," by John A. Lapp and Carl H. Mote, which gives instruction on what boys and girls should know for various occupations; "Vocations for Boys" and "Vocations for Girls," by Eli W. Weaver—practical books discussing the openings in all lines for the boy or girl who wants to get ahead.

"Vocations for the Trained Woman," edited by Miss Agnes F. Perkins, is a valuable publication issued by the Woman's Educational and Industrial Union of Boston, in which experts in each line of trained vocation take up the needed training, the openings, and the chances for advancement in seventy lines; this book also gives the average salaries and the top salaries, which can be reasonably expected, and is a most valuable book for the girl who is starting out to earn her own living.

The Union also publishes many pamphlets on vocations which can be had at a very small cost.

"Business Employment," by Frederick J. Allen, is intended for parents and teachers rather than for the wage seeker, but it contains many helpful hints. "Choosing a Vocation," by Professor Frank Parsons, gives ideas on discovering the proper life work. Meyer Bloomfield, the director of the Vocation Bureau of Boston, has written several helpful books for the teacher, parent or older searcher for a vocation. Among these books are: "The Vocational Guidance of Youth," "The School and the Start in Life," "Youth, School, and Vocation," and "Readings in Vocational Guidance." The Vocation Bureau also issues a number of pamphlets which thoroughly go into the requirements and the possibilities of numerous vocations; they have pamphlets on baking, confectionery manufacture, the work of the architect, the landscape gardener, the machinist, grocers, department stores, banking and law, and have many others in preparation.

Among other suggestive books are: "Vocations for Girls," by M. A. Laselle; "Engineering as a Vocation," by Ernest McCullough; "Vocations for the Trained Woman," by Eleanor Martin; "The Law as a Vocation," by F. J. Allen; "The Young Men and the World," by A. J. Beveridge; "The Making of a Newspaper Man," by S. G. Blythe; "With the Men Who Do Things," by A. R. Bond; "Modern Advertising," by E. E. Calkins; "Talks to Young Men," by Charles H. Parkhurst; "Practical Salesmanship," "Starting in Life," and "How to Get Your Pay Raised," by N. C. Fowler; "How to Get a Position," by S. R. Hall; "Business Education," by C. W. Haskins, and "Vocational Guidance," by J. Adam Popper.

England and America in 1782

O thou that sendest out the man
To rule by land and sea,
Strong mother of the Lion-line,
Be proud of those strong sons of thine
Who wrench'd their rights from thee!

What wonder if in noble heat
Those men thine arms withstood,
Retaught the lesson thou hadst taught,
And in thy spirit with thee fought—
Who sprang from English blood!

But thou rejoice with liberal joy,
Lift up thy rocky face,
And shatter, when the storms are black,
In many a streaming torrent back,
The seas that rock thy base!

Whatever harmonies of law
The growing world assume,
Thy work is thine—the single note
From that deep chord which Hampden smote
Will vibrate to the doom.
                                    TENNYSON

CHILD TRAINING IN HOME AND SCHOOL
THE BOY SCOUT

Why Being a "Good Scout" Is the Making of a Boy

The glorious sun and our glorious flag and the boys all get up about the same time in a Boy Scout camp. The loud, clear notes of the bugle mean another great day of work and fun—the kind of fun that's good for you. When the reveille sounds, every scout bounces out of bed like a soldier on campaign. If he needs any help, his mates are always willing to give it to him. There's no, "Willie, Willie, did you hear me?" business in a Boy Scout camp.

THE Boy Scout Movement developed to meet a real need—a need which always has existed but which was made more pressing by modern social and industrial conditions. This great need which the Boy Scout Movement seeks to meet is that of giving boys effective training in the duties and obligations of citizenship. The Boy Scout Movement accepts the principle that the best way to improve our type of citizenship of the future is to give early attention to the material from which our future citizenship is to be formed; and it has gone to work enthusiastically on that basis. Scouting is interested in the boy of today, not so much because of his present value to society as because of his value as a man in the future—and as the father of the men who will follow him.

What These Young Scouts Are For

1237

Scouting is a long-range proposition but it produces immediate effects of such striking value that the program would be fully justified if the bigger and broader aspects should be entirely forgotten.

How Johnny Lost His "Jobs"

What were the conditions surrounding boys during the several generations immediately preceding our own? For the most part, boys grew up on farms or in small rural communities where plenty of hard work fell to their daily lot. The "boy problem" of those days was solved by making the boy do a man's work at an age that would be unthought of today. Under these conditions, boys had little spare time and little thought was given to boy training.

But as the industrial interests of the country grew in importance, there came a concentration of population in large centers that created new conditions and new problems. There became less of the kind of work boys could do and a large decrease even in the number of chores and tasks that had occupied their time in the home. The result was that the boys found themselves with a lot of spare time on their hands that had to be spent some way and a lot of surplus boy energy that demanded some outlet. No attempt was made to direct the recreational activities of boys or to provide for a constructive expenditure of their time and energy. They were left pretty largely to their own devices, with the inevitable result that many of them were led into recreational activities that were pernicious in their effects on character. Acts of lawlessness increased and the Juvenile Court became a flourishing institution. Boys began to attract attention because of their misdoings and this attention began to grow into a genuine interest in boys and an appreciation of their value and possibilities.

Good Boys Going to the Bad

As a result of this interest a number of organizations for boys were established, among the more important of which were the Boys' Brigade, the Knights of King Arthur, The Woodcraft League, the Sons of Daniel Boone, the Boy Pioneers, and the Boys' Work Department of the Y. M. C. A. Each of these organizations accomplished splendid results, but no one of them seemed to be capable of assuming a commanding position of leadership in work among our boys.

The Work of Baden-Powell

Just about this time, Sir Robert Baden-Powell, a British military leader in the Boer War, became impressed with the deplorable lack of direction in boys' training in England, which was brought home to him by the inefficiency and helplessness of the recruits that were sent to him in South Africa. Baden-Powell was forced to the conclusion that if these men had had proper training as boys, they would have been better soldiers. But, what was of more importance still, he realized that they would have been better citizens in any sphere of life.

In order to solve the problem of training these recruits, he inaugurated a system of "scout" work that produced remarkable results. Upon his return to England at the close of the war, he applied himself to the task of giving the boys an opportunity to become the right kind of men—vigorous, reliable, resourceful.

A Soldier's Campaign for Character

THE BOY SCOUT
Learning to Scale a Wall

Wall-scaling is one of the features of Boy Scout field meets that is always very interesting. The usual method is for teams of eight to race, running fifty yards, scaling a ten-foot barrier and then running another fifty yards. This has been done repeatedly in less than one minute. The picture shows boy scouts scaling a wall in a field meet on the Harvard University stadium.

With this end in view he made a careful study of the existing programs for boys' work, including that of the public school system. This study confirmed him in his belief that the fundamental need in boys' education is character training. He then began his task of outlining a program that would meet this need, and the result was the Boy Scout Movement.

In devising his plan for boys' work, Baden-Powell used many of the features of other organizations, but his program of "Scouting for Boys," as finally developed, was more than a mere regrouping of tried ideas; it contained vital elements that were new in boys' work, the fundamental value of which has been proven by the wonderful growth of the Movement in which they are incorporated.

The "Rights" and "Lefts" of the Scout Idea

The two cardinal principles through which the program of scouting for boys seeks to accomplish its purpose of character development are Honor and Service.

The idea of honor is impressed upon the Scout by means of the scout oath, which he promises "on his honor" to obey. The oath is:

"On my honor I will do my best—

1. To do my duty to God and my country, and to obey the scout law;

2. To help other people at all times;

Waking Up the Muscles in the Morning

Since Boy Scouts don't make use of military drills, many camps have gymnastic exercises to develop the boys physically and to teach them how to obey commands quickly and to manage their bodies skilfully. In an out-of-door camp like this one where the boys are active all day long, the drills are short and are held the first thing in the morning.

3. To keep myself physically strong, mentally awake and morally straight."

The Scout law which is referred to in the oath is as follows:

1. A SCOUT IS TRUSTWORTHY.

A scout's honor is to be trusted. If he were to violate his honor by telling a lie, or by cheating, or by not doing exactly a given task, when trusted on his honor, he may be directed to hand over his Scout badge.

2. A SCOUT IS LOYAL.

He is loyal to all to whom loyalty is due; his scout leader, his home, and parents and country.

3. A SCOUT IS HELPFUL.

He must be prepared at any time to save life, help injured persons, and share the home duties. He must *do at least one good turn to somebody every day.*

4. A SCOUT IS FRIENDLY.

He is a friend to all and a brother to every other scout.

5. A SCOUT IS COURTEOUS.

He is polite to all, especially to women, children, old people, and the weak and helpless. *He must not take pay for being helpful or courteous.*

6. A SCOUT IS KIND.

He is a friend to animals. He will not kill nor hurt any living creature needlessly, but will strive to save and protect all harmless life.

7. A SCOUT IS OBEDIENT.

He obeys his parents, scoutmaster, patrol leader, and all other duly constituted authorities.

8. A SCOUT IS CHEERFUL.

He smiles whenever he can. His obedience to orders is prompt and cheery. He never shirks nor grumbles at hardships.

9. A SCOUT IS THRIFTY.

THE BOY SCOUT

Airing the Bedding

It doesn't take long for a Boy Scout in camp to get into his clothes. He isn't bothered with many and there is always a friendly rivalry among these wide-awake lads to see who can get dressed first. Then the cots with their bedding are set out to air in the fresh morning breeze.

Lining Up for the Morning Mess

There's many a millionaire who would give a small fortune for what every one of those boys has under his belt—a keen appetite for breakfast. You see they are lining up for the morning mess. Think how good it must smell with the odor of those woods for flavor! Doesn't it fairly make your mouth water?

PICTURED KNOWLEDGE
The Boy Scout as a Naturalist

A true scout should have whole volumes of woodland lore at his finger tips and tongue's end. Only by long practice and careful study can this knowledge be acquired, however. It takes skill to get good pictures of little forest creatures, but kodaking them is one of the best ways of learning about them. A good scout knows where the birds build their nests; where and when fish can be caught and just how to land them successfully. He knows, too, what to do if a companion is bitten by a poisonous snake.

He does not wantonly destroy property. He works faithfully, wastes nothing, and makes the best use of his opportunities. He saves his money so that he may pay his own way, be generous to those in need, and helpful to worthy objects. *He may work for pay but must not receive tips for courtesies or good turns.*

10. A SCOUT IS BRAVE.

He has the courage to face danger in spite of fear and has to stand up for the right against the coaxings of friends or the jeers or threats of enemies, and defeat does not down him.

11. A SCOUT IS CLEAN.

He keeps clean in body and thought, stands for clean speech, clean sport, clean habits, and travels with a clean crowd.

12. A SCOUT IS REVERENT.

He is reverent toward God. He is faithful in his religious duties and respects the conviction of others in matters of custom and religion.

The Emphasis on "Service"

In both the oath and law the idea of service is emphasized. And it is emphasized still further by the scout motto "Do a Good Turn Daily." These "good turns" are acts of service performed voluntarily without reward. Still further emphasis is placed on the idea of service through the scout motto "Be Prepared!" The ideal of preparedness for service in any emergency is constantly held before the scout. He is taught that it is the natural thing for a scout to help whenever he is needed. He is taught how to do things and to prepare himself, not only for service in emergencies but for every day service to society and to his country, by keeping himself, "physically strong, mentally awake and morally straight."

These principles of honor and service are naturally appealing to boys, but they are made most effective when given expression through a program of activities remarkably adjusted to boy psychology and boy interests.

Practically every interest that appeals to boys is utilized in the Boy Scout program. To begin with there is the suggestive word "scout," and the promise of the word is carried out in such activities as stalking, tracking, woodcraft, camping, hiking, etc. Other activities that are strongly emphasized are first aid, handicraft, signaling, cooking knot-tying, swimming, pioneering, horsemanship, conservation, and many others, each of which serves its definite purpose in character development.

Putting a Lesson to Practice

Here they go off into the surf. This is probably about ten o'clock in the morning, to judge from the slant of the sun on the boys and the shoulder of the big fellow in the stern of the boat. It is about this time of the day also that the land begins to be quite a little warmer than the water, so that there is just the kind of a gentle on-shore breeze to set the waves playing like that.

Instruction in Using Oars

Here, in quiet waters, where nothing serious can happen even if you chance to spill out, one of the older boys is giving a group of boys instruction in using the oars. The boys will work in pairs, each with a single oar, so they must learn to pull together.

These activities have been included in the scout program on the assumption that it is as easy to interest a boy in activities that are helpful and constructive as it is to interest him in those which are harmful and destructive; and the success of the program has demonstrated the truth of the assumption. All the boy needs is wise and genuinely interested leadership.

Without such leadership the scout movement could never have been developed. Baden-Powell recognized this truth and wisely included in his program the safe-guard of competent adult supervision. As a result of this foresight the Movement is made a vital, living, growing force by the host of splendid men who are giving to the work their best of unselfish, volunteer service. It is not hard to teach boys the principles of service when they are taught by men who live these principles in their daily lives.

These are the main reasons why the Boy Scout Movement met with such instantaneous approval, and why it soon developed in England to a point where it attracted worldwide attention.

Boyce of Chicago. Prior to this time a number of troops had been started in various parts of the country by men who had been impressed with the possibilities of the scheme, through reading Baden-Powell's "English Handbook." It is significant that Mr. Boyce's interest was occasioned because of an actual service rendered him in true scout spirit by a London Boy Scout, who, because of his obligation to do a good turn daily and the rule against the acceptance of tips, greatly astonished and impressed Mr. Boyce. After the conference with Sir Robert Baden-Powell he secured the cooperation of friends in Washington, D. C., and proceeded to incorporate an organization of the Boy Scouts of America under the laws of the

The Stomp Dance

The "stomp dance" was taught the Boy Scouts by Cherokee Indians who visited the Boy Scout camp at Tulsa, Oklahoma. In the foreground a group of boys beating on a hollow log with sticks are furnishing the dance music.

The Movement in This Country

The development of the Boy Scout Movement in the United States has been equally remarkable. In the beginning of 1910 the idea of introducing the Movement along lines similar to those that had made the Movement so successful in England was first proposed by W. D.

Story of the London Scout

THE BOY SCOUT

Like Ducks to Water

Off for a Dip

It's doubtful if a row of frogs ever plunge into their favorite swimming holes with more zest than these boys are doing. Of course, the frogs don't make a run and jump of it, as the boys do; they just jump!

Lining Up After the Dip

After a swim the boys form a line and go through exercises that warm them up. This picture was taken on the shore of Lake Michigan in a summer camp of some Chicago Scouts.

PICTURED KNOWLEDGE
A Pleasant Way to Go to School

Before becoming a first class scout, a boy must describe fully from observation, ten species of trees or plants (including poison ivy) by their bark, leaves, flower, fruit or scent; or describe six species of wild birds by their plumage, notes, tracks or habits; or describe six species of native wild animals by their form, color, call, tracks or habits; find the North Star and name and describe at least three constellations of stars. The boys in the picture are learning about plants under the direction of the scout master at the right. Notice the clothing of the boys—some are in bathing suits, one is barefooted. One of the charms of scout camps for the boy is that little or nothing is required of him in the way of formal covering.

District of Columbia. This was effectively accomplished on February 8, 1910. Headquarters for the Boy Scouts of America were temporarily established at 124 East 28th Street, with the co-operation of representatives from a number of National organizations having headquarters in New York City.

Simultaneously with this effort, other organizations established National Headquarters for themselves. Happily, however, before the middle of July, 1910, all of these organizations with the exception of the American Boy Scouts merged with the Boy Scouts of America. It was largely through the efforts of Mr. Edgar M. Robinson that the different organizations were brought together. From the very beginning he saw the possibilities of the idea; his wide experience in boys' work enabled him to give wise counsel in his endeavor to have the Movement inaugurated under satisfactory conditions. Since the very beginning the organization in the United States has made rapid progress along all lines.

The form of the Boy Scout Movement in the United States differs only in detail from the parent organization in England. It is based on the same proved principles that have made the work successful wherever tried, with such minor changes as were necessary to make the program fit peculiar American conditions and institutions.

The general policy of the Movement is shaped by a National Council composed of men of national reputation who are interested in work for boys. The honorary president of the organization is the President of the United States. This Council meets once a year for the election of officers and the transaction of regular business. The executive direction of the Movement is entrusted largely to an Executive Board which meets once a month. The National Headquarters of the Movement is maintained in New York City with the Chief Scout Executive in active charge, assisted by an able staff which devotes its entire time to the work of the Movement.

The units of organization next below the National Council are the *Local Councils and Their Work* Local Councils. These are formed in the larger scout centers and have general supervision of the work in their particular districts. Many local councils employ a scout executive who devotes his entire time to developing and directing the work of the Movement.

The unit of organization to which the scout himself belongs is the troop. The standard troop has a membership of 32 boys divided into three patrols. Each troop is in charge of a scoutmaster, who must be a man of good moral character, and a troop committee of three men who are interested in scoutcraft and who are willing to give some time and thought to the work of the troop. Most troops also have one or more assistant scoutmasters, who must be at least eighteen years of age. The patrol officers, who are boys, are the patrol leader and assistant patrol leader. There is no maximum age limit for scouts, but no boy under twelve years of age is admitted.

A Good "Cook Stove" Built of Bricks

When a party of scouts expect to camp in one place for any length of time, they usually make their fire in a "cook stove" like this. Several things can be kept cooking at once, and with openings left on all sides the fire is sure of a draft no matter which direction the wind is coming from. And Boy Scouts pride themselves on being able to light a fire in less than a minute by the Indian method of rubbing sticks together.

How to Become a Scout

In order to provide a strong incentive to progress in scouting, there are a number of classes of scouts. The lowest class is the Tenderfoot. No boy is admitted to the scout brotherhood until he has passed the tests for that rank which includes the following requirements:

1. Know the scout law, sign, salute, and significance of the badge.
2. Know the composition and history of the national flag and the

PICTURED KNOWLEDGE
Isn't This a Neat Little Cabin?

Did you ever see anything more spick and span? This log cabin is in the woods near Dorchester, Mass. The boy, looking out of the window, built it and this is how he did it: He first built it on paper—the way in which all good houses and ships and things are built. That is to say he figured out the size desired and carefully drew his plans. Then he secured a piece of ground 12x14 feet. Then, from dead pines and oaks back in the woods there, he got his material. He laid the foundation of oak because of its durability. The pine logs for the walls were hauled during the winter when the snow was on the ground. They were cut 14 feet long and 6 inches in diameter and then notched near the ends very carefully—notice how snugly they fit into each other. The following spring the roof was put on. This was done by nailing boards over the logs on the roof and then putting over the boards a good grade of roofing paper. Then came the building of the fireplace which consisted of rough field stone. The stones were properly fitted and cemented into place with portland cement. This cement mixed with coarse sand was also used to fill the cracks between the logs. Last of all, the windows and doors were carefully fitted in while inside a floor of pine boards was laid. The name of the boy who built it is Howard Upham and he belongs to Boy Scout Troop 36. He says his idea was to build a log cabin that would accommodate "two or more fellows." You will notice that he not only has the cabin, but the "fellows."

customary forms of respect due to it.

3. Tie four out of the following knots: Square or reef, sheet-bend, bowline, fisherman's, sheep shank, halter, clove hitch, timber hitch, or two half-hitches.

The next higher scout rank is that of Second Class, in order to attain which a boy must pass these tests:

1. At least one month's service as a Tenderfoot.

2. Elementary first aid and bandaging: know the general directions for first aid for injuries; know treatment for fainting, shock, fractures, bruises, sprains, injuries in which the skin is broken, burns and scalds; demonstrate how to carry injured, and the use of the triangular and roller bandages and tourniquet.

3. Elementary signaling: know the Semaphore, or the International Morse alphabet.

4. Track half-mile in twenty-five minutes; or if in town, describe satisfactorily the contents of one store window out of four observed for one minute each.

5. Go a mile in twelve minutes at scout's pace—about fifty steps running and fifty walking, alternatively.

6. Use properly knife or hatchet.

THE BOY SCOUT
Trestle Bridge Built by Scouts

This is a fine example of what Boy Scouts learn to do in the way of building and engineering. It's a great trestle bridge across a big valley; that is to say, it's a large bridge on a small scale. It is built on exactly the same principle as are the long railroad bridges across deep valleys.

7. Prove ability to build a fire in the open, using not more than two matches.

8. Cook a quarter of a pound of meat and two potatoes in the open without the ordinary kitchen utensils.

9. Earn and deposit at least one dollar in a public bank.

10. Know the sixteen principal points of the compass.

A Second Class Scout can advance to First Class rank by complying with these requirements:

1. Swim fifty yards.

2. Earn and deposit at least two dollars in a public bank.

3. Send and receive a message by Semaphore or International Morse alphabet, sixteen letters per minute.

4. Make a round trip alone (or with another scout) to a point at least seven miles away (fourteen miles in all) going on foot, or rowing boat, and write a satisfactory account of the trip and things observed.

5. Advanced first aid: know the methods for panic prevention; what to do in case of fire and ice, electric and gas accidents; how to help in case of runaway horse, mad dog, or snake bite; treatment for dislocations, unconsciousness, poisoning, fainting, apoplexy, sunstroke, heat exhaustion, and freezing; know treatment for sunburn, ivy poisoning, bites and stings, nosebleed, earache, toothache, inflammation or grit in eye, cramp or stomach ache, and

1249

PICTURED KNOWLEDGE
First Aid and Life Saving

These sketches show some of the emergencies in which a scout should be prepared to be of assistance—carrying an injured person on a stretcher, binding a broken arm, reviving a lady who has fainted, rescuing a drowning man.

chills; demonstrate artificial respiration.

6. Prepare and cook satisfactorily, in the open, without regular kitchen utensils, two of the following articles, as may be directed: Eggs, bacon, hunter's stew, fish, fowl, game, pancakes, hoecake, biscuit, hardtack, or a "twist" baked on a stick; explain to another boy the methods followed.

7. Read a map correctly, and draw from field notes made on the spot, an intelligible rough sketch map, indicating by their proper marks important buildings, roads, trolley lines, main landmarks, principal elevations, etc. Point out a compass direction without the help of the compass.

8. Use properly an ax for felling or trimming light timber; or produce an article of carpentry or cabinet-making, or metal work made by himself. Explain the method which he followed.

9. Judge distance, size, number, height, and weight within 25 per cent.

10. Describe fully from observation, ten species of trees or plants, including poison ivy, by their bark, leaves, flowers, fruit, or scent; or six species of wild birds by their plumage, notes, tracks, or habits; or six species of native wild animals by their form, color, call, tracks, or habits; find the North Star, and name and describe at least three constellations of stars.

11. Furnish satisfactory evidence that he has put into practice in his daily life the principles of the scout oath and law.

12. Enlist a boy trained by himself in the requirements necessary to become a tenderfoot.

What Breadth of Practical Education!

Still further incentive to progress is provided by awarding badges for special merit in the following subjects: Agriculture, Angling, Archery, Architecture, Art, Astronomy, Athletics, Automobiling, Aviation, Bee Keeping, Gardening, Handicraft, Horsemanship, Masonry, Mining, Bird Study, Blacksmithing, Bugling, Business, Camping, Carpentry, Chemistry, Civics, Conservation, Cooking, Craftsmanship, Cycling, Dairying, Electricity, Firemanship, First Aid, First Aid to Animals, Forestry, Music, Painting, Pathfinding, Personal Health, Photography, Physical Development. Pioneering, Plumbing, Poultry Farming, Printing, Public Health, Scholarship, Sculpture, Seamanship, Signaling, Stalking, Surveying, Swimming, Taxidermy.

Note that the whole scheme of education—and observe the breadth of it—is based on *doing* things, not merely *reading facts about things*.

There are several special groupings of merit badges which entitle scouts to special honors. A Life Scout is one who has passed merit badge tests in the following subjects—Personal Health, Public Health, First Aid, Physical Development or Athletics, Life Saving or Pioneering. A Star Scout has all the badges for a Life Scout and any five others in addition.

The highest rank in scouting is that of Eagle Scout, in order to attain which a scout must pass tests in twenty-one of the merit badge requirements, which must include First Aid, Life Saving, Personal Health, Public Health, Civics, Pioneering, Cooking, Camping, Bird Study, Pathfinding, Athletics or Physical Development and any ten others.

There are now in the United States many thousands of these volunteer leaders serving as scoutmasters, assistant scoutmasters, members of troop committees, members of local councils, etc. It is due very largely to the splendid services of these men that the Boy Scout Movement is making such striking progress.

Some Big Things the Scouts Have Done

It is impossible to estimate the value of the tremendous amount of helpful work that has been done by scouts, for the bulk of it has been in the form of individual daily "good turns," few of which are ever reported. It is easier, however, to ap-
The Scouts preciate the value of the
and Com- acts of community serv-
munity Work ice which are carried out
as troop enterprises. In hundreds of cities and towns, scouts have

A Good "First Aid" Bandage

Handkerchiefs and a rolled up magazine make a first class bandage for an injured arm or leg. The scout's training equips him in resourcefulness in emergencies, so he knows how to improvise what is needed out of whatever material may be at hand.

worked diligently in clean-up campaigns, swat-the-fly campaigns, and other civic enterprises; they have established rest rooms and first aid stations at fairs and carnivals, killed tent caterpillars by the million, constructed and tended bird-feeding stations, assisted in charity work on

The Scouts and the Salem Fire — When Salem, Mass., was visited by a disastrous fire, the first relief to reach the city came in a huge auto truck loaded with food and clothing which had been collected by Boy Scouts. During the period immediately following the fire, when the

Restoring a Half-Drowned Boy

The boys in the picture are practicing the Schaefer method of bringing a partially drowned person back to life. It requires only one operator, as you see. The patient is laid on the ground, face downward, with arms extended above the head, the face turned a little to one side to admit free passage of the air from the lungs to the mouth. The operator kneels astride the prone figure and lets his hands fall into the spaces between the short ribs. By allowing his weight to rest upon his hands he forces the air out of the lungs. By relaxing the pressure, the chest cavity enlarges and air is forced in by atmospheric pressure to take the place of that which was expelled. This operation should be performed fifteen times a minute.

Thanksgiving and Christmas, co-operated with the veterans on Memorial Day, assisted in "safety first" efforts, conducted Fourth of July celebrations, aided in the distribution of Red Cross seals, searched for missing persons, fought forest fires, cared for community parks, distributed circulars—there is no end to the things scouts have done. Whenever an opportunity to serve has been presented, they have taken advantage of it eagerly.

normal life of the city was completely interrupted, Scouts rendered invaluable service as helpers in the relief stations and as messengers for the various organizations that directed the work.

The Scout Executive for Richmond, Va., was requested to mobilize the Scouts for relief work at a train wreck near the city. Twelve minutes after the notice was sent out, the first group of Scouts reported ready for duty. In twenty-five minutes 200 Scouts were in line, in charge of scout-masters, fully equipped for first aid or other relief work. Seventy-five picked Scouts were rushed to the wreck in automobiles furnished by business men. Fortunately the reports of the seriousness of the wreck were exaggerated and there was little for the Scouts to do. But this splendid demonstration of "preparedness" was effective, nevertheless.

In Knoxville, Tennessee, 1,300 children were massed on the steps of their school-house to have a photograph taken. The steps collapsed and there were numerous injuries of a more or less serious nature. By good fortune there were present at the time, a number of Scouts who immediately turned their attention to the work of rescuing the injured and applying first aid. The work of the Scouts was so effective that the superintendent of the school at which the accident occurred, wrote the following letter to the Scout Commissioner of the Knoxville Local Council:

"God Bless the Boy Scouts!"

"I have your favor of the 5th inst. before me. In reply, beg to say that Scouts Fred Chandler, Hale Thomas, and others rendered signal first aid service on the occasion of our unhappy accident here last week. I do not see how we could have gotten along without them. It seems providential that we had on hand, at the time, supplies and Boy Scouts to render this first aid. Too much praise cannot be given the boys for what they did until the doctors arrived. Let us have more Boy Scouts and more trained for first aid service. God bless the Boy Scout Movement. Long may it live to bless mankind with its beneficent object."

Such tests prove that the principles of the Movement are right and that the Scout program for putting them into effect is right. Scouting *works*.

The "Chair Carry" for an Injured Boy

All Boy Scouts have to know something about first aid and to learn more about it before they can advance their rank. The picture shows two boys carrying a supposedly injured comrade in what is known as a "chair carry."

The Stormy Petrel

A thousand miles from land are we,
Tossing about on the roaring sea;
From billow to bounding billow cast,
Like fleecy snow on the stormy blast.
The sails are scattered abroad like weeds;
The strong masts shake like quivering reeds;
The mighty cables and iron chains,
The hull, which all earthly strength disdains—
They strain and they crack; and hearts like stone
Their natural, hard, proud strength disown.

Up and down! Up and down!
From the base of the wave to the billow's crown,
And amidst the flashing and feathery foam
The Stormy Petrel finds a home—
A home, if such a place may be
For her who lives on the wide, wide sea,
On the craggy ice, in the frozen air;
And only seeketh her rocky lair
To warm her young, and to teach them spring
At once o'er the waves on their stormy wing.

O'er the deep! O'er the deep!
Where the whale, and the shark, and the swordfish sleep,
Outflying the blast and the driving rain,
The Petrel telleth her tale—in vain;
For the mariner curseth the warning bird
Which bringeth him news of the storm unheard!
Ah! thus does the prophet of good or ill
Meet hate from the creatures he serveth still;
Yet he ne'er falters—so, Petrel, spring
Once more o'er the waves on thy stormy wing!

Barry Cornwall.

CHILD TRAINING IN HOME AND SCHOOL

CAMP FIRE GIRLS

The Camp Fire Girls and the Women of Tomorrow

GIRLS are just like boys—only different. They like to do things for the same reasons that boys like to do them, only they also like to do different things, and to do them in different ways. The spirit of adventure, the joy of effort and attainment, the love of all of the things that make life interesting and worth while is just as strong in the girl as in the boy.

Purpose of the Organization

The purpose and aim of the Camp Fire Girls is to help girls to grow into true, brave, efficient, womanly women, just as the purpose and aim of the Boy Scouts is to help boys to grow into true, brave, efficient, manly men. The boys are to be men—"doctors, lawyers, merchants, chiefs," while the girls are to be women—mothers and home-makers, for even the teachers, social workers, stenographers and business women are primarily mothers and home-makers none the less. The Camp Fire Girls, therefore, is not modeled on the Boy Scouts, for the

Development of Womanhood

very simple reason that the purpose and the results of the two organizations are different, and different means must be taken to reach these results.

Camp Fire Girls had its origin in the understanding of the heart of girlhood, gained by Mrs. Gulick through intimate association with her own daughters and their girl friends. For years Dr. and Mrs. Gulick, with their little family, had *World-Wide* camped each summer *in* on the banks of Lake *Its Scope* Sebago, in the Maine woods. Gradually the group was enlarged through the coming of girl friends, and out of the camp activities planned to help her own girls to develop into the kind of women which Mrs. Gulick felt that every girl could develop into—true, brave, efficient and womanly—came the inspiration for the great organization of the Camp Fire Girls, which in a few years has become world-wide in its scope and interest, and has influenced the lives of tens of thousands of girls. Every state and territory has its Camp Fires, even far-off Alaska and Hawaii, while Canada, Japan, with nearly all of the Western European nations are represented in the rolls of the National office.

Ideals and Symbols of the Order

Mrs. Gulick's ideal for Camp Fire centered in the three words— Work, Health and Love. Out of *The Watch-* these she took the first *word and* two letters of each and *Its Meaning* made a new word— "Wohelo." This is the watchword of Camp Fire Girls everywhere, and in its symbolic meaning is found the spirit and inspiration of Camp Fire.

The symbol of the Camp Fire Girls is Fire. Men first gathered around the central camp fire for food, for warmth, for mutual protection. The fire thus became the center of the camp of group and tribal life. Separate groups, having the bond of individual interests and love, gathered about smaller fires built apart from, but near the central fire, and so the first homes came to be. So Camp Fire is the symbol of the home.

Camp Fire finds its purposes and interests in the home. It makes the daily task interesting, and gives honors for common-place things well done. It recognizes the spirit of romance and adventure, the quest for beauty and the desire for social life in the heart of youth, and meets all of these by giving the things of every-day life new and fascinating interest. It uses beautiful ceremonies, has an appealing ritual, and bases rank and honor upon personal attainment.

Becoming a Camp Fire Girl

The Camp Fire Girl takes no oaths, makes no vows or pledges, but she does something which is far greater than these—she expresses a desire, an inspiration to be and to do, and inspiration is as limitless as is the eternal in the soul.

"It is my desire," announces the candidate (who must be at least twelve years old) standing before the Council Fire, "to become a Camp Fire Girl, and to obey the Law of the Camp Fire, which is

Seek beauty
Give service
Pursue knowledge
Be trustworthy
Hold on to truth
Glorify work
Be happy.

This Law of the Camp Fire I will strive to follow."

But it is not enough to express a desire—she must now work toward its attainment. In this is one of the fascinations of Camp Fire—a girl must do something worth while in order to attain to something worth having. There are no idlers about the camp. The first rank is that of Wood-Gatherer, and the Camp Fire Girl must attain to this rank before she has the right to wear the little silver ring with the fagots of the Seven Points of the Law with the three raised points for Work, Health and Love.

No Idlers in the Camp

There are six general requirements for this rank: two months' membership, with attendance upon six weekly meetings and two ceremonial meetings; the selection of a Camp Fire name and symbol; the preparation of the headband and the ceremonial gown; the payment of the annual dues; and the winning of at least ten elective honors. These requirements test the girl's sincerity of purpose and interest. When she has complied with them, she may rise at the Council Fire and repeat the Wood-Gatherer's Desire, which is an expression of loyalty to the Law of the Camp Fire and to her Camp Fire Sisters, and a wish "to be true to the truth that is in me and pure in my deepest desire."

How Much of This Could You Do?

The next rank is that of Fire-Maker. To attain to this rank the girl must be at least thirteen years old, and, as the rank carries with it more of dignity and responsibility, she must have won 14 required honors and 20 elective honors. From this list of required honors one gets some idea of the purpose and scope of Camp Fire: (1) To help prepare and serve, together with other candidates, at least two meals for meetings of the Camp Fire; this to include purchase of food, cooking and serving the meal, and the care of the fire. (2) To mend a pair of stockings, a knitted under-garment, and to hem some necessary article requiring at least a yard in length of hem. (3) To keep a written, classified account of all money received and spent for at least one month. (4) To tie a square knot five times in succession correctly and without hesitation. (5) To sleep with open windows or out of doors for at least one month. (6) To take an average of at least half an hour daily out-door exercise for at least one month. (7) To refrain from chewing gum or eating candy, sundaes, sodas and commercially manufactured beverages between meals for at least one month. (8) To name the chief sources of infant mortality in summer, and to tell how and to what extent it has been reduced in one community. (9) To know what to do in the following emergencies: (a) clothing on fire;' (b) person in deep water who cannot swim (both in summer and through the ice in winter); (c) cut foot; (d) frosted foot; (e) fainting. (10) To know the principles of elementary bandaging and how to use a surgeon's plaster. (11) To know what a girl of her age ought to know about herself. (This includes the laws of hygiene, diet, regularity and exercise, and "those intimate things which careful mothers tell to their daughters.") (12) To commit to memory any good poem or song not less than twenty-

To Earn a Fire-Makers' Rank

five lines in length. (13) To know the career of some woman who has done much for her country or state. (14) To know and sing all the words of the national anthem.

When a girl has done all of these things—and it is no light task—she may rise at the Council Fire and repeat the Fire-Maker's Desire:

"As fuel is brought to the fire
So I purpose to bring
My strength
My ambition
My heart's desire
My joy
And my sorrow
To the fire of humankind;
For I will tend
As my fathers have tended
And my father's fathers
Since time began
The fire that is called
The love of man for man
The love of man for God."

The last rank is that of Torch-Bearer. To attain to this rank a girl must be at least fifteen years old, and "must be approved by the guardian as ready to bear the torch *The Rank* of life and light to guide *of* others." For this rank *Torch-Bearer* she must also win certain required and elective honors by which she proves herself worthy and capable of leadership.

The Winning of More Honors

Aside from the required honors for each rank, there are over two hundred elective honors from which a girl may select the things which she wants to do in order to win the rank to which she aspires. Nor does the winning of honors stop when she has won the rank of Torch Bearer—indeed, she is more anxious than ever to win them, for she understands their significance and value better than ever before.

For each honor won, a bead is given when it is reported at the Council Fire. The conferring of the beads is a part of the ritual of the Council Fire, and is an impressive ceremony. The honors are di-*For Each* vided into seven classes, *Honor* each class having its *a Bead* distinctive bead. The beads are usually strung on a long string, with all sorts of modifications according to the fancy of the girl, and this string is a part of her ceremonial costume. It is, indeed, a record of her Camp Fire life and attainments, and becomes one of her most cherished possessions. Honors are given for:

Home-craft: Flame colored honors (fire is the symbol of home).

Health-craft: Red honors (the red blood).

Camp-craft: Brown honors (the brown of the bark and the heather).

Hand-craft: Green honors (the green of new life, of creation).

Nature-lore: Blue honors (the blue of the sky).

Business: Gold honors (money).

Patriotism: Red, white, and blue honors (the flag).

By this honor list it will be seen that no matter what a girl may do or where she may live, she can still win her Camp Fire honors. The business girl may walk to her work every morning for a week and win a Health-craft honor, and report her *How These* work in store or office *Honors* faithfully done and win *Are Won* a Business honor. The stay-at-home girl may keep her own room in order for one month and win a Home-craft honor. An honor in Patriotism may be won by helping, through actual work or by influence, to clean a dirty alley, or by

CAMP FIRE GIRLS

joining in a pure milk crusade. "There is romance and adventure in everyday life," says Mrs. Gulick. The girl is given honors for doing there may be a local Camp Fire. The girls must be at least twelve years old, and the Guardian not less than twenty-one. There is no "upper

Big Sister and Her "Blue Birds"

Little girls between 6 and 12 join Camp Fire by becoming "Blue Birds." The older girls teach them simple craft lessons, beadwork and other things and the older girls unconsciously develop unrealized talents in story-telling, teaching and motherliness.

the simple, homely things, and she learns to love to do them. One must study the lists of tasks for which honors are won to realize how far-reaching is the influence of Camp Fire, not only in the development of the growing girl, but in the life of the home and community in which she lives and wins the honors.

The Camp Fire Guardians

Wherever there is a group of from six to twenty girls interested in Camp Fire, with an older woman, preferably a mother, to lead them, age" limit put upon Guardians, and many a mother whose children have found their own places in the world has renewed her own youth and given inestimable gifts to her community by acting as Camp Fire Guardian.

Qualifications for a Guardian

The girls should belong to the same social group, and the Guardian should be a woman in touch and sympathy with the mothers of the girls. She should be a Camp Fire Girl, or should become one. She should wear the ring of bound faggots and the Guardian's pin. Wherever a Camp Fire girl sees these two emblems of her order, she should know that she has found a friend. The Guardian should be a woman who loves girls and who is interested in the things of their lives and capable of being a leader among them.

The very nature of the service makes it appeal only to those women who have real love of girls and high ideals for them, and who are themselves women of attainment and character. Of the Guardians, forty-two percent are college graduates; seventy-three percent of them have some training beyond a high school course. Writers, musicians, librarians, social workers, high school teachers, pastors' assistants, women of leisure, and mothers are numbered on the rolls. There is a challenge about the work which few without special training or fitness dare to accept, while the limitation for each Guardian to not more than twenty girls in her group gives her a position of real personal influence. She may give something of herself to every girl, which may count for strength and power all the years of her life.

The Guardian is responsible to the National organization for conducting the affairs of the local Camp Fire and for maintaining its standards. She can have but one group under her charge. When interest is extended, new groups can be organized, with new Guardians for each group. When the number of groups is sufficiently large, the Guardians may organize a Guardians' Association, selecting one of their number as Chief Guardian, and they may have meetings as often as they desire to confer together. They may also bring all of their groups together in a Grand Council Fire, at which the Chief Guardian shall preside.

Camp Fire Girls is a national organization, and it is usually best not to organize within other organizations, as subject to them, or to have Guardians who are paid officers in other organizations, as they must be responsible to the National organization for the work pertaining to Camp Fire.

How Often Meetings Are Held

The Camp Fire Girls meet once a month around the Council Fire. This meeting is usually held at the home of one of the girls or of the Guardian, or it may be held at any specially selected place indoors or out. It is not a public meeting, but the intimate coming together of the group; and outsiders, except special friends or mothers, are not invited. For it, the girls don their ceremonial gowns and wear their headbands into which are woven their symbols, and the string of beads showing the honors which they have won.

The ceremonial gown is made of inexpensive material and simple pattern, and, while it may be most beautifully decorated, each decoration must have a meaning, and must be the symbol of some special attainment or worth-while Camp Fire experience—decorations to which any girl may *win* the right, and which no amount of money can buy. The ceremonial gown thus brings the girls together as Camp Fire sisters with no artificial distinctions of money or family position.

The Council Fire ritual is very beautiful and impressive. The songs have been written especially for Camp Fire, and mysterious symbolism has a part in it all. The fire is, when possible, lighted by the primitive method of rubbing sticks together, while the group chants the Fire Song. If the meeting is held out of doors, a real camp fire may be lighted three times from this flame, but if it is an indoor meeting, three candles arranged in triangle are lighted for the three Lights of Camp Fire,—Work, Health and Love. Honors are conferred with appropriate ceremonies, new members are admitted with mystic words, and Wood-Gatherers, Fire-Makers and Torch-Bearers are initiated.

The Beautiful Ritual

A record, or count, of each meeting is kept, usually written in the beautiful Hiawatha measure, in which Camp Fire Girls everywhere have become wonderfully proficient. This count is read at the next meeting. After any special service—Guardian's instructions, music, or story which may be a part of the meeting—all stand and sing America, and then the Council Fire is closed with the Camp Fire Girls' Good Night song.

No one who has ever attended a Camp Fire Girls' Council Fire will ever forget the solemn beauty of the meeting.

Weekly meetings are more informal. Some one of the crafts is taken up, according to the girls' interests. Many of the honors can be won co-operatively, and with so many honors to be won there is no limit to the possibilities of these meetings. Here the mothers often find their opportunities; and the wise Guardian plans for and urges these opportunities upon them. The one who is known as the best breadmaker of the mother-group may invite all of the girls to her home to learn the mysteries of this art; another who is expert with her needle may teach them plain sewing or beautiful embroidery. If nature-lore is the purpose of the meeting, it may be held out of doors, and trees, birds and all of the things of woods and fields offer endless possibilities of honor-winning as well as interest and pleasure, with Health-craft honors to be won at the same time.

What Variety and Interest

Health-craft honors are won on the long tramps and "hikes" which the girls love to take, often camping out for the night, cooking their own suppers and breakfasts in the woods, winning Camp-craft honors as well, and remembering as long as they live the first night under the stars. Often meetings are held several times during the week because the girls enjoy being together. Camp Fire thus becomes the interest around which the social life of the group centers. The advantage of this can be appreciated by any one who studies the work of the organization or observes the girls who come under its influence.

A Night Under the Stars

Camp Life and "The Hike"

Perhaps there is no need of our modern life so great as that of getting away from the crowded, noisy streets and skyscrapers of the cities which we have builded, back to the woods and the fields—out under the open sky. It is to be questioned if sane, normal development for children is possible without something of this elemental contact with the things of nature, without, as the old legend has it, touching the ground to renew their strength.

Back to the Woods and Fields

For this reason camp life is not to be regarded as a luxury but as a necessity for those who live in cities or in the scarcely less crowded and artificial suburban towns.

The founders of Camp Fire have realized, as perhaps few educators have done, this need in the life of youth and the denial of it to them by modern conditions. Summer camps, therefore, are a part of the plan by which girls are led to a better understanding of themselves by the return to primitive conditions through which the race has developed, and so are fitted for larger usefulness. Honors are given for all forms of outdoor life—for sleeping in the open, for cooking by the camp fire, for quick thought and action in outdoor emergencies, for control of their own bodies in swimming, diving, rowing—all forms of water-craft and wood-craft, into which it is not the intention to have the girls enter blindly, getting what they can from experience, but as has been the custom in all races and all tribes since time began, to have them instructed by the older folk of the "tribe."

When the home was in the woods, the boy or the girl went with the father or mother, or head of the family group, and learned the secrets of hunting and trapping, or caring for the various animals and birds; of preparing food, staking camp and caring for themselves and each other in the open. This is what is done in the summer camps. The Camp Fire Girls learn to work together, to camp and tent together; they learn team work and co-operation. They learn to do simple, primitive things, the doing of which has made our complicated civilization possible.

Each Camp Fire Girl chooses a name and a symbol. In this new name she strives to express her own special, personal desire to be and to do. Her symbol is a picture of this desire-name, and she weaves it into her headband, puts it upon her ceremonial gown, and marks with it all of her cherished possessions. It soon comes to have a very real influence upon her thought and action, for, with the symbol of her inmost desire always before her, her daily life becomes an unconscious struggle towards the attainment of that desire. Usually the meaning of the name and the symbol is told at the Council Fire when the new name is formally conferred upon her, but sometimes the girl prefers to keep this meaning secret, even from the Guardian of the Fire.

Camp Fire is full of symbolism and love for the beautiful, and imagination and creative power have full play.

There are special signs by which one Camp Fire Girl knows another, by which she is admitted to the meeting of the Council Fire and to her own special group. Perhaps the most beautiful of these signs is the Sign of Fire, where the girl places the crossed fingers of the left hand upon the right to indicate the crossed fagots, and then slowly raises the right upward in graceful full arm curve to indicate the mounting of the smoke of the fire to heaven.

Big Sister and Her "Blue Birds"

Little girls between six and twelve years of age may join Camp Fire by becoming Blue Birds. Each Guardian may have a nest of Blue Birds, and her girls help in caring for them. In this way the instinctive desire of the little girl to imitate and go with the older sister is met,

Preparing for the Council Fire

The Council Fire Ritual is beautiful and impressive. The fire is, when possible, lighted by the primitive method of rubbing sticks, while the group chants the Fire Song. A Fire Guardian is here preparing the apparatus for making the fire. She has in her hand the drill sockets and the bow, and at her feet you see a fire drill and a fire board. Notice the string of beads showing the honors which she has won, the head-band and the designs on head-band and gown. Each of these has a meaning. As soon as she has started the fire, all the members of the group will gather around it and chant the Fire Song.

PICTURED KNOWLEDGE

Suggestions for Camp Fire Girls' Symbols
(Reading from Left to Right)

1. Su-no-wa—Sun on the water; friends, music, happiness. 2. Can-zu—To be firm of heart. 3. Ma-na—Grow like the green pine. 4. Kani-da-ka—A lover of nature. 5. Ca-du-za—Strong current. 6. Ga-oh—Spirit of the wind. 7. Ki-lo-des-ka—Water-bird. 8. He-wan-ka—To brood over. 9. Kee-wee—Rainbow maid. 10. Te-ca-ya—To make new. 11. Loh-ah—Reaching toward the sun.

and often the home problem of care for the little sister, solved. They are taught simple craft lessons, bead work and other things in which they are interested, and the older girls unconsciously develop unrealized talents in story telling, teaching and motherliness.

Why Camp Fire Appeals to Girls

Camp Fire offers a natural outlet for the cravings and longings of the growing girl. It gives her a new *Dignifying Common Duties* zest and interest in life —she cannot get away from the old, commonplace things, but Camp Fire honors give them a new interest, and homely tasks which she has "hated" become all at once worth doing and worth doing well.

The girl of Camp Fire age is self-centered—she is thinking of herself and of the girls about her. The world appeal has not reached her, in its larger sense, though Camp Fire Girls have proven that they can respond to this, too. But she wants to be happy, and to be a part of a happy group. She wants the spur of effort and the joy of doing—she is not yet ready for the larger joy of giving.

The social approval of girls of her own age means more to her than that of adults, and she will strive for this when other inducements to *Appeal to the Social Spirit* effort fail. There is a new interest given to the daily task in that she is to report it, not to older folk who will regard it but as a part of her duty, but to her mates, who understand and appreciate the effort, and who confer honor upon her for her attainment.

Camp Fire helps the girl to a new appreciation of that most precious possession—health. She does not yet understand all that it means to her, but Camp Fire takes her out of herself, gives her something new to think about, gives her new interests through the out-of-door sports, hikes *Growing into Health* and camping, and gives her new motives to health attainment in the realization that she cannot do as her mates do unless she, too, is strong and well. Unconsciously she "grows into health," and comes to realize the importance of right living and the conservation of her own health, without which no attainment is possible.

It prepares her, too, for the highest fulfillment of her life—wifehood and motherhood. It gives a new meaning to the home life and relationship, a new realization of how the Home has grown up out of the deepest instincts of the soul. Her own home is no longer a thing to be taken for granted—it represents the Love upon which all of the homes of the world have been builded, and gives to her new and holy ideals upon which she shall build the home of her own unconscious dreams.

Why Camp Fire Is of Interest to Mothers

It brings the girl back into the home from which so many of the things of our modern life are beckoning her. It lifts the old ideals of home-making and motherhood back into the first place in the thought of the growing girl, and gives her, through the winning of honors for simple tasks well done, a new share in the home life. It dignifies the mother's task through giving back to her the place of leader and instructor, and gives the daughter a new understanding of the mother and her work, and so brings them closer together.

Exalting the Love of Home

It helps the mother in the solution of one of her most difficult problems—the care of the health of the growing girl. With its supervised outdoor sports, it carries the girl through that critical period of physical development upon which the efficiency of all of her after-life depends.

It satisfies the unconscious restless

Camp Fire Girls Canoeing

This picture illustrates the camping life of the Camp Fire Girls. They are rowing to a rhythmic song, "Yet as one we raise our paddles." Each girl has on her paddle her chosen symbol. "The Camp Fire Girls learn to work together, to camp and tent together—they learn teamwork and co-operation."

craving for romance, adventure; the quest for the mysterious and the unknown, and the love of the beautiful which is in the heart of every girl, and which, rightly directed, leads to all that is most beautiful in the life of woman, but which, ignored or allowed to develop in wrong directions, is the source of her greatest sorrows. Not the least of the value of Camp Fire is that it helps the mother to understand all of these things—she who, perhaps, never understood them in herself—and to direct aright what, without this understanding, she may have thought harmful tendencies. In re- uniting the mother and the daughter in the home interests, in giving them a new bond of understanding, sympathy and love, Camp Fire is doing its greatest work for womanhood.

Camp Fire Membership

Camp Fire Girls is an independent, self-supporting organization, with a national board, president and other officers having general direction and supervision over the local organizations. The dues are fifty cents a year for each girl. Further information can be secured by writing the National Headquarters at 461 Fourth Avenue, New York City.

The Work of the Poets

We are the music-makers,
  And we are the dreamers of dreams,
Wandering by lone sea-breakers,
  And sitting by desolate streams;
World-losers and world-forsakers,
  On whom the pale moon gleams:
Yet we are the movers and shakers
  Of the world for ever, it seems.

With wonderful deathless ditties
  We build up the world's great cities,
And out of a fabulous story
  We fashion an empire's glory:
One man with a dream, at pleasure,
  Shall go forth and conquer a crown;
And three with a new song's measure
  Can trample an empire down.

We, in the ages lying
  In the buried past of the earth,
Built Nineveh with our sighing,
  And Babel itself with our mirth;
And overthrew them with prophesying
  To the old of the new world's worth;
For each age is a dream that is dying,
  Or one that is coming to birth.

ARTHUR O'SHAUGHNESSY

CHILD TRAINING IN HOME AND SCHOOL
MANNERS AND ETIQUETTE

Manners Makyth the Man

"MANNERS makyth man" is the motto of Winchester School, one of the most famous of the great boarding schools in England, which has for centuries been noted for the men it turns out. We have chosen this old motto to head our article as it is so universally true. Good manners *do* make good men, because good manners are only an outward expression of inward qualities, which we all need to cultivate.

George Washington, when a boy of fourteen, prepared under the supervision of his tutor, a "code of honor and civility" by which he hoped to regulate his behavior. Benjamin Franklin did the same thing; in fact, drawing up rules of conduct was a favorite school exercise among our forefathers. Perhaps that was why old-fashioned manners were so much more courteous than they are today. Nowadays we are likely to hear more about "efficiency" than about civility. But good manners—and by this we mean an attitude of mind as well as the observance of a few formal rules—are the foundation of all successful and happy living. It would be well indeed if some of our young people would follow George Washington's example

Efficiency versus Civility

and draw up a little code of their own.

Safe Guides to "The Proper Thing"

When we first begin to be self-conscious and think about the impression we make on other people, we are apt to be troubled by our anxiety to do "the proper thing." We sometimes think that if we only had a book to tell us what to do or to wear on such and such an occasion, we would be perfectly successful in our social relations. But the first thing to make plain is that good manners are based wholly on two fundamentals—
1. Common sense;
2. Consideration of others.

If we possess those valuable qualities, we cannot go far wrong. For instance, it would not be common sense to go to a picnic dressed as if for church; nor would it be common *Common Sense and Consideration* sense to go to dinner with a friend, dressed as if for an afternoon romp. Therefore both these errors would be bad manners. Nor would it be considerate to prolong a visit at a friend's home until your presence became an inconvenience to other members of the household. No matter how much you were enjoying yourself, that would be bad manners. Except in the case of a few conventions of "etiquette" that grown-up people have to observe—such as leaving visiting cards, wearing evening dress, etc.—the two principles of common sense and consideration will solve every problem of manners that arises.

There are two words that often bother young people—*etiquette* and *tact*—and it may be helpful to explain them simply. *Etiquette* is a French word which originally meant *ticket*. It is really a piece of old French slang which has since come to have an exaggerated importance. *The "Ticket" of Good Form* It referred originally to the ticket or card on which were written the rules of ceremony to be observed at court. In the days of Louis XIV of France these cards were handed by the chamberlain to each guest who was to be presented to the king. We have a survival of the same phrase in our own slang when we say, approvingly, "That's the ticket."

Tact is a more interesting word. It comes from the Latin and means the sense of touch. When you touch another person's sensitive feelings you naturally hurt them; therefore, a person who has "tact" knows instinctively how to avoid this. We have a similar phrase in our slang word "touchy." Tact implies a delicate understanding of the feelings of others, and a willingness to adapt one's self to them. It may be defined as an instinctive appreciation of what is fitting. It is nearly the same thing as adaptability. The chameleon is supremely tactful. There is no quality more to be envied than tact.

Manners and Mannerisms

It will be seen that problems of good manners continually hark back to the fundamental principle of consideration for others. The old rhyme so popular with parents and teachers:

"Politeness is to do and say
The kindest thing in the kindest way"

holds a helpful message. But there is another side to the matter. Manners may be exaggerated until they become mannerisms. The true good manners forbid clownish liberties on the one hand, just as they avoid affectations and self-conscious posing on the other. A natural and unaffected simplicity is the most attractive of all.

Be Simple and Natural

Any one who is by nature easy, fluent, and natural in a gathering of strangers is much to be envied. Friends and happiness will cluster around him or her as if by magic.

Good manners are not merely "company manners." Good manners are, as we have said, only an outward expression of the personality within, and the manners that are worth cultivating are those that stay with us at all times. The best place to practice good manners is in the home. Unfortunately it is at home that we are most likely to be careless. Untidy clothes, ungracious words, thoughtless ways, are only too easy when we let down all the barriers of restraint that we feel in the presence of strangers. Let your company manners be your home manners. It will not be a hard rule to live up to when once you have formed the habit. Surely we owe as much respect and courtesy to our own family, who have done everything for us, as to outsiders, however important they may be. And as you grow older you will find that the world has no delights equal to the joys of a happy home.

Home Manners and Company Manners

In the course of our schooling we are apt to come upon puzzling contradictions. Some of the great men, whose lives we are told to study and imitate, prove queer examples indeed on the score of manners. Oliver Goldsmith was freakish and odd; his clothes were of all colors;

Bad Manners of Great Men

his promise unreliable. The great Dr. Johnson was even more unconventional; if he found a mouthful of tea too hot, he was only too likely to eject it into the saucer; his clothes were so extraordinary that when he dined with his publisher and important guests were present, his meal was served to him behind a screen. And yet these were among the world's great men, and men of fine character, too. We can only conclude that the eccentricities of genius can be excused, but they must not be imitated.

Students of animal life have discovered a principle which they call "protective coloring." By this they mean that all living things tend to take the hue of their natural environment. This helps to protect them from their enemies, who would see them the more readily if their colors were conspicuous. Thus the polar bear, living in regions of continual ice and snow, is white; the tree-toad looks like a piece of bark; the katydid is as green as the leaf he rests on. The same principle holds good in the realm of social intercourse. The person who is conspicuous by mannerisms or loud behavior becomes a target for criticism. Refinement seeks a kind of "protective coloring" by blending itself with the surroundings, and thus is happily inconspicuous in any gathering. "When in Rome, do as the Romans do," if properly applied, is an excellent maxim of good manners.

On Not Being Conspicuous

Difference Between Boys and Girls

Good manners are the same for both sexes and all ages; but there are certain natural differences between the conduct of boys and that of girls. The old nursery rhyme,

telling us that boys are made of
"Snakes and snails and puppy-dog's tails,"
whereas girls are compounded of
"Sugar and spice and everything nice,"
is perhaps ungenerous to the males; but the doggerel has a certain truth. There is more mixture of animal spirits in the boy than in the girl, and a greater freedom and bluntness of behavior is natural to him. No one wants him to be the Eric or the Lionel of the sunday school stories. But for his own sake it is fair to ask that he remember that man is the stronger animal, and that he must not abuse his privilege. The highest word of praise we have for the masculine being is "gentleman." Similarly the highest praise for woman is the fine, old word "lady," which in its original meaning denotes the person who kneads the bread—that is, one skilled in the arts of the home. A boy may be as wild and frolicsome as an Irish terrier when he is on the playground, but to elders and those weaker than himself he ought to be gentle and chivalrous, as his Boy Scout rules tell him. And girls may be as sweet and dainty as caramels, but they too have their duties of being helpful in the home. It is not by learning artificial rules from "books of etiquette," but this habitual thoughtfulness for others and for our duties that develops the bearing, the manner of the cultivated man and woman whom everyone admires, and to whom everyone instinctively defers.

A Real Man a Gentle Man

There is a poem by O. Henry which is not well enough known. It should be in the heart of every boy as he grows into manhood. Two stanzas run as follows:

Test of the man, if his worth be
  In accord with the ultimate plan,
That he be not, to his marring,
  Always and utterly man;
That he bring out of the tumult,
  Fitter and undefiled,
To a woman the heart of a woman,
  To children the heart of a child.

Good, when the bugles are ranting,
  It is to be iron and fire;
Good to be oak in the foray,
  Ice to a guilty desire;
But, when the roaring is ended,
  Tenderly, unbeguiled,
Bring to a woman a woman's heart,
  And a child's to a child.

This little poem teaches the first law of good manners for the boy, which is gentleness to those weaker than one's self. The second law—Baloo, the wise old brown bear who was Mowgli's teacher in the *Jungle Book,* calls it the *first* law—is obedience to those who have a right to command. Out of this law of obedience grows a third principle in the boy's code of manners—respect toward all elders. The last great law in the boy's code—and the girl's too, for that matter—is, *tell the truth!*

Five Good Places for Good Manners

There are five different divisions in which a boy may well consider his manners—at school, at home, at play, traveling or visiting, and in public places.

At School—There are many temptations at school for boys to indulge in conduct "unbecoming an officer and a gentleman," as they say in the army. Bullying or "ragging" weak or unpopular boys, harassing an easy-going teacher, slovenly preparation of lessons, chattering in class or in study periods; these are all different forms of bad manners. To do badly in lessons is not generally considered poor manners, but to be slovenly in one's business is like being slovenly in one's dress, and your business at school is to get your lessons and show a gentleman's appreciation of the help the teacher is giving you in getting the education and the training of a man and a gentleman.

At Home—As we have said, the home is the best laboratory in which to practice experiments in courtesy. Good manners are the most potent chemistry to solve many of the problems of life. J. M. Barrie suggests a good rule to remember—"always to be a little kinder than is necessary." Doing an unexpected helpfulness is one of the best ways of having a good time ever invented. Try it on your mother today!

At Play—When one is in the thick of the glorious excitement of play, be it marbles, baseball, skating or what not, manners are likely to be forgotten. The only kind of manners that show then are those that live under the skin and are a real part of you. That's just the time to watch yourself and if you're not living up to Boy Scout tactics, why —get a grip on yourself! Courtesy counts, even on the playground.

Traveling and Visiting—It's pretty easy to be well mannered when you're staying away from home, because you're on your good behavior anyhow. But even so, one or two rules are worth remembering. Don't forget that it is the parents in the house who are your real hosts, and your utmost courtesy is due to them.

Remember You Are a Guest Don't take the best chair in the living-room, or the biggest piece of cake on the dish. Be polite to all servants—even other people's servants. Don't throw your clothes all round the guest room you're stopping in. Don't dawdle in the bathroom. Don't be late to meals, and keep an eye on your table manners. Are those suggestions too juvenile? If so, invent better ones to meet your own case.

And when traveling, keep an eye out for other people to whom you can give a friendly hand. Helping an old lady with a heavy suit-case, or amusing a child on a tedious railway trip, or picking up a package that somebody drops—cultivate your instinct for that kind of thing.

Public Places—A gentleman is always revealed by his conduct in public places where presumably no one knows him. Don't crowd people on the street. Don't talk so loud at the movies that you annoy your neighbors. Give up your seat in the street-car to women or old men. If you must chew gum, don't do it in public.

Don't forget, too, that there is such a thing as good manners to animals. No gentleman will be cruel to animals.

Good Manners for Girls

Girls need to remember a few rules just as much as boys. The things we have just said about boys apply equally to them, but they have problems of their own in addition. Girls generally have better manners than their brothers, as far as the little courtesies of life are concerned; but they are more likely to be narrow-minded, "stuck-up" (as the boys put it), and to talk faster than they think.

As to Being "Stuck Up" and Snobbish Very often girls at school tend to be snobbish, by which we mean, to judge others by outside appearances. Girls sometimes are very "down" on another girl because she is poorly dressed, or awkward, or comes from a family of "common people." Joan of Arc was a peasant girl; and one of the most cultivated women in this nation today came to America in the steerage as a little Russian waif not so many years ago.

Girls have many things in the way of amusements and parties with their friends, to tempt them to undervalue the life of the home and the duties of the home. The old-fashioned upbringing which used to prepare for being cast on an imaginary desert island was not such a bad thing. Without some expert knowledge of cooking, sewing, housekeeping and good books, no girl has earned a title to self-respect. The great movement for the wider influence of women does not mean that they are to leave undone the tasks that tradition has allotted to them.

Ladies and Gentlemen, and Fathers and Mothers

Few of us realize the sacrifices and the unceasing devotion that our parents have lavished on us. Aren't you, yourself, apt to take these things as matters of course? It cannot be too strongly repeated that our first and greatest duty lies toward our parents. Too often, as soon as we begin to live and reason for ourselves, we magnify the importance of our own views and forget what they have done for us. There is nothing sadder to look back on, in later life, than the fact that we have not done everything we could to pay back some of our debt of affection to father and mother.

There is now a national Mother's Day; perhaps some time there will be a Father's Day, too. In any event, there would be no harm in celebrating every day as Father's Day as well as Mother's Day in *Celebrating Father's and Mother's Day* every family. We all look forward to our own birthdays with pleasant anticipation. Do we do as much to celebrate the birthday of Father or Mother? As they go on in years, and the time grows nearer for us to leave home and branch out in life, the thought of parting is more and more painful to them. Let us not forget that, and do all we can, while we can, to show them our feelings. Life gets rather lonely for parents as their children grow older. We ought to remember that some day the memory of every cross word and unkind deed toward them, will hurt us like a stab. Never do anything that you would be ashamed to have your parents hear about. That is a pretty good rule to follow.

Good manners toward our own parents necessarily imply good manners toward our friends' parents, and so to all older people. You not only owe it to them but you owe it to yourselves. You will notice in reading the lives of great men that they universally showed great respect not only for their parents, but they looked up to people older than themselves. It is the pert boys, the over-smart young people of both sexes who make failures in life. Andrew Carnegie tells us how proud he was when he first began to earn a little money so that he could be a "partner" (as he puts it) with his father and mother.

Good Manners on Paper

Politeness in written form is subject to more formal rules than personal civility. When people meet face to face, the form of words or the manner of expressing courtesies may be left to the inspiration of the moment, but where invitations or announcements are to be sent, it is well to follow convention more closely. An invitation to an informal meal or entertainment of any kind may, of course, be phrased in any terms of cordiality that occur to the writer, and answered in the same strain. Such a note would run as follows:

600 Byron Avenue
February 14th

Dear Mr. Brown:

We are going to have a few friends in for dinner on Washington's Birthday at seven o'clock, and would be delighted if you can come. It will be a very small party, and most informal. Mr. Patterson has to be in the city that day and will not return until late, so he charges me to say particularly, no evening dress.

We hope very much you can come.

Cordially yours,
Isabel Patterson.

A More Formal Invitation

A more formal invitation to dinner would be worded as follows, either written on note paper, or engraved on a card (with the guest's name, the date and hour, filled in by hand).

Mr. and Mrs. Carter Patterson
request the pleasure of
Mr. John Brown's
company at dinner
on Wednesday, February
twenty-second
at seven o'clock
Six Hundred Byron Avenue

Replies to invitations should always be written in the same style and degree of formality as the invitation itself, using the first or third person, as the case may be, following the style of the original invitation. Mr. John Brown's acceptance of the invitation above would run as follows:

Mr. John Brown
accepts with pleasure
Mr. and Mrs. Carter Patterson's
very kind invitation to dinner
on Wednesday, February
twenty-second
at seven o'clock
1422 Denver Street

The day and hour mentioned in the invitation should always be repeated, as this assures the hostess that there is no misunderstanding. If the hostess wishes to reveal the particular nature of her entertainment (such as *Music, Dancing, Theatricals, etc.*), this may be written in the lower left-hand corner of the invitation.

The word "informal" is often used in a rather misleading way. Its appearance in an invitation ought to warrant the guest in coming in informal garb,—i. e., not in full evening dress—but hostesses frequently speak of a dinner as "informal" even when they plan quite an elaborate affair. The form of the invitation, however, should always convey the kind of entertainment one may reasonably expect. The interval between the date of the invitation and the dinner is also an indication. Two weeks is the usual period of notice for an invitation to a formal dinner; and about ten days or a week for an informal dinner or luncheon.

Wedding and Dinner Invitations

Wedding and dinner invitations are always issued in the name of both host and hostess; but in the case of all afternoon receptions and teas, and all dances, the name of the hostess alone appears. For instance:

  Mrs. Carter Patterson
  requests the pleasure of
  Mr. John Brown's
 company on Thursday evening,
   March the seventh
    at ten o'clock
Dancing
  Six Hundred Byron Avenue

If it is a dinner dance, two sets of invitations must be issued. Those who are desired as guests at dinner receive a special note, or the regular engraved dinner card with the name written in and "Dancing at eleven" written in the lower left-hand corner. Those invited for the dancing only, receive an "At Home" card with the words "Dancing at eleven," in the corner.

The At Home card is usually in this form:

  Mrs. Carter Patterson
    At Home
  Thursday evening, March
  the seventh at ten o'clock
Dancing at eleven
  Six Hundred Byron Avenue
R. S. V. P.

The usual form of wedding invitation is as follows:

  Mr. and Mrs. Cameron
   Jones Joyce
  request the honour of
 ....'s
 presence at the marriage
  of their daughter
    Elinor
     to
 Mr. Ralph Henry Edward
    Thomas
 on Tuesday, the twenty-first
    of March
   at twelve o'clock
  at St. Thomas's Church

Invitations to weddings, receptions and afternoon teas require no acknowledgment. If unable to attend an afternoon tea or reception, cards should be sent (enclosed in an envelope) on the day of the reception—while it is in progress, if possible. It is a fairly safe rule that acknowledgments are not necessary unless the invitation is to a sit-down meal where places are to be counted, or to a dance or party where partners are to be numbered by couples.

The initials R. S. V. P., an abbreviation for the French "Repondez, sil vous plait" ("please reply"), are said to be going out of fashion. As they are only a reminder of what courtesy and good manners dictate to every one, perhaps it is as well. The English formula, rather more courteous, "The favour of an answer is requested," is perhaps preferable.

Good Manners and Letter Writing

After giving these examples of formal invitations and acceptances, it may be well to show that it is not always necessary to be stiff, to be polite. The art of writing easy, friendly letters is one to be diligently cultivated by every intelligent person. The use of clean, unscented note paper (without over-elaborate monograms) and a carefully chosen pen and ink, should be a matter of course. We cannot all write letters as whimsical and charming as those of Robert Louis Stevenson or other great authors; but we can all practice a simple, direct and tidy style which conveys a message of news and friendship, without too many words, and without blots and scrawls.

Do You Write Such Letters?

A Letter to Mother

The type of letter a thoughtful boy might well write to his mother

MANNERS AND ETIQUETTE

(and boys cannot write to their mothers too often) would be like this:

24 Oak Avenue,
Hempstead, N. Y.
March 25

Dearest Mother:

A Good Letter to Mother

I reached Hempstead very comfortably yesterday afternoon. Never having been on Long Island before, naturally the train ride from New York was very interesting to me. The country is as flat as a table, with a great many nice houses. Spring is just beginning here, and it is nice to see the buds on the trees. As we got near Hempstead we crossed a wide, empty plain where the view was splendid: there was a fine red sunset, and an aeroplane flying high up in the "pink" air.

The first thing you see in Hempstead is a cemetery, which is right beside the railroad station. But the town is not a dead one by any means. Uncle Bob met me at the train, showed me a busy street with attractive shops, and then treated me to a chocolate soda (ice cream) that was as good as any thing I ever had in Burlington.

Aunt Helen is very well, and sends her love. I have a little room in the attic, and Roger (the dog, a big Airedale terrier) slept up there with me. It rained in the night, and the rain on the roof sounded as it did on the old tent down in the orchard last summer.

My best love to Dad and everybody. Tell them how much I am enjoying my adventure.

Your ever loving son,
Edward.

There is nothing stilted or formal about Edward's letter; it is just a sensible, happy little note, such as would gladden any mother to get. In informal letters of this kind the pen may run as it will, and the only rule to remember is cleanliness and neatness in the writing itself.

A pleasant little note for a girl to write would be the following, sent by Emily to her friend Dorothy, who had asked her to a Thanksgiving party.

At Home, Monday

Dearest Dot:

It's awfully sweet of you to ask me to come to Thanksgiving Dinner, but you know I just can't. You see we always have a big family party at Thanksgiving, with a turkey and all sorts of extras, and if anybody weren't there, there would be trouble, I can tell you! Ben and Daisy come all the way from Akron every year just for that Thanksgiving Day feast, so you see I know Mother wouldn't dream of letting me come to you on that day; and I feel the same way about it. But it's just as sweet as possible for you to want me, and I do thank you, and your dear Mother, too, for thinking of it.

Yes, I've had a nasty time with a cold and swelled throat (don't get too close to this letter, perhaps it has germs!) and I guess I won't be back at school until next week, because I'm going to take good care of myself. I want to be in A1 shape for that turkey.

Your most loving chum,
Emily.

These two real letters, written by a real boy and girl, are worth study as examples of simple, friendly messages conveyed on paper.

So you see, as we said at the beginning, throughout the maze of social entertainments, we find the two first principles—common sense and consideration—still guiding the apparently arbitrary conventions of the code. Such matters as introductions, visiting cards, the etiquette of calling, chaperons and engagements, and the customs of balls, house parties and theatre parties, must be left to the books on manners and etiquette (which are many and good). But before leaving the subject, let us close with a word of advice which cannot be too rigidly enforced: Answer invitations promptly!

A Few Final Dos and Don'ts

It is not good manners to carry food to your mouth with a knife or to pick your teeth in public; to drink noisily, or with the spoon left in the cup; to help yourself to bread with the aid of a fork, and to rest both elbows on the table while you are eating. An awkward way of handling your knife and fork shows lack of breeding. It is not polite to help yourself to food first instead of offering it to your neighbor, or to start eating before the others at the table are ready. Cultivated people eat daintily, without soiling the tablecloth or their clothes, and they do not tuck their napkins under their chins or tie them around their necks. All these are some of the commoner forms of bad table manners that one sees in public places.

There are a few other small courtesies that are frequently overlooked. It is courteous for men and young women to rise when an older woman comes into the room, especially if she is the hostess. And when you have been a guest in some one's home, you must not forget to express your appreciation and enjoyment of the hospitality shown you, before you leave. In introducing several people to each other, begin by presenting the others to the oldest lady present. Men should tip their hats in acknowledging an introduction to a woman, and shake hands with the men to whom they are presented. Women may shake hands or not, as they wish. Failing to recognize these little rules of behavior may stamp you as a rude, uncultivated person.

CHILD TRAINING IN HOME AND SCHOOL
TRAINING THE MIND

How to Remember Not to Forget

"LOOK into the window of that school store. There are many different things in it. Now turn your back and see how many you can remember."

That is one of the first things a Boy Scout is told to do. Is it a game? You know the Boy Scouts have a lot of fun.

How a Boy "Scouts" With His Eyes

Yes, it's a mind-training game, and very interesting. Boys are surprised to learn how little they really see of the things they look at. At first, of a hundred objects in a window, a boy may see ten. But by daily practice he will find that he sees twenty-five, forty, or more, out of a hundred. He is training the attention and memory, and strengthening the will power by holding himself to the task.

"Playing Ball" with Your Mind

You know you have to practice running, jumping, skating, swimming, rowing a boat, or playing baseball a long time before you can do them well. So you may have a good mind, but unless it is trained it will not work well or win any of the prizes of life. All games of skill train the mind as well as the body. To become good at anything—to remember what to do and do it—a boy must give attention, remember what he has learned, and be determined to ex-

Training Your Mind to Go Straight

cel. By putting the same amount of effort into it, he can break himself of bad habits of walking, standing and eating. He can cure himself of bad mental habits, too. Some of these are forgetfulness, fault-finding, ill-temper, putting things off that should be done now, indecision, laziness, which is mental rust, having the "blues," self-pity over every little hurt. He can train himself in such good habits as truthfulness, courage, cheerfulness, industry, orderliness, attention, will power.

When a boy, Washington made up a list of maxims, or rules of conduct, and then stuck to them. A greater general, but a less perfect character, might have lost the Revolutionary War.

The three most valuable mental habits are attention, memory and will. Let us study each of these separately, and learn how we can train ourselves in them.

Attention!

You must give your whole mind to anything you are doing, whether it is work or play. To do this you must learn to let nothing disturb you. In every schoolroom some pupils really study. A hard lesson may be learned in twenty minutes of close study; it is unlearned in an hour of fidgeting, staring about, having the attention distracted by

How to "Unlearn" Your Lesson

every little thing. Try a few attention games at home. Lay a domino on the table an instant, cover it, and tell how many spots were on it. Try two dominoes. Use small coins and tell the designs. Read the titles on a row of books and see how many you can remember. Out of doors observe flowers, birds, insects and trees.

Here's the secret. Be interested! That is why you play baseball well. It interests you, so you give your whole mind to it. Think of everything you have to do as a kind of baseball.

Remember!

To remember a thing you must understand it. Merely repeating a thing, like a parrot, makes little impression on the mind. Lincoln, who said so many wise things, said that he never got hold of a thought until he had bounded it, north, south, east and west. For instance, in your geography lesson you may learn that New York is the largest city in the United States. Find out *why* it is the largest city and you will not forget it.

Why Parrots Are Poor Scholars

Fix things in your mind by your five senses. If you have a letter to mail, shut your eyes and *see* yourself putting the letter in the mail box. *Say* to yourself: "I must mail that letter." *Feel* it in your pocket, with your hands. *Write down* the spelling lesson; *prove* a sum in arithmetic, *draw* maps, *model* objects. *Group* things in your mind that belong together. In going to the grocery for mama, group bread and butter, soap and starch, tea and sugar, thread and needles. Help the memory all you can with these short cuts.

You can remember best when the mind is rested. It is at its best after a good sleep. The hardest lessons in school are given in the morning session. And change of work is a rest. Writing, drawing and music relieve the mind between arithmetic, grammar, and history. Cramming for examinations is very bad. It tires the mind. It is better to forget all about it, play hard, sleep soundly and come to the task fresh.

Why Arithmetic in the Morning

It's Will That Wins!

"I can't" never did anything. "I'll try" sometimes succeeds, but "I will" *wins*—always!

Did you ever find yourself arguing with yourself? It is as if there were two people inside of you, a sort of "Katy Did" and "Katy Didn't."

The Katydids in Your Head

"I'll do this," one of them says.
"Better not," says the other.
"Why?" impatiently.
"It isn't right."
"Well, I know; but I *want* to."

How do you decide? The *real* you, the *best* you, is the one that points out the right. You must obey yourself before you are fit to give orders to others. Older people are always watching to see how young ones choose to act. Of two boys a mother says: "I can trust Donald anywhere, but Herbert must be watched."

Which of You is You?

Set Yourself to Watch Yourself

If you don't want to be watched, watch yourself, or some one else will always have to be paid for watching you. In the military school at West Point, where army officers are trained, boys spend four years learning punctuality, obedience, courage, honor, order, courtesy and trust-

TRAINING THE MIND

worthiness. Every hour is a discipline, a training of habits of self-control and choosing the right line of conduct.

A West Point cadet, when called answers "Yes sir," and comes at once. He does not say "Yes, in a minute," and then forget all about it. He does not offer "I forgot" as an excuse for something undone. He does not have to be called six times before getting up. He is never late to meals or in school. He is ashamed to be a coward; he is disgraced by a lie.

What "Yes Sir" Means at West Point

Do you see? Mind training is moral training, too. A bright boy must remember that he needs the balance wheel of choosing the right, if he is to become a good, useful, and trusted man in the business world.

Good and wise people are careful about the company they keep, the books they read, the amusements they seek. But many of them live with dreadful thoughts — hatred, worry, anger, fear, sorrow.

Thought has a great deal to do with health, happiness and effective work. "A merry heart goes all the day; a sad tires in a mile." Do not go to bed worried, or "mad" at anyone. Such thoughts poison sleep and wake up with you in the morning. Did you know that a thought can stay with you all night? Some people have trained their minds so they can wake up at any hour. On going to bed they say: "I must wake at five o'clock." Students know that what is read late at night, is remembered and more clearly understood in the morning.

Guess Who's Hurt When You Get Mad

Thoughts with Aches in Them

Doctors know that thinking about pain makes it worse. A sick person who thinks he is going to die is more likely to do so than if he thinks he is going to get well. A child should not cry for every little tumble, or be "poor babied." The bump should be attended to, and forgotten in a romp or a picture book. Self-pity is a very bad habit of the mind.

Showing the Door to Thoughts

As we form habits of thought from those about us, we should keep away from loafers, people of evil mind and foul speech.

If you have the "blues," get a canary bird, or put a "cheer-up" card in your toilet looking-glass. Smile, look pleasant, and presently you will feel so. Say: "I mean to succeed." If you find thoughts in your mind that you would be ashamed for anyone to see, put them out.

How? Why, just put them out. It's *your* mind, isn't it? Show the door to unwelcome, harmful thoughts. Then invite in all the pleasant things you can think of, about other people; cultivate purity, cheerfulness, faithfulness to duty, unselfishness and self-confidence. This is to the mind what robust health is to the body. The greatest and best use is made of the mental, as of the physical powers, only by exercising them.

CHILD TRAINING IN HOME AND SCHOOL
PARENT-TEACHER ASSOCIATION

How Parents and Teachers Work Together

The Public School the Hope of the State

This beautiful and significant picture adorns the walls of the Franklin Public School, of Trenton, New Jersey. On the right is shown a group of immigrants who have just come to this country.

In the center, sits the teacher. On her right is a figure representing Civilization holding the torch of liberty, and behind her stands a figure holding an olive branch, typifying the rewards of noble ambition. Through the arch on the left can be seen the tall chimneys of factories and public buildings of a great city, toward which the young college men are moving. Back of them are young people of various grades, including the little kindergartener seated on the floor.

THE Parent-Teacher Association is one of the most far-reaching educational movements of the present time. It is a nation-wide organization of parents for child study and child welfare. Its purpose is to reach every home and every parent, and open them to opportunities for the best information obtainable on good home-making and bringing up children.

Declaration of Its Principles

When the Congress was first organized there was no way for parents to procure the knowledge of child nature and home-making, and even those who had received *The Home the Best School* the best education were woefully ignorant on these important duties of life. The place of parents as educators had not been considered in the educational system, yet it is true that the home has the largest work to do in the education of children. From birth until the child enters school, parents are the sole teachers of the child, and even when school days begin, the home still has the larger responsibility, for the school has the care of the child about 800 hours in the year, while the home has the care 7,460 hours.

Teachers are well provided with opportunities for preparation for their educational work, and each year higher standards of preparation are demanded. Most parents on the other hand are plunged into their great educational work without preparation, without knowledge concerning health, infant hygiene, mental development, or the formation of moral habits, and with nowhere to turn to in order to learn the fundamental principles of successful child-training—yet without such information, the lives and future well-being of their children are jeopardized.

Saving the Children

To provide opportunity for parents to learn how to guard a child's health means a great reduction in child mortality. To provide opportunity to learn the best methods of guidance of little children during the most formative years of their lives, to answer the thousands of educational questions the children ask, to understand the great transition period between childhood and youth, to make the home a constructive educational force, means the building of mind and character on a firm foundation.

The method adopted for this education concerning child nature and child nurture was the organization *Methods and Results* of parents in connection with every school, thus doubling the educational use of the school system, making the schools a meeting-place for parents as well as children, and thereby securing a hearty co-operation between the home and the school.

A school principal in Oklahoma says: "In my school of twenty-two rooms whose patrons are working people, I find at the end of two years that the Parents' Club has cut the work of discipline in half since the parents began to come to the school and understand matters."

This is typical of the work throughout the country.

Proper Limitations of the Work

The work of the Parent-Teacher Association is educational and co-operative, and it is in the long run far more useful if it confines its activities within these limits.

A prominent educator, commenting on Parent-Teacher Associations, said they have greater possibilities for good or evil than any other phase of near-school work. One superintendent praises them highly; another says he would as soon have His Satanic Majesty let loose in his community. The proper management of a Parent-Teacher Association is therefore of the utmost importance.

All classes of patrons should belong, and there should be no more meetings than a large number will attend. Too few or too many meetings destroy interest. No meetings of parents alone should be held. In smaller communities, members of the school board, the superintendent, and all of the teachers should be present. The purpose of the organization should be entirely constructive. The parents should not criticise the teachers, nor the teachers the parents.

One important purpose is to inform school patrons of the purposes and methods of the school, so that they may co-operate most efficiently with the teachers.

Do not be discouraged if everyone is not interested at first. An association of three members sometimes does better work than an association of fifty.

One important function is to organize and crystallize public sentiment with regard to public legislation and to let legislators know what their constituents want done for the schools.

Every community has abundant resources to make the work of an association interesting and effective. The pastor, physician, business man, banker, the veterinarian, the farmer, the mechanic, and men in business offices can be induced to help, not only on the programs, but with other work and enterprises of the association.

Among the opportunities for useful service may be named the question of school attendance. Any rural school whose attendance is below eighty-five per cent, or any town school whose attendance is below ninety per cent is not up to the proper standard. Find out whose children are not attending school and why, and what can be done to get them into school. Get the parents to understand the seriousness of the injury they are doing to their children's future. If there is no health inspection in the schools, see that such work is inaugurated. Statistics show that twenty per cent of children attending school suffer from eye trouble, and sixteen per cent from ear trouble.

Increasing School Attendance

Union of Community Activities

Parent-Teacher Associations should enter heartily into such community activities as debating clubs, singing schools, spelling schools, declamation contests, athletic contests, Chautauqua courses, extension courses, vacation schools, corn and gardening clubs, evening classes, farm accounting, the beautification of the school grounds, the providing of proper lunches for children, looking after cases of destitution, establishing school savings banks, the consolidation of schools in rural communities and school sanitation, teaching of domestic science, vocal music, manual training, and the furnishing of vocational guidance where the schools do not provide it. These are among the numerous activities that are successfully carried out by Parent-Teacher Associations.

Provision of Educational Helps

Since 1897 the National Congress of Mothers and Parent-Teacher Associations has collected a vast amount of information on child welfare of practical help to every one having the care of children. Programs of scientific value, yet simple enough for all to understand, are supplied.

Books for both parents and children have been recommended, libraries have complied with the request that they procure the books, and in response to the demand created, much valuable literature on children has been written, and greater study of children developed.

Government Co-operation

The valuable educational help given to farmers by the Department of Agriculture, and to school leaders by the Bureau of Education, inspired the hope that parents might have the same privileges, and the co-operation of the Department of Agriculture was readily secured.

The request, that the home as an educational institution of fundamental importance receive equal atten-

PARENT-TEACHER ASSOCIATIONS

tion from the Bureau of Education that is given to teachers, met with a favorable response. The Home Education Division of the National Bureau of Education was established in September, 1913, and plans for reaching parents were made.

Work of the Bureau of Education

1. To further their own education by recommending to them interesting and valuable reading matter.
2. In regard to the care and home education of their children, with reference to: (a) Physical care and health, sleep, food, etc.; (b) games and plays; (c) their early mental development; (d) the formation of moral habits.

Through the co-operation of the mothers and the state and local branches of the association, many thousand mothers of babies have received the valuable bulletin on "The Care of the Baby" published by the United States Public Health Service, and the information given has been the means of saving the lives of thousands of children.

Light and Help Brought to Mothers

Reading Courses for the Home

A Reading Course for Parents, with certificate given by the Bureau of Education to every parent completing the course, has filled such a need so that thousands every month have been requested and are being used.

Reading courses for boys and for girls, and literary courses for adults have been printed and are doing much to establish habits of home reading after school days.

Many school principals are recommending these reading courses for boys and girls to their graduating classes. A certificate is given by the Bureau of Education, and two years is allowed for completion of each course. The libraries of the country have been asked to co-operate, and in many these Reading Courses are posted.

A valuable bulletin on "One Thousand Good Books for Children," graded by age, has been published, and investigations made as to the agencies outside of schools that are offering educational opportunities in child nurture and home-making.

Book Selections for the Children

The Crying Need for Help

"Send all the information you can to these mothers. We are fifteen miles from a doctor. So many women die."

"Many women in this district live fifty to one hundred miles from a physician."

"We are forty miles from town and need help for ourselves and our children."

"We are twenty-eight miles from the nearest postoffice. We need help."

Appeals like these received by the Bureau of Education from thousands of women throughout the United States, indicate the need which mothers, especially in remote rural districts, feel for advice in the care and training of their children.

How to Organize a Local Association

The organization of a Parent-Teacher Association is very simple.

First of all, the Superintendent of Schools should be consulted and his approval secured. If he is not fully informed concerning the movement, literature can be obtained, giving such information by writing to the National Congress of Mothers and

Parent-Teacher Associations, 910 Loan and Trust Building, Washington, D. C. The interest and co-operation of the principal of the school is also necessary.

The interest and co-operation of the superintendent and principal being assured, the initial steps may be taken. Where this co-operation cannot be secured at the outset, it is better to form a Mothers' Circle or Parents' Circle, meeting in the homes or in some other place than the school, until such time as the co-operation of the school authorities has been secured.

Notice of the meeting should be sent to every parent, either by an invitation written by the children during the writing period, or by notice in local papers.

A short, interesting program should be arranged by the committee of parents and teachers who have planned the meeting. The national scope of the movement and the aims and objects should be given, as well as some of its achievements.

Model of a Constitution

The constitution appended below may then be presented to the meeting, and if approved, a motion to adopt the constitution as read, may be made. It is then read, section by section, the presiding officer asking, after each section, if there are any amendments.

It is then adopted, section by section, and, finally, as a whole. Then the report of the nominating committee is made and permanent officers elected.

CONSTITUTION

Article I

This Society shall be called The Parent-Teacher Association of the .... School. It shall be the local branch of the National Congress of Mothers and Parent-Teacher Associations.

Article II

Its object shall be to study the welfare of the child in home, school and community, and create a better mutual understanding between parents and teachers and their co-operation in all work for the interest of the children.

Article III

Any one interested in the purpose for which the society is organized is qualified for membership.

Article IV

The officers of the society shall be a President, Vice-President, a Secretary and a Treasurer, elected annually at the .... meeting of the year.

Article V

Regular meetings of the society shall be held on the .... afternoon (or evening) of each month. Special meetings by order of ....

Article VI

This constitution may be amended at any annual meeting, or by unanimous consent at any regular meeting when previous notice has been given.

The by-laws should contain the rules of the society, as to dues, duties of officers, method of election, etc.

There should be an annual due of not over twenty-five cents.

Payment of Dues

All Parent-Teacher Associations, Mothers' Circles or Child-Study Circles are admitted as members of the National Congress and the State Branch, on payment of ten cents per capita annually to the treasurer of the state branch.

The organization applying for membership should send a duplicate list of the names of officers and members to the Treasurer of the State when there is a State Congress, and to the National Treasurer, 910 Loan and Trust Building, Washington, D. C.

Ally your association with others, through membership in State and National Congress of Mothers and Parent-Teacher Associations, thus securing the knowledge and suggestions gained by the experience of others.

What Children Have Done to Help

Children have written the invitations for parents' meetings.

In some cases they have cut out cards in the shape of cradles, writing on one side "The hand that rocks the cradle rules the world," and on the other side the invitation.

Children hasten home from school to care for younger children in order that mothers can leave.

Children have voluntarily visited mothers who have not come to the meetings, personally asking them to do so.

Questioning one mother as to the cause of this interest, she replied, "The children notice the difference in me since I've been going to the Parent-Teacher Association. I'm more patient with the children and see more in the work than the drudgery of it."

Topics for Parent-Teacher Programs

Advantages of parental co-operation with teachers. (Have a local teacher present this.)

Wider use of school buildings for community purposes.

Available Open Places for Play.

Available Libraries and Reading Rooms In and Out of School.

Quality of Moving Pictures.

Social Life of School Children.

Temptations—Pool Rooms, Saloons, Poor Theaters.

Use of Children's Leisure.

Prevention of Truancy.

Treatment of Erring Children.

Foreign Children and the School.

Teaching English to Foreign Mothers.

Children Whose Parents Work Out All Day.

Fire Prevention in Schools.

Sanitary Conditions of Schools.

Simple Dress for School Girls.

Children Who Do Not Fit the School System.

Circulating Libraries in Schools.

School Luncheons.

Use of School Grounds as Play Grounds.

Kindergartens—Their Value in Education.

Why Children Lie.

Training in Honesty.

Developing Initiative and Responsibility.

School Credit for Home Work.

Earning and Saving.

Physical Development.

Continuation Classes.

Work for Children.

Home Gardens.

Vacation Occupations.

KEEPING WELL
FOOD VALUES

What Shall We Have for Dinner?

What Science Has to Say About What to Eat and What to Avoid, and the Proper Variety to Have With Each Meal

Proteins, as you know, are building foods. It is protein that most Americans eat too much of—they are over-nourished. The two ounces of boiled ham contain 1/4 of an ounce of protein and supply 180 calories. The boiled egg weighs nearly 2 ounces, contains 1/5 of an ounce of protein, but gives only 80 calories. The four squares of American cheese weigh 1 ounce, contain as much protein as the ham and yield 135 calories. The glass of milk contains an equal amount of protein, but yields more calories than the cheese—160. The lamb chop represents 2 ounces of lean meat. It has half an ounce of protein and supplies 120 calories.

A CHINAMAN, who had never before seen a locomotive, asked what made it go. The engineer replied: "Heap strong man inside. Drink plenty water. If no give water, man no work."

Even our school children know that this explanation is not quite accurate, for no matter how much water is poured into the engine, it will do no work unless this water is turned into steam. To do this a fire is needed under the boiler—a fire kept up with wood, or coal, or oil. Any fuel will do, though some kinds of fuel give more heat than others. Engineers have found a way of measuring the amount of heat which can be got out of different fuels. Thus they say that one cord of oak wood (about 4,000 pounds) gives as much heat as 1,500 pounds of coal, or as 1,000 pounds of kerosene.

The Engine You Live In

You may ask why a story about foods should begin with a discussion of steam engines, and coal and fuel value. Have you never wondered what makes your body do its work; what keeps the heart going, the muscles moving? Have you never thought it strange that the body always keeps warm?

In many respects our body is very much like an engine. It, too, requires fuel to keep it going. To be sure it cannot make use of coal, or wood, or kerosene, but instead of these it burns sugar,

1286

FOOD VALUES
Why We Need the Fruits

Fruits are the kind of food we need a great deal of to offset our over-supply of meat. The apple weighs 6 ounces and supplies 85 calories. Bananas are very nutritious; they give 140 calories apiece, but weigh just 7 ounces. The orange weighs 8 ounces and supplies 90 calories. Fruits, moreover, are the most delicious of all foods and good friends of every other wholesome food.

starch, and butter, and other fats. Foods like these, whose main purpose is to supply heat and energy are, therefore, called "Fuel Foods." Like other fuels they vary in heat value, and just as an engineer can measure how much heat is yielded by a ton of coal, so chemists can measure how much heat is yielded by a pound of sugar, or a pound of butter. Thus, the chemist tells us that 1 pound of butter contains 3,600 calories; 1 pound of sugar, 1,860 calories; 1 pound of American cheese, 2,100 calories; 1 pound of oysters, 235 calories, etc. By a "calorie" is meant the amount of heat which will raise 1 liter of water (slightly more than a quart) one degree Centigrade; or to express it somewhat differently, which will raise 10 cubic centimeters of water (about a thimbleful) from freezing to boiling point.

The Fuel in Your Engine

It is also interesting to know that the fuel foods are burned in the body, exactly as though they were fed into a fire, and that the end products are the same, namely, carbon dioxide and water.

There is, however, a very important difference between the body and the ordinary steam engine. What would you think of an engineer who, when his engine showed signs of breaking down, attempted to repair it by adding iron, or copper, or other material to his ordinary fuel? How absurd that would seem! Yet the body is able to keep itself in repair by doing just this. In other words, by combining meat and milk and eggs with the fuel foods, we supply the body not only with the materials for making heat and energy, but also with the materials needed to keep it in repair. Such foods are, therefore, called Repair Foods or Building Foods, since they not only repair the body, but also make it grow.

An Engine that Repairs Itself

In man and other animals, these building foods are highly complex substances; in plants they are relatively simple chemical compounds. Plants build up their bodies by laying hold on the nitrogen in the air, the salts and water in the soil, and combining all these they form plant tissue. Animals, in turn, use plants for food, and so secure, as building food, material previously manufactured by the plants. Finally, there are some animals, such as the lion,

PICTURED KNOWLEDGE
Two Nutritious Salads

At the left is one portion of banana salad served with whipped cream. It supplies 155 calories. At the right is a plate of "Waldorf" salad and mayonnaise. It gives 280 calories. The variety of salads is almost endless and the making of salads one of the finest of domestic accomplishments.

tiger, etc., who secure all their food, both for fuel and for building purposes, by eating the flesh of other animals.

Plant and Animal Food

Man, too, secures most of his building food from the meat of other animals, though he also makes large use of other animal products, such as milk and eggs. Man's use of foods of animal origin is largely a matter of convenience, habit and instinct; it is possible for man to subsist wholly on a vegetarian diet. In this connection it may be well to point out that almost all who call themselves "vegetarians" make use of two convenient and concentrated building foods of *animal* origin, namely, milk and eggs.

Nature adapts the body very closely to the kind of food habitually used. We see this clearly by comparing the structure of the digestive system of the tiger with that of the cow. In the latter there is an enormous spiral-shaped portion of intestine called the cæcum, evidently intended to serve as a place where large quantities of food can be retained for a long time, and so enable

The Lion and The Cow

the body to extract most of the available nourishment. In the tiger, on the other hand, there is no such spiral-shaped enlargement of the intestine. Since this animal eats practically nothing but meat, he has no need of any place for slowly extracting all the available nourishment from the food.

Attention has often been called to the relation existing between the character of the food, whether animal or vegetable, and certain characteristics of temperament. Speaking generally, it is well recognized that meat-eating people are more energetic than are those who live principally on vegetables. On the other hand, the nations living principally upon rice, while lacking energy, possess an untiring capacity for work. Nervousness is also less prevalent among them.

Is Your Fireman Wasting Fuel?

If you had been running a steam engine satisfactorily for some time on half a ton of coal a day, and found your new fireman burning over a ton of coal daily for the same work, you would probably discharge him for not knowing his business. Yet many of us are doing an equally stupid thing every day by eating much more than our bodies require. On the other hand, some people eat too little, and in consequence are thin, pale, and undernourished. Mistakes like this frequently arise from ignorance of the nourishing value of different foods, and of the amount required by the body under different circumstances.

Eating Too Much and Too Little

Scientists have discovered that ordinary persons doing moderately hard work—for example, clerks, bookkeepers, tailors, seamstresses—require food sufficient to supply each day about 2,500 calories. Just as a 10 horsepower engine requires more fuel than one yielding only 5 horsepower, so persons doing hard physical work require more food than those doing light work. The following table shows the number of heat units actually used up in a test conducted some years ago on persons working eight hours per day at their trade.

	Calories		Calories
Tailor	2200	Metal-worker	3200
Shoemaker	2600	Painter	3500
Bookbinder	2700	Stone-worker	4600
Carpenter	3100	Sawyer	5100

Women, in general, require somewhat smaller rations than men. Measured in calories, the following figures will serve as an example:

	Calories		Calories
Hand-sewer	1800	Machine-sewer	2000
Bookbinder	1900	Waitress	2400
		Wash-woman	2800

In order to form some idea of what these figures mean, study the information about the relative amount of calories in different foods under the pictures.

A person who habitually eats much more food than his body requires, grows fat, i. e., he becomes over weight or grows dyspeptic. This in itself is not only a decided handicap, but it throws considerable extra work on the internal organs.

Classification of Foods

If this were all that had to be considered in the science of nutrition, the whole matter would indeed be simple. To supply 2,500 calories, would merely need to eat twelve and one-half ounces of butter, or twenty-five bananas, or swallow twenty tablespoonfuls of olive oil. As a matter of fact, this would be certain to lead to starvation, for the foods mentioned would fail to supply the building material needed to maintain the body structure. We need, therefore, to learn something about the different kinds of foods, and about the needs of the body in this respect. Foods are conveniently classified as follows:

Carbohydrates
Fats   Mineral Salts
Protein   Water

The carbohydrates and the fats are the fuel foods of which we have already spoken. The protein is the building food. Both water and the mineral salts are also indispensable articles of food.

Starch, flour, and sugar are typical examples of the group called carbohydrates. Butter, lard, and olive oil are typical examples of the group called fats. Meat, eggs, milk and cheese are typical examples of the group called proteins. Most of the common foods, however, supply constituents belonging to several of these groups. Such foods are generally classed according to their most plentiful constituent, though this is not always satisfactory. The following examples will illustrate the point:

Good Fuel for the Engine

Here are some cereals containing carbohydrates which are useful chiefly as fuel food. Two of the shredded wheat biscuits supply 220 calories. Two slices of white bread, each weighing an ounce, supply 160 calories—as much as the glass of milk and more than the lean meat. Five crackers yield 125 calories, as do also the two French rolls.

An egg contains both fat and protein; in fact, two parts of fat to one of protein. Yet we generally class eggs with the protein foods. A potato contains both carbohydrate and protein, about eight parts of carbohydrate to one of protein. Cornmeal contains protein, fat, and carbohydrate, about one part of fat, two of protein, to eight of carbohydrate.

Carbohydrates and Fats

We have already spoken of these foods in speaking of the fuel needs of the body. To a large extent they are interchangeable in the diet, so that it makes little difference whether we supply fat or carbohydrate as fuel, so long as sufficient calories are provided. Attention is called to the high fuel value of the fats as compared with that of the carbohydrates.

Protein

As a result of much study, scientists generally agree that the diet of the ordinary person should include sufficient building food to supply about three ounces of dry protein daily. In this country most of us eat much more protein than this. Next to the English we are, perhaps, the greatest meat-eating nation on the globe. In addition to this we make extensive use of other foods rich in protein, such as eggs, fish, fowl, beans and cheese. As a matter of fact, this excessive use of protein foods is decidedly undesirable, for not only are protein foods expensive, but when eaten to excess they tend to the accumulation within the body of uric acid and allied substances.

Don't Eat Too Much Meat

It may be profitable to sketch in simple fashion what happens when protein food—for example, white of egg—is taken into the body and is eventually built up into muscle tissue. In the first place, the protein is acted on by the gastric juice in the stomach. This breaks the material up into a number of somewhat simpler substances, which then enter the small intestine. Here these are acted on by other ferments and are broken down into very simple substances

FOOD VALUES

which are called amino-acids.

Finally, in some mysterious way, the amino-acids are again combined and built up into a new form of protein, almost as complex in structure as that which was taken in as food. The whole process has been likened to the tearing down of a house, rearranging the building stones and timbers, and then rebuilding them to form a new house. Let us bear in mind that in the case we have imagined, the chicken protein needs to be formed in some way into human protein. In rebuilding, therefore, the body is erecting a structure different architecturally from that presented to it. It is therefore likely that there will be many unavailable pieces to discard, and that the new building will be smaller than the old.

Building New Houses With Old

There is reason to believe that animal protein is more readily utilized than protein from vegetable sources; it would seem as though the architecture of the former molecule were more closely related to that of the protein of the human body.

When thinking of protein foods, most of us think only of meat, milk and eggs. While these, of course, do supply a large proportion of protein, many other foods can serve the same purpose. Wheat, corn, rice, and other cereals contain about ten per cent of protein. Oatmeal contains over fifteen per cent, and beans, peas, and lentils almost twenty-five per cent of this valuable ingredient.

What Water Does for Us

Very few people regard water as a food; nevertheless this is one of the most important articles of the diet. Water is needed to dissolve the food elements so that they may be taken up by the body; water is needed to replenish the blood, and finally, without plenty of water the waste matter could not be washed out of the system through the kidneys. We take in water in many different ways. Almost every food we eat contains some water, and many of the common foods are almost all water. Here, for example, are some familiar foods and the percentage of water they contain:

Apple ....80 per cent water.
Cabbage ....90 per cent water.
Peach ....90 per cent water.
Bread ....35 per cent water.
Milk ....87 per cent water.

Should water be drunk with meals? Much nonsense has been written in answer to this question. The highest authorities now agree that it is well to drink a moderate quantity of water with meals. Some even go so far as to say that a little too much water with meals is less injurious than none taken at all at this time. Women often avoid drinking while eating, for fear they will become stout. This theory has long ago been discarded—and they may safely drink water freely so long as they do not overeat.

About Drinking With Meals

The Savor of Salt

Mineral salts make up an essential part of our bodies and must therefore be supplied in the food. As a matter of fact, if we see that our diet is an ordinary mixed one, containing milk, eggs, meat, cereals, fruit, vegetables, and water, we shall never have to consider the matter further. There is, however, one exception to this, namely, the addition of salt to our food. We add this instinctively, and scientists have discovered that it is necessary to all whose food is largely or entirely vegetable. Wild

PICTURED KNOWLEDGE
About the Coffee and the Tea

Neither coffee nor tea, alone, contains nourishment. But with a pitcher of cream weighing one ounce, a cup of either supplies 110 calories. If the three pieces of Domino sugar are added, they will yield 75 calories more.

animals such as deer or buffalo, will often travel many miles to a salt lick. On the other hand, Stefannsson found that the Eskimos, who live entirely upon a diet of flesh, have a strong dislike for salt.

You Need Vitamins, Too

A mild form of scurvy is often seen in infants fed exclusively on boiled milk. The symptoms rapidly disappear when a little orange juice is added to the baby's diet. In the Orient, a disease known as beri-beri is observed among people who subsist on a monotonous rice diet. Experiments on pigeons have shown that beri-beri can be produced by limiting the pigeons to a diet of "polished" rice, that is rice from which the husk has been removed. If the unpolished rice is fed, no beri-beri results. We see then that some essential food substance is present in the raw milk and in the husk of the rice. The name "Vitamin" has been given to these necessary constituents of food, without which the body cannot thrive. Many

Polished Rice and "Beri-Beri"

absurd statements have been made about vitamins, especially concerning the alleged danger of eating polished rice. In those eating polished rice as part of a mixed diet, the vitamin is supplied by other portions of the diet, and so we rarely find beri-beri developing in this country, despite the fact that we consume large quantities of polished rice, but observe the condition f r e q u e n t l y among those whose main article of food, day after day, is polished rice.

Why Food Must Have Bulk

Entirely aside from the diet's fuel value or from its content of protein, or salts, or vitamins, we must be careful to provide a certain bulk of food. In this way we supply woody fibre, or cellulose, which although containing little or no nourishment, is highly important in promoting a proper action of the bowels. The term "roughage" is often applied to this necessary part of the diet. There is considerable cellulose in spinach, celery, lettuce, corn, apples, pears, peaches, plums, whole wheat and oatmeal. When the diet contains too little of this cellulose, as in a diet composed largely of meat, constipation is apt to result.

Some Well-Balanced Menus

In order to give the reader a clearer picture of what constitutes a proper diet, the following well-balanced menus are presented. It is to be noted that they supply (for one meal) approximately 1,000 calories and from twenty-five to thirty-five grams of protein (30 grams equal one ounce).

organs and bones. Gradually, as active growth diminishes, the proportionate amount of protein required decreases, so that at about the age of fifteen years, the proportion is nearly the same as in adults.

Different Kinds of Protein

When we recall the many things that food must do, namely, supply fuel, building material, mineral salts, water, vitamins, and so on, and if we bear in mind that a normally healthy infant thrives for about a year on nothing but mother's milk,

Low Cost Balanced Rations

	Quantity	Calories	Protein
Macaroni and cheese	3 heaping tablespoonfuls	350	16.5 grams
Bread	2 slices	125	5.0 grams
Butter	½ oz.	110	
Cocoa	1 cup	253	3.0 grams
		838	24.5 grams
Steamed rice, raisins, and maple syrup	2 heaping tablespoonfuls	353	6.2 grams
Bread, whole wheat	2 slices	125	5.0 grams
Butter	½ oz.	110	
Glass of milk	7 oz.	160	7.0 grams
Ice-cream	2 heaping tablespoonfuls	190	5.0 grams
		938	23.2 grams

High Cost Balanced Rations

	Quantity	Calories	Protein
Clam chowder	½ pint	100	4.2 grams
Salmon croquettes	2 croquettes	380	23.2 grams
Baked sweet potatoes	1 medium size	205	3.0 grams
Bread	2 slices	125	5.0 grams
Butter	½ oz.	110	
Custard pie	⅙ pie	245	5.5 grams
Coffee	1 cup		
		1165	40.9 grams
Tipperary stew	4 oz.	175	10.0 grams
Bread	2 slices	125	5.0 grams
Butter	½ oz.	110	
Egg salad	1 egg	170	7.0 grams
Ice-cream	2 heaping tablespoonfuls	190	5.0 grams
Chocolate cake	1 slice	225	4.3 grams
Coffee	1 cup		
		995	31.3 grams

Feeding the Baby

In proportion to its body weight, an infant requires more protein than an adult. This is readily understood, when we remember that a normal infant is constantly growing, adding to the size of its muscles,

we cannot but marvel at the perfection of this food. Where infants cannot be nursed at the breast, fairly good results are obtained with cow's or goat's milk. That these are not perfect substitutes, however, is indicated by the fact that the proportion

PICTURED KNOWLEDGE

"Roughage" for the Human "Live Stock"

Vegetables are our most valuable source of "roughage." Most of us need to eat more of them, too, than we do. The tomato weighs 6 ounces and supplies us with 40 calories of nourishment. One carrot weighs 4 ounces and yields 50 calories. The potato weighs the same as the carrot but gives over twice as many calories—110. The onion weighs 2 ounces and supplies 25 calories.

of deaths of 162 infants under one year is considerably higher in infants fed on cow's milk than in those nursed at the breast. At one time it was thought that cow's milk could be made human mother's milk by merely diluting top milk with a solution of milk sugar. This was before we knew as much as we now know about the composition of protein. Now we know that the protein of each species of animal is peculiar for that animal, although it is probably somewhat similar to that of a closely related animal.

If an infant cannot be nursed at the breast, the following modifications of cow's milk may be used. All the milk should be of the highest grade obtainable, and should be pasteurized, either by the dealer or in the home. To make up for the loss of vitamins as the result of pasteurization, a little orange juice or barley water should be given each day. The latter is used in the formulas here given, but orange juice may well be given in addition.

"Bills of Fare" for Babies

Baby 3 days to 2 weeks old: Milk, 1 tablespoon; *Barley Water, 3 tablespoons. Feed the baby 2 tablespoonfuls at first and increase until the full amount, two ounces, is given at the end of 2 weeks. Feed baby every two hours.

Baby 2 weeks to 3 months: Milk, 1 ounce; *Barley Water, 2 ounces. Feed the baby this amount every 2 or 3 hours. Give only 7 to 8 feedings in 24 hours.

Baby 3 to 6 months old: Milk, 3 ounces; *Barley Water, 3 ounces. Feed the baby this amount every 3 hours. Give only 6 feedings in 24 hours.

Baby 6 to 9 months old: Milk, 6 ounces; *Barley Water, 3 ounces. Feed the baby this amount every 4 hours. Give only 5 feedings in 24 hours, the last one at 10 o'clock p. m.

Baby 9 to 12 months old: Milk, 8 ounces; *Barley Water, 2 ounces. Feed the baby this amount every 4 hours. Give only 5 feedings in 24 hours, the last one at 10 o'clock p. m.

How to Feed Young Children

Let your children have plenty of fresh milk. It is one of the cheapest and most nourishing foods they can have. It makes the children grow. Milk can be used with cereals, vegetables, in soups, in cocoa and puddings. Give your children plenty of water to drink; it is necessary to their health.

Never give children beer, tea, or coffee. Do not let them have cake, candies, or other sweets before meals; it takes away their appetite.

For young children the day's meals may consist of:

*Barley Water is best prepared from Patent Barley, which can be purchased in any drug store. Full directions are given on the box.

FOOD VALUES
Desserts That Taste Good and Do Good

Half a banana, sliced, and with one ounce of cream added, supplies 230 calories, which is 10 less than that given by a baked apple with the same amount of cream. The milk chocolate is cheap and highly nutritious. The piece of apple pie—1/7 of the pie—yields 300 calories, and the small portion of ice-cream gives 140 calories.

Breakfast—Cereal very well cooked with a little sugar and milk.
Lunch—Strained cereal with milk.
Dinner—A soft-boiled egg and a slice of stale bread and butter.
Supper—Strained cereal with milk.

Feeding the School Child

Investigations have shown that a large number of school children suffer from malnutrition. Considering the circumstances, this is not surprising. Away from the eyes of their parents during the lunch hour, many of the children eat only sweets and other dainties, often spending for candy and toys, money which is given them to buy a glass of milk. If at all possible the child should take his lunch at home, for the walk to and from school, if not excessive, will be invaluable in providing fresh air and needed exercise. On the other hand, if the school is more than half a mile from home, the time consumed in walking encroaches seriously on the time required for eating. Under these conditions, it is quite necessary, unless school lunches are provided by the authorities, to give the child a lunch to eat in school. It is important to provide a wholesome, appetizing diet with sufficient variety. A monotonous repetition kills the appetite and often leads to malnutrition.

Food Variety and Exercise

How often should an active school-child eat? This, of course, will vary, but most children will relish a bite to eat on coming out of school, especially if after this they run out to play in the open air.

Is candy good or harmful? Eaten in moderation, and not shortly before meals, candy constitutes a valuable article of food and may safely be allowed to most children. In active children playing much out of doors, candy and other forms of sugar constitute a valuable source of fuel. The great danger is that most children, unless controlled, will eat

Between-Meal Eating and Candy

1295

excessive quantities of sweets, and will spoil their appetites for their regular meals. Perhaps the safest plan is to allow one or two pieces of candy after a meal, as a kind of second dessert.

The following diet is recommended for children of school age:

Breakfast
1. An apple, orange, apple sauce, stewed prunes, or other fruit.
2. Cereal: Oatmeal, wheat food, rice, or any of the cooked breakfast foods, sweetened to taste and served, preferably with cream, otherwise with milk.
3. Dry or milk toast, bread and butter, with jam, jelly, or marmalade.
4. Cocoa or milk.

Lunch
At Home
1. Milk or cocoa.
2. Bread and butter.
3. Cold meat, hashed meat, fish, eggs, macaroni, meat, pea or bean soups, stews.
4. Baked or stewed potatoes, rice, green salad with oil.
5. Nuts, candy, bread or rice puddings, fruit (fresh or stewed).

At School
If the child cannot go home for lunch and none is regularly provided at the school, a simple lunch should be packed in a ventilated box or basket, and supplemented by a few pennies to buy a glass of milk.
1. Sandwiches: bread and butter with jam, cold meat, lettuce, egg, nuts, or cheese; boiled egg, jelly.
2. Fruit.

Dinner
1. Meat, vegetable, or milk soup.
2. Beef, mutton, lamb or chicken.
3. Potatoes, rice, cauliflower, macaroni, peas, beans, tomatoes, squash, celery, spinach, or other vegetables in season.
4. Green salads with oil, vinegar, and sugar.
5. Plain cake, candy, rice, sago, tapioca, bread or custard pudding, stewed fruits, prunes, apple sauce, cranberries, etc.
6. Milk.

Diets in Old Age

With the coming of old age and the general slowing-up of the body's various activities, the need for food gradually diminishes. A celebrated English physician, Cheyne, in discussing this period, advised that every man after fifty, should begin to decrease the amount of his food, so that finally he would pass out of life as he had entered it, even on a child's diet. During this period, it is especially important to see that the digestive system is not overburdened, and that constipation is avoided. In recent years the use of fermented milk has been much discussed, and while many of the claims made for this food have been exaggerated, there is no doubt that it constitutes a very valuable article of diet. The milk can be eaten in the form of "clabber," sprinkled with sugar and cinnamon, or it may be purchased in the form of Zoolak, Matzoon, Kumyss or other commercial products, or finally the milk may be fermented by means of culture or tablets obtainable in drug stores.

Back to Childhood Food

For People Who Grow Too Fat

With a few exceptions, most cases of obesity are due to the eating of greater amounts of food than can be consumed by the body. In order to bring such individuals back to a normal condition, we must, therefore, so plan their dietary and mode of life that the intake will be proportionate to the output. In fact, during the period of reduction proper, the intake of food must be smaller than the output of heat and energy. The method of conducting such a reduction cure depends, not only on the degree of obesity, but also on individual characteristics, and should in every case be supervised by an experienced physician. Most of the much-advertised anti-fat remedies are worthless, some are positively dangerous. Beware of so-called reduction cures that do not restrict the

Beware of Anti-Fat Remedies

diet. Exercise is important, especially hill climbing, rowing, swimming, and sea bathing, for all of these use up considerable energy.

Foods Allowed

Lean meat once a day, fish, cheese.
Green vegetables, such as string beans, peas, spinach, lettuce, celery, cabbage, and tomatoes. Potatoes in small quantities.
Stale or toasted bread.
Coffee and tea without milk or sugar.

Foods to Avoid

Butter, cream, oil, and other fats.
Sugar, candies, and other sweets.
Beer, cocktails, and other alcoholic beverages.
Rich gravies thickened with flour.
Pastry and puddings.

For People Who Grow Too Lean

Since the causes of leanness are varied, treatment of the condition will vary in individual cases. Any underlying worry, anxiety, overwork, lack of sleep, etc., should be remedied. If the appetite is defective, a course of out-door living may be required. Instead of three meals a day it may be well to give five. The diet should be made to include large amounts of fuel foods, especially fats and sugars. Cream and butter can be added in many different ways. The morning cereal should be served with cream, and griddle cakes with generous quantities of syrup and butter. Lettuce and other salads can be made a vehicle for giving large quantities of mayonnaise dressing. Creamed vegetables are of value. Milk and chocolate may be serviceable. Coffee and tea should be served with cream and sugar. Mashed potatoes should be prepared with milk and butter. Desserts should include puddings, made with milk, butter and sugar. In some instances malt extracts will be found very useful. In order to tempt the appetite, all foods should be daintily served, and there should be plenty of variety.

Remarks on Certain Common Foods

Milk.—Attention has already been called to the perfect character of milk as a human food. Unfortunately, it is an equally good food for bacteria, and the greatest care must therefore be taken in its production and subsequent handling. *(Hidden Dangers in Milk)* Experience has shown that the precautions to be taken to ensure a really safe, raw milk, one which can be relied upon to be free from disease germs, are so costly that the price becomes almost prohibitive. Milk of this grade is usually sold under the designation "Certified" or "Guaranteed," and retails for from fifteen to twenty cents a quart. In order to provide a safe milk at moderate cost, pasteurization is employed. This consists, or should consist, in heating the milk for thirty minutes to 140°-150° Fahrenheit and then rapidly cooling it to about 40° and keeping it cold. In New York City, no milk, except the equivalent of "certified" grade, may be sold without having been pasteurized. Since this law was enforced, there has been a marked reduction of typhoid fever in the city.

Eggs.—The amount of nourishment in an egg corresponds to that contained in a cup of milk. Cooked eggs are more easily digested than raw eggs, those boiled for fifteen minutes are probably *(About the Hard-Boiled Egg)* even more easily digested than soft-boiled eggs. Eggs are rich in phosphorus, and for this reason, they have been recommended as a brain food. The very great popularity of eggs as an article of food is due, in a large

PICTURED KNOWLEDGE
Good Bricks for Little Buildings

Here are some foods that are simple in form but that yield a great deal of nourishment. The ounce of American cheese supplies 135 calories, the ounce of butter, 240 calories. The quart of milk gives 680 calories. The pint of cream contains 36 per cent butter fat and yields 880 calories. The egg weighs twice as much as the butter and cheese but gives only 80 calories.

measure, to the ease with which they are incorporated in the dietary in a large variety of ways.

Cheese.—The value of cheese as an article of diet is still but little appreciated in this country. As a matter of fact, cheese is probably the most nourishing of our foods and contains more protein than meat. According to Lorand, cheese is an easily digested food for a healthy person, and it assists in the digestion of other foods. Thus, macaroni is more easily digested when finely grated cheese is sprinkled over it. On the other hand, cheese is not well tolerated when the stomach is weak, and this applies especially to the various hard cheeses. Fresh, soft varieties of cheese are generally more easily digested.

Fish.—The flesh of fish in general is not only much more tender than beef, mutton, lamb or pork, but it is more easily digested. Moreover, fish contains less extractive substances and so gives rise, in digestion, to fewer harmful products. This makes fish a valuable article of diet for patients suffering from kidney and liver disorders, or from gout. It is important, however, to see that the fish is absolutely fresh, for no kind of meat spoils as rapidly as fish. Where fresh fish is plentiful, there is probably no other animal protein, with the possible exception of cheese, which can be purchased at so moderate a price.

Oysters.—Since oysters are so frequently eaten raw, it may be well to warn against eating any which have been subject to the process called "floating" or "drinking." This consists in keeping the oysters in a crate placed in a stream of partly salt water. The oysters absorb water and become plump and white. They appear to have fattened. It has been found that this "floating" or "drinking" often leads to the infec-

Avoid the "Fat" Oyster

tion of oysters with typhoid germs. Instead, therefore, of preferring plump, "fat" oysters, the consumer should insist on getting the natural gray, rather lean oysters, having a fresh, clean, salty taste.

Cereals.—While the cereals are primarily fuel foods, containing, as they do, from 60 to 70 per cent of carbohydrate, they also furnish considerable protein. Moreover, some of the cereals—for example, wheat and rye—are rich in mineral salts. In milling wheat flour, much of the bran is lost, and, since this contains the greater proportion of protein and mineral salts, much is said about the advantages of whole wheat bread over the ordinary white bread. As a matter of fact, the bran is very poorly digested in any case, so that the additional nourishment provided by eating whole wheat bread is almost negligible. For persons who ordinarily do not secure enough woody fiber (i. e., cellulose) in their diet, the use of whole wheat bread is undoubtedly desirable, principally, however, because of the mechanical action on the bowels.

Peas, Beans and Lentils.—The leguminous foods, such as peas, beans, and lentils, contain considerable nourishment. As ordinarily cooked, however, they are but poorly digested. According to some authorities almost one-third the food value is wasted because of improper preparation in the kitchen. To obtain the best digestive results, these legumes should be served in the form of a puree or a puree soup. Since they impose considerable work upon the digestive system, peas, beans and lentils should not be given to persons suffering from indigestion. Neither should they be allowed to those suffering from gout, for all of the legumes mentioned are rich in substances which lead to the formation of uric acid.

Coffee, Tea and Cocoa. — The effect of coffee, tea, and cocoa is similar. They all decrease fatigue and create a temporary feeling of alertness and increased strength. In other words, they are mere stimulants. This action is due to caffein, in coffee, thein in tea and theobromin in cocoa, three substances almost identical in chemical composition. As ordinarily prepared, neither coffee nor tea has any nutritive value apart from the sugar, cream or milk which may be added. Cocoa, however, contains some real nourishment, even apart from the milk and sugar with which it is usually prepared, but the amount of this nourishment is much less than is popularly supposed.

As in the case of all mere stimulants, tea and coffee should not be given to children, although chocolate made with milk may be allowed after the fifth year.

A Parable

Worn and footsore was the Prophet,
  When he reached the holy hill;
"God has left the earth," he murmured;
  "Here His presence lingers still.

"God of all the olden prophets,
  Wilt Thou talk with me no more?
Have I not as truly loved Thee
  As Thy chosen ones of yore?

"Hear me, Guider of my fathers.
  Lo, a humble heart is mine;
By Thy mercy, I beseech Thee,
  Grant Thy servant but a sign!"

Bowing then his head, he listened
  For an answer to his prayer;
No loud burst of thunder followed,
  Not a murmur stirred the air;

But the tuft of moss before him
  Opened while he waited yet,
And from out the rock's hard bosom
  Sprang a tender violet.

"God, I thank Thee," said the Prophet.
  "Hard of heart and blind was I,
Looking to the holy mountain
  For the gift of prophecy.

"Still Thou speakest with Thy children
  Freely as in Eld sublime,
Humbleness and love and patience
  Give dominion over Time.

"Had I trusted in my nature,
  And had faith in lowly things,
Thou Thyself wouldst then have sought me,
  And set free my spirit's wings.

"But I looked for signs and wonders
  That o'er men should give me sway
Thirsting to be more than mortal,
  I was even less than clay.

"Ere I entered on my journey,
  As I girt my loins to start,
Ran to me my little daughter,
  The beloved of my heart;

"In her hand she held a flower,
  Like to this as like may be,
Which beside my very threshold
  She had plucked and brought to me."

JAMES RUSSELL LOWELL

KEEPING WELL — CARE OF BABIES

How the Public Saves the Babies

Prize Babies in a Better Babies Contest

THREE hundred thousand babies under one year of age die in the United States each year. At least one-half these lives could be saved if the knowledge we have regarding baby care were used. There has long been an idea, which still seems deeply rooted in some parts of the country, that each mother is wholly responsible for the health of her baby. In all places where saving babies has received the attention of public health officials, it has become evident at once that this is only partly true. Someone has said that, in the last analysis, each mother must save her own baby, but we know now that she can do this only if the whole community in which she lives is alive to the importance of keeping babies well, and prepared to give the mothers not only the knowledge of how to care for their babies, but also to see that all of the health conditions in the community are such that the mothers may take advantage of them, and the babies receive the care which is their birthright.

Cruel Waste of Little Lives

In days of war, the whole world is horrified when even two or three babies are killed, even though it may be inadvertently, by any of the combatants, yet the death of one hundred fifty thousand babies in the United States each year is equally needless and equally wrong. From a humanitarian point of view, the loss is appalling; from an economic point of view, it strikes at the most basic principle of the welfare of the country. No country, which allows its infant death rate to increase at the same time its birth rate is decreasing, can ultimately survive. Although this situation of a decreasing birth rate in Europe is being met by extended efforts to reduce the baby death rate, in this country we have seemingly not realized the great importance of the fact that, while our birth rate is decreasing, our infant death rate is abnormally high.

To save babies is one of the simplest public health problems, and there is no other kind of community health work that is so sure and so satisfactory. The finest type of national preparedness lies in seeing that our babies are not only kept alive, but that they are cared for so intelligently that they will be well and strong. Healthy baby life brings healthy childhood, which involves better scholarship; and healthy childhood, both physical and mental, means almost certain prevention of ill-health in adults.

Good Work Certain of Results

The Mother, the Baby, and the Community

The baby death rate is the index of the sanitary condition of any community, for the conditions which allow babies to die will inevitably increase the death rate of older children and adults. These conditions are community problems. They include the supply of pure water and pure milk, decent housing with plenty of sunlight in rooms, an abundant supply of fresh air, no overcrowding in living apartments, clean streets, proper disposal of sewage and garbage, and clean, outdoor places for recreation. Every community not only owes every one of these to each mother and baby, but it also—and this is of great importance—must make it possible for every mother to obtain all the information that is needed regarding baby and child care, and the means of keeping babies well and strong.

Many counties, cities, towns, villages, and rural communities have already started splendid campaigns for saving babies, and in every instance this work has shown a decided decrease in the baby death rate. This decrease has been just in proportion to the intelligent effort that has been used by the community. Three big lessons have been learned and applied by every body of people who has successfully carried on this work,— first, that saving babies must be the combined work of everyone in a community,— men, women and children; second, that public health education in its broadest aspect is the means that must be used; and, third, that saving babies does not mean curing sick babies, but it means assuring babies the right to be born healthy and to keep well.

The Three Great Lessons

Baby Saving in New Zealand

New Zealand is the most striking evidence we have of governmental baby-saving. In the United States, approximately one hundred twenty-five out of every thousand babies born —or one out of eight—die before the end of their first year. In New Zealand, where the baby death rate was almost as high, the government co-operates with private agencies in sending out nurses to instruct mothers in baby care and in controlling sanitary living conditions so that, within a few years, it has reduced its baby death rate to fifty-one out of every thousand babies born, and now has the lowest baby death rate of any country in the world.

It is a mistake to believe that it is only in the cities that babies are dying unnecessarily. The small towns and rural communities that have neglected baby-saving work have, in many instances, a higher baby death rate than the large cities. This is because the latter have nearly all realized the great importance of keeping babies alive and well, and have worked steadily towards that end. In New York City, for instance, the baby death rate has been reduced in the last thirteen years from one hundred eighty-one deaths to ninety-five deaths out of every thousand babies born, and the pres-*Baby Death Rate in the Country* ent baby death rate is also lower, in that big, congested city, than it is in all the rest of New York State combined, and lower than that of any other of the ten largest cities of the United States.

There are many ways in which various communities have worked out this problem, but they are all based on the same idea, that is, first, education of the public and, second, education of the mother. It would seem that the women of any community might be the logical people to start such a campaign and to stimulate public opinion regarding its need. The main point to be achieved is the forcing of the public authorities to assume control of this important phase of public health work. In too many places boards of health have been entirely negligent of this part of their work. Even our United States government is extremely backward in this respect. We have in Washington a most efficient Children's Bureau under federal government control, yet the United States spends three million dollars in caring for animal babies and only one hundred sixty-five *Doing Most for Animal Babies* thousand dollars in caring for human babies. This disproportion is one of the first things the people of this country should have changed. The government sends out experts and information in regard to breeding and care of animals, and helps the people of the farming communities not only with their live stock but also with their crops, but until this very modest appropriation was made for the Children's Bureau, no concerted attempt had been made to afford any aid whatever to the conservation of the most important resource of the country—the baby.

The Shaping of Public Opinion

It has been shown that community action must be back of any effective baby-saving work. The most important thing back of community action is, of course, public opinion. Any community that wishes to save its babies should start out, first, by getting some interested body of people to back the campaign. This may be done through a woman's club or *The Children and the Babies* through the public school. School children have shown themselves to be one of the most efficient aids we have in saving babies. There is no reason why they should not be prime movers in this work.

Usually, the best way is to let the people in any town know at once how many babies are dying, and why, and in what part of town they have lived. To do this should not be difficult, nor need it cost any money. Such records should be on file in the office of the health officer in any town. In order to make an appeal to the citizens, however, something besides statistics must be used. Very few people will read statistics, and they have little or no interest for the average person. It is best, therefore, to get a map of the town, showing the streets, paste it on a board, and then put in a pin with a colored cloth or glass top in the location on the map representing *Pictured Knowledge of Conditions* the place where each baby died in the previous year. Different colors may be used to represent different causes of death, such as blue for stomach and bowel disorders, red for contagious diseases, yellow for diseases of the lungs, green for the babies dying from congenital diseases, which means deaths occurring during the first month of life of babies who were not born with sufficient vitality to live longer. Such a map might also have white-headed pins to represent places where babies are born, and the number of such babies in town. The map then could be placed in a window of some prominent store and the attention of the newspapers called to it, if they have not already considered its importance. Newspaper interviews with physicians of the town regarding the matter make excellent items for publication. Letters to newspapers, and opinions of prominent citizens all stimulate discussion. As soon as possible a meeting should be called. Addresses could be made by local physicians, clergymen, and others, and a determined effort made to raise enough money to employ at least one public health nurse.

Don't Stop with a Mere Beginning

The mere appointment of a public health nurse, however, will not alone keep the babies alive and well. The community must be aroused to action in all of the matters that pertain to decency and sanitary conditions. A "clean-up week" is an excellent thing to start with. Such weeks have consisted in plenty of publicity regarding the necessity for cleanliness in maintaining health in any community; the distribution of literature on methods of cleaning up; an arrangement whereby, on a certain day, all the refuse in back yards and vacant lots may be cleaned up and removed, all discarded household utensils taken away, mosquito-breeding pools cleaned out and covered with a thin layer of kerosene and all outdoor receptacles which might collect water, cleaned and either disposed of or kept under constant observation.

In a "clean-up week" any organization of boys may take a most active part. The Boy Scouts have done excellent work in several of our large cities in the big clean-up campaigns, by notifying householders of the conditions which should be remedied and by actually lending a hand to help the work of cleaning-up.

Story of the Milk Station Baby

This is the picture of a poor little baby when he was first brought to one of the public milk stations.

Have a Clean-Up Week

CARE OF BABIES

The publicity gained by a "clean-up week" may then be used to further a great and concerted movement for a pure water supply, a pure milk supply, continued clean streets and proper refuse disposal and decent housing. It is a curious fact that the maligned tenements in large cities are frequently in a much better sanitary state than the slum sections of many smaller towns. This is due

Town Slums Worse Than City Slums — to the fact that the city authorities maintain such constant and rigid supervision over sanitary conditions among the tenement population, whereas, in small towns, little or no attempt is made, in many cases, to clean up the filthy back yards, dirty shanties and general insanitary conditions. Spots like these are inevitable breeding places, for not only baby deaths, but for a vast amount of sickness among the people who live in them, and this sickness and its effects extend not only to the people who live in such degrading surroundings, but to the entire community. No city which has slums can be exempt from the effects of those slums. It cannot evade its moral responsibility and, inevitably, must bear the burden of the ill-health that comes to any community which is so thoughtless as to allow such a condition of affairs to exist.

The Same Baby Ten Months Later

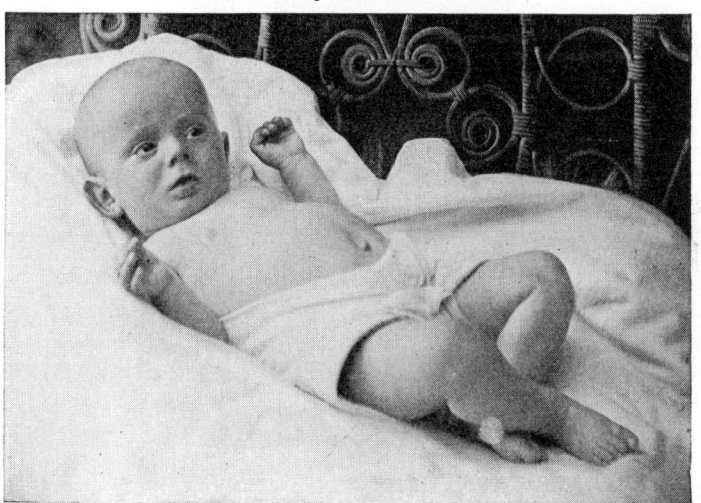

This is the same baby ten months later, after he had been fed with milk cared for according to the simple but scientific methods which poor mothers are taught by the skilled attendants at the public milk station.

Pure Milk and How to Get It

In this general consideration of how the public saves the babies, limited space does not permit a lengthy consideration of the problem of pure milk in a community, but it must be understood that very definite attention should be paid, first of all, to this important health feature. If adequate dairy inspection, with the scoring of the farms, dairies and creameries, cannot be maintained or adequately supervised, then the community should insist upon proper pasteurization of all milk which is consumed within its limits. Within the home, there are three points to be remembered regarding the care of milk. These are easily remembered, for they can be put into the form of a slogan: "Keep the milk clean, covered, and cool." Milk drawn from a healthy cow, by a clean and healthy milker, placed immediately into a sterile container which is at once sealed and kept at a temperature below fifty degrees from the time it leaves the cow until it reaches the consumer, fulfills the main requirements of a safe milk supply. The best milk in the world, however, may deteriorate in the home. After a supply of fresh milk is assured by community action, definite instructions should be given to all mothers and householders as to the necessity of keeping the milk below the required temperature of fifty degrees and keeping it continuously covered until it is used.

Not Easy, but Much Worth While

It is not an easy matter to conduct a campaign of this sort and make it have permanent results, but it is worth all the time and effort that may be expended. In the meantime, the value of the community nurse must not be overlooked. First, she should have some headquarters to work in. In many of our larger cities, the so-called "infants' milk stations" or "baby welfare centers" are elaborately equipped and furnished. This makes them very attractive places for the mothers of the neighborhood, and their clean white and blue interiors, with the white enamel furniture and the many utensils, have a distinct advertising value, but they are not necessary. Just as effective work in baby-saving can be done in one room, with simple equipment of a table,

Establishing Baby Welfare Centers

chairs, a pair of scales, and the double boiler, measuring glass, bowl, spoon, and pitcher that are needed to demonstrate the proper modification of cow's milk. Such a room should, if possible, be painted white. The idea of cleanliness must be taught, not for one lesson, but continuously, morning, noon, and night, and must always be associated in the mind of the mother with baby care.

At such a baby welfare center, the nurse might well arrange to have regular office hours, each morning if possible; if not, at least two or three mornings each week. The volunteer aid of physicians can usually be obtained, each doctor taking one morning or afternoon each week for the purpose of giving advice to the mothers whose babies need medical care, and holding conferences with the mothers in groups to demonstrate the various methods of keeping babies well.

The Many Duties of the Public Nurse

The nurse will find that her duties are multitudinous. Each baby should be weighed each week. The mother must be taught how it should be bathed, how it should be dressed, about its general surroundings and care and the need of fresh air, the making of simple clothes and the arrangement of a clothes basket or box for a cradle. If the mother is unable to nurse her baby, after every effort has been made towards that end, she should be taught how to modify cow's milk in accordance with a prescription given by the doctor. Such public health centers rapidly become real community welfare centers, and the nurse is called upon for every type of advice relating to the care of children. In the afternoons, she must visit the homes of her mothers

CARE OF BABIES
At a Public Welfare Center

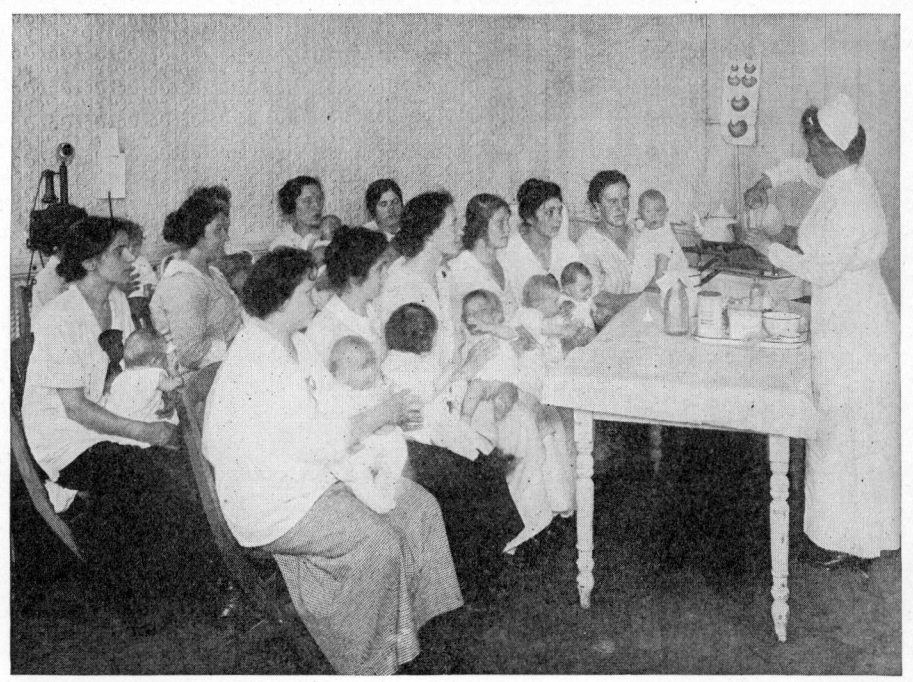

This picture shows mothers listening to a little talk by one of the attendants at a public milk station on how to care for baby's milk.

and see that the instructions she has given are carried out. The nurse must be in close touch with the local health officer, if not under his actual guidance, and she should obtain from him each day a list of all babies born in the town the previous day, and each mother should either receive a circular of instruction or be visited at once. It cannot be too strongly stated that the only way in which the baby death rate can be reduced is to reach the mothers either before or immediately after their babies are born, and to see that they know how to use the methods that will keep the babies well; in other words, the work must be purely that of prevention and education. Sick babies need the care of a doctor, but babies need not be sick in the majority of instances if their mothers can be taught how to care for them.

Teaching the New Mothers

It is interesting to know the causes of baby deaths, because only by studying these causes can we find the way to prevent their occurrence. In general, the causes of infant deaths fall into four broad classes, those from so-called "congenital diseases," respiratory diseases, diarrheal diseases and contagious diseases, with all others grouped in a class by themselves. Although, for many years, the majority of babies who died did so because of some stomach or bowel disturbance, such as are classified under the heading of "diarrheal diseases," at the present time approximately thirty-five per cent, or over one-third of all babies who die in their first year, die from what are known as "congenital diseases"; that is, a majority of them die during the first week or the first month of life, from conditions which are dependent very largely upon the health of the mother before the child is born. These babies are either born with actual disease or they have not vitality enough to survive the first few weeks of life.

To combat such conditions is exceedingly difficult, because it involves adjustment of conditions which may concern the mother during the period before the baby comes. Such adjustment may include the wages of the father, the entire living conditions of the family, the question of whether or not the mother may work, definite treatment of the mother for diseased conditions, provision of proper food so that she may be well nourished. All of these things can be attended to, however, by public health nurses, and the result in those places which have tried this particular work, which is known as prenatal nursing, has been a reduction by about one-half in the death rate during the first month of life among babies born to mothers who have been under supervision during the prenatal period.

The second main causes of deaths of babies are the so-called "diarrheal diseases." These are the ones which have shown the greatest reduction in the campaigns for saving babies, because the provision of a pure milk supply, the teaching of the importance of breast-feeding and the hygiene of babyhood, to mothers, has resulted in a very distinct lowering in the death rate in this class of cases. They furnish at present about twenty-five per cent of the total infant deaths.

Next in order, comprising about twenty-two per cent of all baby deaths under one year of age, are the respiratory diseases. These include bronchitis, whooping cough, and pneumonia. The greatest number of these deaths are from pneumonia, and large numbers of these cases follow attacks of measles or whooping cough. Prevention of such illness is much more difficult than the prevention of diarrheal diseases, but very much may be done by direct education of the mother and by a proper system of quarantine of contagious diseases in the community.

The fourth class—the contagious diseases themselves—comprise only about four per cent of the total and, generally, instruction in sanitation and healthful living, with the proper enforcement of quarantine for cases of contagious diseases, will do much to lower the death rate from this cause.

The Little Mothers' Leagues

Because the work of caring for babies is of such immense importance, the Department of Health of New York City originated the movement to have the girls in the schools taught the simple methods of baby care. As the school authorities were not ready to take up this teaching, the Department of Health inaugurated "Little Mothers' Leagues." These leagues are groups of girls, between ten and fourteen years of age, who volunteer to become aids of the Department of Health in saving babies. They are grouped either in connection with the school or with the local milk station, under the supervision of a trained nurse, who gives them, at weekly intervals, talks on the care

Teaching the Little Mothers

CARE OF BABIES
Preparing Baby's Milk

Here is a Little Mother preparing baby's milk. You see, she must have quite an equipment, but most of the things needed are already in the kitchen and the others are not expensive.

of babies and demonstration of some simple method of baby care. A regular course is outlined to be taken. The children write and give plays demonstrating the facts they have learned. No attempt is made to interfere with the manner of presentation of these plays, the only requirement being that the play should be based on fact.

It has been stated by Professor Terman that this work of Little Mothers' Leagues, that is, the idea of having children teach each other in their own words and by their own methods, the application of facts which they have learned from a teacher, is one of the most important contributions to pedagogical science that have been made. Certainly, those who observe the progress of the Little Mothers' Leagues know that they are effective. The girls can be counted upon as very definite aids for the district nurse. They can canvass homes to obtain the consent of mothers to visit the milk stations; they can visit mothers who have not returned, to find out why; they can take babies out for airings, thus giving the tired mothers a needed rest; but, above all else, the teaching of good motherhood comes to them at a time when they can receive it with a lack of self-consciousness and in exactly the same spirit in which they receive their instruction in arithmetic or geography.

Our experience in New York City with these leagues, which have a membership of about twenty-seven thousand children annually, shows *How the Girls Enjoy the Work* that these girls thoroughly enjoy their part in this big work. Children, as well as adults, like to join societies and they are most effective and valuable aids in this particular

1309

direction. If this work can be extended under the authority of boards of education, so that every girl in the elementary schools receives simple instruction in baby care, we may readily conceive that infant mortality will cease to be a problem in the next generation.

The program for the Little Mothers' Leagues may be made elastic enough to suit any locality. If this instruction is carried on under the authority of the Board of Education, it should be combined with the regular lessons in hygiene; as separate leagues, however, it is recommended that no effort be made to carry out this instruction during the winter months but that, beginning in the early spring, lectures be given by doctors or nurses in the public schools, calling the attention of the children to the problem of infant mortality and the aid that they may give in solving it. Volunteers should be asked for and each child should be asked to sign a card, pledging herself to aid in the campaign of saving the babies. The league may then be organized, with a president, secretary, and treasurer. The best results have been found to follow meetings held at weekly intervals during the entire summer season. For such a series of meetings, the following twelve topics are suggested:

1. Growth and development; special senses.
2. Teeth.
3. Water—internally and externally; special baths.
4. Fresh air.
5. Sleep and quiet.
6. Clothing and cleanliness.
7. First care of sick baby.
8. Difference between mother's and cow's milk.
9. Amount and intervals of feeding.
10. Care of milk, bottles, nipples. Articles needed for home modification of milk.
11. Directions for home modification of milk.
12. Instructions for making albumen water, whey.
13. Quiz on previous lessons.

At each meeting a short talk should be given by the nurse, followed by an active demonstration of the subject. The children should be taught not only to observe the methods which are used but should be required to actually carry them out in practice. One feature of the work, which is the only one actually required of each member, is the promise to do some one deed each day to help a baby. At the meetings, essays on baby care, founded upon the work of the previous lesson, may be read, the experiences of the members should be recounted and the features of recreation and entertainment elaborated as much as possible. Only a simple equipment is needed. The articles will probably suggest themselves readily to anyone who has a knowledge of baby care, but the following list is given as a matter of guidance:

Gas stove and tubing
Bath tub
Double boiler
Two-quart dishpan
Two-quart bowl
Two-quart tea kettle
One-quart pitcher
Enameled cup or saucepan, with cover, half-pint size
Tumbler
Eight-ounce graduate glass
Funnel
Scale
Basket

CARE OF BABIES
The Baby's Bath

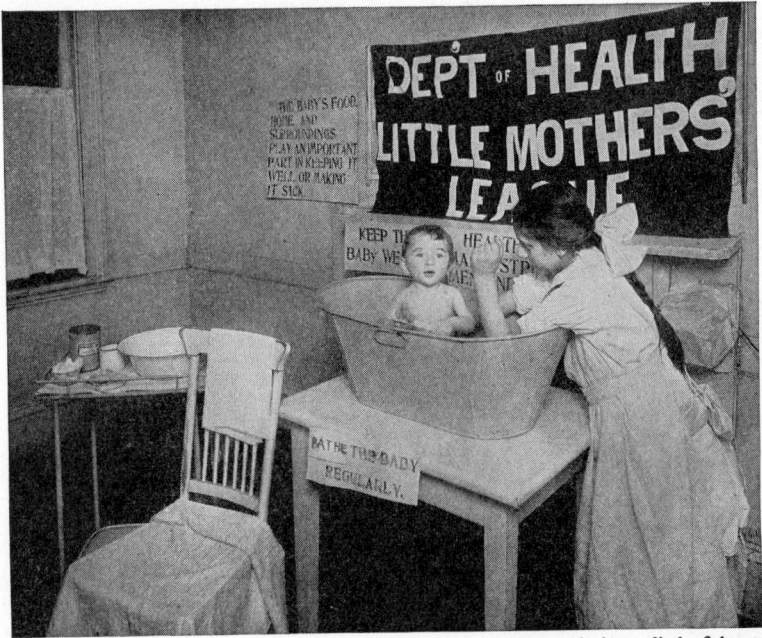

Water, applied externally, is almost as important to little babies as it is to little fish, and they show it by the way they love to paddle in the water. That the baby should have his bath regularly is one of the things that is impressed upon the members of The Little Mothers' League.

Strainer
Bath thermometer
Clinical thermometer
Four nipples
Knife
Tablespoon
Teaspoon
Toothbrush
Safety pins
Piece of castile soap
Piece of rubber sheeting or pad
Two bath towels
Two face towels
Package absorbent cotton, one pound
Package of gauze, five yards
Rice or starch powder
One-half pound borax
One-quarter pound mustard
One package Robinson's barley
Milk sugar
Lime water
Toothpicks
Small bag of salt
Bag of bran
Pad for scale
Tissue paper
Quilted padding, 5 yards, to make cheap mattress and pillow
Large size washable doll
Complete set baby clothes, with patterns for making them.

Work of Publicity in New York State

In New York City and New York State it is the practice to send to the mother of each baby born, a copy of the birth certificate, together with a letter from the Commissioner of Health and a pamphlet descriptive of baby care. Such action stimulates birth registration, as any mother who does not receive a pamphlet is likely to make inquiries as to why it has not been sent. As birth registration is the bookkeeping of the whole infant welfare movement, be-

How the Work Is Done — cause it is impossible to determine the real infant mortality problem until one knows how many babies are born and where they are born, this attempt to stimulate good birth registration is not only worth all the effort expended in sending out the certificates, but it has a very definite value also in calling the attention of the mothers to early and continued care of their babies. All kinds of pamphlets on baby care, including instructions to the mother during the period before the baby comes, and not forgetting pamphlets directed to the fathers on their share in baby-saving, are definite aids in this work. Public lectures, conferences and newspaper publicity should all be used. If the co-operation of a local newspaper can be obtained, it is of value to have, once or twice each week during the summer months, a short interview with one of the local physicians, giving simple directions on some one phase of baby care. This may be printed in a column which has a regular heading, such as "Talks to Mothers" or "The Baby" and may easily be made a valuable feature of the newspaper.

Baby Week and Better Babies Contests

There are two kinds of community work for saving babies which have attracted a great deal of attention within the last few years. These are Better Babies Contests and Baby Week Celebrations. Both have great publicity value. Baby contests may be held at any time during the year, while Baby Week should be an annual affair. In general, any legitimate method of attracting public attention to this problem is of value.

While it must not be forgotten that the direct instruction of the mother through a doctor or trained nurse is absolutely essential, success depends upon the public spirit which can be used to promote methods of sanitary living and proper control of the health functions of the community. Considering, then, that Better Babies Contests and Baby Week may be used in this sense as a matter of publicity as well as actual aids to the babies, a set program for either cannot be advanced, as each community must, to a certain extent, adjust the functions to suit the local needs.

Better Babies Contests have been held in connection with county fairs, or independently in communities. Mothers are asked to bring their babies at certain specified times. The children are then examined by physicians who report, on a standard *How the Prizes Are Awarded* score card, the various points of information regarding height, weight, physical and mental development of the baby. Each factor has a definite numerical count, and upon this count the scoring of the child is based. After all of the babies have been examined, the relative scores are compared and the baby receiving the highest score, that is, the one most nearly approaching the normal development for a child of its age is awarded the prize.

It has been found, in many of our large cities, that while Better Babies Contests have had a definite publicity value, they presented many faults and, in New York City, a few years ago, it was decided to modify the contests. Out of this has grown the *Baby Improvement Contests* "Baby Improvement Contests," which have proved to be very much more valuable than the "Better Babies Contests." In the latter, the child

CARE OF BABIES

is judged upon its status at the moment of examination. In the "Baby Improvement Contest" the babies are brought to a stated place at a specified time, where they are examined by physicians and scored in the way that it attracts the sickly and undernourished baby, as well as the healthy baby, while the "Better Babies Contest" is apt to bring out only the well developed child. The "Baby Improvement Contest" also stimu-

A Meeting of a Little Mothers' League

This is a meeting of a "Little Mothers' League." These leagues are formed in co-operation with the public schools, and these children belong to Public School 42 in New York City. The Little Mothers have been receiving diplomas for the good records they have made in caring for baby brothers and sisters.

that has been described. The mothers are then given definite instructions, both verbally and in writing, as to the future care of the baby. At the end of a specified period—either three or six months—they are required to return, and the babies are again examined and scored. The mother is also given a score, in proportion to the way in which she can demonstrate that she has obeyed the instructions given by the physician. The baby who can show the greatest improvement during the intervening period is awarded the prize. The advantage of this form of contest is lates the mother to greater care of her baby, rather than leaving her wholly satisfied with the methods that she has used. A word should be said here about the inadvisability of awarding money prizes in these contests, as it tends to commercialize them and to promote an unwholesome form of rivalry among the parents, who seem in many instances much more desirous of obtaining the money than of helping their children. Medals, cups, or even certificates, have been found to obviate this difficulty.

The Baby Week celebration is a

much more difficult plan to carry out. Recently, the Children's Bureau at Washington has stimulated this movement by means of the co-operation of the General Federation of Women's Clubs. The idea of a Baby Week is that at some time, preferably during the early spring months, the whole community should be aroused to the importance of providing necessary baby care for all of the babies in the town or city. Usually, a general committee should be formed and every welfare organization in the town asked to serve on such a committee. The chairman of this committee might logically be the local health officer.

The co-operation of the newspapers, advertising men and merchants is essential. If possible, an appropriate slogan should be devised and a special poster or picture provided for the occasion. This picture and slogan should be displayed in store windows, on billboards and featured by the newspapers. Merchants should be induced to advertise any merchandise they carry which may be used for babies. These advertisements will be carried in the newspapers in connection with the news items regarding Baby Week. In return, the Baby Week Committee should furnish the merchants with appropriate literature to distribute with packages of baby clothes or utensils which they sell.

Baby Week itself should have one day assigned for each particular feature. These, of course, must vary according to the facilities which are at the disposal of the committee. In general, however, it should start on Sunday, when the ministers of the town should be asked to preach on some subject connected with the importance of child life and the need of its conservation. The following day — Monday — might well be School Children's Day, when each child in the school receives some pamphlet descriptive of child care and, in addition, each school should receive, if possible, a short talk from some doctor or nurse regarding the part they can play in saving babies. Tuesday might be Fathers' Day, with meetings held, addressed particularly to the fathers as to their civic responsibility in community welfare and, incidentally, in baby-saving. Wednesday might be Visiting Day for day nurseries and babies' wards of hospitals, and Thursday might be the day on which the infant welfare station might be visited. If possible, the Little Mothers' League could arrange to present some of its plays in the schools on this day. On Friday there might be a baby parade, with the presentation of the prizes which have been awarded in previous Baby Improvement Contests. This parade can have many features—decorated floats, carriages or automobiles containing prize babies, baby carriages and many other features which will readily suggest themselves. Saturday should be Mothers' Day, with all-day outings for the mothers and the provision of nurses or volunteer assistants to go along and take care of the babies while the mothers enjoy themselves. Such excursions may take place either in the country or on the water.

The full details of the various methods of public health work in relation to saving babies cannot be given within the limits of this article, but such information may be obtained by anyone who will write directly to The Children's Bureau, Washington, D. C., for their publi-

Features of a Baby Week

cations on baby care and baby week activities, or to the Bureau of Child Hygiene of the Department of Health of New York City for their pamphlets descriptive of infants' milk stations, Little Mothers' Leagues and various methods of baby saving. The American Medical Association, 535 Dearborn St., Chicago, supplies such information and also score cards for baby contests.

Seven Times One

There's no dew left on the daisies and clover,
  There's no rain left in heaven.
I've said my "seven times" over and over—
  Seven times one are seven.

I am old—so old I can write a letter;
  My birthday lessons are done.
The lambs play always—they know no better;
  They are only one times one.

O Moon, in the night I have seen you sailing
  And shining so round and low.
You were bright—ah, bright!—but your light is failing;
  You are nothing now but a bow.

You Moon, have you done something wrong in heaven,
  That God has hidden your face?
I hope, if you have, you will soon be forgiven,
  And shine again in your place.

O Columbine, open your folded wrapper,
  Where two twin turtle-doves dwell.
O Cuckoo-pint, toll me the purple clapper
  That hangs in your clear green bell.

And show me your nest, with the young ones in it,
  I will not steal them away.
I am old, you may trust me, linnet, linnet,
  I am seven times one today.

JEAN INGELOW

"Tea Leaves"

Painted by W. M. Paxton — *Metropolitan Museum, New York*

These two girls are having a cosy cup of afternoon tea together. One of them knows how to "tell fortunes" by the way the tea leaves cling to the sides of the empty cup. Girl-like, she is curious about her "fate," and is trying to read her future from the teacup.

> THE WORLD
> AT ITS WORK
> THE TEA INDUSTRY

The World's "Cup O' Kindness"

A Japanese Tea Picker

Here is a Japanese peasant girl on her way to pick tea. She is a happy, care-free youngster, unlike her city cousin of the overworked, underpaid coolie class.

WHEN anyone says "sky" we think "blue." Some words just jump together. So "tea" makes us think of "party." It's a habit tea leaves have —giving parties. They have a coming-out party when they are living on the gayest little dwarf trees in the tea gardens of Japan. In the

*Polly put the kettle on
And we'll all take tea.*

Tea Blossom Invitations to a Tea Party

season of young hyson, which is early spring, or "before the rains," the pretty white tea blossoms and new leaves send out scented invitations on every little postman breeze. They say:

AT HOME
IN THE NEAREST TEA-HOUSE,
ON THE EDGE OF ANY CITY.
EVERYBODY WELCOME.

1317

At the Curly Roofed House on the Tea Farm

Everybody in Japan goes. If you were visiting in Japan, Nogi and Cherry Blossom would take you out for a treat. The tea house is a curly-roofed pavilion on a tea farm. Polite and smiling people sit on their heels, on mats, with table trays before them. They drink many dolly bowl cups of pale, straw-colored tea. They smell the blossoms and fragrant foliage. They enjoy looking at the little farm of sociable tea bushes, crowded cosily together on the hillside. Tinkle-tinkle, splashes the little brook that waters the garden.

Such a pretty, flowery garden! Tea plants are evergreen shrubs, like our holly bushes. They drop their shabby winter clothes in April, and put on new garden party gowns of pale green, lined with silver down. The leaf is a pointed oval, saw-toothed and net-veined, like a rose leaf; but it is set singly on the twig, like the willow leaf.

Flowers That Remind You of Strawberries

The tea flower is snow white. It flares open and shows a fairy ring of pollen-tipped hairs. It is like the strawberry blossom, except that there are from six to nine petals, and they are thick and waxy. And each one is set on its own short stem in the axil of a leaf. Two or three blossoms may grow from the same axil. The whole stocky little tree is as bright and dainty as a cotton plant. It is no taller than the women and the children, whose busy fingers fly from twig to twig.

Each bush insists upon having four feet of clean soil to grow in, so the sun can get at every leaf. You never would believe that a gay little bush was fifty years old, would you?

The Tea Tree

"Tea plants are evergreen shrubs, like our holly bushes. They drop their shabby winter clothes in April and put on new garden party gowns of pale green, lined with silver down. The leaf is a pointed oval, like a rose leaf. But it is set singly on the twig, like the willow. It is no taller than the women and children, whose busy fingers fly from twig to twig."

THE TEA INDUSTRY

If you parted the lower branches, you would see a stout post of a rough, bark-covered trunk. Tea shrubs are grown like orchard trees. The seeds are planted in nurseries and transplanted. When three years old they give their first crop of leaves. If the dead wood is kept cut out, and the ground is loosened and fertilized about the roots, a tree will live a half century. If allowed to do so, tree plants would grow to be twenty feet high. But a low, bushy shrub bears as many leaves as a straggling tree, and is much easier for the pickers to go over during the harvest season.

Gay Little Tea Bushes 50 Years Old

Miles and Miles of Little Tea Farms

In the warmer parts of Japan, China and India, and on the big island of Formosa, one little tea farm follows another for miles. They seem to make one big plantation. In April the women and children go into the garden to pick the first downy leaves of the year. The work looks easy. With thumb and finger the tip leaf on a twig is nipped. It must be done just right, so as not to injure the tiny leaf bud that nestles like a seed in the axil. That will grow to a new leaf for the next picking, in May, and make a new bud. Down a twig a picker goes, taking from seven to ten leaves and dropping them into a basket that is hung from the shoulders.

Be Careful Where You're Nipping

Four Tea Pickings in a Year

Now the tip leaves are the smallest and make the most delicately flavored tea. After being cured, the leaves are sorted and graded by sifting. From this first picking, several grades teas, both black and of the finest green, are made. The green teas are called hysons, or "before the rains," the black, pekoes, or "white hairs." In May there is a second picking, in July a third, in September a fourth. The bushes "flush" or send out a new crop of leaves, but each picking gives a stronger, cheaper tea than the last.

First Pickings Are the Best

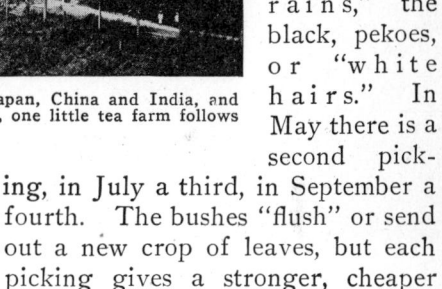

Teas are cured in one of two ways. For the green teas, the leaves are steamed or roasted at once, to wilt them. Then they are rolled. Take some wet leaves from a teapot and try to roll them, from edge to edge, on a table. It isn't easy. But Chinese and Japanese children roll them all day long. Although they can sit before low tables, they get very tired. Out in the gardens very small children sit on the ground to strip the lowest branches. All the work on the small tea farms is done by hand, mostly by women and chil-

The Tea Harvest Is by Hand

View of a Tea Farm

"In the warmer parts of Japan, China and India, and on the big island of Formosa, one little tea farm follows another for miles."

1319

dren. They earn only a few cents a day. The men are doing harder work in the rice fields and factories.

Going Through the Grades — After being dried, or "fired," flowers, twigs and seeds are picked out, and the tea is graded by sifting. The first sieve is so fine a wire mesh that only the leaf tip tea goes through. That brings the highest price in the market.

Why Black Tea Is Black

For making black tea the leaves are wilted slowly in the sun. After rolling, they are packed in baskets and left to sweat, or ferment. Then they are fired in ovens. The slow wilting and the fermenting darkens the leaf and changes the taste. The Chinese and Japanese people like the straw-colored green teas; English people like the bright-brown black teas best. Americans use both kinds. Most of the teas of India and Ceylon are cured black for the English trade. In those countries are big tea plantations, owned by Englishmen, and in Java by Holland Dutchmen. On the plantations, tea is cured and packed by machinery. The work isn't done any better than when done by hand, on the little farms, but it is done faster, and the children have more time for play.

Try Rolling Some Tea Leaves

The Drying Room

Here are trays of unrolled tea leaves in racks, in the drying room of a plantation tea "factory."

Perhaps You Will Invent This Machine

There is no machine for picking tea. Once, you know, cotton seeds had to be pulled from the bolls by hand. A bright American invented the cotton gin. More cotton could be grown then, and cotton cloth was

Tea Growing in Our Own Country

1320

THE TEA INDUSTRY

cheaper. If some man should invent a tea-picking machine, we could grow tea in several of our warm southern states. We have no such cheap labor in our country as there is where yellow and brown people live. We cannot allow little children to work all day. They must go to school, and play, and sleep, so that they grow up into strong men and women.

How the Tea Gets to Market

In the summer the poorest coolies, or laborers, can be seen with boxes of tea strapped on their shoulders, on every country road in the heart of China. They carry the tea to the river boat landings. In Japan, shaggy ponies pull two-wheeled carts of tea to the nearest city market. In Ceylon and Java the rich plantation owners have private railroads to near-by seaports. For sea voyages the tea is packed in tin or lead foil, or in lead-lined wooden boxes, to keep the salt sea air from stealing the delicate flavor.

You Must Keep out, Mr. Salt Sea Air!

Tea That Travels Only by Land

The tea that is sold in Russia does not have to take a sea voyage. It is sent overland, on the backs of elephants and camels to the Trans-Siberian railroad. The Russians drink great quantities of tea, but the people of Western Europe like coffee better. In the British Isles it is the other way around. Wherever the English, Scotch and Irish people emigrate—to Australia, South Africa, Canada, and the United States, they take the tea-drinking habit with them. We Americans are such a mixed people that we like tea, coffee, and chocolate, that we learned to drink from the English, German, Dutch and French people who came to live among us. But we drink more tea than we used to. You see, it is easier to get it, since so many ships go back and forth between our Pacific Coast cities and Japan and China. In almost any large city in our country you can find a Chinese chop-suey restaurant. There you can drink tea on pearl-inlaid teak tables, from little dolly-bowl cups.

Tea, Coffee, and Chocolate Drinkers

"Picking Over" Tea Leaves

© Keystone View Co.

After being steamed, fired and dried, the tea leaves are sifted and "picked over" as mother picks over berries before canning them.

Just Look at These Tea Parties!

As for the tea parties! In Japan and China, tea is offered at once to every visitor, and guests are entertained in public tea houses. In Russia there is a beautiful, old brass samovar, or tea urn, in every drawing room. The tea is flavored with a

Sucking Tea Through Sugar Lumps

1321

slice of lemon. You tuck a lump of sugar between your teeth and suck the hot lemon tea through it. In England everyone—in cottage and castle and palace, even in business houses—drinks tea. Members of parliament, in the summer, have their tea out of doors on the bank of the Thames River. You cannot read a story of English life without coming on a tea party in the drawing room, garden, or nursery. You remember the one in Alice in Wonderland, don't you?

Alice, the Hare and the Hatter

Alice invited herself to the party of the March Hare, the Mad Hatter, and the Sleepy Dormouse. The Hatter sang a song. It ran like this:

> Twinkle, twinkle, little bat,
> How I wonder what you're at,
> Up above the world you fly,
> Like a tea tray in the sky.

Isn't that delightful nonsense? The Hatter said, with a soft sigh: "It's always tea-time, and no time to wash things between whiles."

Always "Tea Time" in England

The author of "Alice" was poking gentle fun at English people for drinking so much tea. It's tea for breakfast, lunch and bed time. And as sure as four or five o'clock come round, a housemaid appears with a tray. The English drink black tea, with cream and sugar. With it they take sandwiches, or plum cake, or muffins, or toast and marmalade. Friends drop in, without being specially invited. Everyone stands around, cup in hand, talking gay nonsense, and changing places "as things get used up," just as the Mad Hatter explained at the party.

"Afternoon Teas" in America

We Americans are getting the afternoon tea habit. It is a nice, cosy custom. One of the prettiest ways to introduce a young lady to society is to give a "Tea," with a bevy of girls

A Malay Girl Picking Tea

"The work looks easy. With thumb and finger the tip leaf on a twig is nipped."

THE TEA INDUSTRY
How the Tea Men Go Down to the "Go-Down"

Here we are looking at a tea curing warehouse in Japan where the tea merchant has just delivered some tea which is being weighed on the scales. The tea merchant buys of the tea farmer up in the hills. The weighing clerk is writing down the amount on Japanese rice paper with a bamboo pen dipped in coal-black native ink, which is similar to our India ink.

His helper, the weighing clerk, is comparing his record of the total deliveries up to date, on a counting frame, with the merchant's record. The merchant, you see, has been keeping track of his deliveries by little notches cut in a stick. The Japanese call these tea warehouses "go-downs" because they go down to them from the farms where the tea is raised.

The initials on the basket are those of the merchant. The merchant's servant is standing by the jinrikisha which contains another load of tea. The bag on the scales, the merchant himself carried on his back. The basket on the cart is covered with matting to protect it from the dirt, as the jinrikisha man trots along the dusty roads with the two shafts in his hands and the cross-piece across his breast.

A Rich Tea Merchant's Store

Chinese stores do not have plate glass display windows as ours do. The light comes in through doorways or through the latticed walls lined with white paper. Some of them, like this one, are elaborately carved and decorated. Chinese signs, you see, run perpendicularly along the store fronts instead of across the sidewalks as ours do.

© *Keystone View Co.*

to "pour" and say: "Do you like tea Russian or English?" Everybody is happy and at ease over a "cup o' kindness." If you feel cross—that "leave-me-all-alone-to-sulk" feeling—an old rhyme tells you what to do about it:

"Take a cup and drink it up,
And call the neighbors in."

The Castle-Builder

It happened on a summer's day,
A country lass as fresh as May,
Decked in a wholesome russet gown,
Was going to the market town;
So blithe her looks, so simply clean,
You'd take her for a May-day queen;
Though for her garland, says the tale,
Her head sustained a loaded pail.
As on her way she passed along,
She hummed the fragments of a song;
She did not hum for want of thought—
Quite pleased with what to sale she brought,
She reckoned by her own account,
When all was sold, the whole amount.
Thus she—"In time this little ware
May turn to great account with care:
My milk being sold for so-and-so,
I'll buy some eggs as markets go,
And set them; at the time I fix,
These eggs will bring as many chicks;
I'll spare no pains to feed them well;
They'll bring vast profit when they sell.
With this I'll buy a little pig,
And when 'tis grown up fat and big,
I'll sell it, whether boar or sow,
And with the money buy a cow:
This cow will surely have a calf,
And there the profit's half in half;
Besides, there's butter, milk and cheese,
To keep the market when I please:
All which I'll sell, and buy a farm,
Then of sweethearts have a swarm.
Oh, then for ribands, gloves, and rings!
Ay, more than twenty pretty things—
One brings me this, another that,
And I shall have—I know not what!"
Fired with the thought, the sanguine lass,
Of what was thus to come to pass,
Her heart beat strong; she gave a bound,
And down came milkpail on the ground:
Eggs, fowl, pig, hog (ah, well-a-day!)
Cow, calf, and farm—all swam away!

JEAN DE LAFONTAINE

THE WORLD AT ITS WORK
THE CHOCOLATE INDUSTRY

Life Story of a Chocolate Drop

CUCUMBERS growing on a tree? Or are they cantaloupes? Well, you would hardly think they were either if you tried to eat one. They pop out of the side of the tree in such a singular way, and they are colored so brightly, you would almost think they were ornaments from a Christmas tree.

Cantaloupe?—No, Cocoa

"Cucumbers growing on a tree? Or are they cantaloupes? Well, you would hardly think they were either if you tried to eat one. And besides, notice the singular way they seem to pop out of the side of the tree."

These bright yellow, and red, and purple pods on this cocoa tree are cakes of chocolate in their beginnings, and although you would never guess it if you did not know, the delicious cocoa you drank at lunch came from the seeds of a tree like this. Perhaps in that one cup of cocoa there were parts of some seeds from trees that grew in Africa, and some from the West Indies, from Ecuador, and Java. In all these countries, as well as all other tropic countries, the cocoa trees grow. In one quick, thoughtless swallow you took your luncheon from countries that circle the world.

Sweet Geography in a Cup

Some day a man will come out to this tree and will look carefully at this queer fruit. He will reach up and feel it, for the tree is not higher than an apple tree, and often much smaller, and then he will decide it is time for the harvest. Negroes or Indians, Hindoos or Malays will cut the pods carefully from the tree. Imagine what a sight it is to see these heaps of pods on the ground like mother's old-fashioned crazy quilt; purple and carmine, orange and olive, brown, canary and dark moss green, all helter-skelter in pile after pile among the trees. What is in them? Well, let's see. This man coming toward us with that big knife will take us into the cocoa's pod house. He swings his machete

Inside the Little Pod House

1325

PICTURED KNOWLEDGE
Cracking the Cocoa

Only two blows of these big, sharp knives are needed to cut the thick, tough cocoa pod cleanly in half. The woman whom you see squatting on the ground is removing the seeds from the opened pods. After the seeds have been taken from the shells they are emptied into the saddle-bags of the patient little burro standing nearby. As soon as he gets his load off he will trot toward the mill.

or cutlass, as the big knife is called, and cuts half way through the pod in one blow. This is what he sees: from twenty to sixty seeds with a very little pulp about them and a thick, hard rind to keep them from harm. His wife and her friends scoop out all these seeds and put them in baskets and they are carried off to the sheds. Now a queer thing happens. These seeds are soft and spongy like a bean just out of any garden and they do not taste any more like chocolate than raw potatoes taste like saratoga chips. Into trenches in the ground or into wooden tanks they are thrown and covered up. This is called fermenting the cocoa.

Threshing with the Feet

After being thoroughly cooked, the seeds are spread on the flat floors of the drying sheds in the hot tropical sunshine. As a shower might come at any moment, the roofs of the sheds are on wheels that can be quickly run over drying seeds. You hear of many new dances from time to time, but in some countries they have a dance that probably will never be popular in your home. It is called "dancing the cocoa" and one of our pictures shows how they dance it. The partly dried seeds of the cocoa are piled up on the dry sheds, and these men you see in one of our illustrations tramp up and down on the piles until the cocoa seeds, now called cocoa beans, are all spread out again. Then they are heaped up and the dance begins again, until they are polished like a shiny pebble. And that is about what they look like when they are packed up in bags of 150 pounds and sent off to the seaport for their long voyage to Amer-

"Dancing the Cocoa"

THE CHOCOLATE INDUSTRY

ica, England, Switzerland or other countries where chocolate is made. Most of them come to America, for we make more chocolate here than in any other country, and yet each man and woman in America eats less chocolate each year (not counting chocolate creams) than in most of the countries of Europe. You see there are so many of us in America.

The Little Beans On Their Travels

Out from the hold of a steamer at a dock in New York City, the bags of cocoa beans are being hoisted. They may have traveled half way around the world. Some of them have come through the Panama Canal from Ecuador, and some through the Suez Canal from Ceylon and Java. They are quickly hurried off to the factories, where there are piles and piles of these bags of cocoa beans. Some of them have cost not more than a dime for a pound, while others have cost three or four times that much.

Those people whom we visited in the Tropics have not been as careful as they might be to keep out all the stems, stones and dust. Such funny things are found with the cocoa—coffee and pepper, all-spice, nails, many strange seeds, chicken feathers and even bones. All these must be separated from the seeds, so that they may be entirely clean.

Funny Things Found Among the Beans

Cross-Section of a Cocoa Pod

"The laborer is ready to crack the cocoa. He swings his machete or cutlass, as the big knife is called, and cuts half-way through the pod in one blow. This is what he sees."

After they are cleaned they are put into long iron cylinders, which are revolved over slow coal fires. Here they steam and roast, the steam gradually passing away and the flavor of the beans becoming more like chocolate. Some of our foods we eat raw, but many of them are cooked. We would hardly care for a raw potato; neither would we care for chocolate made from raw cocoa. The beans are watched very carefully while over the fire, so that they will not burn. They must not be scorched even ever so little, or the chocolate will not be good.

After they are roasted and cooled they must be broken and passed through a blast of air, so that the shells can be blown away. You would not care to eat a peanut, shell and all; and so the shell of the bean, although so much thinner than a peanut shell, would spoil chocolate that was made from it. It would taste bad.

After Roasting Comes the Shelling

The Beans in the Mill

A very wonderful change now takes place in the cleaned and broken pieces of the roasted beans. Brown chippy looking pieces of cocoa bean, more like coarsely ground coffee than anything else, are fed in between two round mill stones and are changed into a smooth, syrupy fluid that runs out from the edges of the

1327

PICTURED KNOWLEDGE
"Dancing" the Cocoa

"You have heard of many new dances this year, but in some countries they have a dance that probably will never be popular in your home. It is called "dancing the cocoa" and this is how they dance it."

Chocolate "Pebbles"

"Then they are heaped up and the dance begins again until they are polished like a shiny pebble."

revolving mill. You see the steel covers of the stones here and between the two pieces of stone, one of which is stationary and the other moving, the cocoa is ground. Everyone wonders why it is that when you put something so dry and hard as *The Answer to the Puzzle* the broken cocoa into the mill, a fluid should come out of it, but the reason is simple enough. These brown dry cocoa beans are half oil, called cocoa butter, and when the mills are warm and the pieces are torn up into very fine particles, the oil is melted and set free, and so makes the fluid. If we should take some of this syrupy fluid and put it into a pan and allow it to cool, it would form a brown cake of bitter chocolate. Put that in a blue paper with a yellow label, and you will at once recognize it as the chocolate mother buys when she wants to make icing for cake; that is just the way that such chocolate is made.

1328

THE CHOCOLATE INDUSTRY
Machines that Change "Pebbles" to Syrup

Brown, chippy-looking pieces of cocoa bean, more like coarsely ground coffee than anything else, are fed in between two round millstones and are changed into a smooth, syrupy fluid that runs out from the edges of the revolving mill. You see the steel covers of the stones here and between the two pieces of stone, one of which is stationary and the other moving, the cocoa is ground.

Making Chocolate Taste Good

So far we have seen nothing that appeals to you as very good to eat. But yet we all know that chocolate is good to eat. So we shall take some of the material that comes from these mills, and mix it with sugar and vanilla in large mixing machines with stone basins and stone rollers moving around in them. Here a paste is formed. It looks as if it would be just right for making mud pies, but it is a little expensive for that. This paste is run between stone rollers until the sugar and the chocolate and the vanilla are all ground together, smooth and even. The paste is then put into little pans of different sizes and shapes, and shaken on machines until the soft paste fills every crevice of the pan. When this has been cooled and wrapped and nicely labeled, you will recognize it at once as the **chocolate** you see in the stores, and of which you are so fond. Sometimes milk is mixed with the sugar. This, as you have guessed, is milk chocolate.

Of course, you know that "lots" of chocolate creams are used nowadays—some with cream centers, some with caramel centers, some with nut centers—tons and tons of them every day.

Now what is the difference between the chocolate in the cake you *Styles in* eat and the chocolate on *Coats for* the chocolate creams? *the Creams* Extra cocoa butter is added in machines like these so that the chocolate will be thin enough to cover the cream, nut, or caramel centers of the candy. Did you ever notice that some of the chocolate

1329

PICTURED KNOWLEDGE
Making the Powder for Breakfast Cocoa

We take some of this liquid (made by grinding the roasted and cleaned cocoa) and put it into these great presses, and part of the oil, or cocoa butter, is pressed out. When we open the press again, where we had formerly placed a liquid, we now find a hard, brown cake. This is pulverized and sifted and the soft powder with the delicious flavor, although very bitter, is the breakfast cocoa we found in our can, and which with its warmth and delicious flavor adds so much to the morning meal.

creams are very light in color, some are darker, and some almost black? The colors of the raw cocoa vary also, from a light yellowish brown to very dark brown. By taking the different colored cocoa beans and blending them together, the chocolate-maker is able to furnish the candy man with these different colored coverings or chocolate coatings.

The Kind of Cocoa We Drink

The red-brown powder that you find in the can, from which the cocoa you drink is made, certainly does not look like any of these things. Where does it come from, and why is it so different from the chocolate? We shall have to go back to the mills where the roasted and cleaned cocoa was being ground into a liquid. We take some of this liquid and put it into these great presses and part of the oil, or cocoa butter is pressed out. When we open the press again where we had formerly placed a liquid, we now find a hard brown cake. This is pulverized and sifted and the soft powder with the delicious flavor, although very bitter, is the breakfast cocoa we found in our can.

How the Cocoa Powder Is Made

It sounds perhaps as though all chocolate were the same, and this might be true if all cocoa were the same and all chocolate were made in the same way. But, you know, there are a great many different kinds of apples; some of them are

1330

THE CHOCOLATE INDUSTRY
Making the Chocolate for Chocolate Creams

"What is the difference between the chocolate in the cake you are eating and the chocolate on the chocolate creams? Extra cocoa butter is added in machines like these so that the chocolate will be thin enough to cover the cream, nut or caramel centers of the candy."

sour; some of them are small and wormy; some are large and fine and beautiful. So with the cocoa. Some is poorly grown and poorly prepared on the plantations. Other cocoa beans are fine and large and prepared on the plantation with great care. There are perhaps thirty or forty different grades of cocoa that the chocolate manufacturer uses, and there are almost as many kinds of cocoa powder to drink and chocolate to eat. When you find one that is really good, you will understand that it is good because it has been made from the finest kinds of cocoa, and with great care and cleanliness.

Nearly everyone is fond of cocoa and chocolate. One reason, doubtless, is that it is not only pleasant to eat or to drink, but it is also so good for food. It is so good a food that the soldiers of all nations are using it, and people who are going on exploring trips and long journeys in the wilderness take it with them to help keep them strong and well.

The Silkworm

Silkworm on the mulberry tree,
Spin a silken robe for me;
Draw the threads out fine and strong,
Longer yet—and very long;
Longer yet—'twill not be done
Till a thousand more are spun.
Silkworm, turn this mulberry tree
Into silken threads for me!

All day long, and many a day,
Busy silkworms spin away;
Some are ending, some beginning;
Nothing thinking of but spinning!
Well for them! Like silver light,
All the threads are smooth and bright;
Pure as day the silk must be,
Woven from the mulberry tree!

Ye are spinning well and fast;
'Twill be finished all at last.
Twenty thousand threads are drawn,
Finer than the finest lawn;
And as long this silken twine,
As the equinoctial line!
What a change! The mulberry tree
Turneth into silk for me!

Spinning ever! Now 'tis done,
Silken threads enough are spun!
Spinning, they will spin no more—
All their little lives are o'er!

Mary Howitt

THE WORLD AT ITS WORK

THE SILK INDUSTRY

Queen Si and the Caterpillar—
The Romance of Silk

© Corticelli Silk Mills

The Birth of a Silk Moth

"A few of the finest cocoons are put aside. The new moths break a hole and crawl out... The others are baked to kill the sleeping grubs." The picture shows the fuzzy, soft cocoons just after the moths have emerged. Notice the shape of the moths—all body and hardly any wings.

THIS is the story of a wise queen and a clever caterpillar, and of a secret that was kept three thousand years, by three hundred million people. It is not a fairy story, but many fairy stories grew out of it.

Once upon a time the Queen of Cathay or, as we would say today, the Empress of China, was sitting in a blue and white porcelain chair in the palace garden of the City of Heaven. This was *The Wriggly Worms in the Garden* Hang Chow Foo, the old southern capital that you will find on the Yellow Sea. On warm spring mornings, the queen spent hours in the high-walled garden to admire the white mulberry trees that were in bloom and new leaf. Clumsy white moths, no larger than honey bees, were crawling on the leaves. Their small wings could not carry their heavy bodies far. The leaves were dotted with pearly eggs as small as mustard seeds. There were worms of all sizes, from squirming black hairs a quarter inch long, to those that were as big as the queen's little finger. They were all nibbling the tender leaves, except the largest ones. They were quite gorged. As pretty an amber as a string of beads, they had a funny hump on the shoulders, a spiny little horn on top of the tail,

1333

PICTURED KNOWLEDGE

and sixteen fat, lazy legs. They were clinging to twigs, spinning and winding cradles in which to sleep.

The Spinners of Sunbeams

All caterpillars make cocoons, but these were so clever about it that the queen watched one. She saw a jet of sunny fluid flow from two holes on the under side of a caterpillar's mouth. They ran together and hardened to a hair, as fine and bright as a sunbeam. Bent backward, nearly double, the worm swung its head from side to side, like a shuttle in a loom. It looped the filament backward and forward, about its body, making the figure eight. You can wind a thread on your thumb and forefinger that way. The gummy floss clung together. So the clumsy creature wound itself up in a gauzy, peanut-shell shaped sac, and closed up the hole in front of its little nose.

Then it went right on weaving inside. For a day the queen could see the little prisoner at work. Then it went to sleep. But its wonder-

A Silk Worm Meal

© *Corticelli Silk Mills*

Here is one of the voracious silk worms eating holes in a mulberry leaf.

ful labors had set the queen thinking.

"That little worm spun and spooled thousands of yards of thread fine enough for a bride's robe. *I wonder if I could unwind it!*"

The New Game at Court

She clapped her hands. Slaves appeared, bearing the little-footed ladies of the court in sedan chairs. The queen had a new amusing game for them—trying to unwind cocoons. They found that the gum softened in hot water, the threads melted apart and the ends could be picked up on twigs. Remembering what the caterpillar had done, the queen joined the filaments of two cocoons, then more. By twisting them together they united into one smooth thread. Hundreds of yards she wound, without a break or tangle.

There was already a loom for weaving cotton and wool, but the queen invented a reeling wheel and set up a small silk mill in the palace grounds. Out of doors many eggs, moths and

This Silk Worm is Just About to "Molt"

© *Corticelli Silk Mills*

"Silk worms eat so much that they outgrow their skins. They seem to feel as you do after that Thanksgiving dinner, when a belt button pops off. They burst out of their skins, take a long breath and run to the table again." This silk worm is just ready to shed his skin.

1334

THE SILK INDUSTRY

How the Mulberries Grow

This branch of a mulberry shows you how the fruit grows among the glossy, green leaves. Mulberries are like blackberries, but sweeter, redder and juicier—they are good food for "humans" as well as for silk worm babies. © Corticelli Silk Mills

French, "silk" in English.

A Secret and a Fairy Story

Strangers were not allowed to travel in old Cathay, so it was not difficult to keep the secret. Besides, it was well known that anyone who told it would have his head cut off. But silk was sold in the seaports, and was carried westward by the camel caravans. In far away Egypt, people wore "silk and fine linens" in Bible days. Many of the nations were as curious about the beautiful fabric as Pandora was about what was in the box. After three thousand years the secret got out. The Chinese accused their neighbors, the Japanese.

"You hired Corean burglars to kidnap Chinese maidens from a silk weaving village and carried them to Japan," they cried.

"Oh, no, indeed!" said the Japanese, who did not want to get anyone into trouble for helping them. Besides, most people in Japan already believed this fairy story:

"On the Yellow River, in Cathay, there lived a wicked ogress. She stole a mandarin's baby daughter, *Ogress and Mandarin's Daughter* tied her in a hollow mulberry log and set the boat adrift. It floated out to sea, and fairies guided it to the shore of Japan. A nobleman found the baby and took her into his castle. She grew up to be a beautiful maiden, so good and gen-

caterpillars were killed by bad weather or were eaten by birds. So she built a silk house. She planted mulberry groves. Then she sent teachers all over southern China to show the poorest people how to grow the trees, care for the worms, reel the silk and weave the beautiful new cloth. By the time she died, silk culture had spread all over south China; Hang Chow Foo was a bower of orchards and was famous for its silks and embroideries or "needle painting." A temple was set up to the queen's memory and the new cloth named for her—"Si." It is "se" in Chinese, "soie" in

PICTURED KNOWLEDGE

tle that everyone loved her. The mulberry log came to life, struck root and sent up a fine tree. From its seeds a grove sprang up along the beach. Before the princess died she asked the fairies to let her live

nature myths. Later the Chinese learned that the Japanese had a temple at Setsu to four Chinese weaving maidens. But they could not punish a whole nation, so they had to make the best of it.

The Silkworm's Lungs

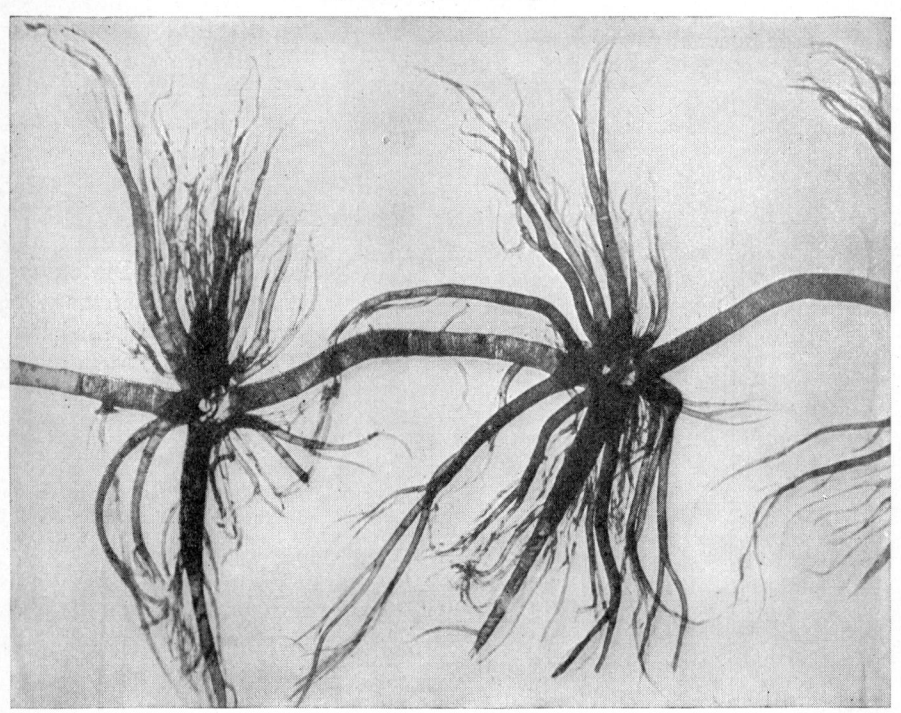

A silk worm's lungs are a system of air pipes going all over its body as our blood-vessels do. Instead of pumping blood to meet the air in the lungs as we do, silk worms carry air to the blood in another way. The silk worm's blood is not shut up in veins and arteries as ours is, but flows freely all through its body. There are slit-like openings at intervals along the body which let the air into the system of tubes. From each breathing-mouth in the main pipe-line, many short tubes run out in all directions, as you see.

in the mulberry orchard forever and to bestow some gift on Japan, where the people had been so kind and she so happy. Then, as the Japanese poets say of one who dies, 'She sucked in her breath and changed worlds.' At once a pretty white moth danced with joy on a mulberry tree. It was the soul of the gentle maiden. She brought the gift of silk to Japan."

This is one of the prettiest of the

How the Secret Spread Around the World

The secret was carried to India by a Chinese princess who married a rajah, or Indian prince. She hid silk worm eggs in the folds of her turban. "To punish me you would have to march an army across the Himalaya Mountains," she laughed tilting her saucy chin. She taught silk culture to her new subjects.

Next, some barefooted monks from Persia slipped over the bor-

1336

THE SILK INDUSTRY

der, filled their hollow staffs with eggs and escaped to their own country. So the secret traveled westward — to Constantinople, Athens, and Rome. In every country it was royal cloth, made first in palaces and worn by kings. The king of France gave prizes to people who planted mulberry trees and raised silk worms.

Today there are silk mills in all European countries and in the United States. But the raw silk is reeled in China, Japan, India, and northern Italy, where there are many poor women and children to do the work. Miles of land are covered with orchards

The Babies Get the Choicest Food

© *Keystone View Co.*
"Thousands of bias-eyed children do nothing else all summer but carry leaves and clean trays." Here are some of them gathering, in big baskets, just the youngest, tenderest leaves for the baby silk worms.

Such Greedy Little Creatures!

© *Keystone View Co.*
The mass of wriggling silk worms will clean up this branch of mulberry leaves that the girl is feeding them, in short order. They are greedy because they do all their growing in the few weeks they are worms.

of little, dwarf mulberry trees that are grown like tea bushes. In thousands of poor homes the eggs are kept on sheets of paper, in cool, dark rooms, all winter. In the spring the eggs are put into a warm place to hatch. Where, do you think? Sometimes between the bed clothes, or inside a very quiet little girl's padded cotton jacket! How would you like that?

A Breakfast of Salted Ashes

In ten days the tiny worms come out for their first breakfast of salted ashes of burned leaves—like salted nuts in a dinner course. For lunch they make a toilet and climb up-

1337

stairs. On the upper side of a sheet of paper that is laid over them, is a feast of chopped leaves and millet flour. Then they do nothing but eat and grow, for thirty days.

Rebecca of Sunnybrook Farm said she believed in babies — "in moderation." Insects have no moderation about the size of their families. Each silk moth mother lays five hundred eggs. How would you like to be nursemaid to millions of babies who were always hungry, and as "mussy" and nervous as human babies? Thousands of bias-eyed children do nothing else all summer long but carry leaves and clean trays. The worms make as much dirt as canary birds. They are given the best room in the poor cottage. They dislike loud noises and smells of cooking and smoke. If disturbed too much they stop eating and "pine away."

My! My! What Big Families!

Making Nests for Silk Worms

© *Keystone View Co.*

When ready to spin, the caterpillars are lifted gently to heaps of clean straw. Each one gums a thread to a straw, as a spider anchors his web, and makes cocoons, small in the middle, like short, glossy, fuzzy peanuts with two kernels. A few of the finest cocoons are put aside.

Eating More Than Their Skins Can Hold

Silk worms eat so much that they outgrow their skins. They seem to feel as you do after that Thanksgiving dinner, when a belt button pops off. They burst out of their skins, take a long breath, and run to the table again. Three times they do this. After the last time, the food they eat does not make them grow. As a bee makes wax of some of the honey it eats, so the silk worm stows away a gummy, golden liquid, in tubes that lie along the side of the body. This is squeezed out by muscles, in spinning, as you squeeze paint or vaseline from a col-laps'-i-ble tube.

When ready to spin, the caterpillars are lifted gently to heaps of clean straw. Each one gums a thread to a straw, as a spider anchors his web. Then the worm bends itself backward, nearly double. The cocoon is only half as long as the worm. The figure eight looping makes most cocoons smaller across the middle, like short, glossy, fuzzy peanuts with two kernels.

How Little Worms Begin to Spin

A few of the finest cocoons are put aside. The new moths break a hole and crawl out in about fifteen days. The others are baked to kill the sleeping grubs. The cocoons can then be kept for months. The last eggs are kept over winter. In

THE SILK INDUSTRY

Three Stages in the Preparation of Raw Silk

The Busy People in the Cottages

cottage door yards on every bright day, whole villages of women reel silk on the foot-power wheel of the Queen of Cathay. A careful child attends to the hot water pan and picks up the ends of silk. Half a dozen ends are threaded into eyelets on the wheel. The co-

© *Keystone View Co.*

The half-naked Japanese in the lower picture is putting the cocoons into the vats of boiling water, which melts the gummy paste with which the threads are stuck together. After the cocoons have been in the water a little while, the ends float loose and can be picked up and the cocoons unwound.

© *Keystone View Co.*

In the first picture the man is examining his "incubator" with its racks of silk worm eggs. The eggs are in the rack above, between sheets of paper. The eggs are so tiny that it takes seven hundred thousand of them to weigh a pound.

The second picture shows the Japanese silk growers separating the finished cocoons from the straw nests where they have lain for a week. This must be done carefully so that the frail fibers of the cocoons will not be broken, because the threads must be long and even to make glossy, smooth silk.

© *Keystone View Co.*

1339

coons bob in the water and unwind like spools. New filaments are spliced on, so a continuous skein of raw silk is reeled. It is a glistening, pale amber, like a dolly's blonde wig. It takes hundreds of cocoons to reel one pound of silk, and the best workers can only reel a pound or two a day. The women dye the silk and weave it on rude hand looms.

Work in the Big Mills

Most of the raw silk, and even the cocoons, is now sent to factories, where reeling and weaving is done by steam power. But the work is done in the same way. Each worker in a mill room full of flying wheels and belts, has a child helper to attend to the hot water pans. The skeins of raw silk are packed into small, linen and matting-wrapped bales. These are sent to the cloth mills in the home countries and over seas. Paterson, New Jersey, near New York, is our largest silk weaving city. We get our raw silk from China, Japan, India and Italy. The workmen are Italians who were taught silk weaving in the mills of Milan. We are able to make one-fourth of all the silk dress goods, velvets and ribbons that we use.

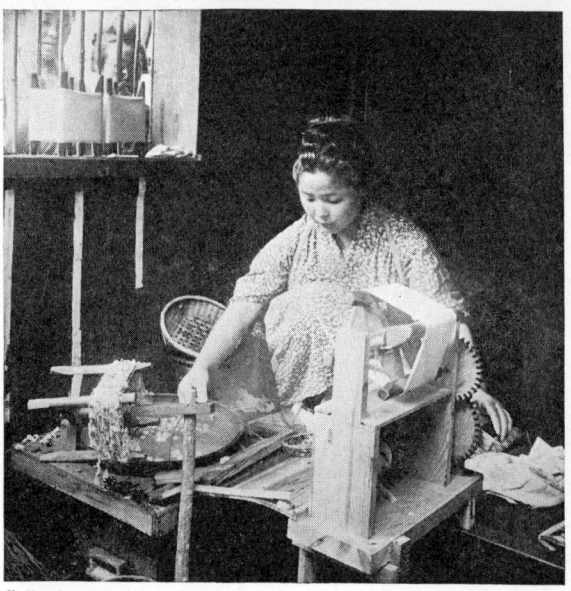

Silk does not have to be combed, but it must be cleaned, freed from knots and twisted into thread. The gum is boiled out and the silk is bleached snow-white and then dyed to the most delicate tints. The silk of the tusser moth will not bleach, but keeps its natural brownish-yellow color. It will take well only the dull, dark shades of blue, green, red and brown. And it makes the flax-like pongee, tussah and rajah silks that are usually homespun. Pongee means homespun. The dull, rich colors, loose, uneven weave and rough texture are very "ar-tith-tic" as a little girl who lithp-ed, said.

A silk loom may weave furniture brocade fifty inches wide, or baby ribbon, a quarter of an inch narrow. After weaving, the nap is singed off. The cloth is brightened by sponging with gum water and ironing between heavy rollers. This gives it a beautiful gloss. Collect your hair ribbons and neckties and study the pretty weaves. There are plain

Reeling Silk in Japan

© *Keystone View Co.*

At the left is the pan of hot water with the cocoons "bobbing" in it. The Japanese girl is winding the threads from their first position on the reel at the left, on to the reel at the right. Notice how she is doing it—by a crank that turns the two wooden cog wheels. The silk on the second reel is smoother and more uniform than on the first. It is in this form, known as "raw silk" that it is sent to the silk mills.

The Different Kinds of Weaves

THE SILK INDUSTRY

Making "Spun" Silk

The coarse, outer threads of silk cocoons and broken threads, too short to use in reeling, are shipped as silk "waste" to manufacturers who spin it into thread, much as cotton and wool are spun. The first picture shows some women sorting and cleaning such silk from the straw packing in which it came.

The pierced cocoons—those in which the moths were allowed to mature and come out—are not so valuable as the perfect ones, because the filaments of silk are broken. They are packed in bales

© *Keystone View Co.*

cross weaves, corded, twilled, pebbled and basket weaves; satin, where the warp threads are thrown up to the surface, or perhaps a cotton back. In "changeable" silks, the

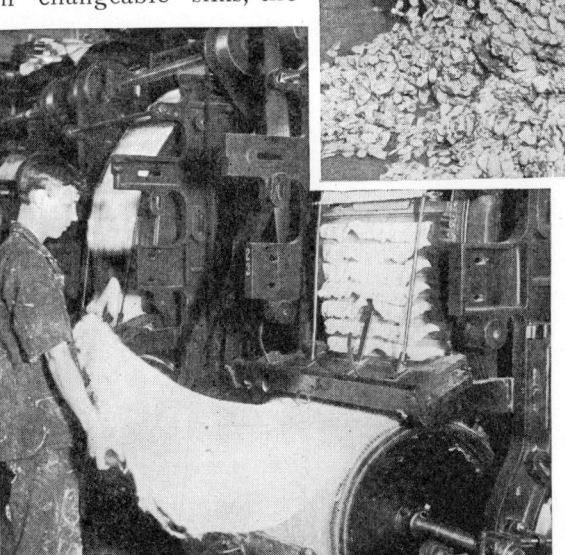

© *Keystone View Co.*

like this one at the right and used to make "spun" silk, too. This silk is not so fine and lustrous as the "reeled" silk made from the filaments that are unwound in unbroken threads from whole cocoons.

The machine in the last picture straightens and combs out the tangled mass of short fibers of waste silk. The drum from which the boy is taking his sheet of silk is called a "porcupine." By means of the steel pegs all over its surface it removes chrysalis-shells, sticks and dirt. The sheets of fibers on the rods at the top are waiting to be combed out by this roller.

© *Keystone View Co.*

PICTURED KNOWLEDGE
Making Silk Yarn

© Keystone View Co.

The combed out, short fibers of waste silk are clamped together into a fringe like the one in the first picture. They are called "flags." Behind the flag in the rack are sticks of fibers waiting to be combed.

The right hand upper picture shows one of the "drawing" machines for combing and straightening silk fiber.

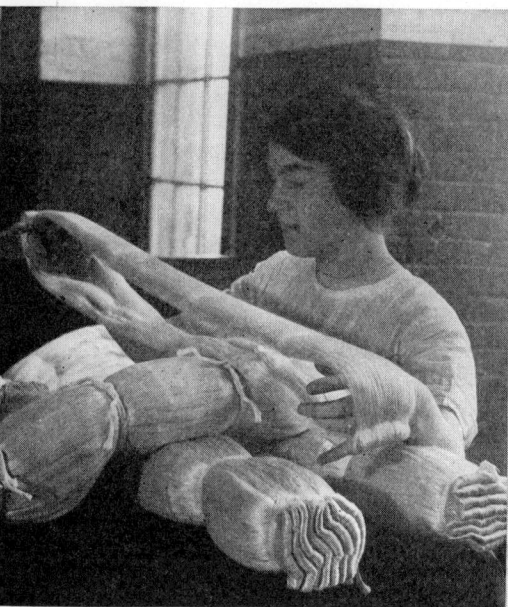

© Keystone View Co

On the left at the bottom are the finished skeins of spun silk. In the next picture they are being wound on bobbins ready for weaving into cloth.

THE SILK INDUSTRY

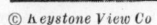

The Last Chapter in the Romance of Silk

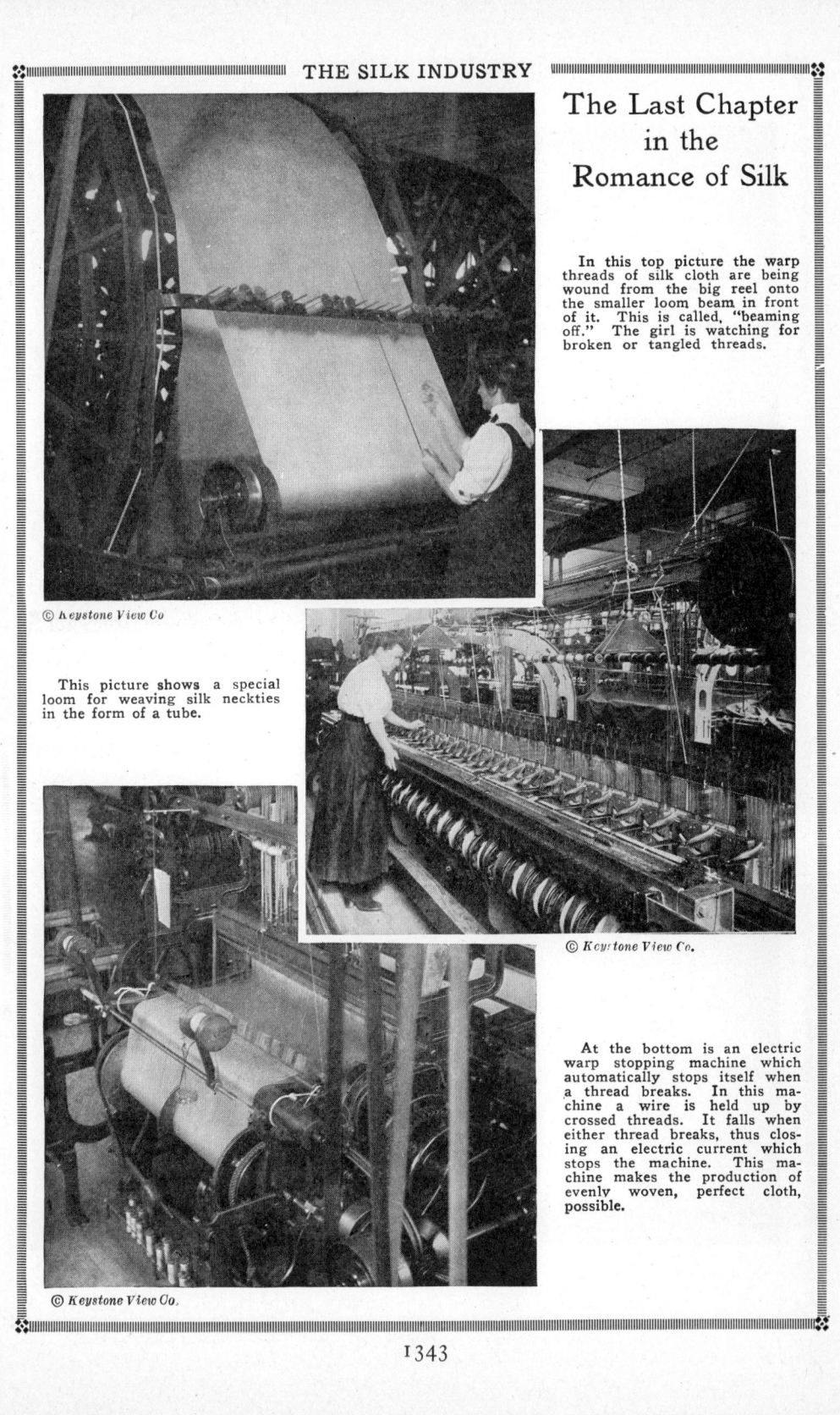

In this top picture the warp threads of silk cloth are being wound from the big reel onto the smaller loom beam in front of it. This is called, "beaming off." The girl is watching for broken or tangled threads.

This picture shows a special loom for weaving silk neckties in the form of a tube.

At the bottom is an electric warp stopping machine which automatically stops itself when a thread breaks. In this machine a wire is held up by crossed threads. It falls when either thread breaks, thus closing an electric current which stops the machine. This machine makes the production of evenly woven, perfect cloth, possible.

PICTURED KNOWLEDGE
A Japanese Artist at Work

© Keystone View Co.

Here is a Japanese artist at work in his studio designing a cut velvet pattern. Whole landscapes as well as human figures are worked out in detail in both silk and velvet by the artistic Japanese silk makers.

warp threads are of one color, the woof threads another. If you ravel a flowered ribbon, you will find that the warp threads were printed before weaving. Foulard silks are printed in colors, like calico and wool challies, after weaving. Velvets have the warp thread woven over wires. When the loops are cut and the wires lifted, a soft "pile" of short threads is left. This is sheared even, and steamed and brushed up. You can steam and brush up velvet that has had the pile crushed and flattened. Stiff, rustly silks have more gum added, and this makes them crack or split. The softer silks wear

More Spun Silk

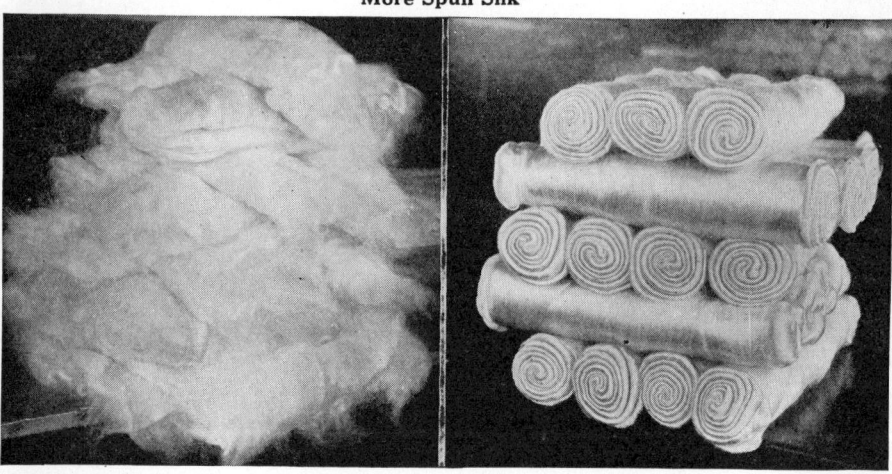

© Keystone View Co.

At the left is a pile of "flags" removed from their frames. The other picture shows a pile of dressed fiber rolls. How soft and glossy they look!

A Jacquard Loom

© *Keystone View Co.*

    This is one of the Jacquard looms that weave the brocades which are so beautiful and costly. The Jacquard loom was invented by Joseph Jacquard, a French weaver of the eighteenth century. It is the best loom for weaving fabrics with large figures.

    At the top of the picture you can see the punctured cards bearing patterns for designs. The Jacquard loom gives the weaver complete control over every thread of the warp because each thread can be raised or lowered without disturbing the other threads.

better, especially in umbrellas, but taffetas make nicer hair ribbons.

The Wonderful Jacquard Loom

Wires are used also to throw up the colors and patterns on damask and brocade. Such weaving is done on the wonderful Jacquard loom that was invented by a French weaver over one hundred years ago. It is one of the beautiful mysteries of the work-a-day world. Wires, passing through perforated paper, guide threads of many colors, even gold and silver, to repeat the designs of lace, embroidery and painting. It is said to be as simple as—well, as the perforated roll that unwinds and makes music in a pianola. But I think that is just sheer magic! Don't you?

What would little Queen Si of Cathay, who lived nearly five thousand years ago, say if she could see our lovely silks and great silk mills? Her best silk trousers and jacket were of rough but lustrous homespun. But I wonder how many little heads of today, that are tied up in her gift of pretty ribbons, will grow to be as wise as hers.

Lullaby! O Lullaby!

Lullaby! O lullaby!
Baby, hush that little cry!
   Light is dying,
   Bats are flying,
Bees to-day with work have done;
So, till comes the morrow's sun,
Let sleep kiss those bright eyes dry!
   Lullaby! O lullaby.

Lullaby! O lullaby!
Hush'd are all things far and nigh;
   Flowers are closing,
   Birds reposing,
All sweet things with life are done,
Sweet, till dawns the morning sun.
Sleep then kiss those blue eyes dry,
   Lullaby! O lullaby.

WILLIAM COX BENNETT

THE WORLD AT ITS WORK
THE GOLD INDUSTRY

Mother Earth's Treasures of Gold

Panning for Gold in California

This is how a miner worked his claim in the early days when gold was discovered in California. All day long these patient men, who had made the long trip over the plains from the East in "prairie schooners," worked at the tedious, back-breaking work in the burning sun, as you see this one doing. Many of them made their fortunes, it is true, but more of them straggled home, sick and discouraged, or remained in the new land to build up their fortunes in another way than by panning gold.

YOU know what "hidden treasure" is in the story books. It is gold dollars, buried on some lonely island, by a miser or a pirate. He meant to come back and get it, but something happened. Then the hero of the story book finds it and digs it up. Isn't it exciting when his pick rings on the iron-bound chest?

It is just as thrilling when a miner's pick uncovers a vein of gold ore. But Mother Earth hid her treasure, oh, ever so much more cleverly! She divided it *How Mother Earth Hid the Gold* into gold dust as fine as flour, and into pinhead grains. Now and then she made a nugget as big as a pebble, as a prize for some lucky miner. Then she tucked that gold into tiny cracks and holes in mountain rocks. Some of it she buried in river beds, under flowing water. She scattered her golden treasure in wild, and lonely, and dangerous places. Then she said to men: "You can have it. But you must hunt for it, and toil and suffer."

Why Gold Is So Precious

Men always were willing to do almost anything to get this beautiful metal. It did not rust or tarnish. It was so soft that it could be shaped into ornaments. It could be drawn into fine wire, and beaten into thin leaves for gilding. Long before the human race had a written history, gold was used to adorn kings, palaces and temples, and was coined into money. And the desire for the precious metal was the subject of wonder stories and fables.

Gold in the Old Wonder Tales

Jason and the Golden Fleece is a Greek wonder story that every child should know. King Midas wished

What Happened to King Midas — that everything he touched might turn into gold. He had his foolish wish and starved in the midst of his yellow treasure. He could not eat gold, of course.

A Siberian Mine

Old-fashioned methods of gold-mining are still in use in Siberia. Here is the way they raise ore from the mine—by a rope and windlass, the windlass turned by the two horses, trotting constantly in a circle. One might say it is the old oaken bucket system of lifting, turned on end.

The Sorrowful Struggle for Gold

Men faced dreadful perils to reach the gold fields of California. You may know some one who joined in the gold rush to Alaska. Miners froze to death on the terrible climb over the Chilkoot Pass. They stood and washed gravel in the icy floods of the Yukon and the Klondike. With hot boulders they thawed gravel out of blue ice in Arctic hillsides. They have scaled the cliffs, and pushed through the tropic jungles of Central and South America. In our early history are stories of cruel wars for gold. Helpless Indians were enslaved and forced to work in the mines of Mexico and Peru.

A Little Gold Almost Everywhere

There is a little gold all through the earth. It is in sea-water and beach sand, in clay and common rock. Only in mountain regions was the gold collected in veins and pockets in the rock layers.

Why the Gold Settled in Cracks

The wrinkling up of the earth's rock crust, as we saw in the geography story of North America, not only makes the mountains, but it does other things. It crushes and cracks the rocks and so leaves open-

THE GOLD INDUSTRY

The Mosquitoes and the Gold Miners

The gold hunters in Alaska are not only obliged to protect themselves against the vigorous cold of winter, but against the vicious mosquitoes in the summer. You see these miners are working with their faces covered by a mosquito net arrangement made especially for the purpose. The summer season is so short that the mosquitoes seem to feel that they must be particularly active to make up for it. It isn't necessary to cover the hands. They are toughened by hard work and besides are in constant motion.

ings all through them. Then in this same crushing and grinding together of the rocks, heat is generated which melts out the gold scattered in small particles all through them and causes it to run down into these cracks, so making the veins in which the gold, usually mixed up with other minerals, is found. In some places also, as the expert geologists are able to tell from the looks of things thereabouts, water has dissolved gold out of the rocks and deposited it in veins and pockets as the water evaporated, much as the water in the teakettle deposits lime.

Where a "fault" was made by rock masses being pushed over one another at a fracture in the crust, the gold was caught in pockets of clay, like raisins in a mince pie. Such pockets are called "bonanzas," a Spanish word that means "good find" or treasure chest. Some famous bonanzas have been found in America. Ask your papa to tell you about the "Comstock Lode."

© *Keystone View Co.*

© *Keystone View Co.*

Placer Mining Near the Yukon

Here Alaskan gold miners are digging loose the bank and shoveling the dirt into the water. The stream carries soil and gold to a sluice which separates the two. Gold occurs in two ways in the Klondike region—in the bottoms of the valleys and in a bank or ledge that runs along the side of the valleys. Mines on the sides of valleys are called "high-beach" mines.

PICTURED KNOWLEDGE
On the Beach at Nome

These miners are panning and sluicing the sands for gold on the beach at Nome. The kind of sluice used in mining is a long inclined water trough, the bottom of which is covered with ridges to hold quicksilver for catching the gold.

When the gold was all locked up in the sparkling crystal caskets of white quartz rocks, in the hearts of mountains, rivers began to dig it out again. Melting snows cut deep channels and washed gold with sand and gravel into the valleys. The heavy gold was dropped in pools and at bars. At Cape Nome, Alaska, it was carried swiftly down to the ocean beach. There the sands were filled with gold, to a bed of clay.

How the Rivers Dug for Gold

In West Australia, desert winds did the sifting. They blew the light dust from dried-up river beds, and exposed the gold. In South Africa, quartz pebbles were washed into a great field, and there embedded in clay and cement.

Work of Desert Winds

The Two Kinds of Gold Deposits

So gold is always found, in quantity, in just two kinds of places. It is found in drift, or placer mines, and in cracks and pockets of mountain rocks. Of course, it is easier to wash gold out of gravel than to dig it out of buried rocks. In every new gold field thousands of miners work small placer claims. All they need is food and a board shack; and for tools, a shovel, a miner's iron pan, and a box cradle, or sluice trough, to wash out the gold.

How the Gold "Pans Out"

Now a miner cannot dig very deep into a river bed with a shovel. In a few years the cream is skimmed from placer workings. To go deeper, machines must be used. Some old placers and new ones, in our western states, are now being dug up with steam dredges. Gold bearing, gravelly hillsides are being torn down by streams of water from hose many times bigger than those used by firemen. The frozen river banks in Alaska are now thawed out with steam. To get at the gold-filled bars of rivers, streams have been *lifted*. The water has been made to flow overhead through "flumes" or

After the "Cream" Is Gone

THE GOLD INDUSTRY
A "Flume"

The water in this stream is made to flow through a trough or "flume." The miner in the background is dumping soil from the creek-bed into the flume where it is washed away, leaving the gold behind.

viaducts, while the river beds were dug out.

Mining in the Old Days

Fifty years ago most of our gold was simply washed out of placers by hand. Even where ore was taken out of deep mines it was often just crushed and washed. Unless a rock *Two Hundred* mine was very rich, with *Dollars a* from one to two hun-*Ton for Ore* dred dollars' worth of gold in a ton of ore, it did not pay to work it at all. When a mine was found, there might not be any timber for roof props, or water for washing the ore. Lumber, tools, blasting powder, chemicals, even food and clothing, had to be hauled a hundred miles or more by wagon. Then everything had to be carried up and down the mountain trails on the backs of pack animals.

Mining Methods of Today

Since railroads have been built, supplies are got more cheaply and quickly. And wonderful machines *How Dirt Is* have been invented, and *Made to Pay* better ways of getting *Nowadays* out the gold discovered. Ore that has only two dollars' worth of gold to the ton, just one-tenth of an ounce, can now be put through a modern gold mill, with a profit of one dollar.

The World of Machinery and Material in a Modern Mine

A great deal of money, sometimes a quarter of a million dollars, is spent before a ton of ore can be treated. Shafts are sunk much deeper than for coal or iron. Some shafts go a mile into the earth.

Equipment That Costs a Fortune

An electric power plant is often built, to generate electricity from a mountain stream. An engine compresses air to work the rock drills. Tons of giant powder have to be bought to blast out the rock. Elevators must be put in to lift the ore to the mill. Furnaces are built to roast ores with sulphur in them. And then there are machines. A gravity machine sorts out light, worthless rock. The crushing is done in huge steel hoppers with hammer stamps that weigh eight hundred pounds. Quicksilver and costly chemicals are used in taking gold out of the crushed ore.

The Sounds of War in a Gold Mill

A row of hoppers and hammers in a gold mill is called a "battery" as if they were cannon on a battlefield. They make as much noise as artillery. "Boom, boom, boom! Rattle, crash! An earthquake jar!" as the ore tumbles into the hoppers, and the giant stampers pound it to powder. A cataract of water flows out, at the bottom, over long, shallow copper troughs that are silvered with mercury. Not an atom of gold escapes. Mercury swallows gold, as water dissolves salt or sugar. But it will take up just so much gold, and no more,

A Burro Train Carrying Gold

© *Keystone View Co.*

Although machinery and private railroad tracks are almost indispensable in the larger mines, the patient burro is still in use in the smaller ones. This picturesque train of burros loaded with ore and driven by the horsemen in the rear, is coming down the mountain side from the Virginias, a Colorado mine that has been worked for over thirty years.

and make a metal paste or dough. This is called an amalgam, or union, of gold and mercury.

The soft amalgam is scraped from the copper plates, and heated. The mercury escapes in vapor, leaving the gold behind. The vapor is condensed in a cold vessel, just as steam is turned back into water. The mercury is used over and over again. The gold is melted and poured into molds about as big as a bar of laundry soap. One bar weighs forty pounds! It is heavier than so much lead. But pure gold is so soft that you could scratch it with your finger nail. It is easily dented and worn away.

How the Gold Is Set Free

Where gold ore is very low grade, with many impurities, other ways of getting it out of the ore are better. It is first roasted and powdered in water and turned into great tanks. Chlorine gas, forced through the liquid, unites with the gold to form a "chloride." Then, when sulphate of iron is put in that, it unites with the chlorine, and frees the gold. As a purple powder the gold settles in the tank.

The Curious Cyanide Process

Still more curious is the cyanide process. Cyanide of potash dissolves

THE GOLD INDUSTRY

Cutting Down a Hill with Water

"Gold-bearing, gravelly hillsides are being torn down by streams of water from hose many times bigger than those used by firemen."

A Gold Dredge

In contrast to the primitive, old-fashioned methods of gold-mining in Siberia, here is a modern American gold dredge that scoops up several tons of river bottom a day.

PICTURED KNOWLEDGE

Ready to Come Up from the "Bobtail" Mine

© *Keystone View Co.*

The three views on this page show workmen in the depths of the "Bobtail" mine in Colorado. Compare them with the pictures of coal miners. Colorado is our greatest gold-producing state.

and boiled. It takes 2,016 degrees of heat to boil gold!

How the Gold is Turned Into Money

A great deal of the gold from our mines is shipped to Uncle Sam's mints to be coined into money. But no matter where it is sold—to jewelers, gold-leaf beaters, gilders, gold-thread and lace makers, or manufacturers of dentists' fillings—gold is worth $20.67 an ounce—always that and just that and no more. It

Fixing the Market Price of Gold

Miners Drilling Holes for Blasting

© *Keystone View Co.*

These miners are drilling holes in which dynamite sticks will be placed.

gold. The powdered ore is mixed with cyanide water, and trickled through boxes filled with zinc shavings. The gold flies to the zinc and plates it. The zinc is melted out. The gold that is recovered is full of impurities. So it is put into a blast furnace with soda, borax, and sand,

Putting Gold on to Boil

Driving a Cross-Cut, or Passage, from One Vein to Another

© *Keystone View Co.*

is not like wheat, cotton or iron, or anything else in the world, in having a changing value. That is because the big trading nations use gold for money. They have agreed on the value and weight of their coins. Of course, when there is more gold, prices of other things have a tendency to go up; which is as if the price of gold went down. But, in buying and selling, more and more money is needed all the time. There has never been more gold than was needed.

A Cross-Section of the Richest Mine in the World

The richest mines in the world are in the Witwatersrand gold fields of the Transvaal, South Africa. They are popularly called the "Rand" and are six thousand feet above sea level, near Johannesburg. In these South African mines many Negroes are employed.

PICTURED KNOWLEDGE
The Ore-Breaking Machine

This is one of the powerful machines used for crushing ore to get out gold. It is called the Gates ore-breaker. The lower picture shows the machine at work and on the opposite page you see a cross-section of it. In the top picture only the top of the crusher is visible above the material that is pouring down onto the feeding platform and into the hopper.

THE GOLD INDUSTRY

A Cross-Section of the Gates Ore-Breaker

The Gates ore-breaker has a big hopper like a coffee mill. The ore goes out of it all broken up very much as the grains of coffee go out in little pieces into the drawer of the coffee mill. The ore, however, is not ground, but is crushed. That huge shaft, D, has an attachment called the crushing head, which moves around in the cavity, C, into which the ore comes from the hopper, and crushes it against the side, as a boy cracks nuts with his teeth. (Only, of course, boys shouldn't crack nuts with their teeth!) The shaft "wabbles" very much as a top does when it is about to fall over. The device that gives the gyratory (wabbling) motion to the shaft is called an "eccentric," and is indicated by the letter A. This "eccentric" is a wheel through which the shaft runs, but instead of going directly through the center, the shaft goes a little to one side of the center, as you can see by the diagram, so that as the wheel revolves it causes the shaft to make a circular and rolling movement inside the throat, as the part of the machinery is called in which the ore is crushed. This "eccentric" is one that is used in a great many kinds of machinery; in the steam engine it works the valves, which, in turn, let steam into the cylinder at the proper time. The combination of the bevel gear with the bevel wheel, B, which here causes the crushing shaft to turn, is operated upon the same principle that is used in automobiles to transfer the motion from the engine to the wheels.

PICTURED KNOWLEDGE

The Sorting Table

The ore is drawn up from the mine and dumped in the bin at the back of the picture. From the bin the larger pieces of ore fall out onto the circular, revolving table beside which the men are standing. As it moves past them the men pick out the pieces of rock that are not gold-bearing. What similar process does coal pass through? The story about coal tells you.

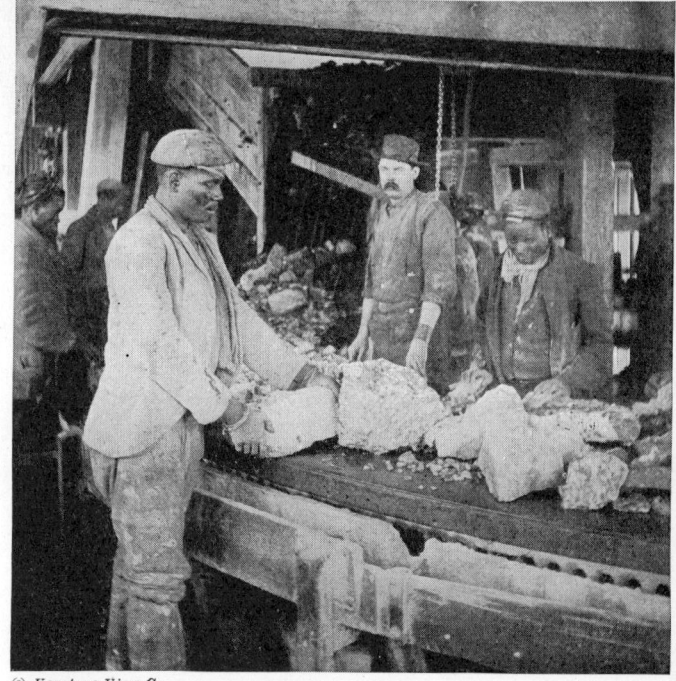

© Keystone View Co.

© Keystone View Co.

The Stamping Mill

From the rock crushers the ore passes on to the stamping mill. The stamp batteries are arranged in groups of five, on the principle of a mortar and pestle. The stamp is a big steel pounder that falls on the ore in the box below. The rods in the upper part of the picture are the shafts of the stamps. Below the spool-like attachments riveted to the stamp shafts are the teeth of the big horizontal shaft. The teeth are called "cams." The flywheels of the shaft can be seen, but the shaft itself is hidden. When the shaft turns, the cams push on the spools and so the vertical shafts and stamps are lifted about eight inches and then let fall again. The head of the shaft with the stamp weighs almost a thousand pounds. When it drops upon the ore in the mortar-box it crushes it to sand. Water is mixed with the ore in the mortar-box and flows out through wire screens and down the table-like troughs. The ore is carried along with the water as soon as it is cracked fine enough to pass through the screens.

1358

THE GOLD INDUSTRY

Cyanide Tanks

"Cyanide of potash dissolves gold. The powdered ore is mixed with cyanide water, and trickled through boxes filled with zinc shavings. The gold flies to the zinc and plates it." These are the cyanide tanks. Amalgamation, that is, combining with mercury, gets about seventy per cent of the gold from the ore. The cyanide process frees about twelve per cent more. These two processes save millions of dollars' worth of gold from being wasted.

The Gold Concentrator

After being crushed to powder in the stamping mill, the gold ore is separated by the concentrator into two parts, one of which contains almost all the gold. This work formerly cost $30 a ton, but now, by the use of improved machinery, it can be done for $4.

© Keystone View Co.

Don't you wish you could see gold and silver bars made into money? The oldest United States mint is in Philadelphia, but there are several others. In a mint there are steel vaults containing gold and silver bullion, and other vaults containing new coins in bags. For coining, gold is melted. A little copper is added to make it harder, or the words and designs on gold pieces would soon be worn away.

© Keystone View Co.

1359

PICTURED KNOWLEDGE
The Huntington Crushing Mill

The picture shows a row of the machines known as Huntington mills which are sometimes used to crush the coarse pieces of ore coming from the Gates ore-breaker. Two- and three-pound pieces are fed into the mill, together with considerable water and are crushed to a thin mud which flows out through screens.

At the bottom of the mill, resting against the side, is a steel ring like a barrel hoop, only, of course, much bigger and heavier than a hoop. Hanging vertically from the framework within the mill are three round shafts to each of which a steel wheel is attached at the lower end. These shafts are so placed that the tread of the wheel rests against the inside of the big hoop. The framework holding the shafts is revolved by a belt wheel outside of the mill and as it revolves the little steel wheels roll around inside of the hoop. The vertical shafts, to which these wheels are attached are so fastened to the revolving frame at the top that they can turn around as the wheel rolls and also can swing sidewise. It is because they are able to swing sidewise that the mill gets its great crushing force. When you swing a weight on a string, the faster you swing the weight, the harder it pulls. This is called "centrifugal" force. In the same way, when the frame moves around in the Huntington mill the small wheel shafts would swing "outwards" if it were not for the fact that the "roller rings" press against the inside of the steel hoop or "ring die." What really happens then is that the "roller rings" press against the "ring die" very hard, and when the pieces of ore get between the two they are crushed to tiny bits. The water which is fed into the mill washes these fine bits of rock and gold out through the screens.

Copper or silver is added to gold that is made into jewelry.

The gold is cast into bars as wide as a twenty dollar gold piece. After these bars have been rolled into strips of the proper thickness, round discs, the size of the coins to be made, are punched out of them.

It's Just Like Cutting Cookies

The smooth, round discs of gold are fed into a machine. They drop between two steel dies and are squeezed so tight that all the letters, figures and design are pressed into them. In putting the new coins into packages they are not counted.

1360

THE GOLD INDUSTRY
Cripple Creek Mines

This is a bird's-eye view of the mines in the Cripple Creek region of Colorado. Notice the big piles of waste material from the mines.

They are just shoveled into scales and weighed. The total weight is divided by the weight of one coin. That gives the number.

Will Our Gold Mines Give Out?

What will the world do when the gold gives out? It is not likely that it ever will give out. It is not like coal—in just a few beds. New gold fields are being found all the time, *The World Still Full of Gold* and new methods are making it possible to re-work old mines. As railroads are built, much more gold will be taken out of Australia, Siberia and Alaska. Deserted mines in Mexico and Peru will be reopened. The deserts of Western Australia will be grid-ironed with steel rails, to fetch out the gold. Mineralogists think that the Western Hemisphere alone could supply the world with gold.

Underneath the grim crags, the snow peaks and frozen cascades, the pines and dancing streams, there is another world of "faery" in our western mountains. The underworld is seamed and veined and laced with glittering dust, locked up in crystal rocks—the world's gold deposits.

The Coppersmith

In the days before machinery was invented, there were coppersmiths in every town of any size. They were usually men who had learned their trade as apprentices when they were boys, and spent their whole lives fashioning by hand all sorts of things from sheets of copper. Some of the things made by these old-fashioned coppersmiths are very valuable today and are handed down as heirlooms. Perhaps you have a copper teapot or candlestick in your family.

THE WORLD AT ITS WORK
THE COPPER INDUSTRY

Long Story Back of a Copper Cent Piece

Undeveloped Copper Mines

Here are whole mountains of copper ore in Arizona, just beginning to be worked. Arizona is rich in minerals. These include, beside copper, gold, nickel, and wolframite from which tungsten is made.

IF YOU have a silver quarter to spend for a Christmas gift for little brother, there is something not many people think of that will outshine everything else in his stocking. Go to a bank and buy twenty-five new copper cents just as they come from Uncle Sam's money factory. They are a bright, red-gold, the color of the Indian whose feathered head is stamped on some of them. On others is the head of our great president, Lincoln. The government put it there where all the people could see it. Few ever see a gold dollar, but everyone uses pennies.

Copper is so much cheaper and more abundant than gold and silver that all countries use it for coins of small value.

Gold, Silver, and Copper First Used of All Metals

Of all the metals in our earth, yellow gold, white silver and red copper were used first. So bright and shining that they could not escape notice, they were often found pure, unmixed with other metals, in glittering dust and nuggets in the sand and gravel of river beds and banks. And they lay in the seams and pockets of rock layers. When the rocks were broken up, the heavy metals were easily washed out, melted and molded into any shape. Iron was much less easily seen, recovered and worked into useful forms, so copper was long used in its place.

Copper stands between the precious and the base metals, with some of the qualities of both. Like gold and silver it can be hammered into thin sheets, drawn into fine wire and used in plating other metals. It readily unites, or forms an alloy with gold, silver, tin, zinc and aluminum; and, next to silver it is the best conductor of electricity. As bright as gold when first mined or minted, it does not remain so. In dry air it tarnishes to a dull brown. In the damp it rusts like iron. Iron rust or ash is red and falls away in dust and scales. But copper rust is a greenish-gray, and forms a light, paint-like coat which protects the metal beneath from further injury. Ornamental articles in copper are often rusted to this beautiful, mottled "verdigris," or green-gray purposely, for the decorative color in making lamp bases and other things. But that rust is poisonous, and as there are specks of it on old coins, children should not put pennies in their mouths. Luckily copper has an unpleasant taste.

There must have been large copper mines in every ancient empire around the Mediterranean Sea, for many people used this metal freely. *How Copper Got Its Name* It got its name Kyprum from the Island of Cyprus. Pronounce the C hard as the Greeks did—Ky'-prus. The name became Kupfer in German and copper in English. The metal had one fault. It was too soft to take a good, cutting edge, and men needed tools and weapons. But it was found that, by melting a little tin, also a soft metal, with the copper, a very hard, yellowish-brown alloy could be made. This was called bronze. Bronze was as great a discovery in its day as the making of hard steel from iron.

The Wonderful Age of Bronze

There was a long and wonderful bronze age. Warriors had armor, helmets, swords and shields of it; workmen had hammers, axes and knives. There were ornaments, coins, medals, jewel caskets, urns, statues, church and palace furnishings, house and ship trimmings. Bronze was made in dozens of colors and degrees of hardness. Gun metal for casting cannon was one variety. Bell metal was given a musical tone by adding silver to the copper and tin. Bronzes in the greatest beauty and variety, some modeled and engraved by goldsmiths, and set with gems, have been dug up from ruined cities, forts and tombs, from Egypt to Ireland, and placed in museums. The Indians of Mexico, Peru, and the south shore of Lake Superior, had no tin, but they made tools, weapons and vessels of copper. We still use bronze for stat-

THE COPPER INDUSTRY
A Mining Camp in the Desert

Here is an Arizona copper-mining camp in the midst of the dry, treeless desert.

ues, gun barrels, building hardware and for ornaments, but with the general use of iron and steel, the Bronze Age came to an end.

Everybody in the Middle Ages had copper cooking vessels; but that made a great deal of work. To cook in dull pots, pans and kettles was *Copper and Cooks in the Middle Ages* dangerous, and housewives were obliged to keep their utensils brightly scoured. We are glad that we have iron, tin, enameled ware and aluminum to use. The only copper thing left in household use is the bottom of the wash boiler. Except in making bronze for gun metal, bell metal, statuary, building hardware and small coins, copper has lost most of its old uses. That is lucky, because we have so many new uses for this wonderful metal that there would not be enough to supply the world's industrial needs.

The Copper of the New World

So much copper was used in the Bronze Age that the richest mines of the Old World were worked out by the time America was discovered. All the copper mines of Russia, Norway and Sweden, Germany, Spain and Great Britain, today, produce only about 20 per cent of the copper in the world's markets. New mines have been found in Japan, Alaska and Australia; but the United States mines 55 per cent of this metal and with Canada, Mexico and South America, about 70 per cent. All our copper is found in three regions: Northern Michigan, the Rocky Mountains and Sierra Nevadas.

On the map of Michigan in your geography, find Keweenaw Point. It is a peninsula, twenty miles wide and sixty long that is pushed into Lake Superior from the southern shore. In this small region was found the largest and most interesting field of native copper in the world. Long before white men came to America, the Indians worked these mines. They picked up nuggets on

PICTURED KNOWLEDGE

The Richest Copper-Mining Town on Earth

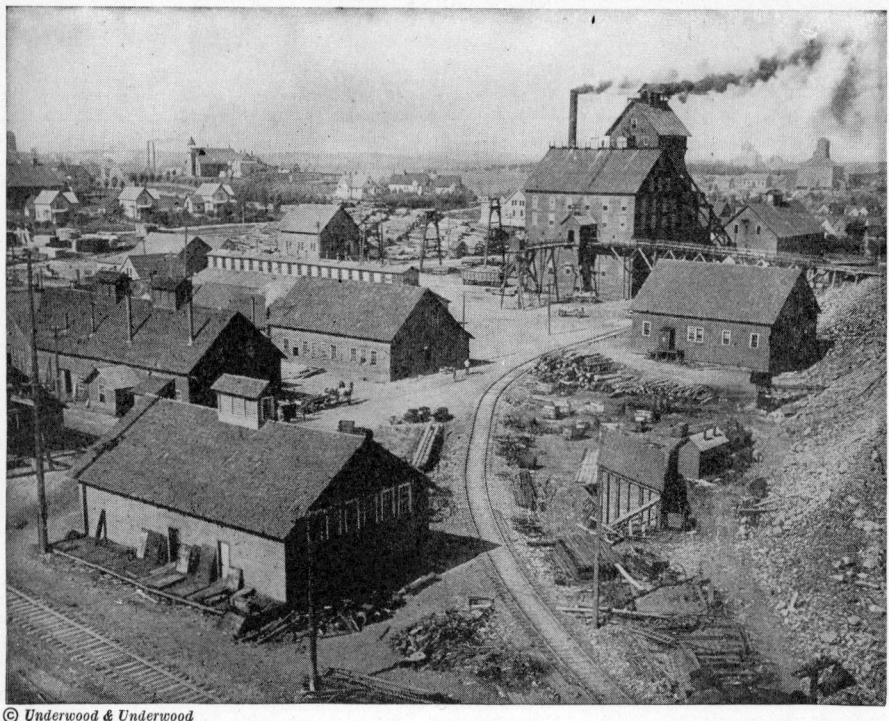

© *Underwood & Underwood*

On Keweenaw Point, in Michigan, "was found the largest and most interesting field of native copper in the world. Calumet is the center of this big, busy copper-mining region. It is a city of tall chimneys, stamp mills for crushing the ores, railroads and miners' cottages."

the beach and broke great masses from their beds in the rocks. Their stone hammers are still to be found on the hillsides. They told the French explorers in Canada that there were mountains of solid copper, and it is true that masses of pure metal of tons weight have been uncovered.

Geologists explain the fact that this vast deposit of copper ore is so near the surface in this way: Lake Superior is a glacier-scooped and water-filled valley of an old mountain system. Today, this old mountain system is a hilly ridge called the **Laurentian Highland**. Lying between the St. Lawrence River system and Hudson Bay, it runs from

Mr. Glacier Is a Copper Miner

Labrador to the Mackenzie River. Lake Superior is almost circled by hills and cliffs which spring to four and seven hundred feet above the water. Iron, copper and other minerals are abundant in these old, worn-down mountains. Buried deep under lofty ranges at one time, these minerals are now near the surface. Some iron mines are so exposed that they are worked like stone quarries. The copper on Keweenaw Peninsula runs both wide and deep, in big veins and pockets of volcanic rock—gray lava and white quartz. The white quartz copper ores are so beautiful that they are much prized for school and museum specimens.

You might get a specimen from the schools of Calumet, Michigan, if

THE COPPER INDUSTRY
How They Burrow Into the Mountains

© *Underwood & Underwood*

Here is a mine where the copper is reached by tunneling straight in from the surface instead of sinking shafts to reach the ore levels, as in the Calumet and Hecla mines. These tunnels are made on the same principle as those which allow a railroad train to go through a mountain.

you can offer something in exchange —sea-shells, corals or cotton plants. Calumet is the center of this big, busy, copper-mining region. It is a city of tall chimneys, stamp mills for crushing the ores, railroads, and miners' cottages. Over a wide field a shaft has been driven straight down into the hills, every thousand feet or so. A mine shaft, you know, is just a very wide, deep well. The main shaft of one of the Calumet and Hecla Mines is over a mile in depth and no bottom has been struck in the rich ore.

The shaft measures about 12x30 feet. Except where it has been driven through solid rock, the sides are walled with timbers or stone to keep them from caving in, and to keep the shaft from filling with water. Partitions to the bottom divide it into four compartments. Two are used for elevators to send workmen down and haul ore up. One is for pumping air in, to ventilate the mine, and one to pump water out of the tunnels and chambers which open from the shaft. The elevating, pumping and fanning machinery is in a big power house built over the mine shaft. In the underground workings, the ore bearing rock is broken in pieces with dyna-

PICTURED KNOWLEDGE
Using the Pneumatic Drill

This picture shows you how they go right through a solid rock, if necessary, in order to follow a vein of copper ore. These men are operating drills driven by compressed air. The air, which is compressed by a steam engine, is sent to the drills through those pipes.

mite charges, loaded on little cars and lifted to the surface. Carried far up the hillside to the tops of tall stamp mills, the ore is emptied into huge hoppers. Like wheat in a flour mill, the ore is crushed to sand and the heavy metal washed out, as it drops from floor to floor. Melted and cast into bars it is shipped by lake and rail to refineries. Most of it is worked up in the factories of Michigan, New York, New Jersey and the New England states.

All copper mining is not as simple as in Michigan. In Montana and Arizona and most copper fields, the metal is found mixed with sulphur, iron, silver, arsenic, and other materials, and has to be purified. Sulphurous copper ores are brassy in color, not red gold. If both sulphur and iron are present, the ore shows such beautiful blue, green and purple lights, that it is called peacock copper. Where the ore has been exposed to dampness and air it is rusted to a mossy, mottled green. This is known as malachite, a beautiful green stone which takes a polish like marble. Too valuable for ore, it is used for table tops, mantels, mosaic work and ornamental articles. It is even carved and used as settings in silver jewelry. A still more beautiful stone is azurite, a blue crystal which gets its color from copper.

Mining Harder in Other Fields

How the Ores Are Separated

Where copper is found almost pure, as in most Lake Michigon ores, it is crushed out of the rock in a stamp mill, and is then washed out over horizontal shaking tables which concentrate the heavy minerals and wash away the worthless rock. Where there are impurities or

THE COPPER INDUSTRY

where the ore contains silver, the impurities are removed and the copper recovered by the "electrolytic" process. That is, it is dissolved in acid and electricity passed through this solution. This causes the copper to settle on plates and allows the impurities and silver to go to the bottom of the tank as "slimes," from which the silver is later recovered. Where ore contains sulphur, the sulphur must be burned out. In handling this "sulphide ore," one process is to heat it so that the sulphur passes away as gas. This is called "roasting." By another process the ore is made to smelt itself, the sulphur furnishing the fuel and being entirely consumed. This is one of the very simple discoveries that have meant so much to the copper industry. Formerly, owing to the poisonous fumes resulting from the roasting process, nothing would grow for miles around a smelter, and the men had a white, bleached appearance. Now this has all been changed by the sulphur being made to act as "fireman" instead of getting into mischief.

Copper is nine times heavier than water, melts at 1,100° C., about the same temperature that melts gold, and stands next to iron in hardness and strength. It is easily hammered, rolled, shaped and drawn into wire. And copper wire is so strong that a wire measuring one-twelfth of an inch in diameter will hold up a weight of three hundred pounds.

What would the world do without copper wire? Next to silver it is the best of all metals for conducting electricity, and silver is far too scarce and dear to use for our telegraph, telephone, ocean-cable, trolley-car, electric light and factory power wires. In the United States alone there are now more than half a million tons of copper in telephone wires. The use of electricity in so many ways is possible because copper is plentiful and can be produced and sold for about twenty cents a pound.

Other Uses of Copper in the Industries

Copper is used in batteries in the generation of electricity; for electroplating in printing works, and, mixed with zinc, in making brass. What countless things are made of brass, from beds, to automobile parts, stair-rails, door-knobs and policemen's buttons. Alloyed with zinc, copper helps make brass; with

A Copper Smelter

The slag is being run off from this furnace. You can see it pouring out of the big spout in the center. Below this another spout or trough is emptying gold, silver and copper, mixed with much sulphur, into the vat.

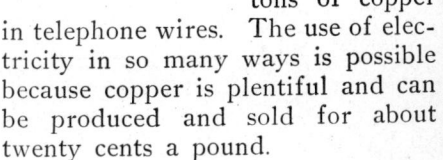

tin, gun-metal; with tin and silver, bell-metal; with tin, zinc and lead, statuary and hardware bronze; with nickel and zinc, German silver; with aluminum, a gold-colored metal for cheap jewelry.

Since you know about that green copper rust, "verdigris," the peacock ores, malachite "marble" and the blue crystal azurite, you will not be surprised to learn that copper furnishes us some beautiful colors for paints, dyes and stained glass. Most green paints and many green calicoes and wall paper get their color from copper and arsenic. These are not always safe to use in houses. Copper paint is fine for ship hulls, for it protects the iron from rust and keeps away barnacles. Copper gives the color to green and blue glass. Blue vitriol, a sulphate of copper, is used to dye wool and cotton black. The verdigris of the market, a green paint, is an acid oxide of copper. Put a penny in vinegar for a few days and see what happens. Another oxide, or rust of copper is so red that it grinds to a crimson powder.

Pure copper is used chiefly for coins, wire, bolts and plates in shipbuilding, where iron would rust, for pipes in distilling vats, in battery charging and electroplating. Aside from those the greatest quantities of copper are used in the alloys — brass, bronze, and gun-metal. Many cities have brass foundries, where the copper and zinc are melted together and then cast into plumbers', building and machinery fittings. The sheet brass is stamped into such things as eyelets for shoes, and caps for shoestrings.

Do you wonder that the world produces and uses over thirteen hundred thousand tons of copper every year and wants more? It is a greater source of wealth to the United States than our gold. And the new copper mines of Alaska, to which a railroad has been built, will make that territory rich even after its gold has all been mined.

Mining at Anaconda, Montana

Anaconda, Montana, has the biggest copper-mining flue and stack in the world. This picture shows them in the process of construction. The stack is 300 feet high.

THE COPPER INDUSTRY

Michigan Copper Ready for Shipping

© *Underwood & Underwood*

This is how the copper comes from the smelter—in bars and thick plates. It is leaving the Calumet and Hecla mines.

A By-Product of Copper Mining

Loads of slag from the copper smelter are being dumped alongside the track as ballast.

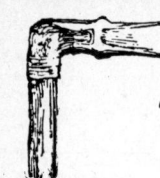

The Grandfather of Grandfather's Ax

A True Story of the Age of Bronze

YOUR grandfather, of course, had a grandfather, but so did his ax. In the days of our ancestors of the Very Long Ago, in the Age of Bronze, when you wanted an ax, a hatchet, a chisel, or other cutting tool, you didn't go to the hardware store and just buy it. You cast it in a mold. That queer looking affair in the center of the page is one side of such a mold. The men of the Bronze Age put the two parts of the mold together and poured the molten bronze in at the top. After the casting had cooled sufficiently, the mold was opened and the casting taken out. Then they hammered down the edge. This made it sharper and at the same time harder. Sometimes they put "eyes" in their axes. (This eye looks more like an ear perhaps or the handle of a jug, in the mold.) Then they ran a thong through the eye, as you see in the right-hand picture, to hold the ax on the handle. And sometimes they didn't; as you see by the picture of the ax on the left which has no eye. These axes also had what are called "stop ridges" between the blade and the part that holds the handle. In the picture on the left you see what it was that the stop ridge stopped; it prevented the thong which helped to hold the ax in place from slipping up and down. (Can you find in the mold the part that cast this ridge?)

But the queerest part of this story is about that little square hole in the top of the mold. This is the place where they put in what foundrymen call a "core." A core is a separate shape or filling that is put inside a casting to make that part of it hollow after the core has been removed. So in the ax when this core at the top was taken out it left a hole right in the top of the ax. Then the axmaker cut a hardwood stick with an elbow in it, fixed one end in the hole and bound the handle on with thongs.

The three things at the bottom are waste pieces from the castings that were left on the outside of the mold. Foundrymen call them "jets." The hole in the one that looks like a doughnut is where the core in the ax stuck up through so that it could be pulled out when the metal had cooled. (When you eat an apple the "core" is what is left; but when you make a casting, the "core" is what isn't left, you see!)

But why did these ancient axsmiths make a hole in the top of their cutting tools instead of a hole running straight through, as we do now? Then any good stick would have answered for a handle and they wouldn't have needed the thongs. (Ask the foundryman or the blacksmith, or the man at the hardware store which kind of a core it would be easier to fit and hold in its place in the mold—a core that would make a hole straight through or a core that would leave a hole in the top.)

The Jets

THE WORLD AT ITS WORK

DIAMONDS

The Diamond Industry

Cleaving the Precious Stone
This picture shows the first treatment of a diamond in the rough, the insertion of the wedge-shaped steel knife in the V-shaped groove. The diamond cutter has just struck the knife a blow with the mallet.

WHEN you go into a store to buy a hat or a suit of clothes you have noticed, of course, how your image is repeated in the mirrors they have for showing how you look at the sides as well as in front. You seem to be several people at once. In the same way the many flat faces, called facets, on a polished diamond, catch and repeat the light. "Brilliants," as the most valuable diamonds, such as you see in the picture, are called, have an eight-sided surface in the center and around it thirty-two facets reaching to the edge of the stone. You see how these would make one sunbeam repeat itself in innumerable flashes.

Another thing that makes the diamond sparkle is the fact that the rays of light, passing down into the stone as the light passes through a window pane, are refracted—that is, bent back—and come out again at the surface multiplied many times. It's like putting money into a savings bank and drawing it out again with interest, isn't it?

Diamond's Multiplication Table

Sometimes you seem to see many colors in a diamond—red and blue, among others. This is because the diamond acts as a prism, breaking the rays into the different colors of which light is composed.

To children and other poets, dew drops are diamonds and a star is a "diamond in the sky." Both the star and the dew drop being round, are many-sided as the polished diamond is, and so the sun's rays are multiplied.

How are Diamonds "Taught to Sparkle?"

Haven't you heard people say

1373

PICTURED KNOWLEDGE
Diamond Polishers at Work

This shows the interior of a diamond polishing plant, full of little diamond lathes. The workmen are polishing the faces of the diamonds.

that some one was "a diamond in the rough"? This meant that the person referred to was like a diamond as it comes from the mine—a rather unattractive, dull stone—but that, like the stone, he had fine qualities of mind and heart which only needed shaping and polishing. The diamond itself must go through the same process in order to bring out its best qualities. To "put the sparkle into a diamond" not only requires great skill, but each separate stone has a character of its own, like people, and must be treated in a different way. It must be ground so as to put the faces where they are wanted, with as little waste of the diamond, in the grinding, as possible.

The most important piece of machinery used is the gem cutter's brain; the rest of the machinery is comparatively simple. You have heard the saying "diamond cut diamond." That expression really tells just how they do it. First two diamonds are put into holders and

How Diamond Cuts Diamond

rubbed against the other so the original rough surface is removed and you get the plain, unpolished stone.

That part of the diamond which is ground away—it looks so much like slate pencil dust that you could not tell the difference—is saved and used in the next step, which is that of putting on the facets and polishing them. When one of the faces is ground, the diamond is unsoldered from its holder, put into another position and another face ground against a revolving wheel which is covered with olive oil and diamond dust.

The Story of the Wonderful Pebble

The greatest diamond fields in the world are in South Africa, and it was through a child playing with pebbles that these wonderful mines were discovered.

The children of a Dutch farmer, named Jacobs, used to gather pretty pebbles along the banks of a shallow little stream running into the Orange River. One of these stones of a peculiar shape was so bright that it attracted the attention of Mamma Jacobs. She took a look at it, said how pretty it was, handed it back to the children, and forgot all about it until one day an old friend of the family, named Schalk Van Niekirk, was calling on the Jacobses. Mrs. Jacobs mentioned the pretty stone. With the help of the children it was found in the garden, and as Van Niekirk took a fancy to it the Jacobses laughingly gave it to him and told him to sell it and make his fortune. Van Niekirk had the stone examined, found that it was a diamond, and sold it for $2,500. Then he found other gems of the same kind, bought others from the natives, and became a rich man. One stone was sold for over $50,000. What he did for the Jacobses or whether they went into the diamond business too and got rich, the story doesn't say.

Making Diamonds Out of Sugar

But more interesting than the story of the Jacobses and the wonderful pebble is the story of how a man actually made diamonds.

First I must tell you that diamonds are found in the fissures of rocks, rocks which originally boiled up out of volcanoes; that is to say, these rocks are lava which has hardened. The diamonds were formed under immense pressure and were originally just the carbon in the earth melted. Lava is virtually melted iron, and the clay in which the diamonds are found is this iron rusted and weathered away.

A Diamond Polishing Lathe

Now imagine that we are in the shop shown on the opposite page. Here we are looking at one of the diamond lathes; you can see a diamond, that has been polished, near the lathe and another in the machine, being held against the steel disk which is turning at the rate of 2,000 revolutions a minute.

In order to make diamonds, all you have to do is to take a piece of carbon, heat it forty times as hot as the hottest day in August—say 4,000 degrees—and under a pressure of about ninety-five tons to the square inch.

In Paris, between 1852, when he was born, and 1907, when he died, there lived a very eminent chemist, Henri Moissan. After doing a number of other wonderful things in chemistry he took up the question of the making of artificial diamonds. He believed that if he could reproduce the conditions under which nature made diamonds, he could make them too. So what did Professor Moissan do but take a piece of pure sugar, burn it into black charcoal—thus getting pure carbon—mix this carbon with pure iron, just as the carbon was mixed with the iron in the fiery furnace we call a volcano, put the mixture in a crucible, heat the crucible until the lime with which it was lined began to melt and the iron to go up in clouds. Then,

The Professor's Toy Volcano

with the proper instruments he plunged the fiery white crucible into cold water, as a blacksmith plunges a white hot horseshoe into his tub. The surface cooled and hardened, so

long process the iron was dissolved away, just as the iron in the diamond fields rusted away, and these artificial diamonds were taken out.

But here's the trouble. As soon

Another View of a Diamond Polishing Plant

Here is another view of a diamond polishing plant with rows of workmen at their benches. Notice in this, as in the previous picture, how very light the place is, as polishing diamonds is a very delicate operation and requires plenty of light.

forming an iron shell that held the contents in its grip under immense pressure. As the melted mass inside cooled the carbon separated from the iron in liquid drops.

Now, iron is like water in one respect. You know, as water turns into ice it expands. So iron, in passing from a liquid to a solid state, expands, and this expansion produces enormous pressure. The iron cooling inside the casing could not expand outwardly because of the shell, so it did all its expanding inwardly and so subjected these liquid drops of carbon to enormous pressure and they became solid crystals of diamonds. Then, by a

as the pressure is removed these "home-made" diamonds break up into fragments. The diamonds found in the earth are not so easily broken because, so to speak, they have got *used* to being diamonds; *they* were subjected to pressure for ages and ages. However, these magicians of the world of atoms—the chemists—are still working on this problem, and it is believed that in the course of time they will be able to make diamonds of sufficient size to compete with the natural diamonds.

Then, being so common, perhaps most people will not care much more for diamonds than they do now for

DIAMONDS
Three of the World's Greatest Diamonds

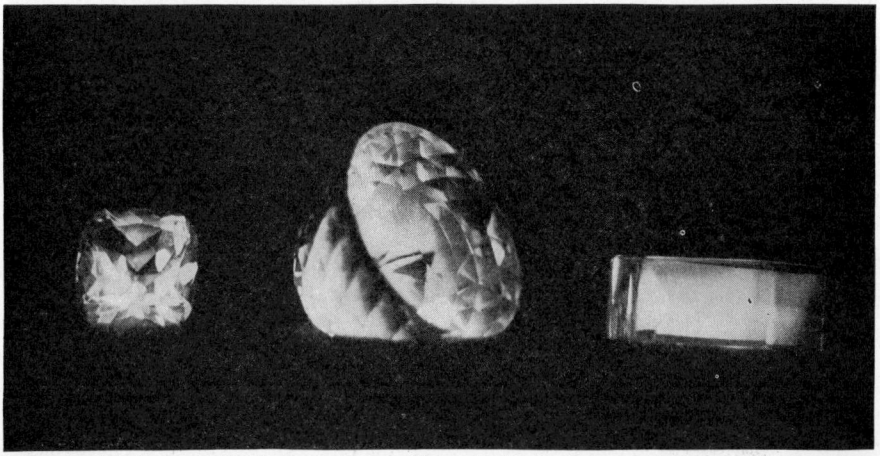

On the left is the Polar Star, a 40-carat diamond of rare purity and luster, without a flaw. (Maybe your big sister has a diamond ring that is a whole carat in weight. She is sure to be very proud of it.) This diamond was bought in England for the Russian collection of crown jewels and once belonged to Joseph Bonaparte.

The stone in the center is regarded by some people as the world's greatest diamond. It is known as the Great Mogul and was mined in India about 1640. It was as big as a hen's egg before being cut, and weighed 900 carats. Jemla, a wealthy diamond merchant, presented it to Shah Jehan of the Mogul dynasty of Hindustan—hence its name—GREAT MOGUL! It was the rarest gem in the ruling family's collection until Delhi was sacked by the Persians, when it passed into the possession of the Persian royal house. It is now in the royal museum at Teheran, Persia.

The Shah, on the right, also belongs to Russia, and is remarkable for its oblong shape. It is almost the same as when it was mined, that is, it needed very little cutting. The Shah belonged to Persia in its earlier history and is engraved in Arabic with the names of three Persian rulers. There is no cloud or flaw in this beautiful diamond, which weighs 86 carats.

dewdrops; for the preciousness of precious stones is due in part to the fact that there are so few of them.

There used to be still another reason; people thought precious stones would *do* things for you. Not only in the old days of Greece and Rome and the older days of Egypt, but in the Middle Ages, men— and some of them very wise and learned men —had these superstitions about stones. For example, they thought the diamond was deadly poison but that it protected the wearer against all poisons. Benvenuto Cellini, an eminent sculptor, writer and some other things not so creditable, tells us in his memoirs about how some enemy—he had many enemies, for he was a bad man—put what he thought was diamond dust in Cellini's salad. But it turned out to be

Story of Cellini's Salad

the dust from another kind of stone and so Cellini "thanked his stars" and wrote the story into his memoirs.

When you see in the portraits of some grandee of the Middle Ages, a finger ring prominently displayed, it is probably that he is wearing it not only because it is handsome, but because he believes in "safety first."

Opals were considered unlucky; and they are still so considered by foolish people. The story is told of a prominent man who had met with business misfortune and thought the opal was in part the cause of it; but, when he took the opal to a jeweler, he found it was not an opal at all, but what is called a "star stone."

A ruby is supposed to warn you of impending danger by turning black; emeralds expose false witnesses, and

The Diamond in the Dop

a jacinth is a great help to anyone who is ambitious to be "rich, wise and honorable." To be sure, jacinths *would* make you rich —if you had enough of them; but that's like catching a bird by putting salt on its tail, isn't it? The great difficulty is to catch the bird in the first place.

This shows the diamond cemented in the brass dop in which it is held while its face is polished.

The Sea

The Sea! the Sea! the open Sea!
The blue, the fresh, the ever free!
Without a mark, without a bound,
It runneth the earth's wide regions 'round;
It plays with the clouds, it mocks the skies,
Or like a cradled creature lies.

I'm on the Sea! I'm on the Sea!
I am where I would ever be—
With the blue above, and the blue below,
And silence wheresoe'er I go.
If a storm should come and awake the deep,
What matter? I shall ride and sleep.

I love—oh, how I love—to ride
On the fierce, foaming, brusting tide,
When every mad wave drowns the moon,
Or whistles aloft his tempest-tune;
And tells how goeth the world below,
And why the south-west blasts do blow.

I never was on the dull, tame shore
But I loved the great Sea more and more,
And backwards flew to her billowy breast,
Like a bird that seeketh its mother's nest;
And a mother she was, and is to me,
For I was born on the open Sea.

BARRY CORNWALL

THE WORLD AT ITS WORK
CEMENT INDUSTRY

Making Stone to Order

Making Models for Cement Decorations

This is a clay modelling room where designs are being made which will later be cast in cement. Some of them are for decorations on cement buildings, others are outdoor vases and urns. The process is identical with the modelling in clay which precedes the casting of a figure or bas-relief in bronze.

CEMENT is a binder. It is anything that holds other things together without the aid of screws, nails, rivets or cords. Glue, plaster of Paris and mortar are cements. But what is now commonly meant by cement is the artificial stone used in sidewalks and buildings. This is Portland cement. To make it, lime and clay rocks are crushed, burned and ground to a flour.

Why "Portland" Cement?

It is called Portland cement because it looks so much like a building stone much used in England which comes from the quarries on the Island of Portland. It was a brickmaker of Leeds, England, who made the first Portland cement and gave it its name. He mixed limestone with clay from the bed of the Thames.

Portland cement, when used, is mixed with water, sand and crushed stone, or gravel, and the mixture is known as concrete. This mixture is easily made to take almost any form you wish as easily as you mould clay in

1379

school. But you mustn't "stop on the job," for if you do the mixture will harden to stone and that's the end of it, so far as taking any further shapes is concerned. The concrete, instead of being shaped by hand as a sculptor shapes his little clay models, is poured into moulds. These moulds are made of wood, iron or plaster. Within a day after the mixture has been made, the concrete has hardened so that the moulds may be removed, and within a week you have a stone that is as hard as the sedimentary rocks on which nature has worked for ages in the stone presses of the sea.

Why You Mustn't Stop on the Job

More than that, this artificial stone grows harder and harder every year for some time and is much less affected by the weather than natural stone. You can have ivy wandering, in its picturesque way, over walls of concrete without doing any harm, while the acids from roots and from the decay of dead leaves eat into the stone of old buildings—like the ancient walls of Oxford, for example. But where, owing to the sinking of foundations of buildings and the settling of the ground under concrete walks, cracks are formed, Jack Frost gets into them and with his ice wedges pries them apart. Freezing water expands and if confined on all sides, exerts a pressure of 28,000 pounds to the square inch. No rock, either natural or artificial, can stand that!

How Cement Resists the Weather

By mixing ground up fragments of real rock into the cement, natural stone can be so closely imitated that it is difficult to tell the difference between the real and the artificial. The addition to Gore Hall, as the library building of Harvard College is called, is made of this imitation granite. The imitation matches the original building better than real granite would do, because the old granite had weathered and it takes some time for fresh granite to show the effects of weathering so that it will blend with an old building.

Cement and the San Francisco Earthquake

For underground foundation work, bridge and other piers, dams, reservoirs and great warehouses and docks, reinforced concrete is used. This is made of Portland cement, sand, gravel and broken granite, strengthened by twisted rods of iron or steel. This strong material, that stood best the earthquake shocks in San Francisco, is cheaper than stone or brick. It is fire and vermin proof, cool in summer, warm in winter and free from damp. It can be moulded into balustrades, basins, vases, benches and statues, to reproduce all the forms of ancient architecture and sculpture, at small cost. City parks and wealthy people are now using it in these ways, made of very white lime stone or marble dust. By and by, as lumber becomes more scarce and costly, we shall see more cement and concrete houses.

Beautiful Things Made of Concrete

How Concrete Helped the Engineers

Not only is this artificial stone so adaptable to every building purpose, but it has helped the architect and the engineer to work out building and engineering problems which would otherwise have been almost insurmountable, such as the building of the concrete walls of the Panama Canal, the tunneling of rivers, the construction of subways under the

CEMENT INDUSTRY

The Mountain They Blew Up

This is one of the mountains from which sections are blown out from time to time in order to get material for the cement mill. It is made almost entirely of limestone which you can see exposed on the mountain side. Limestone is made from the shells of ancient sea creatures.

streets of our great cities, and the immense irrigating plants in the arid regions of the West.

Use of Concrete on the Farm

Concrete is getting to be used more and more on the farm. It is employed for making almost everything you can think of that a farmer wants—a bridge across the run, fence posts, walks, barn floors, water troughs and tanks, lawn rollers, drains, posts and floors for corn cribs, foundations for the windmill, root cellars, hot houses, silos and buildings for the pigs. (The only way you can teach a pig to be neat is to give him a nice, clean house.)

Stone Mansions for Hens They even make concrete hens' nests, casting them in moulds that look like the little round-topped trunks people used to have in Grandmother's day. Just think of a little stone mansion for a hen's setting place and her babies to be born in!

"Laying" Stone with a Hose

One interesting way of laying concrete is to spray it out of a hose. The machine for doing this is called a "cement gun." The mixture is sprayed on walls either of stone or concrete that have cracked and need repairing and it is also used to change a frame house into a house of stone. They simply spray the cement on the weather boarding to the required thickness.

And, by the use of concrete, it is also possible to build a house first and set it up afterwards. That is to say, the walls are first cast in horizontal moulds and then they are raised to a vertical position.

By adding pigments a house can be given any color that is fancied. A stone gray Colonial or Italian villa cement house, with white pillars and trimming, and a red or green tile roof, is as beautiful as one could wish.

At first all Portland cement was imported, most of it from Germany, but American manufacturers now make more Portland cement than any manufacturers in the world and the quality is also the best in the world.

Blowing Up Mountains to Make Concrete

One of our illustrations shows a mountain which is made almost entirely of the limestone which you can see exposed on the side. The rest of the rock is covered with a sparse growth of vegetation. The rock in this mountain happens to have almost the exact proportion of clay already mixed with it to make cement, when properly treated. But, of course, you can't haul a whole mountain away to a cement mill; so the stone makers have to do something to such mountains before they can start on grinding them up in their mills. The next picture shows you what they did to this one. They bored holes in it here and there, put in sticks of dynamite and blew it up.

How They Blow Up the Mountain

This picture shows you how the cement makers blow up mountains; by boring holes here and there like the ones shown in the picture and inserting sticks of dynamite.

It took 50,000 pounds of dynamite to break up the rock as you see it. It is estimated that 300,000 tons, that is to say, 600,000,000 pounds of rock were thus broken up and made ready to be hauled away to the cement mill from this particular mass of rock. At the bottom of the picture you can see the opening of another tunnel into the rock. Men go into this tunnel to bore more holes for the dynamite sticks.

A Visit to a Cement Mill

In the next picture we are in one department of the mill in which this rock is ground. You will notice an electric motor at the bottom of the picture on the left. This motor turns what is called a conveyor, which carries the crushed rock from one machine to another. The conveyor is a belt run on pulleys that are curved out to hold it in the shape of a trough, so that the

CEMENT INDUSTRY
A Corner in the Drying Room

This is the department of a cement mill in which the rock is ground. The electrical motor which you see operates the conveyor which carries the crushed rock from one machine to another.

crushed rock or cement, as the case may be, will not spill out. You see they use these conveyors all through the mill from the beginning to the end of the process. First they carry crushed rock, ground to greater and greater degrees of fineness as it passes from one part of the mill to another; and finally they carry the finished product to the bins where it is stored.

You will notice that wherever there is a belt, it is carefully protected by screens reaching five feet from the floor. This is done so that workmen will not be caught in the belt. Notice also that arrangement over the shaft like the steps of an old-fashioned stile between country fields. This stairway is to enable workingmen to cross that shaft without the danger of being caught.

Now we are standing before the giants who stir the fires in the mill. They stir it by rolling over and over, because the fire is inside of them. The part of the kiln that is most prominent in the picture does not turn. The part that turns is the cylinder just back of these round fronts. You can see it plainly in the second kiln. These cylinders are enormous things, from 60 feet to 170 feet long, set on rollers, and they keep turning continually, like the wire cylinder of the cornpopper man. They are lined with firebrick to protect the outside from getting too hot, and are heated with pulverized coal. This coal is sprayed into the kiln right through the crushed rock, by a special spraying apparatus; and because it is in dust form and forced in with the proper proportion of air, it burns instantly, and goes off almost as quickly as gun powder. On account of this arrangement, they can feed

PICTURED KNOWLEDGE
The Giants That Stir the Fire

Here we are in the kiln room, looking down a long row of "giants that stir the fire."

in the coal in just the proper quantities to give the right heat.

Where the cement makers are fortunate enough to obtain limestone rock in which clay is already so well mixed that it is ready for the burning, just as it comes from the ground, it is simply dumped into the kilns without having much done to it. But in the case of ordinary limestone, clay must be added in the proper proportions.

How and Why the "Clinker" is Seasoned

When the rock and clay have been sufficiently heated in the kiln —that is to say to about 3,000 degrees—they melt and run together in the form of clinkers. These clinkers are made in much the same way that clinkers are made in a stove or a furnace. At this point in the proceedings, the heating is stopped and the clinker dumped out, while still hot, through a blast of steam. The steam, getting into the clinker, swells it full of little holes so that it becomes much like a sponge, and still more like pumice stone. This puffed-up clinker from the cement works kiln is carried out along the horizontal track you see in the picture, in steel buckets which are attached to an endless chain. At the proper point these buckets are tipped up by a device set there for the purpose. You see one of the buckets emptying just above that pyramid on top of the pile before us. This mass is called a storage pile, because the clinker is stored here for a certain length of time so that it can be seasoned by the weather. This makes it crumble more easily, and also gives it a certain amount of "experience" which stands it in good stead when it is finally made into cement, and must spend the rest of its life out of doors in the shape of sidewalks

CEMENT INDUSTRY
The Hot Clinker Going to the Seasoning Pile

Notice the bucket emptying just above the pile. Here the clinker is exposed to the weather in order to get "experience."

and things. As we shall see, however, it is given still further "experience" before it's sent out into the world. In the storage pile it is simply going through the "elementary grades," as it were.

The Journey Through the Tube Mills

After the clinker has seasoned sufficiently in the storage pile, it is taken back to the cement mill again and fed through enormous hoppers into what are called the tube mills.

Feed End of the Finish Tube Mills

This shows the part of the mill in which the cement is fed into the tube mills through the great hoppers which you see here, and on down into the big "coffee grinders."

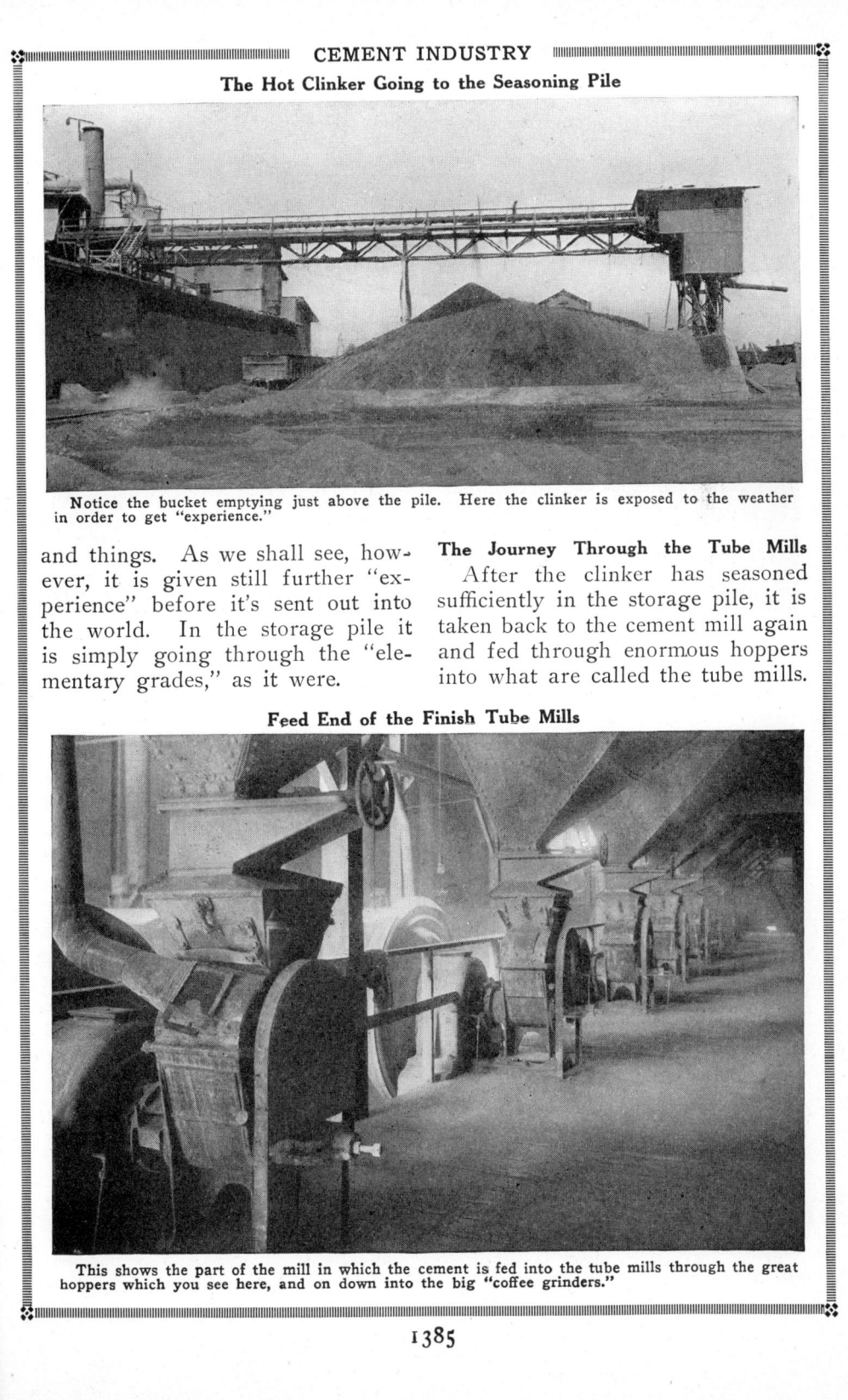

PICTURED KNOWLEDGE

In the Stockhouse Tunnel

Here we are inside of the tunnel through which runs the conveyor that carries the cement to the stockhouse.

In one of the illustrations we are looking into the department containing these tube mills. The clinker goes down through those hoppers into the front end of the mill, which, as you see, looks much like the coffee grinder in the grocery store, and is operated by a belt which runs inside of the protecting frame in front. In these "coffee grinders" the clinker is ground into pieces from the size of a walnut to the size of your fist. From the grinder it pours into what are called the "finishing tube mills," one of which is shown plainly to the left of the second grinder from where you are supposed to be standing. These tube mills are much like the kilns but they are not heated, and are much smaller. Their purpose is to grind the clinker into fine powder.

The grinding is done in a very curious way; something like the way in which the hen grinds up her food in her gizzard. To be sure, Biddy does not roll over and over —wouldn't that be funny?—as the tube mill does, but the mill is filled with little hard round things just as Biddy's gizzard is filled with gravel. These little round things are either flint pebbles or small steel balls made for the purpose and grind up the clinker as the mill turns.

In the Stockhouse Tunnel

In the picture of the stockhouse tunnel, the long covered trough on the right contains a belt conveyor similar to the one described under our fourth picture. You see the bottom of the trough is curved to conform to the shape of this belt. On this belt the cement, which is now finished with the exception of its final seasoning, is on its way to the stockhouse where this seasoning

CEMENT INDUSTRY
Concrete Foundations for Cannon

Courtesy Scientific American. © *Munn & Co*

Concrete is widely used in building foundations for cannon. Our illustration from the Scientific American shows a type of coast defense gun, which is mounted on wheels and runs on a track so that it may be quickly shifted from one point of attack to another. This is a cross section of the cannon platform and shows the base of the gun mounting locked in position, and the gun ready for firing.

takes place. The cement is coming through those inclined chutes just above the conveyor. You will notice that these chutes have covers with handles. This is to allow the inspector-man to pull down the cover at any time and take a sample of the cement from time to time.

The stockhouse to which the cement finally goes is just a series of bins with walls made of cement. Here the cement is left for ten days or more in order to season—until it is, it is apt to show some variation in the setting time. When it has been properly seasoned, it is carried by conveyors to the sacking machines, which weigh it into 100 pound sacks; or, if it is shipped in carload lots, these sacks are dispensed with and it is conveyed and weighed directly into the car.

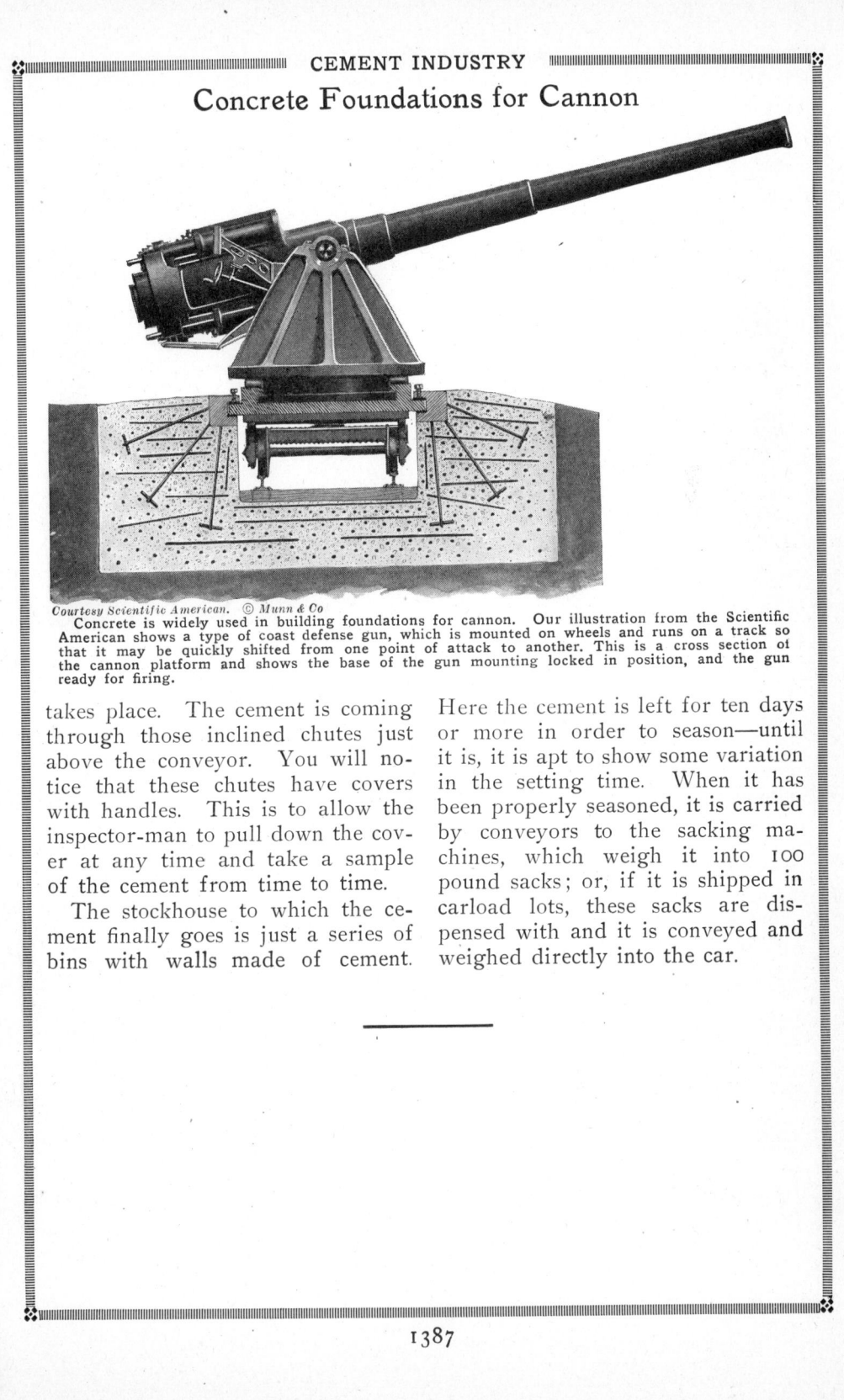

Down in a Salt Mine

The most wonderful salt mines in the world are those of Galicia, in Polish Austria. This picture shows a passage in one of these mines. The salt deposits there are 500 miles long, 20 miles wide and 1,200 feet in thickness. The salt walls of this passage look like a mass of icicle-coated fungi from the woods.

THE HOW AND WHY OF COMMON THINGS
THE SALT INDUSTRY

Story of a Pinch of Salt

In the Salt Mine

Sometimes the solid salt in a mine has to be blasted to loosen it. Here are men at work on it with pickaxes and shovels and a compressed air drill. The tube leading upward conducts the air which operates the drill.

Mr. Salt's Big Family

FOR one thing it is very interesting, because it is our only mineral food. It is one form of a metal called sodium. When you study chemistry in high school you will be told to call salt "chloride of sodium." The soda that is used in cooking is "bicarbonate of sodium," borax is a "biborate" and saltpeter "nitrate of sodium." Sodium furnishes us a big and useful family of chemical products.

The metal sodium is not found in nature, but always in one of its compounds. It is found oftenest as salt. Melting easily in water, this salt has been washed out of the earth and carried to the ocean. Then, when the waters of the sea were evaporated by the sun, salt, lime and other minerals were left behind. Ancient ocean beds that have dwindled down to lakes with few inlets and no outlet, like Great Salt Lake and the Dead Sea, have become as salt as brine. Away down in the earth are salt beds, covered with stone and pressed into rock salt crystals, that were made by such salt lakes drying up. When water falls to these beds, washes over them and then comes to the surface, we have salt springs.

1389

PICTURED KNOWLEDGE
This Is "Rock" Salt, Indeed!

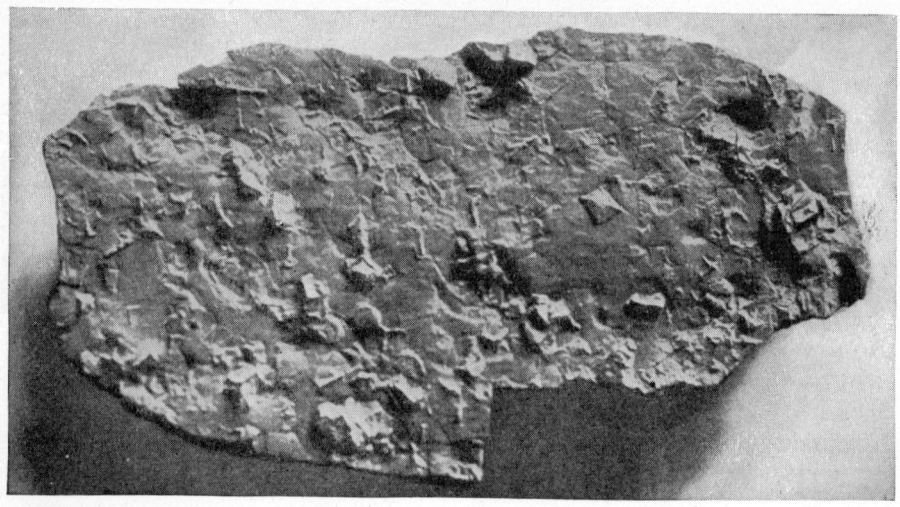

This stone was once part of the shore of a salt lake. The hot sun dried the briny water into little crystal pyramids of salt and hardened the sandy soil to rock.

The Geography of Salt

The salt we use is taken from mines, or is made by evaporating sea and salt-spring water. Over three million tons of salt are made in this country, from mines, springs and sea water, chiefly in New York, Michigan, Ohio, Pennsylvania, Illinois, Kansas, Louisiana, Utah, West Virginia, Texas and California. A good deal of it is changed into soda in factories.

Mexican Salt Venders

© Keystone View Co.

Here is a group of Mexican salt merchants squatting on the ground, and a man buying some of the big, coarse lumps from them.

The Chemistry of Salt

When the salt in the earth is exposed to the rain, sun and air, though it retains its white, crystalline form, the certain something in the salt which gives it its peculiar taste disappears—it has "lost its savor."

This is probably due to the great attraction of salt for water. You know how the salt cellar cakes and refuses to "give down" in rainy or hot summer weather. This characteristic is particularly noticeable in moist climates or on the

THE SALT INDUSTRY
The Salt in the Little Dead Seas

These men are working in a salt-pond; one of a series leading up to a salt refinery near San Francisco Bay. This must be the last pond in the series because it is only in the last pond that water has become so salty that it is allowed to dry out entirely and so leave the salt ready to be shoveled.

How and Why They "Spill the Salt"

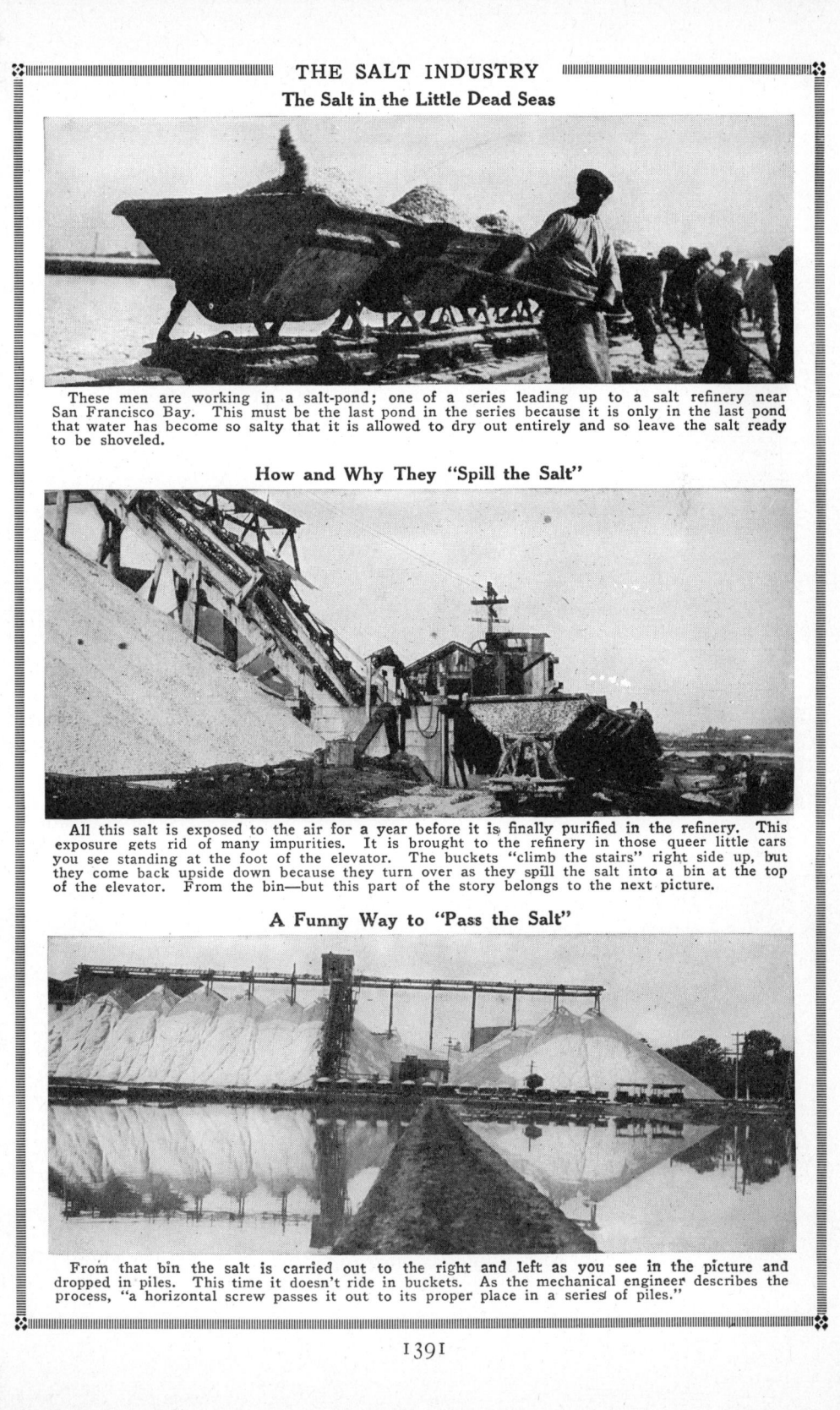

All this salt is exposed to the air for a year before it is finally purified in the refinery. This exposure gets rid of many impurities. It is brought to the refinery in those queer little cars you see standing at the foot of the elevator. The buckets "climb the stairs" right side up, but they come back upside down because they turn over as they spill the salt into a bin at the top of the elevator. From the bin—but this part of the story belongs to the next picture.

A Funny Way to "Pass the Salt"

From that bin the salt is carried out to the right and left as you see in the picture and dropped in piles. This time it doesn't ride in buckets. As the mechanical engineer describes the process, "a horizontal screw passes it out to its proper place in a series of piles."

Making Basket Salt

Basket salt is a coarse grade of salt that takes its name from the cone-shaped baskets used in making it. As the salt crystallizes from the vats of brine it is collected into the baskets by workmen. At the right of the picture is a shallow pan with its handle attached to the middle. It is used to skim impurities from the top of the crystallizing brine. Each vat is fed by a branch pipe leading from the large one running through the center of the room. The flow of brine is controlled by the wooden plugs you see in each pipe.

Heating Tanks for Brine

1—Heating tanks
2—Boiler room
3—Tanks for fire purposes

After the crude salt has been changed to brine, it is settled and clarified, then run into the heating tanks marked (1). It begins to evaporate and crystallize here. When it has been heated to the temperature of the vacuum pans which you see on the next page, it is drawn off into them. Back of the heating tanks is the boiler room. The chimneys are very high, as you see, so that the soot and smoke will be carried away. Each heating tank holds 75,000 gallons.

THE SALT INDUSTRY
Vacuum Pan for Crystallizing Salt

1—Upper section of pan
2—Condenser
3—Vapor line
4—Water pipe
5—Discharge pipe

Here are the upper and lower sections of one of the vacuum pans. Coils of steam pipes run through the upper section of the pan and keep the temperature high. When the air pressure is lessened, liquids boil and evaporate more readily, so part of the air in these pans is pumped out to make the salt crystallize quickly. There is a partial vacuum in them, hence their name, vacuum pans.

sea coast. Pure sodium chloride does not take up water from the atmosphere in this way, but certain other mineral salts which are always found along with it, collect moisture and make it gather in lumps instead of keeping the perfect granular form. This is why it is a good plan to keep the salt dish on the stove in the kitchen—it is continually drying out, losing by evaporation the moisture it may collect.

Long ago, cakes of very hard salt were used as money in Abyssinia, possibly because salt is essential to everyone. In early times, before the process of mining it or obtaining it from the ocean was thoroughly understood, it was a luxury which only the wealthy could afford.

1—Lower part of pan
2—Pipe carrying brine
3—Discharge chamber

Where the brine passes out of the pan.

PICTURED KNOWLEDGE

Collecting the Salt from the Brine

This is the method of collecting the crystallized salt in another salt manufacturing plant. Notice the kind of shovels used. They have holes in them through which the brine can drain as the salt is lifted up.

The Last Chapter in the Story of Salt

The air-tight cartons of table salt that you buy from the grocer are filled by a machine like this. It will fill twelve hundred cartons an hour. After filling, the girls put on the cover of each carton and seal it shut.

THE HOW AND WHY OF COMMON THINGS
ALUMINUM

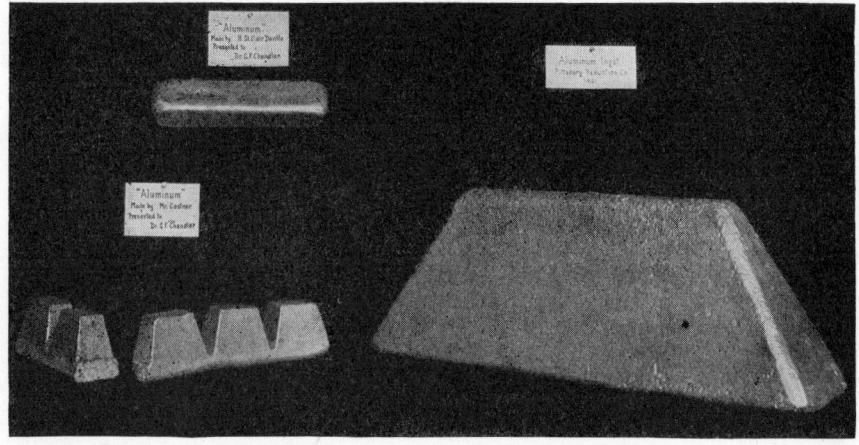

What Is Aluminum?

Aluminum As It Comes from the Smelter

Molten aluminum is run into molds just as copper and silver are. The shape of the mold varies according to the purpose for which the metal is to be used. The large block or ingot of aluminum is about 12 inches long, 5 inches high and 1½ inches wide at the base. If it were of silver or gold, it would be so heavy that you probably could not budge it from its resting place. But since it is aluminum you could easily pick it up, for it weighs only about five pounds, while a silver ingot of the same size, would weigh over 25 pounds, and a gold one almost 50 pounds.

"WHAT is aluminum?"

"Oh, that's an easy question," you say. "Aluminum is some kind of a metal that they make into teakettles and things."

So far, so good, but where does it come from and how does it get into the teakettle, so to speak?

When you know that aluminum is almost as common as dirt, because it is in the rocks and the soil everywhere, you might wonder why aluminum ware isn't still cheaper and why aluminum works aren't almost as common as tin shops used to be. The reason is that while aluminum is even more common in the earth than iron, it is not found everywhere in sufficiently concentrated form to make its extraction profitable and the process of extraction is expensive. Iron itself is another example of the same thing. While so widely distributed, it is only where it is found in the concentrated form of iron ore that it pays to mine it.

Going still deeper into the history of this aluminum teakettle, we run right into that Fairyland of Change known as "Chemistry." It was while he was making some experiments in what high school and college boys call the "lab" for short, that a certain college boy hit upon the process by which practically all the aluminum in the world is now made. This young man's name was Charles M. Hall, and he was a student at Oberlin College. In his

PICTURED KNOWLEDGE
The Plump and Cheery Teakettle

As bright and shiny as the copper teakettles of our grandmothers, with only half the labor necessary to keep it so, much lighter and more durable than the enameled pots of our own day, and always free from rust, the aluminum kettle is truly the housewife's joy.

study of chemistry he knew of the old process invented by a German chemist in 1827, but this process was so slow and expensive that the extracted aluminum was a scientific curiosity rather than an article of commerce. He got to thinking why couldn't aluminum be taken from the ore by using electricity for heating purposes. In the old process the aluminum ore was put into a pot or vat of molten metal which "soaked up" the aluminum, as the warm water in a cup of tea absorbs the sugar.

So Hall made a rectangular iron pot and lined it thickly with carbon, the material out of which those "burning sticks" are made in an arc light. He suspended cylinders of the carbon above these pots with the ends of the cylinders dipping into the pieces of metal to be melted. When the electricity was turned on, it passed through the metal and into the cylinders and in so doing, melted the metal and kept it in this molten state. When anything is heated by electricity—the filament of an incandescent lamp, for instance —the heating is due to what is called "resistance," that is to say, the resistance made by the substance heated to the passage of the electricity. It seems to be a kind of friction.

After the metal in the pots has been reduced to a molten state, the aluminum ore, properly ground up, is added from time to time. For some reason this reduces the resistance which the electricity encounters, and the workmen can tell when the aluminum ore has been dissolved; for there is an incandescent lamp attached to each melting pot and when the light which goes out when the aluminum ore is first

ALUMINUM
Forms of Aluminum

Aluminum that helps mother in the kitchen.

stirred into the "bath" (as it is called) brightens up again, the workmen proceed to stir in a fresh supply.

When the aluminum is dissolved the bottom of the pot and is drawn off while the rest of the material in the ore remains as dross.

The carbon cylinders and the carbon lining of the pots are charged

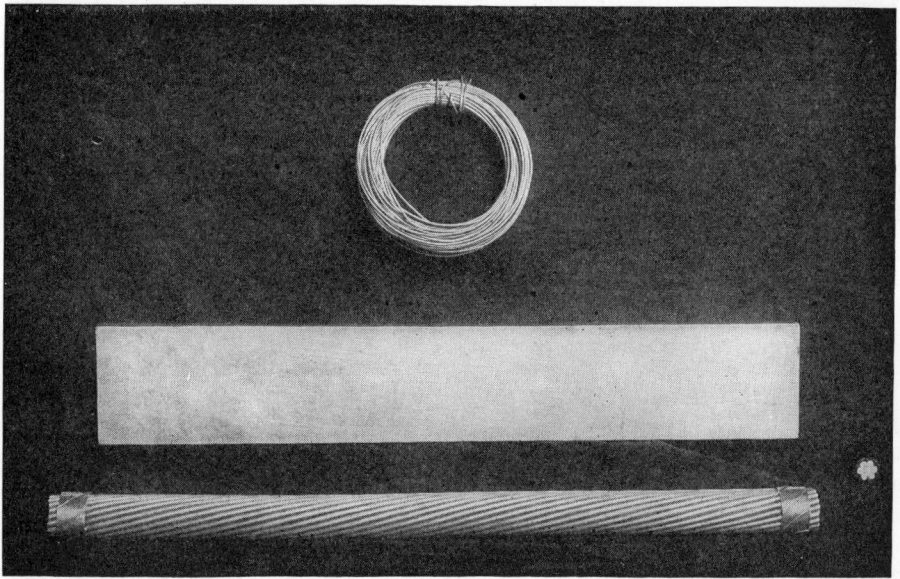

Besides being so conveniently light, aluminum can be drawn into wire and rolled into sheets, though it lacks the strength of some of the heavier metals. At the top is a roll of fine aluminum wire and below is a cable of heavy wires. A cross-section of aluminum wires bound together by a gutta percha band is shown at the right. In this form aluminum is used instead of copper for carrying electric currents when lightness is desirable.

it is a kind of "dissolution of partnership," such as sometimes takes place in business affairs; the pure, or nearly pure, aluminum sinks to with two different kinds of electricity—the carbon cylinders being the negative and the carbon lining, the positive. The result is that the

1397

PICTURED KNOWLEDGE
A Metal Basket

Aluminum is so light and pliable that it can be woven like reeds, into a basket. And a basket made of aluminum will last a lifetime.

aluminum is attracted by the carbon in the pot, while the dross is attracted by the carbon cylinders. The theory is that substances which yield to electric action in this way, are made up of what are called "ions," and that these ions are at first held together in pairs, one ion being negative and its partner positive. The assumption is that when acted upon by electricity, these positive and negative chums of the invisible world of the ions, separate because they are more strongly drawn by their opposites in the negatively and positively charged carbon of the melting pots and the carbon cylinders.

So all this is how you came to have that nice aluminum teakettle and things. Before it could finally be shaped into the teakettle and saucepan and all, it had first to be rolled, of course, into sheets like tin and then shaped by what are called "stamping machines."

But what would you say if I told you that that sapphire in Mother's ring owed its beautiful red color to aluminum? It is the oxide or rust of aluminum that gives the beautiful blue to the sapphire and red to the ruby. You know that even rusted iron has a reddish tinge.

Yet, one of the advantages of aluminum when pure, as it is when made into the metal of commerce, is that it will not rust.

The Pageant of History

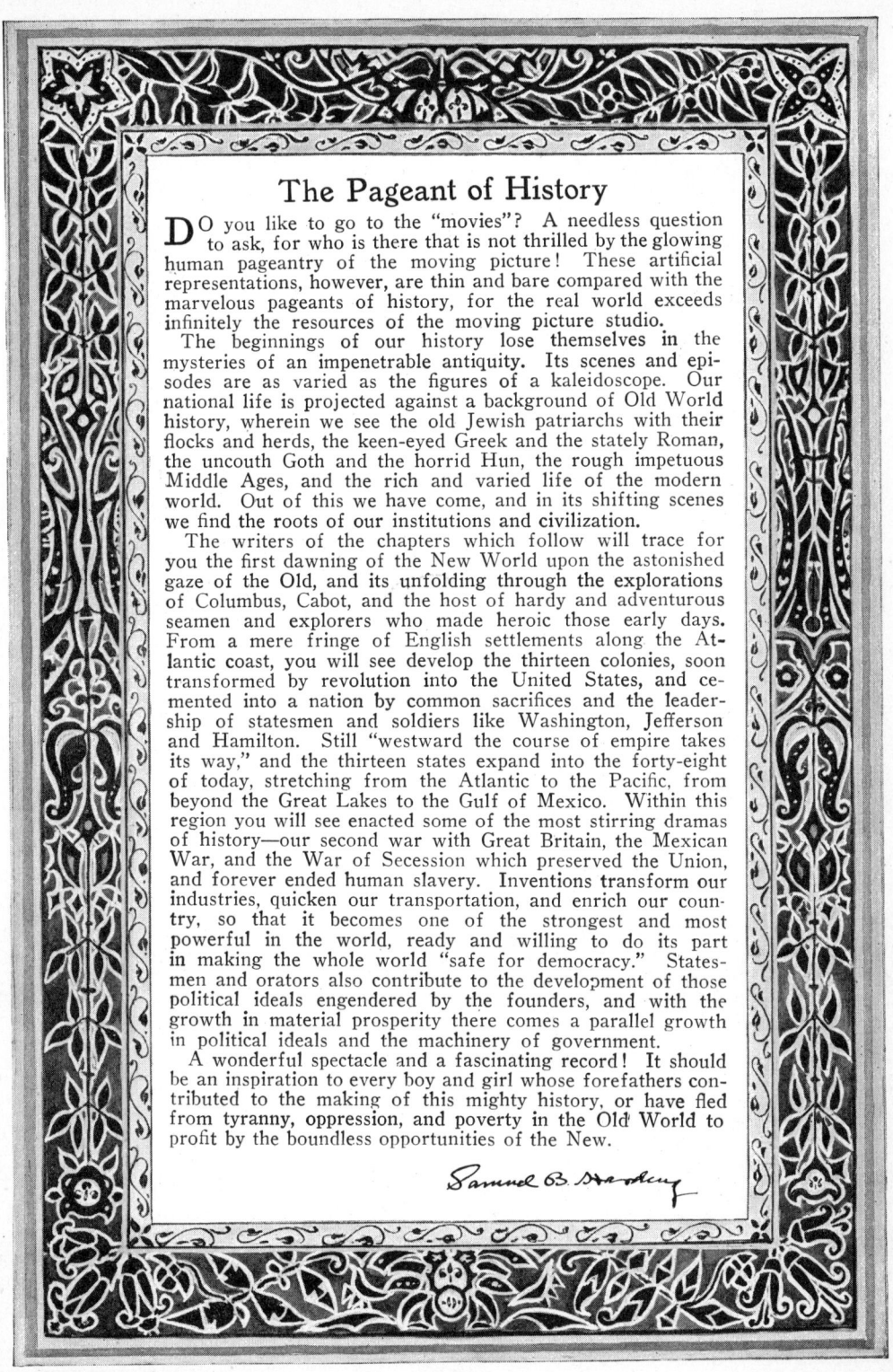

DO you like to go to the "movies"? A needless question to ask, for who is there that is not thrilled by the glowing human pageantry of the moving picture! These artificial representations, however, are thin and bare compared with the marvelous pageants of history, for the real world exceeds infinitely the resources of the moving picture studio.

The beginnings of our history lose themselves in the mysteries of an impenetrable antiquity. Its scenes and episodes are as varied as the figures of a kaleidoscope. Our national life is projected against a background of Old World history, wherein we see the old Jewish patriarchs with their flocks and herds, the keen-eyed Greek and the stately Roman, the uncouth Goth and the horrid Hun, the rough impetuous Middle Ages, and the rich and varied life of the modern world. Out of this we have come, and in its shifting scenes we find the roots of our institutions and civilization.

The writers of the chapters which follow will trace for you the first dawning of the New World upon the astonished gaze of the Old, and its unfolding through the explorations of Columbus, Cabot, and the host of hardy and adventurous seamen and explorers who made heroic those early days. From a mere fringe of English settlements along the Atlantic coast, you will see develop the thirteen colonies, soon transformed by revolution into the United States, and cemented into a nation by common sacrifices and the leadership of statesmen and soldiers like Washington, Jefferson and Hamilton. Still "westward the course of empire takes its way," and the thirteen states expand into the forty-eight of today, stretching from the Atlantic to the Pacific, from beyond the Great Lakes to the Gulf of Mexico. Within this region you will see enacted some of the most stirring dramas of history—our second war with Great Britain, the Mexican War, and the War of Secession which preserved the Union, and forever ended human slavery. Inventions transform our industries, quicken our transportation, and enrich our country, so that it becomes one of the strongest and most powerful in the world, ready and willing to do its part in making the whole world "safe for democracy." Statesmen and orators also contribute to the development of those political ideals engendered by the founders, and with the growth in material prosperity there comes a parallel growth in political ideals and the machinery of government.

A wonderful spectacle and a fascinating record! It should be an inspiration to every boy and girl whose forefathers contributed to the making of this mighty history, or have fled from tyranny, oppression, and poverty in the Old World to profit by the boundless opportunities of the New.

Samuel B. Bradley

The Eskimo Boy's "Shot Gun"

In order to be reasonably sure to get something to eat, most of the time, when he got to be a man, one of the first things an Indian boy had to learn was how to hunt. This picture shows how Eskimo boys got birds for food, by throwing at them a bunch of small ivory balls which they could use over and over again, because they were fastened to thongs. Being tied together at one end, these little balls would spread out so that they covered more space and were more likely to hit the bird, acting in this respect much like a shot gun as compared with a rifle.

STORIES OF AMERICAN HISTORY
THE INDIANS

How the Red Man Lived Before the White Man Came

In the Big Chief's House

Here we are looking into the house or tepee of a chief. It reminds us something of the hall of one of the great barons of the Middle Ages, with its groups of shields and weapons. On the right you see the buffalo head-dress used for the buffalo dance. Among the spears leaning against the wall are some poles with scalps attached which were used during special ceremonies. The bones you see lying about the floor were probably thrown down by the Indians while eating, and immediately appropriated by the dogs. Even the fine lords and ladies of the Middle Ages, you remember, when at table, threw the bones on the floor. Hanging from the post is a willow basket used in fishing, and below, a hand-decorated paddle, used by Indians in canoeing. On the floor are a mortar and pestle for grinding corn and another for grinding colored earth with which the Indian painted himself. You can also see wooden bowls and Indian pottery. The chief is apparently holding a council with other members of the tribe and the pipe is being passed.

OUR histories begin by saying that before Columbus, America was inhabited by Indians. But in the crowding events of the settlement of our continent, there is room to speak of them only as they affected the lives of white colonists. So they appear to us as painted savages on the warpath. This image is true, but incomplete. Indians had to make a living, and under much harder conditions than white men. So you may be sure they had many other absorbing interests and activities beside fighting.

Again, most of us think of all Indians, simply as "Indians"; as if they were all alike.

Think a moment and you will see that this could not be so. White people are not all alike. Many nations came to America from the Old World; English,

French, Spanish, Dutch, and others. Some were tall and fair, some small and dark. They differed in manners and customs, education, natural ability, dispositions and ideals; and they differed so very much in language that they could not understand each other. The Indian nations of America varied as widely, and in similar ways. There was, indeed, more reason why they should vary. Europe was thickly settled, and travel and trade were easy and constant, so that people acquired habits and knowledge from one another. But in all North America there were no more than a half-million people, separated by large areas of heavily forested mountains, deserts and sterile coasts. There were no horses for rapid travel and only the Eskimos and some Canadian forest tribes had trained dogs. All land journeys were made on foot, and water travel was in small boats and canoes. Tribes and even nations were isolated.

Do All Indians Look Alike to You?

The Different Types of Indians

While the Indians all belonged to the red-skinned, semi-barbarous race, and were at the Stone Age in development when the white man came, they differed in nearly everything else. On the basis of languages there were one hundred and twenty nations, and within a nation there were as many dialects, often, as there were scattered tribes. Even those close enough to fight and trade, differed in appearance, in disposition, in intelligence, in their skill as hunters and in the arts and crafts. The degree of progress was determined by character, but the direction of this progress, by climate and natural feature belts. Within a given region all tribes would have to learn the same things and use the same materials.

Many Nations and Tongues

Fishing and Photography

When the Indians went out to spear fish in the winter, they put hoods over their heads while watching for the fish through the ice, very much as the photographer covers his head when taking your picture, and for a similar reason. By shutting out the light they were able to see the fish more clearly. You see the Indian in the foreground is just taking his fish off the hook. These hoods didn't fit close around the head but were held up by sticks. To attract the fish, the fishermen had a stone image of a fish on the end of a pole which they thrust down into the water.

THE INDIANS

This is to be seen most plainly in the Eskimos. Their land was that broad, northern end of our continent, a five-thousand-mile belt of frozen, treeless plains, that stretches from Greenland to Alaska. Uninhabitable by white men or by any other Indians, it has for unknown ages been occupied by small scattered bands of hardy Eskimos. They form a real nation, distinct from all other primitive peoples of America, and may, indeed, have a different origin. It is thought they may have crossed to Alaska from the Arctic shores of Siberia. A small people, the men are seldom more than five feet high. While they have the straight, coarse black hair and high cheek bones of the red race, their features are flat and their skins a yellowish-brown. As a rule they are good-tempered, and wars among them are practically unknown.

To provide themselves with food, clothing, shelter, tools, weapons and transportation in that barren land of bitter cold, these people had only snow, sea and land animals, a little driftwood that floated to their desolate shores from blown-down trees and wrecked ships, the ledges of stone and fields of moss and stunted bushes that were uncovered in the brief summers, and packs of wolfish dogs. Yet what wonders they have accomplished. Some think them the cleverest of all American tribes. With the least material, and under the hardest conditions they have done most.

Cleverness of the Eskimos

The Indian Warrior and His Striped "Uniform"

This is the kind of military costume an Indian put on when he was ready for the warpath. The painted designs on an Indian's body usually indicated that he belonged to a certain society; for the Indians had fraternities just as college boys do. Sometimes, however, the designs were symbols of some dream he had had, telling him that he was going to distinguish himself in battle, and he wore them to remind the dream spirits of the success they had promised so they wouldn't forget him in the day of trial.

They build a warm, half-buried igloo, framed up with drift timbers and whale ribs, and covered with turf. Lacking these, they build equally well with snow blocks, so cut and fitted that the walls rise spirally and close with a key-block in a perfectly arched, round dome. The animals they kill furnish their food and clothing, summer tent, boat and sledge covering, and dog harness. Out of the bones they make the frames of their boats and sledges, the handles of tools, shafts of harpoons and spears, their snow-saws for building their houses, and skin-dressing knives. The sinews are made into thread and cord, and the fat gives them light and fire.

Explorers say that the Eskimos' stove-lamp, while extremely simple, is the greatest of all Indian inventions. It is made of a slab of soapstone, of which there are long worked quarries. Three feet long and half as wide, it is a clam-shell shaped tray with an upturned rim. When this shallow vessel is set up on a block, filled with seal oil and fitted sling-shot ivory balls on strings, for killing birds, that are his own inventions. He can make good snowshoes of whalebone and strips of sealskin, and a fire-drill of bone and

Why the Indians Struck the Post

When the Indians were about to go on the warpath they made it a point to work up as much enthusiasm as possible, and the ceremony called, "Striking the Post," was part of this preparation. The post was painted red, symbolic of war, and the musicians of the tribe, sitting on the ground, sang songs of war-like deeds while others beat on the drums and shook rattles. If you had been at one of these performances, after this had gone on some little time, you would have heard a sharp yell. This would mean that some warrior felt moved to get up and recite his exploits. The music would immediately stop and he would have the most profound attention while, dressed in his bravest feathers and paint, he would step out with his club or lance and strike the post to illustrate what he meant to do to the enemy. When the warrior finished his story of what he had done and what he meant to do, the whole crowd of warriors would join in yells of victory and defiance. Then the music would be resumed until another warrior took the stage. This ceremony lasted for several hours. The early Greeks had war dances similar to those of our American Indians and no hero in Homer showed more fire in words and acts.

with wicks of dry, twisted moss, it warms a big igloo for several families, cooks the food and gives the light of several kerosene lamps.

The Eskimo also makes a harpoon with which he can kill seal, walrus, whales and polar bears. The long, narrow blade of chipped flint is set in a slot in a wood, bone or ivory tusk shaft, and securely fastened with fish glue and sinews. He has the smaller, ordinary Indian spear for killing land animals; and a spring dart and a cluster of

His Many Other Inventions

sinew. The squaws make needles of fish bones, and household vessels and baskets of tusks, whalebones and split roots. The rib-framed, skin-covered kayak is a true canoe that, in workmanship and usefulness, is second only to the birch-bark canoe of the Great Lakes.

When he has open water, as on the west coast of Alaska, the Eskimo makes the umiak. This is a square-bowed, row and sailboat, big enough for thirty people. It is covered with seal skins and the sail, fitted to a twelve-foot mast, is made

THE INDIANS

Carrying Away the Wounded

The Indians used to carry the wounded from the battlefield much as wounded soldiers are carried on stretchers today. The litter was made of two poles lashed together, with a blanket fastened to them. It was carried partly with the hands and partly by the supports you see across the men's shoulders. Indians would carry a wounded comrade miles and miles in this way when they were retreating from an enemy.

"In the Trenches," Among the Aztecs

This looks a good deal like one of the trenches on the battlefields of the European War. Although it is a fortification instead of an entrenchment, it is constructed on much the same principle as the trenches with its in-and-out angles, called in military language, "salients and re-entrants."

PICTURED KNOWLEDGE

A Luxurious Indian Water Craft

Here we have quite a luxurious way of traveling employed by the Indians. Boats like this were called balzas by the whites, after a Spanish word. The Indians had the balza under another name before the white man came. With the balza the Indians could undertake voyages that were not possible with a canoe. Notice how the balza is supplied with a comparatively smooth floor, a place of shelter and a place for keeping a fire and cooking the meals to be served in the "dining room," which was under that grass-covered roof. Notice the pilot, and how the keel is fastened to the raft, projections being thrust between the logs and held with wooden pins.

of seal intestines, split into ribbons and sewed with sinews.

The Dawn of the Fine Arts

And the Eskimo is an artist. He ornaments his favorite tools. On the top of his harpoon and spear he carves little heads, claws and tusks in ivory. The work is crude, but it is a striking example of the deep instinct for art in the human mind. There emerges this sense of beauty, in spite of the stark world around him.

Every Indian tribe in America had some artistic ability,—in carving, engraving, modeling, embroidery, painting or picture-writing. The most advanced tribes had several of these arts; some only one, but that highly developed. The North Pacific Coast Indians, who lived immediately south of the Alaskan Eskimos, were expert sculptors of

Various Forms of Art

wood. The mountainous shores were covered with cedar, fir, hemlock and other straight-grained trees that were easily worked. With stone axes and chisels they felled trees, split them into planks and built good timber houses. And they made canoes of hollowed and spread cedar logs, with sharp prows for bucking ice. They covered everything they made with carvings.

Before their doors they set up totem poles from twenty to fifty feet high that, in grotesque human masks and the figures of birds and beasts, set forth the historic emblems of a family. The carving was in bold relief and was colored black, red and yellow, with clay pigments. Totem poles were made by no other Indians, but similar sculpturing in stone was done by the Aztecs and Mayas of Mexico; and the geometric designs appear on the baskets, blankets,

Family Coats of Arms

THE INDIANS

Gathering the Rice Crop

While the Indians had gardens and farms in a small way, they depended as much as possible on the free gifts of nature for their food. Here you see the Indian women gathering wild rice which was found in the shallow waters of regions and lakes in the upper Mississippi region. It ripened in September. Usually two or three women worked together. One took the bow and the other the stern of a moderately sized hunting canoe, previously cleaned and made perfectly water-proof and dry. Pushing the canoe into the wild rice field, they bent the stalks in handfuls over the side and beat out the grain with paddles. Besides being served as we serve rice, it was roasted. Children were particularly fond of it in this form and the hunters carried a supply with them. It was put in bags of vegetable fibre and kept throughout the winter.

wampum belts and pottery of distant tribes. Together with certain root-words found in all Indian languages, these point to a common origin for the most widely separated and dissimilar tribes.

Toboggans, Snowshoes, and Canoes

To find other Indians as clever as the Eskimos you must go down to the Great Lakes. The forest tribes of Central Canada made just two good things—the flat-bottomed toboggan sled and the snowshoe. As the snowshoe was used in all the colder parts of America, *How the Snowshoes Were Made* you should know how it was made. The frame was a slender, split sapling, of some light, tough wood that could be bent to an oval, with the ends bound together in a point at the back. Braces across the middle served as a foot rest. The entire space was filled in, like a tennis racket, with a netting of rawhide. With such snowshoes securely tied on, hunters could skim over frozen lakes and streams, across prairies, through open woodlands and up and down hills. They could outrun wolf-packs and overtake deer, buffalo, moose and caribou.

The snowshoe and birch-bark canoe were possessed by all the tribes of Southern Canada and Northeastern United States. East of the Mississippi from the St. Lawrence to the Gulf of Mexico was one of the two most populous regions of America. Game, fish, nuts and berries were abundant, and crops of corn, beans, pumpkins and tobacco could be grown in the fertile soil; and there were the best of waterways for travel. Here the Indian dians for neighbors. The Iroquois, known as the "Six Nations," occupied New York State, between the Hudson and Lake Erie.

Like the Algonquins, they had

How the Women Guarded the Corn Fields

Here is another example illustrating the interesting variety of things the Indian women had to do. They are "shooing" the birds out of the corn fields by beating on pans and shouting and waving pieces of cloth. Birds, you may be sure, were very thick in those days. The boys and girls also helped and enjoyed the work hugely. In the spring the children also helped to plant the corn. Mother, although she never studied the art of teaching, was very clever at keeping them interested and showing them how. The work was done in the spirit of gaiety and frolic. Whenever a little papoose missed the hill in which he should have planted corn, mother and the other children laughed at him and he laughed too, but he took particular care not to do it again you may be very sure. Who would think of the wild Indians having little kindergarten schools of their own like that.

reached his finest physical development. He was tall, lean, coppercolored, with bold features and proud bearing. The braves were a race of hunters, fishers, tool and weapon makers, and fighters; the squaws skilful at farming and the handicrafts.

The Three Great Nations East of the Mississippi

East of the Mississippi were three great nations. The numerous tribes of the Algonquins were scattered along the St. Lawrence River, from New England to Minnesota and southward to the Ohio. A peaceable people, if unmolested, they had the ill fortune to have the Iroquois Indians for neighbors.

farms and the best of hunting and fishing grounds. Every year they stored quantities of food in their tribal "long houses" that were fortified with stockades. Their trade with Atlantic Coast Indians, exchanging dried meat, skins, arrow-heads and tobacco for salt, wampum shell beads, dried clams and oysters was highly developed; and so was their political organization. A true, strong confederacy, they had a trained army, and leaders skilled in war and statecraft. Naturally ferocious, they raided villages from Montreal to the Mississippi. The Algonquins fled before them to refuges along the upper lakes.

Government and Commerce

THE INDIANS
In a Dakota Village

The Dakotas had two kinds of houses. One was the cone-shaped wigwam which could easily be taken down and moved, and which was used when the tribes were moving in search of game. The other kind of house, shown here, made up their permanent villages. The houses in a village like this were covered with bark, usually from the elm tree. The framework for the walls and roof was made of saplings fastened by withes or the sinews of the buffalo. On this the bark was laid and secured by a framework of saplings resting on it.

How the Chippewas Built Their Bee-Hive Huts

This picture not only shows you how the Chippewa's hut looked when you got up close to it, but also how these huts were built. The shape is very much the same as that of the Eskimo ice hut. You notice who is doing all the work, don't you,—the women; while the two plumed warriors are sitting on the ground enjoying their pipes and either discussing international affairs among the tribes or remarking what a fine day it is.

The Algonquins could fight, run away, gather a host of warriors and return because they made the most and the best canoes in America, for they possessed the land of the yellow birch tree. For gunwale, ribs and stiffening strips they used the same light, tough, bendable wood that was used in snow-shoe and hunting-bow. The frame was lashed together with deer tendons. Over it was stretched the cover of birch bark, sewed with sinews, and with holes and seams filled with pitch and spruce gum. The sides were often decorated with painted figures or porcupine quill embroidery. As Longfellow says in Hiawatha: the birch-bark canoe lay on the water "like a yellow leaf in autumn." In these frail boats Indians made voyages of hundreds of miles, crossing wide lakes and twisting through foaming rapids. There were no birch trees in the South. The Natchez Indians of the lower Mississippi, and the Florida or Mobile tribes of the Gulf Coast could make nothing better than the pirogue. The pirogue was a clumsy, hollowed cypress log which they pushed along with poles on every sluggish stream.

The Arrow Straightener

The Indian straightened the shafts of his arrows with a piece of horn like this. It had holes of different sizes for different arrows. Through one of these holes, however, was a string to which was tied a cross stake held to the back of the hand by a string between two fingers, so that it would not slip while in use.

The northern Indians of the forests and prairies made the best bows and arrows. Several skilled crafts went into the making of them. Certain light, tough, flexible wood had to be found, seasoned and shaped for the bow. Only a rod of service tree, a reed or cane would do for the arrow shaft, and this was straightened by heating and drawing repeatedly through a hole in horn or stone. The toughest deer sinew was used for a string. Feathers carefully selected and adjusted to the shaft gave lightness and speed. Each tribe had its expert workmen who could chip flint into perfect arrow-heads—plain for hunting, barbed for war. A few tribes around Lake Superior and in Mexico hammered copper nuggets into arrow-heads. The weapon was made in several sizes, suited to different purposes. The forest Indian's bow was short for ease in

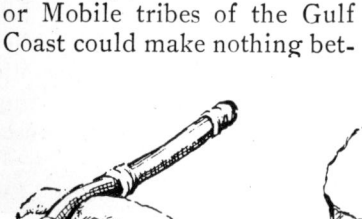

Stone Ax   Wooden Dipper / Stone Hand Mill   Spear Head

managing under trees. The prairie hunter had a long, strong bow, with an arrow-head like a double edged knife-blade, for killing the buffalo. There were small bows for boys to practice with. In the war weapon the arrow-head was often steeped in poison and set horizontally to the bow, to strike between the ribs of an enemy. The hunting arrow-head was set vertically.

The fire-drill, too, whether twirled between the palms, or with a bow or string, was a skilfully made tool, with its rigid shaft, rough stone point, and pitted fire-board where, by friction, dust was heated to sparks in a few seconds. And there were stone spear-points, chisels, knife-blades, axes, and tomahawks of obsidian, a glass-like volcanic rock that could be brought to perfect shape and edge only by long and patient chipping and grinding. The chief source of obsidian was the cliffs of Yellowstone Park, so there must have been trading between the eastern Indians and the Shoshones of the northern Rockies. It is known that the Algonquin tribes went to the head of Lake Superior in their canoes and had dealings with the Dakotans, Sioux and Mandans to the west. They had, besides, to make the stone or wood planting stick,—a pointed spade—hoes of deer and buffalo shoulder blades, skin-scraping knives of clam shells, needles of fish bones and thorns, and stone and wooden troughs and mortars for pounding corn. Life in the American wilderness was complicated and toilsome for both braves and squaws.

Grinding the meal.

The Algonquin tribes built the big, domed wigwam, like a circus tent. Often fifty feet in diameter, it sheltered several families. The frame of saplings was covered with bark or with grass mats woven by squaws. Mats divided it into family compartments around a central fire. The Iroquois Indians built the better, square-sided "long house" of timber and bark, often inclosing a village in a stockade of posts. Each village had its council house, quite one hundred feet long, where all the warriors could gather. In the South, where canes and willows covered every river bottom, the house walls were often woven in basket work over a frame of timbers, and plastered with clay. Out on the prairies, where wood was scarce, the Omahas set up the tent tepee of poles and buffalo hides. On the grassy plains hunting journeys were long, and the tepee could be carried on drags and set up anywhere. In the deserts of the Southwest, where cool shelter was needed from burning suns, the thick-walled house of adobe, or of stone was built.

Long Houses of the Iroquois

PICTURED KNOWLEDGE
Indians Playing Ball, Everybody to Bat

When the Indians played ball, everybody went to bat at once armed with those crooked sticks. This is the game we now know as Lacrosse. It was played in the winter when the hunts were over, or in the summer when the game was unfit to kill. The opposing sides often came from two different villages, so you see they even had the beginnings of a league. The game began midway between two goals. At the start one of the older men of the tribe threw the ball into the air and the players all endeavored to catch it on their bats. The one who caught it threw it in the direction of the goal of the opposite party and if caught by one of the same side it was carried on in the same direction; if by one of the other side, of course, it as started back toward the opposite goal. The one who caught it had the right before throwing it to run as far as he could until overtaken by one of the other party. Then he must throw it. You see it was a kind of combination of baseball, basket ball and tennis.

Indian Women Playing Plum Stones

Men, women, and children among the Indians played what the Dakotas called Kun-tah-soo, "Game of the Plum Stones." Either plum stones or pebbles were used and each stone was marked differently and had a different value. One stone would have on it the picture of a turtle, for example, another a sparrow-hawk, and so on. The sparrow-hawk ranked high and if two sparrow-hawks were turned up in a single throw, that alone won the game. The stones were either thrown in a little pit in the ground or shaken in a wooden bowl and thrown out on a robe. That is the way the women are playing it here. The bowls were often ornamented with figures similar to those on the stones. This was to bring good luck. Of course, if it brought as much good luck to one player as it did to the other, these "good lucks" would cancel each other, wouldn't they? It seems the Indians didn't think of that.

THE INDIANS
Indians on Their Travels

"Every-once-in-a-while" was moving day among the Indians. If you are fond of traveling, perhaps this is one of the things about being an Indian you might have enjoyed, for the Indian's life was one of almost perpetual travel. He traveled with the change of season, moving south in winter and north in summer. He traveled in pursuit of game. If he had bad luck in hunting or fishing, or there had been a good deal of death or sickness in the tribe, or some chief had a bad dream, down came the wigwam, the family belongings were strapped to the simple "moving van" such as you see attached to the horses in the picture, the head of the family mounted the horse, and his wife trudged behind, carrying things for which there wasn't room on the "moving van." As the head of the family used to expose his life in battle and endure hunger and cold in his long and often fruitless tramps for game, it was considered fair that his wife should do the larger part of the other heavy work. And no matter whether they had much or little they never complained.

Arts of the Tanner, Weaver and Potter

Various Uses of Leather — Wherever deer were plentiful all tribes had the art of dressing skins. The hair was loosened by soaking the hides in lime water. Then hair and flesh sides were scraped clean with clam shells. When stretched, dried and rubbed full of oil the skins were as soft as cloth, and looked like the pretty yellow chamois skins you buy in a drug store. They were made into shirts, petticoats, leggings and moccasins, and were decorated with cut fringes and embroidery of colored porcupine quills. It formed the foundation of the war bonnet of eagle feathers, the arrow-case and the wampum belt.

Basket and mat weaving, of grasses, reeds, fiber plants, palm leaves and flexible bark, was a universal art. The Algonquins of the upper lakes and the southwestern desert tribes still make baskets that are prized for their workmanship and beauty. When the strong, coarse *Pottery and Baskets* baskets were filled in with pitch they were used for water jars. When coated with clay they became cooking pots, for the clay hardened in the fire. Basket weaving led to both cloth weaving and pottery. The Navajos still call their earthenware cooking pots "mud baskets." But good pottery was made only by a settled, advanced people. The Algonquins and Iroquois were both great travelers, making annual journeys to distant hunting grounds, and were often on the warpath.

PICTURED KNOWLEDGE

Indian Pottery

Pottery is heavy and easily broken. If very good it is too valuable to be left behind. So they never took much pains with their pottery.

The Vanished Mound Builders

Around the Great Lakes there were, at some remote time, tribes that were more settled. They built the mounds of Ohio and Wisconsin and left fine pottery behind them. Every trace of their buildings is gone, but their houses and fortifications were probably of timber. Most of the mound builders must have perished, but it is thought that a few reached the lower Mississippi Valley for, when found by white explorers, the Natchez Indians were building on elevations and artificial mounds in the flood bottoms of the great river. And they were making pottery similar to that found in northern mounds. They shaped their vessels by coiling slender ropes of clay, turning their work on trays and smoothing it neatly inside and out. Only a soft, unglazed ware, burned in the open because they had no furnaces, it was variously and artistically shaped and decorated with engraving and low relief modeling.

Indians of the South and Southwest

The Natchez Indians spun cotton and hemp and wove coarse cloth on rude looms. And they made beautiful feather mantles, covering webs of net, on both sides, with overlapping swan and duck feathers. Such work was one of the arts of the Aztecs of Mexico. The Natchez claimed to have come from the Southwest, and they may, indeed, have been the remnant of an old and large migration that reached the Great Lakes and built the mounds. All over the continent there were such shiftings of the population. The wanderings of the Shawnees, an Algonquin tribe, in historic times, from the Suwanee River, Florida, where

A Yepiti Grape Juice Factory

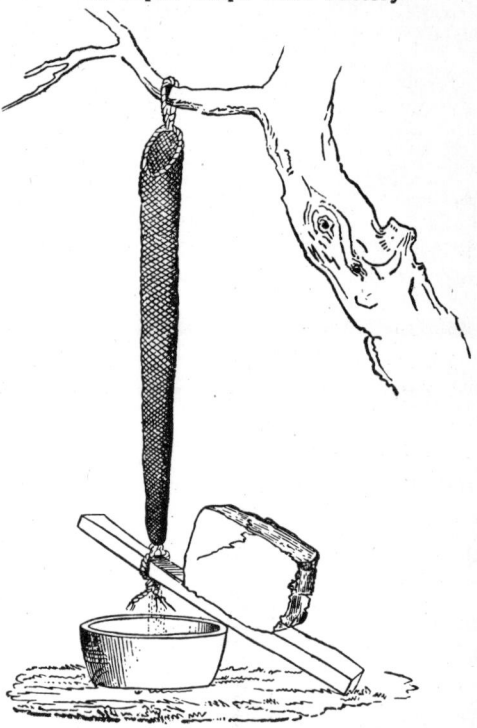

Suppose you lived in the woods where there were plenty of wild grapes and you wanted to save some of their delicious juice for winter, how would you go about it? Do you think you would figure out this ingenious way of doing it, practiced by the Yepiti Indians? They cut slips of thin cane, plaited them into a course basket-like tube closed at one end. Then in this tube they put the grapes and hung it from a limb, fastened a stick of wood to the lower end, as you see, put a heavy stone upon the stick and the grape juice factory began to operate! The juice was caught in a big bowl made of clay and stored in jars.

1414

THE INDIANS
The Spirits and the Doctor-Prophets

The Indians, of course, didn't know anything about microbes, those queer little things that get into the blood and cause the spread of disease, but they did believe that diseases were spread by all sorts of invisible evil spirits, and it was the business of their doctor-prophets to chase them away with the help of good spirits. Here you see one of these professional gentlemen at his work. He is calling to the good spirits, North, South, East, and West, and you see them in the air coming to his aid. The owl hasn't come yet, but he will, for turning to the North, the Prophet has cried, "Holo, koko, koko, kisagasweigo," which means "Owl, thou art invited to smoke." The people you see sitting on the ground have replied for the owl, "Ho, ho, ho," which means "Yes, yes, yes." The turtle was supposed to be the interpreter between man and other creatures.

they got their name, to the banks of the Delaware and then westward into Ohio, would fill a book. Indians emigrated as well as white people.

Certainly the Natchez Indians of Mississippi were superior to all their neighbors; their language was foreign, their political organization higher, and they had the sun-worship and the arts of pottery and weaving that we do not find again until we near the Mexican border. In what is now New Mexico and Arizona were the building tribes of the Pueblos, Zunis, Moquis and Navajos.

The Navajos wove every kind of fiber—wild flax, yucca, the bark of sage brush, cotton which they culti-*Weavers and Builders* vated, milk weed, the hair of jack rabbits and the wool of mountain sheep. Their looms were rude affairs—just two posts set up in the ground with cross pieces lashed to them. On these they wove their soft, thick blankets and rugs, with

PICTURED KNOWLEDGE
Indian Doctor Preparing His Medicine

The Indians relied on two things to cure them of wounds and sickness. One was magic, the other medicine. Here you see an Indian doctor mixing his medicine by the help of magic. He is stirring up a mixture in a vessel while he shakes a rattle and recites certain magic words. The sound of the rattle, which was a gourd with pebbles in it, was supposed to make the medicine work better.

On the Long Voyage

Primitive peoples, like the Indians, did not draw any sharp distinction between sickness, sleep, and death. In case of sickness they thought the good spirits had left the body, and the prophets and medicine men used to do things like those shown in the picture of the prophet's lodge, to bring them back. When a warrior ceased to breathe, it was believed that his spirit had gone into another world and that he would need there the same things he did in life. So they buried his weapons with him and brought food to his burial place. This picture shows how the Chinook Indians on the Pacific Coast buried their dead in canoes, because they thought they would need these canoes in the other world. Attached to the canoe, you see vessels containing food. The female relatives have come to visit with the dead just as if they were still alive.

THE INDIANS
The Feast of Mandamin

This is what you might call Thanksgiving Day among the Indians. It represents a scene in the land of the Dakotas. When the first ears of green corn were ripe, they gathered in one of their houses, had a feast of roasting ears, and offered prayer and thanks to the great spirit whom they acknowledged as the source of all good gifts. Corn was the principal grain food of the Indians and one of the most famous chiefs of the Iroquois was known as Corn Planter because it was his policy to have large fields in cultivation so that his people could not only meet their daily wants, but were better prepared than other tribes for war because of their large corn supply.

designs in black, white and red on the natural gray ground. They and the Zunis wove the same figures into their beautiful baskets.

Fortress Homes of the Cliff Dwellers

The Pueblos were noted as builders and potters. The desert furnished a dry, powdered clay for brick making, and the crumbling cliffs, slabs of sandstone. All Indian shelters were community houses with a central fire. So the Pueblos built a number of rooms adjoining, arranged in a semicircle or strung along a cliff for better defense. The roofs being flat the houses were piled on top of each other, wherever the space was limited. The upper rooms were reached by ladders, and the village became a fortress. Except in their location the cliff-dwellings are much like other villages of the Pueblos. The mound builders, no doubt, built as extensively, but of timber which decayed in the rains and snows of centuries, while the brick and stone work of the cliff-dwellers was preserved by the dry air of the desert.

From this region all the arts of weaving, pottery and building increased steadily in quantity and quality southward into Mexico and *Culture Center of the Continent* Central America, the cultural center of the continent in pre-Columbian days. And to these arts was added metal working in gold, silver and copper, sculpturing in stone, modeling in stucco, paper making and the development of picture-writing into characters that approached an alphabet. In pottery and terra cotta, the Aztecs of Mexico and Mayas of Yucatan made vases with necks, jugs with handles, and bowls with feet; funeral urns, water pipes, and statuary figures. And they ornamented their work by pinching, engraving, painting, relief modeling, and inlaying of colored clays. They built cities, temples and palaces of adobe and stone, set in mortar and covered with stucco and carvings. They wove many grades of cloth, made a wadded armor, coated cloth with rubber, and worked the metals into weapons, ornaments, house trimmings and furniture.

The Sign of the Red Hand

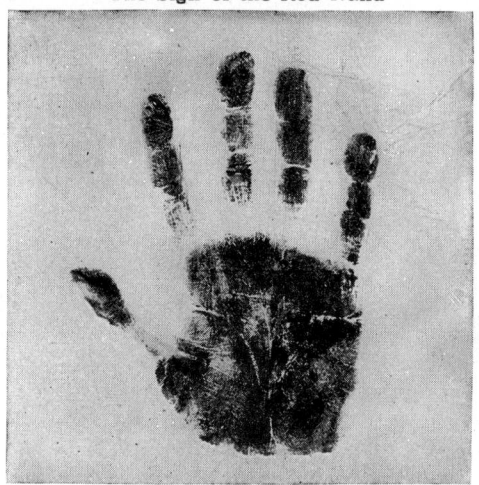

This is just what it looks like—a human hand. The Maya Indians of Yucatan smeared their hands with red paint and then printed them on the stones of their temples. This red hand was intended as a symbol, the seal, of the No Hock Yum, the great Master, or Lord. "I shall never forget," says Professor Thompson, of Harvard University, who supplied this picture of the red hand and the information for readers of Pictured Knowledge, "my first sight of the red hand at Chichen Itza, 'The City of the Sacred Well.' The expedition reached the base of the great edifice, the Nunnery, just as a tempest was about to break. Leaving the rest of the party to unpack the mules and get the things under the safe shelter of the lower chambers, I climbed the shattered stairway to the upper story and got our bearings. As I peered into the chamber entrance in the massive end wall, a bright hued motmot* flew out, hoarsely scolding, a big iguana† clambered clattering up the roof, and a single lurid ray from the half eclipsed sun, glancing through the doorway to the opposite wall illumined, in a quivering panel of light, the outline of the red hand. Then the gathering darkness blotted out the gleaming vision, while all the empty chambers of the structure echoed to the rattling and the crashing of the tempest."

*A tropical bird which looks like a blue jay with a very long tail.
†A large lizard.

The Artists in Stone

The best architects and sculptors in stone were the Mayas of Yucatan. They built on artificial mounds such as we find in Wisconsin and among the Natchez Indians of Mississippi. The roofs and openings of their ruins still show the pointed arch. The walls are thick and covered with carved figures and grotesque masks of men and beasts, a higher development of the carving on totem poles of the rude tribes of British Columbia. Everywhere we find traces and proofs of a common origin of the race. Halls, monoliths, tablets and temples were raised in profusion and variety. The Mayas had only stone tools for carving in stone, but in execution their work has been compared to that of ancient Egypt.

Beginnings of an Alphabet

And these people came very near to forming an alphabet and a written language. Practically all Indian tribes used picture writing to mark springs, trails and camping places, to give warnings and to ward off evil. The Swastika was the universal sign of good luck. They painted family and tribal emblems on their tent cov-

The Red Hands and the Ruined Portal

This is all that is left of a small temple on an island off the coast of Yucatan, which was formerly inhabited by the Mayas. The first thing that catches your eye is that queer kneeling figure, but strangest of all, what are those three things above the figure? They look like the prints of a hand, don't they? The picture on the opposite page tells you what they are.

erings and beaver blankets, and tatooed them on their bodies. The Algonquins recorded journeys, historical events and ceremonial rites in pictographs, worked them into wampum belts, and wrote messages on birch bark. Some tribes kept clan rolls. Many a cliff and canyon wall of the Southwest still shows elaborate scratchings that, no doubt, tell old Indian stories. The Aztecs' writing was purely pictorial; but that of the Mayas was phonetic. Their characters alone represent, not objects but sounds, and were meant to translate speech into writing.

This was a long, upward step, and the people who made it understood its importance. They made parchment of sheep skins, a smooth cotton cloth, and a tough paper of the maguey plant, on which to preserve their writings. They wrote on both sides of long strips of cloth, paper or skin, painting the characters in brilliant colors, then folded the strips into books and covered them with ornamented boards. These books were often kept in temples, or buried with the priests who wrote them. The Spanish conquerors, considering them works of evil, have confessed that they destroyed great numbers of them.

The Figure on the Tiger Throne

In the middle of the wall opposite the doorway of one of the Aztec temples, is what remains of a figure, nearly life size, seated on a throne, ending on the right and left in tiger heads and supported by two legs, modelled to represent the feet of the animal. Although only about one-third of the original figure remains, it gives a sufficient clue for students of such things to conceive what the whole figure was like, and this picture shows how it would look if restored, according to the eminent sculptor, Waldeck, who made this restoration. While the style of the restoration is a little too refined to be true to Aztec art, it is said by Professor Holmes of the Smithsonian Institution, who has devoted his life to the study of such matters, to be a very fair representation of what the figure must have originally looked like. Just think of Indians being capable of work like that!

These books seem to have been texts, calendars and calculations in numerals and in time. All the people south of the Rio Grande to Peru, South America, where dwelt the Incas, were sun-worshippers and learned in astronomy. The most remarkable work of the Aztecs was the calendar stone, now in the museum of Mexico City.

Now the Aztecs conquered the Mayas and learned many of their arts before white men came to America. Both would have risen higher. In another century, perhaps, they would have mined and smelted iron, developed an alphabet and written the Indian epic of hero stories. In their upward climb they were arrested by the Spanish conquerors who crushed them and the Incas of Peru, destroyed their works, and reduced them to slavery in field and mine. Three hundred years of

The Ruined Temple of the Sun

The Aztecs and the Mayas, like so many other people in various parts of the world, worshipped the sun. This is what is left of one of their Sun Temples. The roof as you can see, was very thick and it seems strange that it has not caved in long ago from its own weight. So strongly knit, however, was the masonry, that the roofs remained except where the wooden lintels over the doorway have decayed. On top of this is a pigeon-hole affair, called a roof comb, of which you shall learn more later.

A Maya Gentleman in Full Dress

This is a portrait of a Maya gentleman in full dress. Undoubtedly he was some lord; for the lords of the Mayas dressed like that—not all the time, but on great occasions. As they had no portrait painters in those days, his picture was carved in relief on the walls of one of the temples.

The kings and the lords among the Mayas, as you can see, wore girdles about a hand's breadth with ends falling down in front and behind. The ends of these girdles were ornamented by the Maya women with embroidery and feather work. In the monuments, you will see them covered with the most elaborate designs. The commonest of these designs was a face uglier than a hallowe'en mask, supposed to represent one of their water gods. For the Mayas and the Aztecs had gods for nearly everything in nature—the sun, the moon, the wind, the rain; gods of war, gods that helped them with the corn crop, and so on. See the many strange faces worked into or hanging upon this lord's costume, as distinguished foreigners nowa-days wear medals. But in addition to wearing them as decorations, the Mayas wore these things much as foolish people wear charms; that is with the idea that if you had them on, the gods they represent would keep a friendly eye on you in case of any trouble in their line; for example, the god of rain would protect you from lightning but he could not help you in war. There was a separate god for that. Look at the funny little idol this lord seems to be drawing along on the ground behind him. No doubt these lords learned to carry such things about with them as gracefully as a European army officer can dance with his sword on at a court ball.

And the feathers they wore! See them? The North American Indians, you know, wore feathers in their hair and often in a long strip down their backs, but you see his lordship here has feather plumes sticking out of him everywhere. These elaborate feather devices were worn by the different classes of the Mayas to indicate their rank, much as army men have different kinds of marks on their uniforms today. Not content with ornaments of the feathers themselves, the Mayas had them fastened in ornamental holders, and the more important lords kept feather artists of their own and these artists ranked high among the skilled workers of the Mayas.

THE INDIANS
How the Aztecs Built Their Roofs

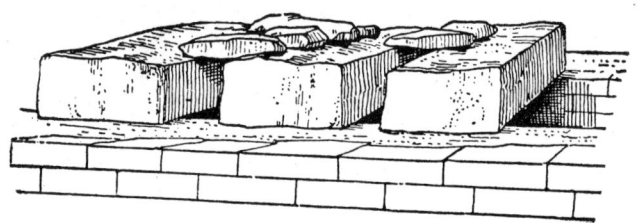

The Bridges Between Ceiling Stones
Often among the Aztec ruins, explorers come across stones arranged like this across the big slabs. They are supposed to have been so placed to support the ceiling.

Spanish rule left them degraded, their arts and origin forgotten.

Ruins of a High Civilization

We know how Egypt, Carthage, Greece and Rome in the Old World, rose to power and glory and then fell into ruin. Here in America, too, civilization, or something very near it, was destroyed. No descendant of the Aztecs, today, could understand the calendar stone. Mayas who guide scientists to the splendid ruins of works built by their ancestors, in the forests of Yucatan, stare at sculptured temples without interest or comprehension.

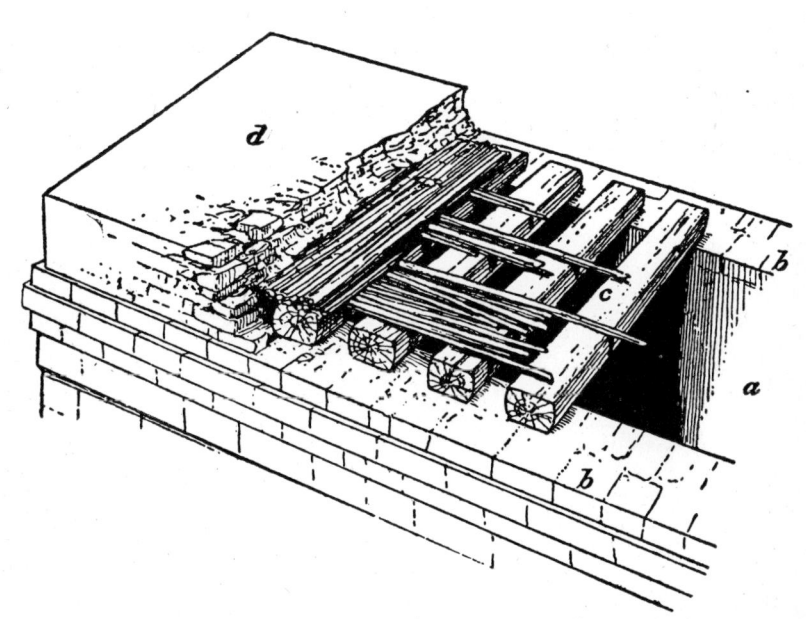

How the Aztecs Built Their Roofs
This picture shows how the Aztecs built the roofs to their wonderful buildings. (a) shows a chamber space to be covered; (bb) side walls. Across these walls beams, as at (c), were laid and across these at right angles small timbers or canes; across these again at right angles more canes; then above all, (d) a covering of cement and stones with a smooth surface.

One of the Triple Doorways

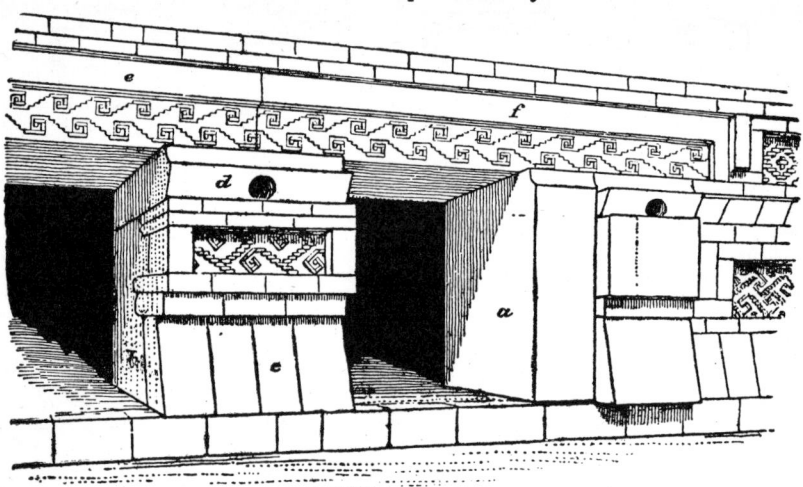

As a rule the doorways to the Aztec Temples were simply constructed and had the appearance of square holes about seven feet high and six feet wide in the walls. A single doorway was formed by a single lintel from one side to the other and supported the structure above.

In the more pretentious temples, however, the builders took more pains and built more elaborately. Here the doorways were often made double and many times triple, and occupied the center of the fronts of the buildings, which faced upon the courts. In some temples this entire side was made up of a series of doorways.

A favorite method of accomplishing the triple doorways, by one section of the Aztecs, was by the use of large round columns representing feathered serpents, the heads appearing at the bottom. These columns supported the ends of huge lintels, which in turn supported the mass of masonry above.

In another section of the Aztec country, instead of using round columns, massive square pillars were used as you see in the picture above.

This is one-half of a triple doorway, and shows a side pillar and one of the central ones. Each doorway is approximately seven feet high and six feet wide. From these dimensions one can realize how massive are the pillars.

The long lintel here shown is typical of all the doorways, made in three sections neatly fitted together and embellished with a mosaic design.

The pillars, as you can see, were very plain with the exception of a small mosaic design on the face and here almost invariably were found the holes in the capstone into which were secured porch beams.

The most striking features of these doorways were the lintels which were made sometimes upwards of fifty feet long.

Explanation of above illustration: (a) Lateral jamb stone; (b) and (c) piers separating doorways; (d) capstone for supporting porch or awning beam; (e) part of middle lintel; (f) end lintel.

Cord Holders for Awnings

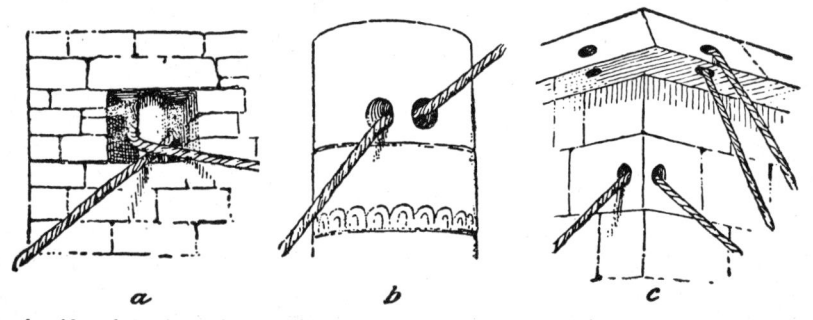

At the sides of the Aztec doorways were sunken cord holders, carved or built into the masonry, for the purpose of holding awnings which could be raised or lowered just as we have them today. (a) Shows one of these built into one of the masonry walls; (b) a cord holder in the back of a column; (c) the cord holders as used in moldings and corners of jambs and walls.

THE INDIANS

Stones Used by Mosaic Workers

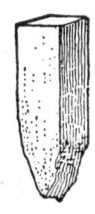

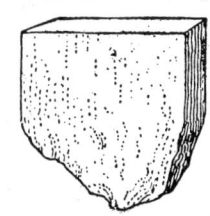

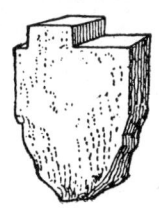

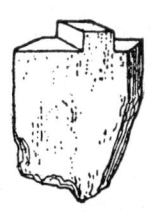

Here you see the different forms of the little stone blocks used by the Aztec mosaic workers. The number used, of course, was very great. A single room in one of their temples contains over 13,000, and all the rooms in a single temple must have contained nearly ten times that number. Think of the enormous amount of labor required to cut and dress these little picture blocks, or rather picture-making blocks; for the Aztec artists in mosaic "composed" pictures with them as you spell words with letters.

Work in Mosaics

What the Maya Ladies Did to Their Faces

Back in colonial times, you remember, the ladies, when they dressed for a ball or anything like that, used to put little patches of court plaster on their faces. Discs, scars, crescents—just a tiny spot here and there. That's why this plaster is called "court" plaster to this day. The custom originated at court, in England. And these patches really do seem becoming on the faces of the beautiful women of colonial days, as you see them in their portraits, but what would you think of a lady with that queer little monster on her face? You would probably say, "How ugly!" But perhaps that is because we are not Mayas; for the Maya ladies used to put these things on their faces whenever they wanted to look particularly attractive. First they painted their faces a lovely rich yellow; then they stamped on them these patterns in red. The stamps were made of pottery.

The Aztecs did not have a great variety of styles in mosaics, but they used them with great artistic effect, as you see by the designs here reproduced.

PICTURED KNOWLEDGE

How the Stone Slabs "Walked" Out of the Quarry

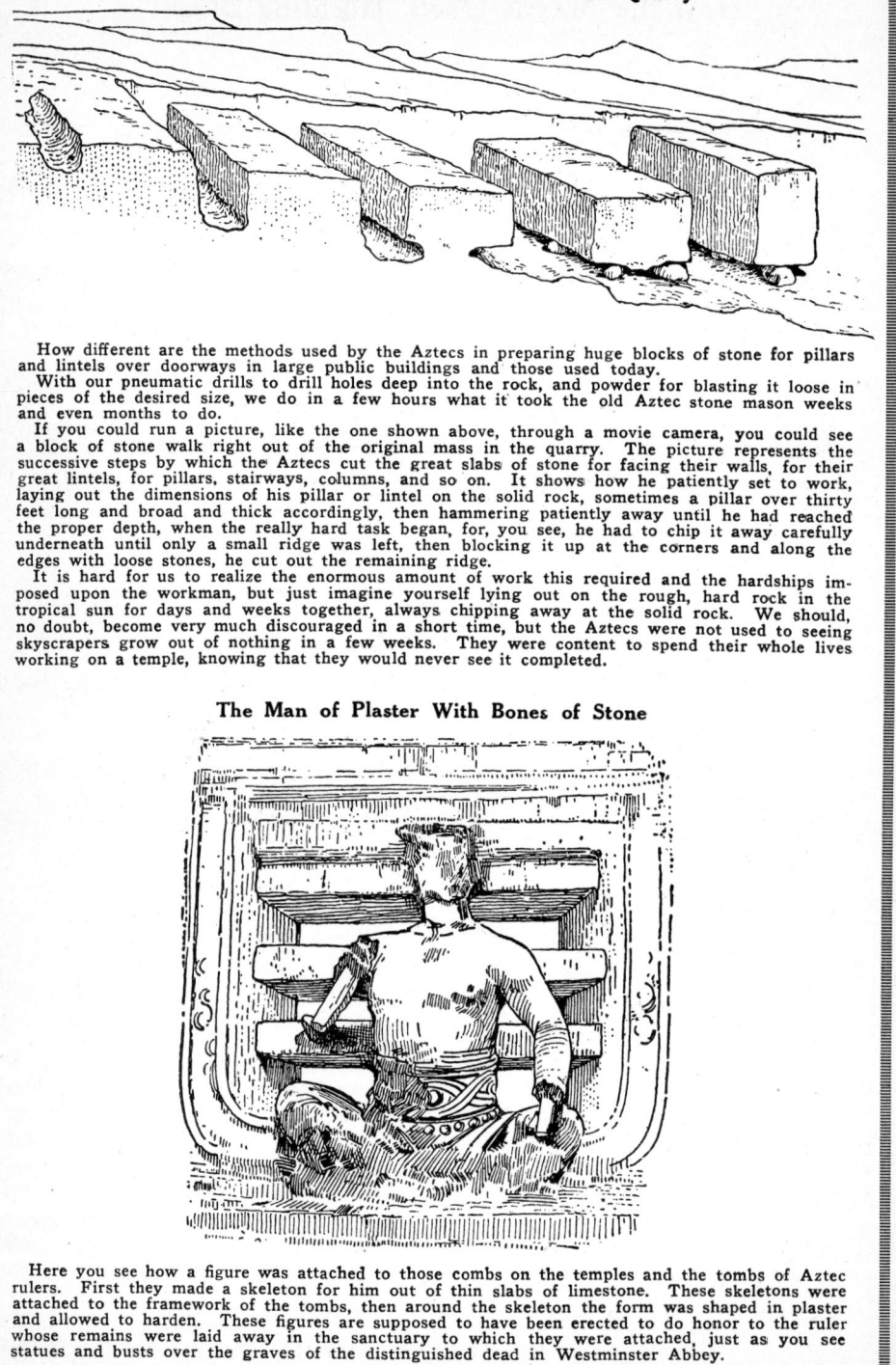

How different are the methods used by the Aztecs in preparing huge blocks of stone for pillars and lintels over doorways in large public buildings and those used today.

With our pneumatic drills to drill holes deep into the rock, and powder for blasting it loose in pieces of the desired size, we do in a few hours what it took the old Aztec stone mason weeks and even months to do.

If you could run a picture, like the one shown above, through a movie camera, you could see a block of stone walk right out of the original mass in the quarry. The picture represents the successive steps by which the Aztecs cut the great slabs of stone for facing their walls, for their great lintels, for pillars, stairways, columns, and so on. It shows how he patiently set to work, laying out the dimensions of his pillar or lintel on the solid rock, sometimes a pillar over thirty feet long and broad and thick accordingly, then hammering patiently away until he had reached the proper depth, when the really hard task began, for, you see, he had to chip it away carefully underneath until only a small ridge was left, then blocking it up at the corners and along the edges with loose stones, he cut out the remaining ridge.

It is hard for us to realize the enormous amount of work this required and the hardships imposed upon the workman, but just imagine yourself lying out on the rough, hard rock in the tropical sun for days and weeks together, always chipping away at the solid rock. We should, no doubt, become very much discouraged in a short time, but the Aztecs were not used to seeing skyscrapers grow out of nothing in a few weeks. They were content to spend their whole lives working on a temple, knowing that they would never see it completed.

The Man of Plaster With Bones of Stone

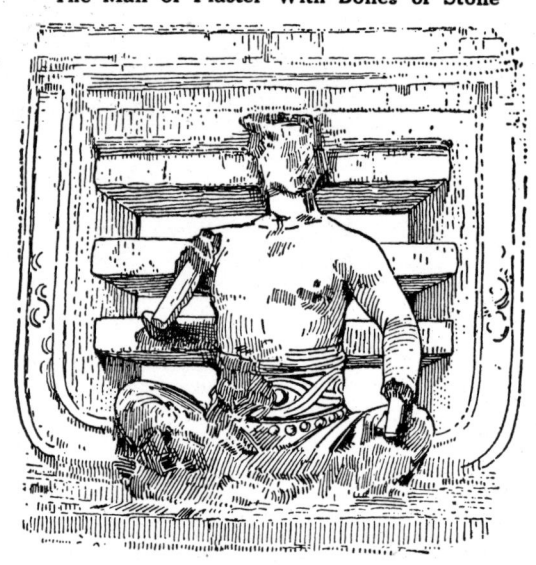

Here you see how a figure was attached to those combs on the temples and the tombs of Aztec rulers. First they made a skeleton for him out of thin slabs of limestone. These skeletons were attached to the framework of the tombs, then around the skeleton the form was shaped in plaster and allowed to harden. These figures are supposed to have been erected to do honor to the ruler whose remains were laid away in the sanctuary to which they were attached, just as you see statues and busts over the graves of the distinguished dead in Westminster Abbey.

How the Mayas Used "Building Blocks"

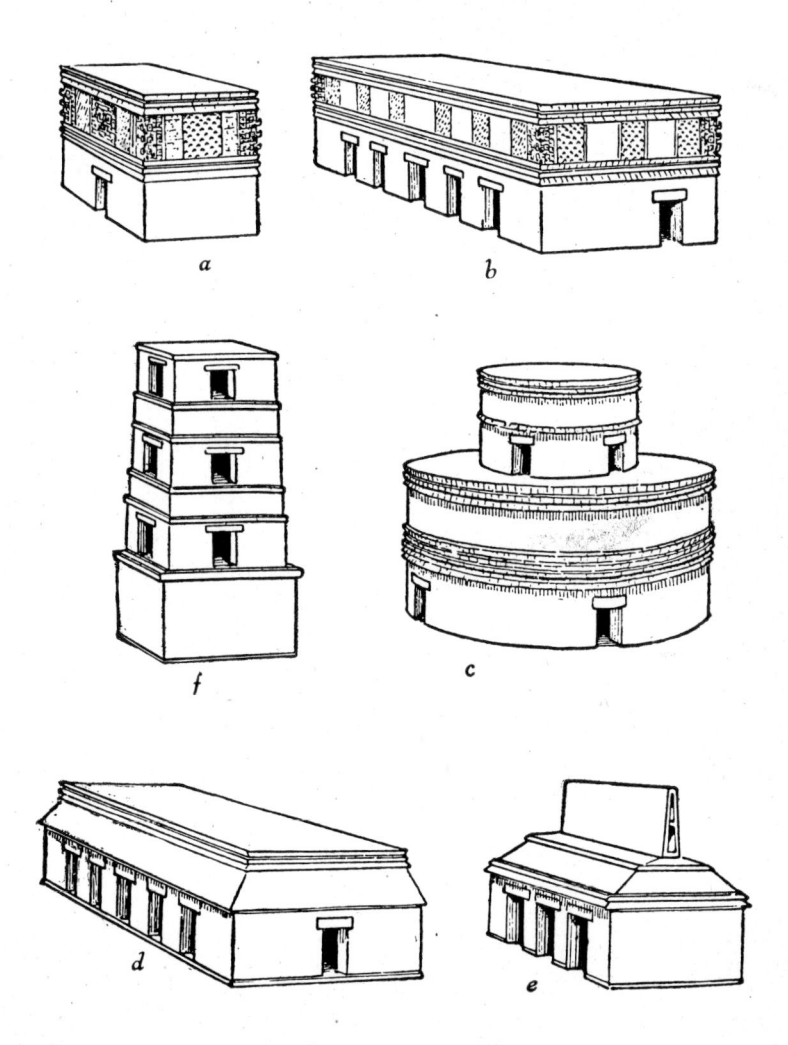

a

b

f

c

d

e

This page will give you a clear idea of the different styles of architecture employed by the Aztecs and the Mayas. The Aztecs and the Mayas belonged to the same race of highly civilized Indians, the Mayas living in Central America and the Aztecs in the country to the north, including what is now Mexico. At (a) you see a single chamber building—the unit of construction. The next picture (b), a multiple chamber building, is an assemblage of twelve or fourteen of these units, much as a little boy makes different shaped buildings with one style of building blocks; (c) circular building; (d) building with sloping roof similar to the modern mansard; (e) temple with roof comb; (f) square tower of four stories.

PICTURED KNOWLEDGE

The Cookies and the Spinning Lesson

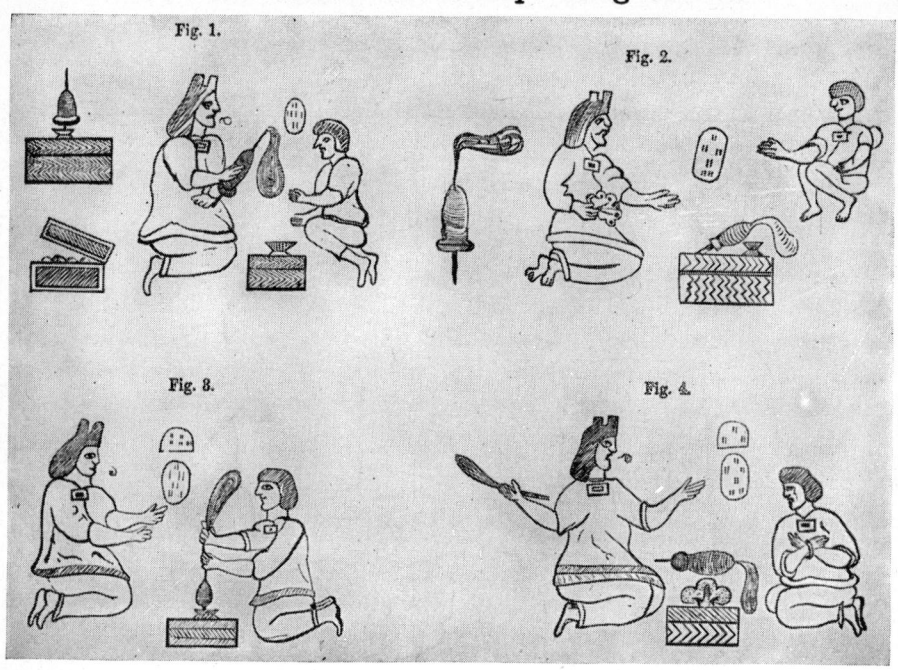

A Vivid Picture Story of Home Life Among the Aztecs

Here is a picture story by an Aztec artist which gives us an increasing insight into Aztec home life and the work of the women. In the first picture mother is handing daughter a spindle of wool and is going to teach her to spin. Back of mother is a "work box" in which the materials and things for spinning are kept. On the upper box sits a spindle with a disk weight attached to increase the momentum when it was twirled. The curl in front of the lips means that mother is talking. Notice the dutiful attitude of daughter. The little round thing just above her head represents a sweet cake which mother has promised to give her if she does her work well.

But, Oh, my! Just see what is happening in the next picture, and notice the expression on mother's mouth. You can see she is put out. Daughter, instead of kneeling down by the spindle box, is shrinking back and yet reaching out for the cake, meaning that she wants the cake first, but mother, you see, sternly points toward the work. She says, "No, little daughter, you must do your spinning lesson first and then you can have the cake." Mother is so vexed that she has stopped fanning herself with the fan which she holds in her right hand. You notice both mother and daughter are wearing amulets on their breasts. This is not only for good looks, but for good luck.

But now, as you see in Figure 3, daughter has decided to be a good girl, and kneeling down by the spindle has already commenced to spin the thread. This pleases mother so much that she has quite a different expression on her face and you see she is saying something which pleases the little girl. Notice how she smiles. Can you guess what mother is saying? There it is as plain as day. She says, "Now that you are going to do as Mama says, she intends to give you a cake and a half!"

Figure 4 tells what would have happened to the little girl if she hadn't done as her mother said. She would not have received the cake and a half and she would have been given a whipping. No doubt when she finished her spinning lesson and got her cookie, she thought how much nicer it is to do your work and think how nice it is to get a cookie than it is *not* to do your work and think how nice it would be to get a cookie.

But little son as well as little daughter had home lessons to get in the days of the Aztecs. On the next page is one of the picture stories that tells how a goldsmith taught his son his trade. The letters A

1428

THE INDIANS

How the Goldsmith Taught His Son

and B show how the blow pipe was used. One kind of a blow pipe had a wide mouth so as to spread the blast for annealing. A pipe with a narrow mouth was used for soldering. In the picture marked C the goldsmith holds in the left hand a pair of pincers made by bending strips of hollow copper. With the pincers he is holding a piece of gold jewelry which he is annealing, in the flames. You see little son is watching all this and the curl in front of his mouth means that he is asking questions while father is explaining things. Among the Aztecs a father could always tell what his son was going to be, because whatever his own trade was, the boy was obliged to follow whether he wanted to or not.

Picture Language of the Indians

This is What the Chippewas Asked

A delegation of Chippewas went to Washington from Wisconsin, carrying with them this picture petition to be presented to the president. They wanted back certain land which they had ceded to the United States. The Chippewas who made up this delegation were represented in the picture by the figures of their clans, just as the Scouts have their clan symbols today. The totem of the chief who led the delegation was a crane. You notice there are lines running from his eye to the eyes of all the other totems that are following him. This means that all of the chiefs in the delegation—the marten, bear, catfish, etc.—look at the whole matter just as the chief does. In the same way all their hearts are connected, which means that they all have the same feeling about it. The line from the crane's eye forward points to Washington and the line leading to No. 8 refers to a group of small rice lakes near a river, marked 9, to which the Indians wanted to be moved.

PICTURED KNOWLEDGE
The Bible in Picture Language

The chapters in the Indian Bibles sometimes had the contents summarized at the beginning just as you have in your Bible, except that for the Indians, the good missionaries used pictures instead of words. If you don't remember what Chapter 30 of Proverbs is about, you can recall from this picture what it says.

The Handwriting on the Walls

This illustrates the kind of picture-writing done by Indians on big rocks and on the stone walls of mountain sides. The little figures in the lower right hand corner tell us of a beloved Prophet of an Indian tribe who has passed away. You see he is wearing the long garment that the Priests wore. Below him is a heart with shrubs sprouting from one of the lobes. This meant that his people carried sweet memories of him in their hearts. The figures with crosses on them are supposed to indicate towns or forts.

From the Indian Picture Dictionary

Here are some additional examples of how much the Indians could tell each other by a very simple little picture. The first picture tells about a man walking by moonlight, the next how man gets light from on high. You see the sun and the sun's rays expressing intelligence. The next picture tells of a man who is eager to learn and listen. No. 4 represents the sea in its big earthen bowl. No. 5 is how father looks just before Christmas; a man with a load of presents. No. 6 an Indian doctor carrying various herbs.

1430

The Arab's Farewell to His Steed

My beautiful! my beautiful! that standest
   meekly by,
With thy proudly-arched and glossy neck,
   and dark and fiery eye!
Fret not to roam the desert now with all
   thy winged speed:
I may not mount on thee again—thou'rt
   sold, my Arab steed!

Fret not with that impatient hoof, snuff
   not the breezy wind,
The farther that thou fliest now, so far am
   I behind.
The stranger hath thy bridle rein—thy
   master hath his gold;
Fleet-limbed and beautiful, farewell!—
   thou'rt sold, my steed, thou'rt sold.

Farewell! Those free, untired limbs full
   many a mile must roam,
To reach the chill and wintry sky which
   clouds the stranger's home.
Some other hand, less fond, must now thy
   corn and bed prepare;
The silky mane I braided once must be
   another's care.

The morning sun shall dawn again, but
   never more with thee
Shall I gallop o'er the desert paths, where
   we were wont to be;
Evening shall darken on the earth, and
   o'er the sandy plain
Some other steed, with slower step, shall
   bear me home again.

Yes, thou must go! The wild, free breeze,
   the brilliant sun and sky,
Thy master's home—from all of these my
   exiled one must fly.
Thy proud dark eye will grow less proud,
   thy step become less fleet,
And vainly shalt thou arch thy neck thy
   master's hand to meet.

Only in sleep shall I behold that dark eye
   glancing bright;
Only in sleep shall I hear again that step
   so firm and light;
And when I raise my dreaming arm to
   check or cheer thy speed,
Then must I, starting, wake to feel—
   thou'rt sold, my Arab steed.

Ah! rudely then, unseen by me, some cruel
   hand may chide,
Till foam-wreaths lie, like crested waves,
   along thy panting side;
And the rich blood that's in thee swells in
   thy indignant pain,
Till careless eyes, which rest on thee, may
   count each starting vein.

Will they ill-use thee? If I thought—but
   no, it cannot be,
Thou art so swift, yet easy curbed; so
   gentle, yet so free;
And yet, if haply, when thou'rt gone, this
   lonely heart should yearn,
Can the hand that casts thee from it now
   command thee to return?

Return!—alas, my Arab steed! what shall
   thy master do,
When thou, who wert his all of joy, hast
   vanished from his view?
When the dim distance cheats mine eye,
   and through the gathering tears
Thy bright form, for a moment, like the
   false mirage appears?

Slow and unmounted shall I roam, with
   weary step alone,
Where with fleet step and joyous bound
   thou oft hast borne me on;
And, sitting down by that green well, I'll
   pause and sadly think,
"'Twas here he bowed his glossy neck
   when last I saw him drink!"

When last I saw thee drink!—away! The
   fevered dream is o'er!
I could not live a day and know that we
   should meet no more!
They tempted me, my beautiful! for hunger's power is strong—
They tempted me, my beautiful! but I have
   loved too long.

Who said that I had given thee up? Who
   said that thou wert sold?
'Tis false!—'tis false! my Arab steed! I
   fling them back their gold!
Thus, thus, I leap upon thy back, and
   scour the distant plains!
Away! who overtakes us now may claim
   thee for his pains!

                            HON. MRS. NORTON

The Santa Maria and the Liner

This is how the flagship of Columbus, the Santa Maria, would look alongside an ocean liner. Even these enormous liners sometimes succumb to the perils of the sea, as when the Titanic was sunk by striking an iceberg. Think then of the boldness of Columbus in putting to sea in that little cockleshell.

STORIES OF AMERICAN HISTORY
THE EXPLORERS

The Age of Discovery

The First Discoverers of America

Before they were converted to gentler ways by the Christian missionaries, the fierce, bold Vikings were for many years the terror of Europe. Pirates, raiders, and explorers, they even crossed the Atlantic in their strange boats. These vessels were light yet sturdy. They were driven, as you see, by the wind aided by the strong men at the oars, and were carved with terrible dragons' heads. The sails were square and made of flax, bound at the edges with hide to strengthen them. Often they were gorgeously embroidered, as this one is. This was done by the women. Dragons and serpents were their favorite devices. We know a great deal about these old sea rovers from the custom of burying with a war chief, his vessel, dogs, horses and weapons, in one great mound of earth. Several such mounds have been discovered and the old boats brought to light.

The Vikings' vessels were sometimes 80 feet long, but so shallow that they would float in four feet of water. With this kind of boat—in which your mother would probably consider it unsafe for you to take just a pleasure trip on one of the Great Lakes—the Vikings raided all the coasts of Europe and the Mediterranean, and discovered Iceland, Greenland, and America.

THE greatest events in all human history, the ones which changed and advanced the world most, were the birth of Christ, from which we date time, and the sailing of Columbus from Palos, Spain, nearly fifteen hundred years later. Before Columbus three-fourths of the world was unknown, its nature only dimly suspected, the wide oceans, lonely. Except for the open boats of a few Norse adventurers who visited Nova Scotia about the year 1000, no sail had been seen in Mid-Atlantic nor had white men reached its western shores. But within a century after 1492, this ocean swarmed with ships, and two bold navigators—Magellan for Spain, and Sir Francis Drake for England—had plowed their water furrows around the enormous earth, proving that it was in truth a globe.

Your school history tells the brave story of the discovery and

The Outbreak of Discovery

1433

exploration of America, and of the adventurous men who were engaged in it. But really to understand what happened here, we should know something of the Old World from which the New was re-peopled. Why, after so many centuries of land-faring, were all the nations of Western Europe suddenly out on this fearful sea?

The chief reason, no doubt, was that the overland route to India, China and Japan had been closed, after Western Europe had become accustomed to the spices, silks, carpets, gold, pearls and other luxuries of the Far East. But religious zeal came second. The revival of Greek learning and the invention of printing, played their part, too. Men ventured again to believe and to say that the earth was round, and that ships might sail around it. And with the mariner's compass and astrolabe, or "star-finder," introduced from China, navigators were no longer afraid to leave the shore. Greed for gold, love of adventure and belief in fanciful tales about distant lands drew many out to these perilous adventures. The urgent need of salt fish, the chances of profitable trade, and envy of the growing wealth and sea-power of Spain, obliged others to enter the great water-race around the globe.

Two Centuries of Adventures By the age of discovery—and much beside America was discovered—is meant the nearly 200 years from about 1420, when Portugal found the Cape Verde, Madeira and Canary Islands west of Africa, to 1609. Until after Champlain sailed into the St. Lawrence and Hudson went up the Hudson River, very little exploration in the interior of America was done, except by the Spanish, working westward from Florida and north and south from Mexico. In the fifteenth and sixteenth centuries the drama was enacted in Europe and on the oceans. The seventeenth century saw new destinies of Old World peoples being worked out in the settlement of America.

The Daring Rovers of the North

To understand the story of Columbus and those who followed him, we shall have to go back six hundred years, to the Norsemen of the ninth and tenth centuries. The men of Denmark and Norway were the pagan sea-rovers and pirates of the time. The island-fringed, mountainous shores of Norway, heavily forested and deeply indented with glacier-carved fiords, faced the North Atlantic. Much of their land cold, steep, barren rocks, or sand and swampy lakes, the Danes and Norse were obliged to build boats and get their living from dark, fog-veiled and stormy seas. So here was the greatest training school for sailors, fighters and adventurers the world has ever seen. Putting boldly out to sea, they rode the gales and hailed the icebergs. The terror of seaport towns and coastwise traders and fishing boats, they raided every coast from England to Italy. Now and then a band settled on some good harbor in England and Northern France and there started other breeds of sea-faring men. It was the Normans, or Northman-French who, in the year 1066, conquered England; and Norman fishermen, who came from France to Newfoundland in such numbers about the year 1500.

As early as the tenth century, with no compass but sun and stars,

The Face of a Dreamer and a Doer

CHRISTOPHORVS·COLVMBVS·

Genoa is usually accorded the honor of being the birthplace of Columbus by historians of authority. But Spain and Portugal, and other Italian towns besides Genoa, claim him as their son. We are told he had the coloring of a Norseman—sea-blue eyes, auburn hair and a ruddy skin. That he was a handsome man you can see in the picture which this artist has painted. Some recent research workers even claim to have found proof that Columbus was a Portuguese Jew. Dispute as they may as to the facts surrounding the birth and ancestry of Columbus, the fact remains that he was one of the greatest navigators of history, a man of strong, clear faith and determined purpose, of the breed of men who achieve the great things of the earth. Notice the high cheek bones, the powerful nose, the square chin, the stout neck, the high forehead and the big thoughtful eyes—features which express a vigorous personality and a wide vision.

The Stone and Its Story

If you could read the Runic characters on this stone what it would say to you is this: "Eight Goths (Swedes) and twenty-two Norwegians upon a journey of discovery from Vinland westward. We had a camp by two skerries one day's journey north from this stone. We were out fishing one day. When we returned home we found ten men red with blood and dead. A. V. M. save us from evil.

"(We) have ten men by the sea to look after our vessel fourteen days' journey from this island. Year 1362."

THE AGE OF DISCOVERY
How They Explored the Explorers' Stone

Isn't that a queer looking stone? It was found under the roots of a tree on a lonely farm near Kensington, Minnesota, a good many years ago while the farmer was clearing the land for plowing. His two little boys, aged ten and twelve, were looking on. The inscription is in Runic characters, a form of writing used by the Norsemen.

The thought that here is actually a message of history carved in stone by the hands of those brave adventurers who are said to have found America before Columbus came, makes the story of the Norsemen and Vinland seem very real, doesn't it? But what is even more interesting is the story of how a committee of students of history, appointed by the Historical Society of Minnesota—the stone is now in the Society Museum—"explored" the stone itself.

First of all they came to the conclusion that the farmer could not have carved and buried the stone himself, because although a Swede, he was not an educated man, and, so of course, would not know how to write in the language of the fourteenth century. The roots of the tree under which it was found had grown around the stone and its rings showed that it was about forty years old, so that the stone must have been there before the farmer bought the place. The investigators couldn't find any skerries "one day's journey north" from the stone. A skerry is a rock or reef standing out by itself in the water. The inscription speaks of "this island," but the stone was found on a hill and not on an island. Down to the time when the tree began growing over the stone, Vinland was supposed to be either Nova Scotia or Massachusetts; and these are a great deal more than fourteen days' journey—as those Norsemen would have had to travel—from the place where the stone was found.

What the Rings Had to Say

Moreover, although the inscription pretended to have been carved over five hundred years ago, the edges and angles of the chiseling are sharp, whereas if exposed to the weather for only a few years, stone inscriptions begin to decay, as you can see in the marble slabs in any old graveyard.

All this looked pretty bad for the stone, didn't it? But further investigation showed that while there were no rocks standing in the water as described, there were found twenty miles to the North—what would have been a day's journey for the Norsemen—two large rocks, and the geology of the region shows that these rocks were at one time surrounded by the waters of a lake, and also that the hill on which the stone was found must at one time have been an island.

As to the reference to Vinland, it is said that when the Norsemen came to America, the name was applied to the whole known coast of North America, which at that time took in Hudson Bay. So the reference to Vinland as "Fourteen days' Journey" from the island, would be natural after all. As to the inscription showing so little weathering after 500 years, it was learned that it was found lying face downward, and a stone so protected decays very slowly.

A Little Deeper into the Past

But what is regarded as the most remarkable thing in the whole inscription are the three letters, "A. V. M." This is an abbreviation of the Latin invocation in the Catholic service, "Ave Virgo Maria," but the Scandinavians were all Lutherans. Up to 1362, however, they were Catholics.

If the inscription was invented as a practical joke, it must have been by some very learned man who knew these things which only a scholar would know. But why did he put it where he would have to wait so long to know whether he fooled anybody or not? In previous hoaxes, such as the discovery of buried "giants," the man who buried them saw to it that they were discovered. Moreover, learned men get their greatest pleasure in searching for the truth and not in playing practical jokes. And the inventor of this inscription would have to be a skilful writer also. You see it would be very easy for a Norseman to tell this brief and simple tragic story. It is easy to tell the truth, but it is very difficult to invent a story that looks like the truth, and particularly to tell it in such a small space.

Yet, although the members of the committee were satisfied that the stone was genuine, several other scholars were not. They insisted that several of the words used in the inscription were not spelled as they were spelled in the fourteenth century. But, whether the stone is genuine or not, the story of how scientific men explore facts is the most profitable and interesting part of it. It will help you to realize how hard and how carefully students of history work.

History Back of Your Histories

A Map Columbus Studied

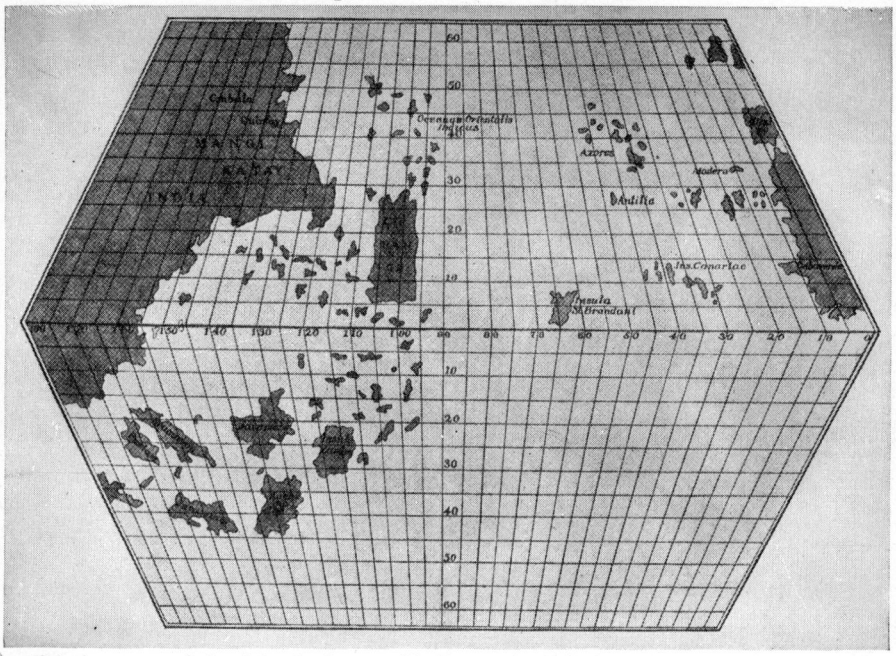

This is a map of the Atlantic Ocean with Europe just peeping over on one side and Asia standing boldly out on the other. It was made by a learned physician of Florence, named Toscanelli. He is said to have corresponded with Columbus and to have made him many valuable suggestions. You see it leaves out North and South America altogether because neither Toscanelli nor Columbus or anybody else at that time knew that North and South America were there. That large island off the coast of Asia marked "Zapingo," we now call "J-a-p-a-n."

no pilots but ravens, they turned the dragon-headed prows of their undecked boats westward, and colonized Iceland and Greenland. A boat blown southwestward by storms, reached the shore of North America.

Guided by Stars and Ravens — Later, Leif Ericson explored our coast in the region of Labrador and Nova Scotia. It is thought that trading was carried on with the Indians, and temporary settlements and missions made during the next three centuries. The Norse had been converted to Christianity and turned their adventurous spirits into spreading the new faith. The formation and wars of the three kingdoms of Denmark, Norway, and Sweden, and more profitable enterprises in barbaric Russia occupied their attention. So the Northman practically disappeared from the sea.

How the Norse Inspired Columbus

But the story of "Leif the Lucky" was not forgotten. It lived in Iceland and elsewhere as a saga—a hero tale of a braver day, to inspire the discoverer of America. Columbus heard the story when he made a voyage from Portugal to Iceland in 1477. It seemed probable to him that the Norse Vikings had reached the northeast coast of China. This confirmed him in the idea that the countries of the Far East could be reached by sailing west.

What was Columbus doing in Portugal? He was a native of Genoa, Italy, which lay in the very center of the known world. Around

THE AGE OF DISCOVERY
Columbus and the Wise Men of Spain

When Columbus made his daring proposition to reach the East by sailing west, he was referred to a council of the wise men of the realms of Spain. Here we see him, map in hand, proving with great eloquence and enthusiasm that he can accomplish what he promises. The learned men, mostly priests and church officials, are telling him he is a madman and a heretic. One of them is showing him the passage in the Bible that refers to the "four corners of the earth" as proof that the world is flat, not round. Another is holding out the writing of some of the early church fathers, whose crude ideas of science were taken as authority by the people of the Middle Ages. These wise men also said that Columbus could never carry enough provisions to sail around the world, and that even if he did get around on the other side he couldn't get back again without sailing up hill which would be impossible. They laughed at the idea of people walking around with heads pointing down and feet up, because they didn't understand the nature of the laws of gravity.

the Mediterranean Sea had risen and fallen all the ancient empires. In the middle centuries the independent republics of Genoa and Venice were rulers of this sea, sharing between themselves the naval power and commerce, and the overland trade with India and China. The fleets of Venice had gone to Egypt and Asia Minor to meet the camel caravans from Arabia; those of Genoa to the head of the Black Sea, to meet the caravans from the Caspian Sea and the Persian Gulf. For three centuries no Italian navigator had had to seek employment in a foreign land. After 1460 they were numerous and needy in Lisbon, Palos, Antwerp and London. Why this change? Let us see.

You know how white settlers in America gradually pushed the Indians westward? Something like that happened in the Old World before Columbus' day. The *The Restless Westward Drive* people of Western Europe were pushed toward the Atlantic by crowding hordes from Asia. The Westward urge began in China. A great military leader, Genghis Kahn, organized the Mongols into an army that conquered the eastern provinces of China. Under his grandson, Kublai Kahn, this Mongol Empire spread westward to the Caspian Sea.

PICTURED KNOWLEDGE
How Columbus Won the Support of Isabella

After Columbus had been refused a hearing several times and referred to councils which always reported unfavorably upon his scheme, Queen Isabella of Castile finally summoned him to her presence. Here he is talking, with all his eloquence and enthusiasm, of the land he will reach by sailing west. The wise men of the realm are there to listen to him, and a few ladies-in-waiting attend the queen. A scribe or notary is beside Columbus to take down in correct legal fashion his promises and demands, as well as the terms of any agreement that may be made between him and Isabella. Isabella was sole ruler of Castile and Leon, and the wife of King Ferdinand of Aragon, and she was a wise monarch.

See how she has leaned forward, she is so interested, and how thoughtfully she is listening to the glowing words of Columbus. If this strange man really can reach the East Indies by sailing west, what a wealth of trade will pour into her dominions! And there will be new lands to conquer, heathen to convert to Christianity and untold wealth for Spain if what Columbus says is true.

The painter of this picture shows Isabella's jewels being brought and laid out upon the table, to furnish money for the expedition—in accordance with the old story of how she raised the necessary funds. But this story has been proved a mistake. Isabella did not pawn her jewels for Columbus—though she was so eager to help him that she would willingly have done so. Part of her jewels had already been pawned to wage war against the Moors, but as that war proved successful, she was well supplied with money at this time.

The first effect of this was to enrich Venice and Genoa, for Kublai Kahn encouraged trade and travel. Italian princes and merchants took service under him and visited the courts of China and of India. One of these travelers, Marco Polo, wrote such glowing accounts of the wealth and splendor of the East that a kind of fever to see those strange lands and fairy courts ran like an epidemic over Europe.

Then something else happened. In pushing his empire westward, Kublai Kahn had to push the Ottoman Turks before him into Asia Minor. These fanatic Mohammedans, enemies of all Christian people, then crossed the Dardanelles into Europe, and after a hundred years captured Constantinople. The trade routes to the East were suddenly closed by Turkish fleets and armies. The ships of Venice and Genoa returned to their docks, many to rot, some to creep timidly out through the Strait of Gibraltar to trade with London and Antwerp. While Greek scholars and artists swarmed into Italy, to add to its learning and build up its arts, Italian merchants, bankers and seamen sought opportunity and employment in every country facing the Atlantic.

Decay of Venice and Genoa

The "New Birth" of Europe

This period was, indeed, such an amazing time of intellectual expansion that it was called the Renais-

1440

THE AGE OF DISCOVERY

The Last Farewells at Palos

Just imagine that it is dawn on Friday, August 3, 1492. After long delays and difficulties, the 120 men and three little ships have been gotten together to embark on this mad voyage to the unknown ends of the earth. Everyone but Columbus has dark fears that the expedition never will return. That is why the women weep as they bid the men farewell, and that is why Prior Juan Perez looks sadly at the enthusiastic Columbus as he says good bye. The Prior was a warm friend of Columbus and helped him many times at court, where he had some influence with the queen, and in getting the much needed ships and sailors in Palos, from which the expedition started. The three vessels are riding at anchor in the harbor of Palos on the broad bosom of the red-brown Tinto. The oarsmen are ready to push off, and the Pinzon brothers, captains of the Nina and Pinta, are saying goodbye to their families. The men have all spent long hours in the church every day for weeks, praying and asking forgiveness for their sins. The first ebb tide of the day will soon carry them out to sea and they will sail westward into the unknown, uncharted Atlantic.

The short tunic, long tight hose, and small velvet cap which Columbus wears were much in use at that time. Notice that he wears his sword hung loosely from his belt on the left side. The little boy clinging to his father, Martin Pinzon, wears striped hose. Sometimes these stripes only ran down one leg, while the other one was a solid color. The Prior, you see, is not clean shaven as the priests of today are, but his clothing is much the same in style.

sance or "new birth" of Europe. With the invention of printing there was a revival of literature. And that was followed by the Reformation or religious upheaval in Northern countries, and by a freeing of the spirit in exploration and discovery. All the powers of men were quickened, their vision enlarged. Great events trod on each other's heels. As Venice and Genoa declined, the fleets of five nations—Portugal, Spain, England, The Netherlands and France—rose in size and power and navigated all the uncharted oceans. Disunited Italy's skilled seamen won empire and glory for every land but their own.

The Rise of Portugal

Columbus went first to Portugal. One of the smallest and poorest countries of Europe, it had taken the leadership on the sea. Early in the century, Prince Henry had set up a school of navigation and naval design. Religion was his motive. For hundreds of years Spain and Portugal had been overrun by the Moors or Saracens of Morocco. To carry the war into Africa, and prevent the return of the Moslem hordes, Portugal built a fleet and opened the Strait of Gibraltar. Then, growing bold, the Madeiras, Canaries, Cape Verde Islands and the Azores were discovered and set-

PICTURED KNOWLEDGE
Columbus Lands in the New World

Columbus has just set his foot on the shores of the little island which he named San Salvador. He is richly clad in honor of the occasion and is accompanied by the brothers Pinzon, bearing the banner of the green cross, and by most of his crew. According to the old account of the event, they all gave thanks to God, kneeling upon the shore and kissed the ground with tears of joy for the great mercy received. Columbus then named the island, San Salvador, and took possession of it for Ferdinand and Isabella.

Columbus Telling of His Discovery

When Columbus returned successful from the voyage which everyone had prophesied would end in ruin, he was loaded with honors and wealth. Here we see him being received in state by Ferdinand and Isabella, who are listening with interest to the story of his adventures. He has brought gold and many implements of Indian manufacture, as well as some of the Indians themselves, to prove the truth of his story. The whole court is gathered here, in one of the big audience halls of the palace at Barcelona, to hear Columbus' account of his discovery.

THE AGE OF DISCOVERY

tled, and Portuguese navigators began to creep down the African coast to lands of dates, ivory and gold. Hearing of the spices of islands

The Santa Maria and How She Sailed

© *Underwood & Underwood*

The famous little vessel of Columbus, the Santa Maria, may be said to have "discovered" America twice; once when it carried Columbus and again in 1893. As part of the celebration of the 400th Anniversary of the first voyage of Columbus, an exact copy of the Santa Maria was built in Spain and sailed across the Atlantic and through the great lakes to Chicago where, moored on the shore at Jackson Park, it was one of the most interesting historic exhibits at the great World's Fair. The trip was made in 36 days, about half the time taken for the voyage of Columbus, but the experienced sailors who made up the crew said that it pitched horribly.

In studying this little vessel, one of the first things that strike us is that it stands so high out of the water and that the masts are so tall for the length of the vessel. This is because the more surface a vessel offers to the wind the faster it will travel—provided, of course, it doesn't capsize. It was necessary to make the masts so high in order to carry the huge sails. That great, high projection at the bow is the forecastle. Almost all of the medieval vessels were built on this plan because all vessels were battleships in those days, liable to be attacked at any moment and this high forecastle furnished a convenient place for men to gather in attacking an enemy vessel. The foresail bears the papal cross and the mainsail the Maltese cross, while the papal cross and the Spanish flag fly from the masts.

far to the east, the Portuguese started for "the bottom of the world." In 1846, six years before Columbus' expedition, they reached the Cape of Good Hope. Then Vasco da Gama sailed around the Cape to India in 1497.

This explains why Columbus failed to get a hearing in Lisbon. Portugal was already putting all her resources into developing a much safer and more promising line of exploration, mission work and trade. His appeal failed in England. Lying far off on the northwestern corner of Europe, neither king nor country had yet awakened to what was going on. Besides, the English had only small coastwise and fishing boats. The city of Bristol, however, did build a ship to be manned by a crew of nineteen, for John Cabot, an Italian navigator who had settled in that seaport town. He, too, sailed in 1497. So it happened that three explorers, sailing south, west and northwest, all seeking the same thing —a sea route to the Far East—were on the Atlantic at the same time.

To Portugal and Spain came the good luck. Da Gama brought back a cargo from India that made Lisbon rich, and Columbus opened the way to lands of gold to fill the empty treasury of Spain. John Cabot discovered only the bleak shores of Labrador, with its icebergs, polar bears, codfish and eider ducks. His voyage created no desire in England for further exploration. His story

Dividing Up the Big Apple

1443

John Cabot and His Son Sebastian

was little known for the next sixty years and, after one more voyage, his neglected son Sebastian sought employment in Spain. Besides, all exploration of other nations was forbidden, when the Pope divided the unknown world between Spain and Portugal.

Nothing Left for Others

The English were still loyal to the Church of Rome and would not disobey the Pope. The French were good Catholics, too, but the King of France had the spirit to protest against this unfairness, and to send the Norman fishing fleets of St. Malo to the banks of Newfoundland, where Cabot's ship had plowed through oceans of cod. In 1523 he boldly sent an Italian navigator, Verrazano, on an exploring expedition. He waylaid a Spanish treasure ship

The idea of sailing west in order to reach the East Indies seems to have occurred to John Cabot about the same time it did to Columbus. And the man who gave England her claim to North America was like Columbus in another respect; he was by birth a Genoese. He moved to England in order to interest the English merchants and king in his project. With the help of Henry VII he made two trips to America and planted the English flag on Canadian soil, thus giving England a claim to the New World which was of great value to her in later years.

Very little is known about the life of John Cabot. He and his son Sebastian are always mentioned together, while Sebastian's other two brothers do not seem to have been so closely associated with their father. Sebastian was a young man in his twenty's at the time of his father's first voyage to America, and probably went with him, though it is not known definitely. After his father's death he led an expedition of his own to South America and achieved considerable fame as a navigator and map-maker. The statue here shows him as a young man, scarcely more than a boy, lovingly pointing out the way to his old father. We can imagine that the Cabots are on their first voyage to America and that Sebastian is enthusiastically urging a venturesome trip into some unexplored river mouth, which the elder Cabot is fearful to undertake. His father is studying the map and thinking over the suggestion with the cautiousness of age.

and explored 2,000 miles of our northeastern coast. Then he was captured and put to death as a pirate. Violent death, disgrace or neglect, was the fate of most of the explorers of all nations in America. Many, indeed, were pirates; and most ships were traders, armed naval vessels and privateers in one. In this wild and lawless time the destiny of nations was decided on the oceans of the world.

France was distracted from further adventures for one hundred years, but stuck to her sober business of bringing fish home from the Grand Banks of Newfoundland for her Friday dinner. But not England. Seeing a profitable business and plenty of adventure in buccaneering, they built swift ships with high forecastles, clouds of sails and long-range cannon and sailed out, alike to explore and to raid the Spanish treasure ships. It was these explorers and pirates, who, in the sixteenth century, opened the sea to England and secured for her the discoveries of the Cabots.

Spain's Undeserved Good Fortune

But in the main, the story of the sixteenth century in America belongs to Spain, although she did little to deserve her good fortune. Unlike little Portugal, she had no interest in the science of navigation, and gave Columbus only a half-hearted hearing, deluding him with false promises. There is nothing more tragic in history than the figure of this poor, discredited genius. A beggar at indifferent courts at fifty-five, ridiculed, gray, broken-hearted, we see him leading his motherless son, Diego, across the lovely landscape of Andalusia, to the monastery of La Rabida to beg the good brothers for food and shelter. And no situation in melodrama seems more wildly improbable than that he should find there a father confessor to Queen Isabella.

Columbus got another hearing because the royal treasury was depleted from long religious war against the Mohammedan Moors of Granada in Southern Spain. There was money in the India trade, but Portugal had the route about the Cape of Good Hope all but completed, and would not share it. There was hope only in the West. The Spaniards believed ardently in old legends of fabled islands and cities in the sea, in mountains of gold and fountains of youth. So the great navigator got his ships and sailed from Palos, Spain. His greatness lay, not in the fact that he discovered America, for he died in ignorance that he had found a new continent, but in his vision and daring in sailing westward at all.

The Navigator and the Dreamers

Other Spanish explorers had only to follow in his path. By 1525 they had explored the coast from Florida around to California, and penetrated the heart of the continents, working westward from Florida and north and south from Mexico. The cross went with the sword into every wilderness they trod. Magellan, a Portuguese in the service of Spain first circumnavigated the globe, and for quite two hundred years Spanish treasure fleets, convoyed by ships of war, plowed the seas.

England's Collision with Spain

But they were not left unmolested. America was too big for one nation to occupy, the oceans too vast to be defended. The geographical situation of Spain had given the Spaniards the best route, in that day of sailing vessels, in the path of the trade-winds along the Tropic of Cancer, and the lands of gold in the American tropics. Above the Carolinas on the eastern coast their ships never cruised, and all the North Atlantic was left unguarded. Quite unmolested by them, the Norman French, descendants of the old Norse Vikings, fished in ever-growing numbers on the Grand Banks of Newfoundland and even followed schools of whales into the St. Lawrence. And the Spaniards used their flood of gold from Mexico to wage war on the Protestant Netherlands, and to threaten England with naval fleets. When the English broke with the Pope and set up a church of their own, Spain, as defender of the Roman faith, undertook to punish them.

England was too small and poor to make open war on Spain, but her rulers aided and abetted venturesome men in building and arming the biggest and swiftest vessels on the ocean. With all sails spread, these men of Bristol and Plymouth braved the fogs, storms and cross-currents of the North Atlantic, and swooped down like hawks on the Spanish treasure fleets. Many seamen left commerce and fishing to engage in this profitable and patriotic business of piracy. The British bred as bold, picturesque and successful buccaneers and slave-traders as ever sailed the seas. As early as 1563, Sir John Hawkins invaded the Portuguese regions of East Africa, sold Negroes in the West Indies, and brought American Indians to London. Sir Francis Drake was bolder, sinking whole fleets, and burning towns and robbing the mule pack-trains on the Isthmus of Panama. From a peak there Drake had glimpsed the Pacific—blue, peaceful, shimmering—that had thrilled the Spaniard, Balboa, half a century before, and vowed to God that he would make a "perfect discovery" of that great ocean. In 1580 he returned from his voyage around the world. Some historians call him the British Puck. He had put a girdle around the earth. The first of all English heroes of the sea, he helped to make it possible to lay claim to the lands discovered nearly a hundred years before by the Cabots, now remembered and honored, and to plant English colonies on the North Atlantic seaboard.

The Good Qualities of Magellan

Does this look like a man of stubborn will, great courage and (for his age) a humane disposition? He was all these things, for this is Ferdinand Magellan, one of the world's most daring explorers. He was born a mountaineer, far away from ships and the sea, but he was of noble descent and went as a page to the court of the king when he was only a boy. There he heard the wonderful reports of the great navigators of that age of discovery as they returned from the far ends of the earth. Fired with the zeal to equal their exploits, he embarked upon an expedition around the Cape of Good Hope to the East Indies. Magellan was a small, homely man, with irregular features and an awkward appearance, but his will was tremendous and his mind clear and active. In the midst of the fierce storms and hardships of the passage through the strait that bears his name, Magellan's men besought him to go no farther. He replied, "I will press on if we have to eat the leather of the rigging." And his statement was proved to be literally true, for in the midst of the vast Pacific, when the biscuit had become a mass of wormy powder and the drinking water was so foul that the sailors had to hold their noses in drinking it, they did cut off pieces of the leather rigging, soak them in sea water to soften them and broiled them over the coals. Unlike most of the explorers for Spain, he was so humane to the natives whom he encountered on the voyage that his men complained because his gentleness didn't give them enough amusement; nor could he be prevailed upon to turn aside from his purpose to look for gold or treasure. He did not live to complete the circumnavigation of the earth, as he was slain by natives in the Philippine Islands in 1521.

Francis Drake was the last and best of a brave and patriotic breed of men who won for England her place on the sea. Before he died on shipboard in the West Indies, the courtly Oxford student, Walter Raleigh, appeared, won the

Magellan Passing Through the Straits

This picture gives you a good idea of how the vessels of Magellan must have looked when they sailed through the straits which bear his name, as the details of the kind of ships in which he is known to have sailed are very carefully worked out. It was considered quite an achievement for the United States to send a fleet of great war vessels through these straits, under Admiral Evans a number of years ago. But several of the battleships of this fleet were of 16,000 tons of burden, while none of Magellan's were more than 130 tons and some were only 60 tons.

Raleigh and "The Drake"

The Terror of the Spanish

Sir Francis Drake's character is easily read in this portrait of him. Not so much the gentleman and courtier as Raleigh, his large eyes look boldly at you, his chin is square and firm. There is not a weak line about his face. And he needed all that boldness and strength in his long voyage around the world, for making such a trip, with the small sailing vessels then in use, and a rich, powerful enemy like Spain to combat, was a very brave thing indeed. But it is to Drake and the men like him that England owes her sea power today, for they broke Spain's cruel rule in the New World and swept her haughty merchantmen off the seas. So greatly did the Spanish fear him that when the great Spanish Armada was sent against the English fleet and its commander, found that the vessel attacking his own ship was commanded by Drake, he struck his colors at once, not even attempting resistance against the gallant Englishman.

Raleigh, the Courtier, in His Gallant Dress

Sir Walter Raleigh lived in a romantic age of stirring events and took no small part in the shaping of those events. As a youth he had his own fortune to make and, being of an adventurous disposition, he went to court. You all know the story of how, when his clothes represented "a considerable part of his estate," he threw his cloak across a puddle so that the queen might not soil her shoes. It was by such acts as this, and by the charm of his handsome face, strong, tall figure, and ready wit in flattery and verse-making that he won the queen's favor. Raleigh was a court dandy and a very fine gentleman indeed, as well as a writer and explorer, so he was dressed in the very latest fashion you may be sure. What do you think of his collar? The ruff had at that time only recently come into fashion. It began to be used in the first half of the sixteenth century as a little cambric collar with a fancy edge.

fickle favor of Queen Elizabeth, explored, named and claimed for England the coast of Virginia, and left a company of ill-fated colonists on Roanoke Island. He and his dream of colonization were brief, for he was overtaken by the tragic end that awaited most explorers. After fifteen years of unjust imprisonment, he was executed on a charge of treason in 1618. He was soon forgotten, for London, Paris and Antwerp were thinking of little but finding the northwest passage to China for which the Cabots had searched as far as Hudson's Bay. Portugal held the route around Africa, and Magellan and Drake had proved the length and perils of the voyage around South America. Both were too long for northern countries. England, France and Holland turned their eyes and hopes northwestward.

THE AGE OF DISCOVERY

Wonderful Story of the Dutch

The Dutch had fairly won their right to a share in the exploration of the New World and of trade in the Far East. A smaller country even than Portugal had been, though enriched by industry and trade, only 800,000 sturdy people dwelt on the sterile sands behind the dykes of Holland on the North Sea. There they had fought their long wars for political and religious liberty against the armies of Spain. In the days of English privateering they decided that their enemy was to be defeated only on the sea. Declaring honorable war, the Dutch, too, raided the treasure ships and brought home gold to pay and feed their little armies. When able to hold their own on the sea the Dutch stoutly disputed the division of the world and started out definitely to find a route of their own.

What this little nation did in the last quarter of the sixteenth century is altogether incredible. The Dutch first sent ships northeast, trying to round Norway and Russia. Some of their ship-wrecked crews spent winters on Nova Zembla and Spitzbergen. Shakespeare speaks of these earliest of arctic explorers in his reference to "icicles hanging on a Dutchman's beard." They cared little for ice, storm or fog, but they were not reckless. When, in Archangel, Russia, they heard of the bitter, endless leagues of Siberia stretching southward around the North Pole, they very sensibly turned back.

Next they tried the southern route. Fighting the Portuguese, tropic storms, the ship diseases of long voyages, and the natives of Java, they brought back cargoes of spices. The orange, white and blue flag of the Dutch Republic was on every sea.

Not contented with these achievements, they rivaled England and France in efforts to find the Northwest Passage, offering a prize and honors to any navigator of any nation who would discover it. This attracted the attention of an Englishman, Henry Hudson, who entered the Dutch service, and sailed westward in the Half-Moon. This was in

A "Type" Picture of Henry Hudson

This is not a true picture of Henry Hudson, for, so far as we know, that brave explorer never had his portrait painted. It is the picture of some unknown man who probably resembled Hudson, and so the picture came to be called a portrait of Henry Hudson and as such has come down to us. Hudson's name is written a good many times on the map of our continent, though he didn't actually discover the regions that are named for him. He and Champlain both proved about the same time that there is no short route to China across North America, and Hudson's voyages were the beginning of the great fisheries and other trade with the New World.

What Hudson Did for the Dutch

Henry Hudson's Last Voyage

Hudson's fourth voyage of exploration, in the service of England, took him into what is now Hudson Bay, where his little vessel, the "Discovery," was frozen in during the winter. When the ice broke up in the spring the ship's provisions were so low that it seemed that all aboard must starve. The men were sick and rebellious, and of course they blamed Henry Hudson for the sufferings they were undergoing. He was still eager to press on in the hope of finding a passage to Asia, but the crew took matters into their own hands. They set him adrift, with eight of the sickest of their number, in a small, open boat, while they made all possible speed back to England. Here you see Hudson, comforting his small son, who is too sick and weak to sit up alone, and at the same time guiding the rudder of the little boat so that it won't be crushed to pieces by the great ice floes of Hudson Bay. One of the sick men is crouching under a fur robe in the foreground. Notice the clear, sad eyes the artist has given the old explorer; he is doing his feeble best to prevent their destruction, though he can see nothing ahead but death from cold and hunger.

The faithless crew of the "Discovery" fared but little better than the captain whom they deserted. Several of them were killed in a battle with the Eskimos, others died of starvation on the return voyage, and the few who reached England were thrown into prison for their crime.

THE AGE OF DISCOVERY

1609, one hundred and seventeen years after Columbus sailed from Palos, Spain.

The exploration of America was far from being finished, but a new era had opened. In 1600 neither England, France nor Holland held a foot of soil in the Western Hemisphere. With the exception of Brazil, which Portugal held, Spain claimed both continents and was in actual possession of two-thirds of the land. But Northern Europe was determined, if not united. A small colony was established by the English at Jamestown, Virginia, in 1607. In 1609, Champlain entered the St. Lawrence River and planted the golden lilies of France at Montreal; Henry Hudson sailed up the Hudson River for the Dutch, and an Englishman, Captain John Smith, explored the coast of New England. All of these explorers were searching for the Northwest Passage to China. Not one of them dreamed of the extent or riches of the continent, whose water gates they had entered, or that a new age of colonization had opened.

How Columbus Landed at Taunton

The school children of Taunton, Mass., gave a pageant in which they acted out the landing of Columbus. Here we see Columbus approaching the new shore, welcomed by a wondering Indian. He landed, you know, "richly clad and bearing a royal banner of Spain, on Watling Island, called by him Saint Salvador." Notice the "F. Y." on the banner. This stands for Ferdinand and Isabella, for in Spanish, Queen Isabella's name began with a "Y."

De Soto and His Romance

De Soto was a poor young nobleman, who as a retainer in the household of Pedrarias d'Avila, the Governor of a Spanish colony in America, fell in love with Avila's daughter, Isabella. Then Avila fell out with him for he had other plans for Isabella. Having failed to secure the assassination of De Soto he readily consented to his coming to America in the hope that he would be killed or disgraced in the fierce struggles for wealth in the new country. But, instead, as we know, De Soto won fame and fortune in the New World. Isabella waited for him faithfully and when he returned to Spain, fifteen long years afterward—Avila, in the meantime having died—they were married and lived happily in Seville for two years, when De Soto embarked on the expedition for which he is chiefly noted and which cost him his life.

STORIES OF AMERICAN HISTORY
THE SPANISH IN AMERICA

The Spanish Gold Seekers and Their Rule of Ruin

NO time in the history of the human race furnishes a more interesting and instructive study than that of the colonization of America by Spain, France and England. Here, on a continental scale, is illustrated the fact that the destiny of a nation is determined less by its outer circumstances than by the character and ideals of its people. In the settlement of America, Spain had all the advantages of time, location and natural wealth. She preceded France and England in the New World by a century, had the most favorable trade route, and found *How Spain Won Wealth and Ruin* gold and silver with which to develop her possessions in the rich American tropics. It is true that she came in contact with, and was opposed by the two most civilized and highly organized of Indian nations—the Aztecs of Mexico and the Incas of Peru — but she was equipped to conquer them speedily and had no long, harassing Indian wars. So one might reasonably expect to find Spanish colonies the most flourishing and progressive. The reverse is true. They sank steadily into poverty, disorder and ruin as the English colonies rose to prosperity, responsibility and freedom.

Presently we shall discover that American colonies failed or succeeded according to the worth of the ideas upon which they were founded. The Spaniards were gold seekers, caring nothing for the lands of their discovery, except what they could take out of them. The French were adventurers, missionaries and conscious empire builders, the success of their plans depending upon the intelli-

The Spanish Soldier's Iron Hat and Its Air Holes

When Cortez led his little force against the great Aztec citadel, he defeated the Aztecs but sacrificed most of his own men. This helmet was lost by one of the Spanish soldiers who died there and was found many years afterward. It is not one of the headpieces worn by mounted knights in full armor, as you see, but probably belonged to a foot soldier who was either a gunner or archer. It is hardly more than a peaked iron hat but it was a good deal of protection to the soldier's head against the heavy wooden or stone weapons of the Indians. Foot soldiers did not wear full suits of mail at any time during the Middle Ages when armor was worn, for it was too heavy for a long march or for quick movement on foot, and it was too costly for a poor man to buy and keep in repair. During the long marches in the hot sun and over the Mexican mountains, the soldiers of Cortez wore no more armor than was absolutely necessary, you may be sure, because it was so uncomfortable. The holes were for ventilation. Imagine wearing a hat like this in the broiling sun!

1453

gent co-operation of the mother country, which was not always given. The English alone were self-reliant, home builders and defenders. They depended on themselves.

Greek and Roman Ideas of Colonization

We must remember that to the peoples of Europe of that day, emigration was an experiment. Since the fall of the Roman Empire there had been few large movements of the population, or undeveloped lands open to settlement. So all their ideas of colonies were got from the histories of ancient Greece and Rome. The Greek colony was founded by a band of voluntary exiles like the Pilgrims of the Mayflower. A brave little company of families departed from their old home, taking seeds, tools and cattle with them. They expected to make *The Loyal Greek Colonists* a living by their own labor, and to govern and defend themselves. Loyal citizens of Greece, they were ever ready to fight for their parent city, and to her they looked, with a confidence that was seldom abused, for help and protection. On this ideal, a wide community of rich farming lands and commercial cities spread around the islands and shores of the eastern Mediterranean Sea and flourished for a thousand years.

The Roman Empire was built up by conquest. Conquering her colonies by the sword, she held them with garrisons of soldiers, but only until lands could be allotted to Roman citizens, who emigrated with *How Europe Copied Rome* their families. The Roman colony was not self-governing. It was always ruled by appointment from the capital. In the settlement of America this Roman idea of centralized power was held by every court of Europe. The new lands were the property of the Crown, to be given or withheld at the pleasure of the king, and it was his right to appoint the governor. But while this theory of the colony was held in all countries, the practical workings of it differed widely.

In England, where there was a measure of political liberty and a surplus of industrious, independent people, emigration was encouraged, and some colonies were granted charters to govern themselves. Only ill-advised monarchs interfered much with colonial liberties or *How the English Differed* imposed unpopular governors or unjust taxes. Thus the English colony was a mixture of the Greek and Roman. It was protected and fostered, and at the same time learned to be self-reliant. The French colony was purely Roman, but lacked strength and definite policy. The Spanish colony was the conquered Roman province at its worst. Captured and ruled by the sword, it was held for three centuries by an army of occupation, while it was systematically parceled out, robbed and oppressed. It existed for no people, but solely to fill the king's treasury. The only redeeming feature was the devotion and self-sacrifice of the missionary monks whose ruined mission villages still dot the landscape of our southwest.

Spanish Men and Methods

Now the early Spanish explorers should be given due credit for their heroism and very great discoveries. They braved dangers and endured hardships such as no English and few French ever faced. And they were not all plumed, mailed and

THE SPANISH IN AMERICA

mounted knights, like Cortez in Mexico, and Pizarro in Peru, leading victorious armies into treasure-filled capitals. Lured on by the hopes of rich rewards from the king, or by phantoms and fables of lands of gold and fountains of youth, they were cruel and relentless, but they failed miserably as often as they succeeded. Gray-bearded grandees of old Aragon and Castile were captured and tortured by savage tribes. They sank in the poisonous swamps of Florida, and found graves in the tawny flood of the Mississippi. We see them afoot and dying of thirst in the cactus desert of Arizona, freezing in the eternal snows of the Andes, and stung to death in the venomous jungles of Panama, which they opened for their treasure-laden pack trains.

It is because of such men as these that Spain was able to explore and occupy all of South America (except Brazil), Central America, Mexico, the southern third of the United States, and the larger islands of the West Indies, within thirty-five years after the first voyage of Columbus. But when the lands were secured, and these early actors were off the stage, Spain ceased to explore, and spent all her energies in establishing strong military rule, and in draining her American colonies dry.

The rapidity and extent of the Spanish conquest is explained by the fact that the precious metals, in varying quantities, mined and unmined, were found nearly everywhere; and each new colony, without help from Spain, furnished the wealth to conquer the next. The island of Hispaniola (Hayti) where Columbus built his first fort of the timber from one of his wrecked ships, alone furnished $2,000,000 of gold. Cuba outfitted ships to explore Florida and conquer Mexico. Mexico, in turn, sent fleets to Panama and the Philippines, and Panama furnished men and ships for the expedition against the Incas of Peru. Mexico and Peru poured rivers of silver and brooks of gold across Panama and the Atlantic into the Spanish treasury.

Long before France and England had any foothold on the continent, Spain had built fortified cities at Havana, St. Augustine, Florida. Vera Cruz, Mexico, and Panama,

The Conqueror of Mexico

At sixteen, Hernando Cortez chose a life of adventure as his career. He went to Cuba and from there he led an expedition to explore Mexico. The stories of the wealth and power of the Aztec emperors made him determined to conquer them, so he burned the ships which brought his force, in order to teach his soldiers that they must conquer or die. By his cunning and his bravery he succeeded in subduing the whole of Mexico for Spain, though his rule was one long tale of torture and oppression. Great wealth and honor were his for a time, but he died disappointed and neglected by the king whose territory he had so greatly increased.

Plunder of the Treasuries

1455

and had erected forts, garrisons, prisons, governors' palaces, cathedrals and monasteries in numerous seaports and colonial capitals. Before the middle of the sixteenth century, she had set up nine widely scattered governments, in Peru, Argentina, Chili, New Granada (now Colombia and Panama), Venezuela, Guatemala, Yucatan, Mexico and Cuba, under viceroys or captains-general, and had complete control of well-established trade routes.

In that time the Spanish planted only one true colony after the English pattern. This was at Santa Fe, New Mexico. This second oldest city in the United States was founded by an American-born Spanish-Mexican, Juan de Onate. Taking 200 soldiers, and as many colonists, men, women and children, with seeds, tools, cattle and sheep, and a band of missionaries, he built a self-sustaining town and the Church of San Gabriel in our mountain and desert country. Santa Fe is proof that the Spaniards might have been useful colonists had the right classes been permitted to emigrate, and had they not been corrupted by finding too much "easy money." This colony was the model of the later mission towns of California. Nominally they were under Mexico, but in reality were too far away to be interfered with.

Spain's Only True Colony

In all her other colonies, Spain kept everything in her own hand—people, lands, revenues, courts, administration, religion and trade. The viceroy or captain-general, was sent out from Spain, and represented the royal ruler. He was supported by troops from home, and had the power of life and death. The very first governor appointed, arrested Columbus and sent the great navigator home in chains. Balboa, who discovered the Pacific Ocean from a mountain-top in Panama, was put to death by a viceroy, who was jealous of his growing fame. Spain's best and bravest were betrayed and ruined.

Cortez in His Iron "Dress Suit"

In the sixteenth century when Cortez and the other Spanish explorers were making their conquests in America, armor had almost outlived its usefulness. But it was still worn on state occasions as a sort of full dress. The portrait opposite shows Cortez in a very handsome suit of dress armor. The ornamental armor of Cortez' day was of thin steel plates inlaid with gold and silver, trimmed with those ridges and engraved in various designs. The short skirt of old-fashioned chain mail which Cortez wears, came into use in the latter part of the fifteenth century. Over this are the tuilles, a series of jointed plates that look like hip pads and swing as the warrior walks. The breastplate of this suit is beautifully decorated, and you can see the origin of the modern epaulets worn on officers' uniforms, in the heavily ornamented shoulder plates. The succession of band-like plates on the upper arm, at the elbow and around the neck, allowed the poor overloaded knight some freedom of movement. Cortez' helmet does not protect his face as the earlier and more useful helmets did. Its great crest of feathers is in keeping with the gorgeousness of his armor, and no fully armed knight would have been ready for battle without his steel gauntlets, like those lying on the table beside Cortez.

Why don't we wear armor nowadays? It isn't altogether because bullets have taken the place of arrows and spears in warfare, though of course a knight's armor would not be proof against modern rifles. By the end of the sixteenth century, armies were no longer made up of steel-encased knights, fighting hand to hand, because the medieval custom of fighting in solid, immovable masses changed. Rulers began to organize armies that they could move rapidly from place to place for surprise attacks and quick raids into the enemy's territory. This required long marches and rapid transportation, something that was impossible for the cumbersome, heavily-armed knight who couldn't even get to his feet without help if he had the misfortune to fall down.

Squeezing the Colonies Dry

The System of Extortion

No Spanish colony ever cost the mother country a penny. Each one not only paid its own civil and military expenses, but showed a handsome profit for the Crown. To many offices no salary was attached, but appointments were eagerly sought, for the holders were privileged to grow rich on what could be squeezed out of the colony after the royal treasury was satis-

Cortez in His Iron Dress Suit

"In the sixteenth century when Cortez and the other Spanish explorers were making their conquests in America, armor was still worn on state occasions as a sort of full dress."

fied. Lands were allotted to nobles, explorers and colonial officials for service to the Crown. The only exception to this was the lands that were given to religious orders for churches, missions and monasteries.

anything that Spain could produce. The only colonial industries encouraged were the building up of large cattle ranches and mining properties, and for the working of these the owners had the free labor of en-

The Story of the Spanish Conquests

Although this painting, the original of which is in the Capitol at Washington, is called "The Discovery of the Mississippi by De Soto," it is rather a summary of the Spanish conquests in America, than a true picture of the historical event. As a matter of fact, De Soto did not discover the Mississippi. It was first sighted by Penedia who sailed a short distance up stream from its mouth in 1519, while De Soto did not reach the Mississippi in his search for the gold that was not there, until 1541. He was an extremely handsome man and it would be hard to conceive a more striking figure than he represents here in his plumed hat on his white charger.

Before him you see, considerably idealized, the Indian maidens and the Indian men with their weapons at their feet and peace pipes in their hands in token of subjection. Behind him are his soldiers with their armor and their serpent-handled cannon. the culverin. In the foreground is a chest typifying the wealth Spain took from her possessions, and further to the right, the priests blessing the cross about to be elevated in the new land. Such pictures, while they do not represent real historic scenes, are very useful. Fix them in your mind and you will be surprised to see how easily you can recall whole periods of history and their lessons for us.

Spanish farmers and mechanics—the best of all classes for true colonists—were discouraged, and even forbidden to emigrate to America. Spain is not a country of skilled industries, and never had any skilled workmen to spare. Besides, more could be made at home, supplying Toledo swords, armor, Cordovan leather for the trappings of cavalry horses, and even woolen cloth, olive oil and wine, to the colonies, which were not allowed to grow or make slaved Indians and imported Negroes.

And while men who would have made useful colonists were kept at home, Spain forced her undesirables to emigrate. Criminals and paupers were drafted into colonial armies, or shipped as crews of the "flotas" or treasure fleets. Columbus was given such a crew of rascals for his first voyage, and was threatened with mutiny. Every colony, of

The Grandees and the Jail Birds

1458

course, had its devoted missionaries, for the Cross went with the sword into every wilderness conquered by Spain. But beside the Brotherhoods we find in all Spanish colonies only the dregs and froth of society — beggars, jailbirds and degraded slaves, and over them the cruel, indolent, greedy and haughty grandees of Spain. So perfect was that organization of tyranny and corruption, so relentless its grip, that it endured for three hundred years; and Cuba freed herself at the end of another century, only with the help of the United States. We can study the colonial system of Spain in the unhappy story of this big, beautiful island near our southeastern shores.

Balboa the Adventurer

Vasco Nuñez de Balboa was a typical adventurer. Soon after coming to the West Indies he involved himself so heavily in debt because of his recklessness, that he had to flee the country in order to avoid arrest, so, taking with him only his armor, he hid himself in a cask of provisions, and was loaded on board a vessel embarked upon an exploring expedition to Central America. He soon rose to be first in command and was counted the strongest lance and the surest shot in the company. Prodigal, generous, and good-natured, he was loved by his men and had more success in dealing with the Indians than any other Spaniard of the period, except De Soto. Under his command the spoils of war were divided equally among all the soldiers, irrespective of rank. It is said Balboa never commanded his men to GO but always asked them to COME with him.

Story of Cuba as a Type

Cuba was discovered by Columbus on his first voyage. A curving bow of land, ninety miles wide and nearly eight hundred long, it had all the appearance of a continent. When he had passed through the fringe of small islands and coral reefs on its north coast, he was struck by the grandeur of its airy mountains and long lines of bold headlands. And no less was he impressed with its tropical forests, fertile valleys, many bright streams and broad coastal plains. Certain that this was a part of the mainland of China, he sent envoys to greet the Emperor. But he found here only friendly natives. In Hayti and other neighboring islands there were tribes of cannibal Caribs, but the Koo-bans of Cuba were far advanced and peaceable. They had a simple religious belief, without barbarous ceremonies, lived on fruit, fish and corn, wove cotton cloth, made baskets, pottery and golden ornaments, and built such good huts of grass, bark and palm leaves, that their model is still used by the Spanish-Cubans of today. Columbus called Cuba the Fortunate Isle. Its misfortunes began with the coming of the Spaniards.

The island was not occupied, however, until Hayti, where a greater quantity of gold was found, had begun to run dry of treasure. By that time the Koo-Bans had become of gold was also soon exhausted.

Cuba's wealth was in its soil, but the island was permitted to grow only sugar, coffee, cotton and tobacco, which Spain could not produce.

Cortez and the Wreck of the Aztec Gods

During the conquest of Mexico, Cortez and his soldiers were driven from the city of Mexico and forced to flee for their lives. At Otumba a great Aztec army blocked the way. They vastly outnumbered the Spaniards and though the Spaniards had a tremendous advantage in their armor, horses, and cannon, the Indians were getting the better of them when Cortez decided he must capture the Aztec commander in order to save the day. This commander was a royal personage, and was directing the battle from a hilltop, borne in a litter by his nobles. The Aztecs thought their royal family the highest representatives of the gods on earth and worshipped them as such. Cortez succeeded in cutting his way through the mass of warriors surrounding their chieftain. The litter was overturned, and the king and his nobles slain. As the Aztec chief fell, a Spanish soldier seized the sacred standard from his hand and gave it to Cortez who was on horseback. When the Aztecs saw the litter, with its sacred emblems, overturned, and the royal banner captured, they were struck with superstitious terror and fled in all directions. It was this victory which decided the fate of Mexico.

The picture shows Cortez just after receiving the banner from the soldier. In the foreground is the overturned litter, the images of their gods that the Indians carried into battle, and the Indians themselves can be seen fleeing in all directions.

alarmed, for news of Spanish methods had been spread. They resisted, but were speedily conquered, and put under a tribute of gold or cotton. Those who failed to pay were enslaved, or branded as cannibals and put to death. No Indian was ever able to endure slavery. Hard labor, disease and despair reduced the native population so rapidly that it practically disappeared in one generation. Their scanty accumulation

Nobles grew rich on their big plantations, by the use of negro slaves. But all around them fertile lands lay uncultivated. Not only were the working classes of Spain forbidden to emigrate, but all foreigners were refused admission. Trade was restricted by high tariffs and by the government's custom of selling the monopoly of it to one city, first Santiago, then Havana, and

Monopoly of Robbery

THE SPANISH IN AMERICA
A Muzzle-Loading Cannon

This is the heaviest gun of the sixteenth century in use in the New World and threw a shot of fifteen pounds. It takes its name, culverin, from a French word, meaning serpent, on account of those crooked handles, on the top, with which the gunners tilted up the gun when loading and which are supposed to look like serpents. You see cannon in those days were muzzle-loaders, like the rifles. When first invented, these cannon threw round stones. In a Turkish cannon, a 600-lb. stone shot was used in the siege of Constantinople. In Dover Castle, England, there is still to be seen a culverin which is known as "Queen Elizabeth's Pocket Pistol."

every necessity had to be imported from the mother country. Commerce with foreign lands, and even with neighboring Spanish colonies, was not permitted. Evasion of this law was punishable by confiscation of property and death. All trade was by "flotas" or royal fleets under convoy of Spanish war ships. Vessels of other nations were even denied refuge from storms in Cuban ports.

Some of these regulations were, no doubt, necessary in the sixteenth century. Spain had many enemies who disputed her arrogant claim to the whole western hemisphere. Her "flotas" were attacked on the Atlantic by the English, Dutch and French. And, as all Spanish ships, to and from the Colonies, stopped in the fortified harbor at Havana, Cuba became the storm center of a wild and lawless century on the sea. Her coasts were raided, her towns burned, her slaves captured, and her many fringing islands and snug harbors furnished hiding places for pirates. But when these dangers no longer threatened, Spain did not relax her grip on Cuba, although all the conditions had changed, and the island could quickly have risen to prosperity.

In spite of all Spain's precautions and restrictions a native-born white population was growing up. Some nobles had chosen to remain; or had left their rich estates to younger sons who married in the island and brought up families. These Spanish-Cubans asked for schools, but were refused any except those kept by religious brotherhoods. None but devotional books were allowed to be imported. The native-born were not permitted to travel abroad, or to send their children to foreign countries to be educated. And, although of pure Spanish stock, they were excluded from office. Rulers from Spain thus formed a privileged caste, a class apart, foreign in feeling and habits, and with no interest in the island. They looked upon the natives as inferiors; on the land as something alien that existed only to be plundered. In four hundred years there were one hundred and thirty-six captains-general of Cuba, most of whom were greedy politicians who went home rich.

This state of affairs bred exasperation, desperation and contempt of the law in the very people who should have been building up a prosperous country and stable government. Smuggling became a flourishing industry. The Cubans needed the salt-fish, meat and lamp-oil of the English colonies, and the North needed sugar, molasses, tobacco, coffee and cotton. So the sailing vessels of good Puritans and Quakers slipped into island bays and carried on a profitable if dangerous trade. The children of rich planters often "disappeared," returning after being educated in Boston or Philadelphia. Discontent seethed under the surface while the burden grew heavier. Spain was never a manufacturing country and could not supply the growing needs of Cuba. She bought of England, France, Germany and even the United States, and reshipped cargoes to Havana. Many a vessel load made two voyages across the Atlantic, Cuba paying double freight, giving a profit to some Spanish merchant, and then paying high import duties. The cost of every imported necessity was doubled. At times Cuban ports were opened to foreign trade, but extra duties and port and tonnage dues made this unprofitable. Export duties were assessed on all the products of the island. Industry was slowly bled to death.

Throwing Off the Spanish Yoke

Early in the nineteenth century all the Spanish colonies in America rose in revolution. Taking advantage of the Napoleonic wars in Europe, in which Spain was conquered and her King lost his throne, every colony from Cape Horn to the Rio Grande River threw off the Spanish yoke and formed republics. Cuba and Porto Rico rebelled also, but before they could win their freedom the old line of monarchs was restored in Madrid. From one of the greatest and richest powers in Europe, Spain had sunk to one of the poorest and weakest, but was still strong enough to hold her West Indian islands. Needing money desperately and with four colonies left from which to obtain it, Cuba was squeezed to the last bitter drop.

Beside the old trade restrictions, monopolies and duties, every industry, trade, profession and art was taxed. Real estate paid 12 percent, so that any Cuban who owned his home bought it again of the government every eight years. There were taxes on the farmers' plows and the workmen's tools, on every beef sold in the market, on the surgeon's instruments and the carrier's cart. Every bill, account, check, note, court claim, deed, will, contract and license had its stamp tax. Printed legal forms had to be bought of the government, the price per sheet running from three to forty dollars, according to the money value of the business transaction. Tax collectors, working on commission, were interested in over-valuing everything. This led to bribery and every form of political corruption. All of Cuba's profits and savings were automatically absorbed into the treasury and the official pockets of Spain. There was no capital for business, no revenues for schools, roads, pub-

Cuba Still Enslaved

lic buildings or for health. Havana and other seaports became pest holes of yellow fever, festering and rotting under the tropic suns.

There were four rebellions in the half century after 1817. In 1868 a ten years' guerrilla warfare was begun that was one long nightmare of massacre, starvation, epidemic diseases and destruction of property. In making peace, Spain promised every reform that was asked for, but she did not keep faith and Cuba staggered up from its devastation to find itself saddled with a war debt of $300,000,000. Spain had borrowed money on Cuban bonds, with which to subjugate the unhappy islanders. After paying the interest on this debt, and supporting a fleet and army of occupation, and the civil expenses, there was now a deficit. Another hundred million of debt was slowly piled up. In 1890 Cuba owed $300 for every man, woman and child of its population, counting the recently freed slaves. Then the island was given a little taste of prosperity. For three years Cuba was permitted to buy and sell freely in the United States. Trade immediately, and to her great profit, flowed to this big, rich neighbor, her natural customer. This so alarmed Spain that the gates were again shut.

Cuba's Final Deliverance

But the island refused longer to submit. In 1895 there was a fresh revolution. With a real leader, in

"Remember the Maine"

When the revolution and famine in Cuba became serious, the United States battleship "Maine" was stationed in Havana harbor. Wholly without warning she was blown up and the 266 U. S. marines on board were killed. A board of inquiry examined the wreck, shown here, and decided that the cause of the explosion was that she had struck a mine, that nothing had gone wrong with her mechanism—that is, that the explosion was planned and not accidental. As a result of this report, President McKinley demanded that Spain withdraw from Cuba. On Spain's refusal, war was declared.

It was believed that the Maine was blown up by the Spanish authorities, but it was also suggested that Cuban revolutionists might have laid the mine, hoping to bring about war between Spain and the United States which would result in freeing Cuba from Spanish rule. There are also those, even in the United States, who think that perhaps the explosion was accidental and was from inside, not outside, the vessel. "Remember the Maine" became the battle cry of the American soldiers.

© Underwood & Underwood

Maximo Gomez, who formed an insurgent government, and whose intelligent plan was to destroy all of Spain's sources of revenue, Cuba was in flames from end to end. The revolutionists soon held all the land outside the garrisoned cities. Unable to cope with this situation, *Weyler's Horrible Rule* General Weyler, who had won fame, or rather, infamy, as "The Butcher of the Philippines," was sent to Havana as Captain-General. He was not a soldier, and, in any case, had too few troops for the task, but he could at least punish the helpless "pacificoes." On the ground that they were feeding and sheltering the scattered bands of revolutionists, he gathered the old men, women and children of the country into concentration camps in decaying cities. There, to the horror of the world, the population of Cuba began to perish of starvation and epidemic diseases.

This aroused the anger of the people of the United States. We had stood these horrors long enough. By buying Florida and Spanish possessions on the Pacific, annexing Texas after that state had separated *Our War with Spain* from Mexico, and giving the protection of the Monroe Doctrine to new and struggling Spanish-American republics, we had helped drive Spain from the continent. Then eighty years longer we had had this piteous little island neighbor at our doors, pleading for mercy and justice. Now, on threat of interference, our government demanded the recall of General Weyler and the release of the "pacificoes." Then the U. S. Battleship Maine, lying in Havana harbor, was blown up with a loss of 266 United States marines.

Congress recognized Cuban independence and declared war on Spain. With the cry: "Remember the Maine," our armies were in the field, our fleets on the sea. Admiral Dewey captured Manila in one short naval battle, and freed the Philippines. Admiral Sampson sank the Spanish fleet at Santiago, and our "rough riders" swarmed up San Juan hill. The war, beginning in April, was over in August.

We had colonies, almost for the first time in our history. We annexed little Porto Rico, to the general satisfaction of its people. The Philippines we undertook to keep and protect until the people could learn to govern and defend themselves. Every government in the world, very likely, thought we intended to annex Cuba. Many Cubans thought so, too, for they had no reason to trust anyone. But we announced our intention to remain only until the island republic could be put on its feet. The Cubans had earned their freedom by four hundred years of oppression and a hundred of struggle.

Within six months the whole country was under American military rule, with General Leonard Wood as governor. The dead were buried, the sick cared for in hospitals, the starving fed, the idle put to work cleaning the cities. Out of Santiago and Havana, four centuries of accumulated filth *What We Did for Cuba* was dug and destroyed. Water works and sewers were put in, and yellow fever stamped out. Then a police force and health department were organized. Money for all this work was found in customs' offices, official palaces and garrisons. Hospitals and

The Hero of Manila Bay

Harris & Ewing

For his brilliant work, Dewey was made an admiral, the highest office in the American navy, and became the hero of the hour. Here we see him in his admiral's uniform, the most marked feature of which is the epaulet of heavy gold cord on each shoulder. These queer ornaments were at one time worn by all soldiers alike. Later they were confined to officers only, and in the last century their use has been more and more restricted to the navy.

PICTURED KNOWLEDGE

In Honor of the Heroes of Manila Bay

This is the famous Dewey medal ordered by Congress to be struck in honor of the victory won by Dewey in Manila Bay. On one side is his portrait and on the other an American naval gunner stripped for action, seated on a gun. Around the sailor is the inscription, "In Memory of the Victory of Manila Bay, May 1, 1898." Around the relief of Dewey's keen and powerful face, this: "A Gift of the People of the United States to the Officers and Men of the Asiatic Squadron under the Command of Commodore George Dewey." Underneath the inscription is an anchor with the laurel wreath and a single star. The medals were the work of the eminent sculptor, D. C. French.

schools were built without extra taxation. People were returned to their farms, with seeds and tools; the press was made free, and the people had the right of free speech and peaceable assembly. The effect was wonderful. Cringing fear held up its head; the ruined took heart and began to build up their businesses; the children, clothed and fed, forgot their misery in clean, bright schools. No laggards there! School was a novelty. "Shining morning faces" were seen on every street. Within four years there were 3,300 public schools in the island, with 143,000 pupils. Civil service was applied to the customs and post office, police, health and fire departments and finances were put into such shape that Cuba could live in self-respecting, progressive ways, build up her industries, and still, in time, with reduced taxes, pay off her debts.

Our motto was "Cuba for the Cubans." A disinterested friend of a ruined and distracted neighbor, we held the island in trusteeship for two years, leaving it clean, well, on its feet and with a million and a half in its treasury. After seeing these newly enfranchised people through an honest election, with a government of their own choosing installed, the United States withdrew. In 1906, when there were charges of election frauds and threatened revolution, we were obliged to interfere and restore order. Three years later we withdrew our forces again, and the island flag flew over the now peaceful and prosperous little republic.

By its action in Cuba the United States gave the world a new idea of a colony. We rebuked the Roman system of gaining and holding lands by conquest, and improved on the liberal system of the Greeks. Our own country founded on the system of "government by consent of the governed," we drove Spanish armies out, put Cuba in order and then restored her to full freedom. And so, a little more than four hundred years after Columbus, Spain's flag disappeared from our hemisphere.

THE SPANISH IN AMERICA
Such a Big Battle in Such a Little Book!

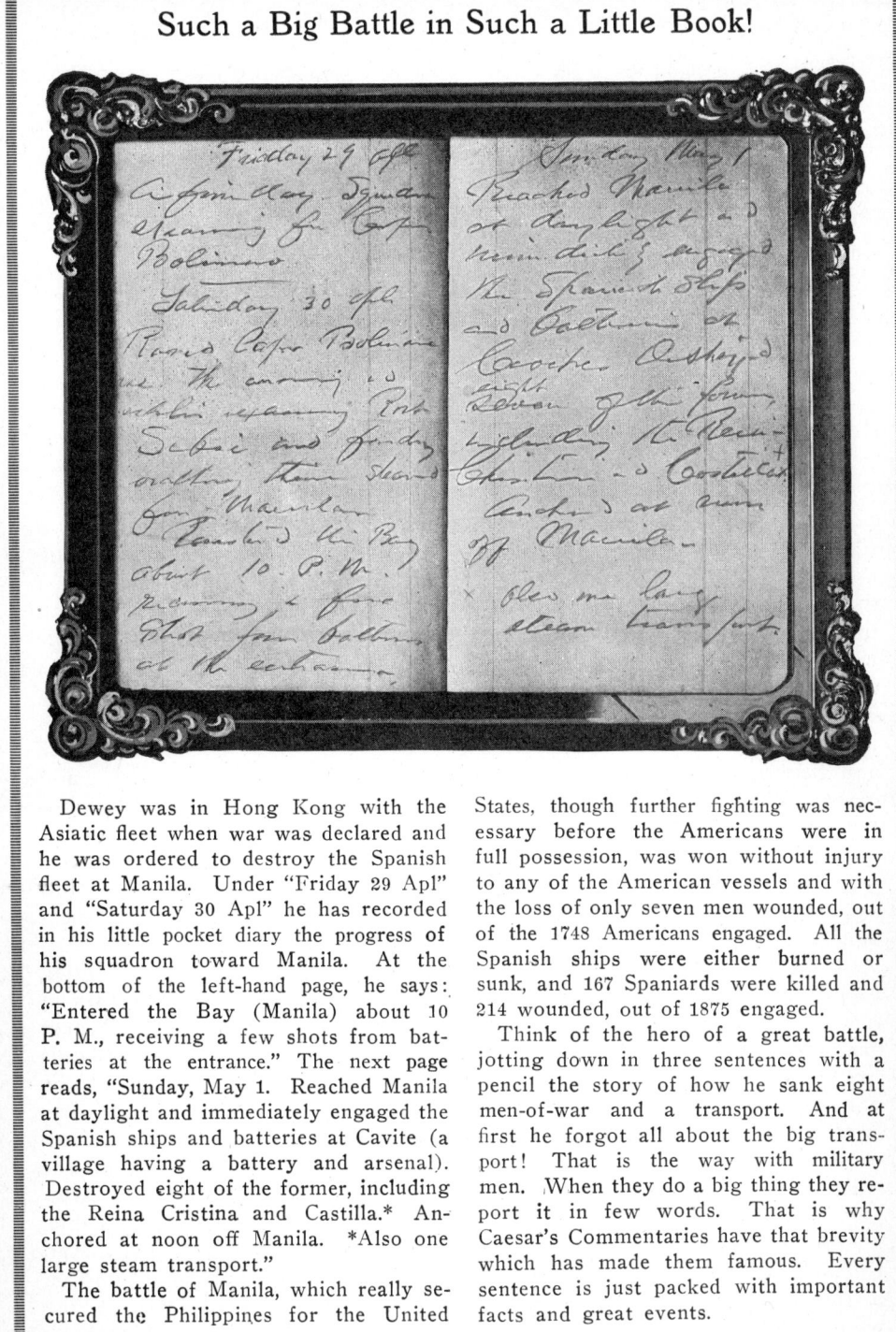

Dewey was in Hong Kong with the Asiatic fleet when war was declared and he was ordered to destroy the Spanish fleet at Manila. Under "Friday 29 Apl" and "Saturday 30 Apl" he has recorded in his little pocket diary the progress of his squadron toward Manila. At the bottom of the left-hand page, he says: "Entered the Bay (Manila) about 10 P. M., receiving a few shots from batteries at the entrance." The next page reads, "Sunday, May 1. Reached Manila at daylight and immediately engaged the Spanish ships and batteries at Cavite (a village having a battery and arsenal). Destroyed eight of the former, including the Reina Cristina and Castilla.* Anchored at noon off Manila. *Also one large steam transport."

The battle of Manila, which really secured the Philippines for the United States, though further fighting was necessary before the Americans were in full possession, was won without injury to any of the American vessels and with the loss of only seven men wounded, out of the 1748 Americans engaged. All the Spanish ships were either burned or sunk, and 167 Spaniards were killed and 214 wounded, out of 1875 engaged.

Think of the hero of a great battle, jotting down in three sentences with a pencil the story of how he sank eight men-of-war and a transport. And at first he forgot all about the big transport! That is the way with military men. When they do a big thing they report it in few words. That is why Caesar's Commentaries have that brevity which has made them famous. Every sentence is just packed with important facts and great events.

The Lotus-Eaters

"Courage!" he said, and pointed toward the land,
  "This mounting wave will roll us shoreward soon."
In the afternoon they came unto a land,
  In which it seemed always afternoon.
  All round the coast the languid air did swoon,
Breathing like one that hath a weary dream.
  Full-faced above the valley stood the moon;
And like a downward smoke, the slender stream
Along the cliff to fall and pause and fall did seem.

A land of streams! some, like a downward smoke,
  Slow-dropping veils of thinnest lawn, did go;
And some thro' wavering lights and shadows broke,
  Rolling a slumbrous sheet of foam below.
They saw the gleaming river seaward flow
  From the inner land; far off, three mountain-tops,
Three silent pinnacles of aged snow,
  Stood sunset-flushed; and, dew'd with showery drops,
  Up-clomb the shadowy pine above the woven copse.
The charmed sunset linger'd low adown
  In the red West; thro' mountain clefts the dale
  Was seen far inland, and the yellow down
Border'd with palm, and many a winding vale
  And meadow, set with slender galingale:
  A land where all things always seemed the same!
And round about the keel with faces pale,
  Dark faces pale against that rosy flame,
  The mild-eyed melancholy Lotos-eaters came.
Branches they bore of that enchanted stem,
  Laden with flower and fruit, whereof they gave
To each, but who so did receive of them,
  And taste, to him the gushing of the wave
  Far, far away did seem to mourn and rave
On alien shores; and if his fellow spake,
  His voice was thin, as voices from the grave;
And deep-asleep he seem'd, yet all awake,
And music in his ears his beating heart did make.

They sat them down upon the yellow sand,
  Between the sun and moon upon the shore;
And sweet it was to dream of Fatherland,
  Of child, and wife, and slave; but evermore
  Most weary seem'd the sea, weary the oar,
Weary the wandering fields of barren foam.
  Then some one said, "We will return no more";
And all at once they sang, "Our island home
  Is far beyond the wave; we will no longer roam."

ALFRED TENNYSON

STORIES OF AMERICAN HISTORY
THE FRENCH IN AMERICA

The French Dream of Empire

Father Marquette's Headquarters in Chicago in 1674

Did you ever see a more inhospitable and dreary winter landscape? And yet this is how a portion of Chicago looked in the year 1674 at the point of the Chicago River where the devoted missionary spent the winter. He had with him, Joliet, two coureurs de bois, and a little band of faithful Pottawattomies whose canoes you see drawn up on the beach and their wigwams clustered about the cabin. The hut is supposed to have been left by a trader in furs who built it and made it his headquarters.

IN the year 1634 a French explorer reached Green Bay, Wisconsin, on the western shore of Lake Michigan, fifteen hundred miles from the ocean. This was fourteen years after the Pilgrims landed at Plymouth. His name was Jean Nicolet. He made the six weeks' journey from Montreal in the birch-bark canoes of Huron Indians. Expecting to find the coast of China over these fresh water "Western Seas," he wore the robe of a Chinese mandarin, embroidered with golden dragons and with brilliant birds and flowers.

As he leaped ashore among the startled Winnebagoes, he fired a pair of dueling pistols in the air. Thus he was clothed in mystery, splendor and power, as was Spanish Cortez in Mexico. But he had no soldiers with him, nor any hostile intentions. His genuine friendliness, trust and charming manners captured the affections of this savage tribe. For two years he remained with his *"frères sauvages"* (wild brothers) as he called them, adopted their dress and habits, learned their speech and went on voyages with them. Once he was within fifty miles of the "Messassibi, Father of Waters," and he carried news of the Great River back to Montreal.

The whole episode is typical of the French in America. All their fur trappers, explorers, missiona-

1469

ries and empire builders, who, for one hundred and fifty years, passed in a splendid, historic pageantry over our two great inland waterways, from the Gulf of St. Lawrence to the Gulf of Mexico, were spectacular and romantic, and endeared themselves to the Indians. They were the first, and long the only ones, to reach the heart of North America.

A glance at any map of the continent will tell you why. In the discovery of the St. Lawrence River by Jacques Cartier, in 1534, the French found the widest water gate on the Atlantic, and possessed a long water highway into the interior, while the English and Dutch colonists, on the Atlantic seaboard, had a mountain wall at their backs, from New England to the Carolinas. But, while their fishing fleets continued to come to the Grand Banks, the French made no attempt at colonization until 1609, when Samuel de Champlain arrived at Quebec, to search for the Northwest Passage to India and China, and to develop the fur trading of the Canadian forests.

The French soon had their settlements in Nova Scotia (then Acadie) on the islands in the Gulf, and along the St. Lawrence between Quebec and Montreal. There are French villages today in Canada and Louisiana that are much like the Grand Pré of Longfellow's Evangeline. They consist of a single, long street fronting the river, and with the narrow farms marching in line back to a bluff or belt of woods. Montreal and Quebec had stone forts, log trading posts, water mills and Catholic churches; and there was plenty of social gayety, and all the comforts of Old France in the cozy dormer-windowed, piazza-fronted log cottages that had their gardens and orchards, and cattle grazing on a common pasture. But the small village farms were not expected to support families. In the winter the men were in the woods with the In-

The Discoverer of Canada

Jacques Cartier was the son of humble fisher folk in the French village of St. Malo. This portrait was painted in 1839 from sources which are now lost and is the only authentic picture we have of him. It shows this earliest explorer of the mainland of Canada, on the deck of a ship, looking ahead with a tight-set jaw and searching eyes. His face is firm and strong; it is that of a man of earnest purpose and iron will. Jacques Cartier's clothing shows us the costume worn by a sea captain of 400 years ago. His thick cloak is gathered in at the waist by a belt which supports a sword and also a dirk, the hilt of which can be seen near his right hand. He wears the tufted Breton cap common among the seafaring men of France. He has no ruff and his shirt is finished with only a small ruffle at the neck and wrists, for Jacques Cartier is dressed for action and rough work, not for a state occasion.

Secret of French Discoveries

Picturesque French Life

THE FRENCH IN AMERICA

dians, hunting and trapping, and bringing their furs into the beaver fair at Montreal in the spring.

The life just suited these Frenchmen, many of whom were blue-eyed, brown-haired descendants of the old Norse sea-rovers. They loved the voyages in frail canoes, over leagues of wild, uncharted waters; the days of stalking bears and moose in the unbroken forests, and the nights by campfires, when they played the violin for the delighted Indians. They often took squaws for wives, with the blessing of the church. Every one of them wanted to be a hero, and dreamed and talked of doing some brave deed for "la belle France." They soon knew every Algonquin dialect, and were as hardy, as skilled canoeists, snowshoe "wood-runners" and hunters as the Indians.

This is how it happened that, as early as 1625, Jean Nicolet was living with the Hurons on Lake Nipissing. Hearing there of the "Western Sea" and fired by the hope of reaching China, he got the mandarin's robe of Champlain, made his will, confessed his sins, and started on his perilous voyage to Green Bay.

The French had no choice but to go westward. They were hemmed into the narrow, rocky valley of the St. Lawrence, on the north by thick woods and Arctic plains, and on the south by the English and Dutch settlements, and by the warlike Iroquois. They had won the enmity of the "Six Nations" in western New York State by allying themselves with the much more numerous, but weak and unorganized Algonquins. They had, besides, poetic imagination. As Champlain stood on the forest-crowned bluff at Quebec, three hundred miles from the ocean, and watched the St. Lawrence pouring its exhaustless flood out of the wooded wilderness, he realized the colossal scale on which the continent had been planned. He thought that across some distant divide the headwaters of the Great River might be found, and with it a passage to India

The Founder of Quebec

Champlain

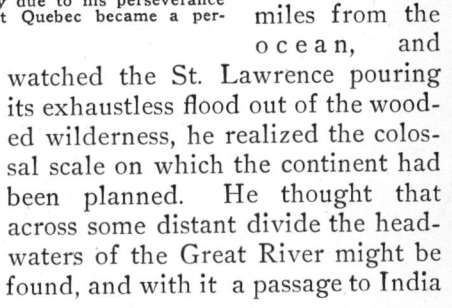

Like Captain John Smith and Sir Walter Raleigh, Samuel de Champlain was not only an explorer but he added to the value of his explorations by the interesting books he wrote about them. His VOYAGES give much valuable information about the customs and habits of the Algonquin Indians as well as about the region he explored.

It was Champlain's daring and perseverance that gave the French their foothold in America. But, on the other hand, it was Champlain's alliance with the Algonquins which turned the Iroquois against the French, and so materially aided the English cause in the long conflict for the possession of America, which followed.

Like most of the French explorers, he was more deeply interested in discovery and in winning converts for the Catholic church than in colonization, though it was almost wholly due to his perseverance and good management that Quebec became a permanent settlement.

1471

and an empire for France. With this end in view he built the fort and trading post at Montreal, just below the rapids, as far as vessels from France could ascend the river.

perior and brought back furs and copper arrow-heads. It was over this route that Nicolet reached Green Bay.

The Mississippi must soon have

Story Told by an Old Lead Plate

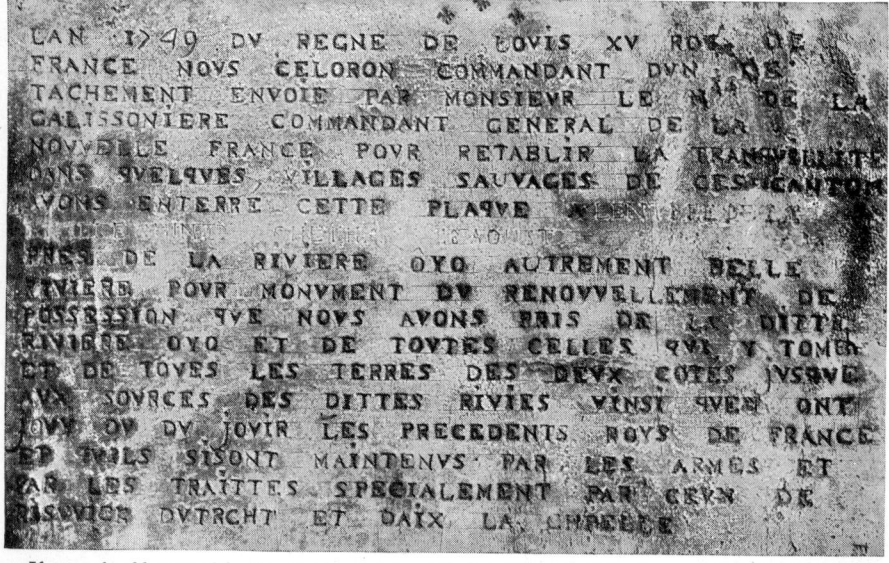

```
LAN 1749 DV REGNE DE LOVIS XV ROY DE
FRANCE NOVS CELORON COMMANDANT DVN DE-
TACHEMENT ENVOIE PAR MONSIEVR LE     DE LA
GALISSONIERE COMMANDANT GENERAL DE LA
NOVVELLE FRANCE POVR RETABLIR LA TRANQVILLITE
DANS QVELQVES VILLAGES SAVVAGES DE CES CANTON
    ENTERRE CETTE PLAQVE         
    DE LA RIVIERE OYO AVTREMENT BELLE
RIVIERE POVR MONVMENT DV RENOVVELLEMENT DE
POSSESSION QVE NOVS AVONS PRIS DE LA DITTE
RIVIERE OYO ET DE TOVTES CELLES QVI Y TOMBE
ET DE TOVES LES TERRES DES DEVX COTES JVSQVE
AVX SOVRCES DES DITTES RIVIES VINST QVEN ONT
JOVY OV DV JOVIR LES PRECEDENTS ROYS DE FRANCE
ET QVILS SISONT MAINTENVS PAR LES ARMES ET
PAR LES TRAITTES SPECIALEMENT PAR CEVX DE
RISWICK DVTRCHT ET DAIX LA CHAPELLE
```

If you should ever visit the Museum of the Virginia Historical Society, one of the interesting things they would show you would be this old lead plate. It was buried by French explorers at the foot of a tree and claims for the French King, Louis XV, all the territory drained by the Ohio and the streams entering into it. As you see, it is written in French and the carving was probably done in the soft lead with a hunter's knife. Time and the acids of the soil have eaten away a good many of the words, but it is still legible, and the English of it is:

"In the year 1749, during the reign of Louis XV, King of France, we, Céloron, commander of a detachment sent by Marquis de la Gallissoniere, commander-in-chief of New France, to restore tranquillity in some savage villages of these districts, have buried this plate at the confluence of the Ohio and . . . this . . . near the river Ohio, alias Beautiful River, as a monument of our having taken possession of the said river Ohio and of those that fall into the same, and all the lands on both sides as far as the sources of the said rivers, as well as of those of which preceding kings have enjoyed possession, partly by the force of arms, partly by treaties, especially by those of Ryswick, Utrecht, and Aix-la-Chapelle."

Those queer little figures at the top that look like a flight of ducks are the lilies of France. If you could see the original plate you would notice that it was carefully ruled with a knife point before the words were cut into the lead. Other plates were buried at other points and two of these were found in recent years sticking out from the river bank by boys.

Through these rapids the Algonquin tribes did not go, nor did they often venture on Lake Ontario. That lake was claimed by the Iroquois, and above it there was a thirty-six mile portage to be made around the thundering waters of Niagara. Instead, they paddled up the Ottawa River, and, by many forest-walled water courses, won their way into Lake Huron. Thence they went to the head of Lake Su-

been discovered from the upper lakes but for the fact that the Iroquois Indians waged unceasing war on the Algonquins and their French allies for the next thirty years. They drove the tribes to the upper lakes and shut the French colonists in their forts. In 1660 there were only three settlements and three thousand French in the St. Lawrence valley. Then Adam Daulac, known as

Dollard's Test by Fire

THE FRENCH IN AMERICA
Champlain's "Gift of God"

© *Underwood & Underwood*

Three hundred years after Champlain sailed up the St. Lawrence to Quebec for the first time, Quebec celebrated his coming with a grand pageant and many impressive ceremonies. Here is a reconstruction of Champlain's ship, the Don de Dieu, manned and equipped as it was in Champlain's time, and surrounded by the canoes of curious Indians. It was one of the most striking features of the Quebec celebration.

"Don de Dieu" means gift of God. The vessel was a small one, as you see, to brave the stormy Atlantic. It was 80 feet long and 20 feet wide, with a draft of 12 feet when fully loaded.

General Fraser and His Highlanders at Quebec

The victory of the English over the French at Quebec was in part due to the valor of the Scotch-Highlanders under General Fraser. In the picture the General is pointing to the enemy and calling on his men to charge. You see with what enthusiasm the order is received. General Fraser himself was a Scotchman and entered the British Army at an early age. He served with distinction in Holland and Germany and accompanied General Wolfe to Quebec. He always showed as great skill in conducting a retreat, as in making an attack.

"Dollard," commandant at Montreal, convinced the Iroquois that the French were unconquerable. With seventeen Frenchmen and four Indians in a little log fort on the Ottawa, he held off 700 warriors for days and killed a third of them before he and his little band were overpowered.

All through that generation of warfare, too, French missionaries had been in the woods with every harried band of Algonquins. They lived on roots and berries, slept on the snow, listened for the midnight alarm, comforted dying warriors, and took squaws and papooses to their scattered kindred. In many a wild island and hidden retreat around the upper lakes they gathered bands of starving fugitives, built bark chapels, and set up the portable altars which they managed to, bring in safety through every peril. There they lit their tall wax candles, burned incense and used the sacred vestments and communion service, in the darkest hours bringing the mystery, splendor, and consolation of religion to despairing tribes. After the war was over, it was missionaries, such men as Nicolet and the defenders of the little fort on the Ottawa, who carried the cross and the lilies of France down to the gulf of Mexico.

Père Marquette and His Work

Père Marquette, a frail young priest of such zeal and consecration that white men and red alike looked upon him as a saint from heaven, had a mission among the Hurons at Mackinac, when in 1671, the sovereignty of France over the Great Lakes was declared at Sault Ste. Marie. Every voyager and Indian stopped at his chapel, in passing, for a blessing. Among them was Louis Joliet, returning from the cop-

The Surrender of Champlain

Champlain, surrounded by his soldiers and the Indians who, you remember, were always friends of the French, is here shown handing his sword to the leader of the British Naval forces, Admiral Kirke. In the background is one of the little Catholic chapels with which the French dotted the wilderness. Kirke, although an Englishman, was born in Dieppe, France, in 1596, where his parents were temporarily located. He was the eldest son of a Scotch merchant. Accompanied by his two brothers, one of whom, Lewis, became the first Military Commandant of Quebec under English rule, he led an expedition of three vessels, in 1627, to break up the French settlements in Canada and Nova Scotia. When he first ordered Champlain to surrender Quebec, the latter concealed his weakness by a defiant answer which so deceived Kirke as to his strength, that Kirke withdrew. When later he attacked the French squadron near Gaspe, capturing all the arms, ammunition and stores intended for Quebec, and again appeared before the town with his squadron, Champlain gave up the struggle.

THE FRENCH IN AMERICA

per mines empty handed, turned back by the warlike Sioux. Père Marquette told him of a band of Illinois Indians who had made a thirty days' voyage from the south, to beg him to come to their villages on the Illinois, near the "Messassibi," and found a mission. He was awaiting the permission of his superiors in Montreal to carry the Cross to the banks of the Great River.

Marquette and Joliet

Thus the way southward was opened to the French. Joliet made a swift return to Mackinac, with the joyful news that he had been commissioned to find the Great River, and that Père Marquette was to go with him. To that saintly soul on his forest and wave-girt rocky point, this news was an answer to two years of ceaseless prayer.

These two, with five Indians, set out in a big canoe, armed only with the Cross, the banner of France, and a peace pipe. Going by Nicolet's route to Green Bay and down the Fox River they entered the Mississippi at Prairie du Chien, Wisconsin, and floated to the Illinois. The year was young; bluff and prairie

Joliet and Marquette at a Portage

This picture shows Joliet and Marquette at the portage from the Fox to the Wisconsin rivers. Father Marquette, as you can see, was a young man; he was only thirty years old when he died, and his character was as beautiful as his face. His whole life was given up to his religion and to doing good. The man on his left is Louis Joliet. French woodsmen and Indian converts carried their canoes and baggage over the portages; that is to say the places where it is necessary to cross the land to get from one river to another. Notice how the Indian at the right carries the baggage strapped to him. Beyond him is a woodsman bringing in a deer.

and tender woods enchanted them. Marquette's journal reads like a romance. The mission was planted at Utica, Illinois. Then, over streams populous with canoes, bordered by fields bright with corn, they were guided to the Chicago River. Joliet returned to Montreal, losing his records in the rapids of the St. Lawrence by the upsetting of his canoe. Père Marquette went back to Illinois, spent one winter on the Chicago River and died. Mournful Pottawattomies carried his body north, to some disputed point—perhaps to Glen Haven, Michigan; perhaps to lay him under the floor of his chapel at Mackinac. His spirit was long invoked by the Indians to still the tempests on the Great Lakes.

La Salle and His Dream of Empire

Now appeared the greatest man that France sent to the New World. He was Robert Cavelier, Sieur de la Salle, poor, unknown, of middle- it he sought out Iroquois chiefs in their villages in western New York. He cut green timbers in the woods, mounted cannon on his floating fort, and spread the first sails to the winds

An Encounter With Hostile Indians

The Indians among whom he worked and who knew his saintly character were very devoted to Father Marquette, but the enemies of these Indians were hostile to him. This relief pictures an encounter with the Sioux, one of these hostile tribes. Father Marquette is shown standing, holding the peace pipe. A cross is stuck in his girdle but he has no gun, for the missionaries went unarmed among the Indians. Marquette and some French Canadian woodsmen are in the canoe with Joliet.

class birth—a handicap in those days of privilege for nobles—when he appeared in Canada. But he won a grant of land by his services, and built Fort Frontenac at the foot of Lake Ontario. He was there when Louis Joliet returned from his amazing voyage of discovery, and saw his records before they were lost in the rapids. For years he had dreamed of the great empire in America to be won for France. With the knowledge now gained he went to Paris, aroused the enthusiasm of the French court, and secured a commission from the King to explore, fortify, colonize and trade in the Mississippi Valley.

But he got very little money. He sold his estate on the St. Lawrence for funds to build a sailing vessel at Niagara. For permission to build of the Great Lakes. It was 1679 when the Griffin dropped anchor in the midst of a hundred canoes at Mackinac, and La Salle went ashore in a scarlet mantle, gold lace, powdered hair and delicate ruffles, to pray at the grave of Père Marquette. No humble petitioner was he, but a man of imperial vision, ambition and resource. To the Indians he was magnificent, for, in triumph or defeat, he trod the wilderness like a king. He had with him but one friend and faithful lieutenant, Henri di Tonty, but the Algonquins gathered around him for protection and helped him set up cannon on Starved Rock—a lordly bluff on the Illinois at Utica, where Marquette had founded his mission. He built another vessel at Peoria, with which to descend the Mississippi.

THE FRENCH IN AMERICA

Misfortune and enmity pursued him. The Griffin, with its rich cargo of furs from Green Bay, was lost on Lake Erie. Count Frontenac, his powerful friend who ruled in Montreal, was recalled to France and help was refused by his successor. Obliged to go to Paris for assistance, he found, on his return, that his Indian allies had been scattered by the Iroquois. Again he gathered 20,000 warriors around his fort, while other tribes kept the Chicago portage open. In 1682 he went down the Mississippi to the Gulf and took possession of the valley, which he named Louisiana, in honor of the King of France. He had won an empire, but was discredited, and forbidden even to pay his own expenses out of the profits in the fur trade.

Pursued by Adverse Fate

With all his hopes crumbling into dust, he returned to France again, got the ear of the King, ships, money, soldiers, colonists and authority over Louisiana. But again he was betrayed. His fleet commander landed the expedition on the coast of Texas, four hundred miles west of the mouth of the Mississippi.

The Final Resting Place of Father Marquette

At the right of this bas-relief is Marquette's principal mission, a little log building at Old Mackinac on the south shore of the straits of Mackinac. Father Marquette died when he was only thirty years old, somewhere on the east shore of Lake Michigan. He was buried where he died, but a few years later the Indians took his body to Mackinac and buried it under the floor of his chapel there. The picture shows the funeral procession approaching Mackinac chapel with a priest in the lead, reading the service, and a little girl by his side swinging the censer.

There he was assassinated by mutineers of his own party.

Continuing La Salle's Work

For the next twenty years Tonty held the Illinois country, built forts and kept the trade route to Montreal open, but in 1700 he gave up the struggle and went down to the Gulf, when d'Iberville from Canada was building forts at Biloxi and Mobile. La Salle lay dead on Trinity River, his work lost. Now France proposed to do that task all over again, by pushing up the river from the new capital of Louisiana at New Orleans.

There were still Frenchmen in Illinois, keeping the lamp of religion and civilization burning in the wilderness. Just as missionaries had led harried bands of Indians to the upper lakes sixty years before, so

1477

now they went with fugitive tribes down to the banks of the Mississippi, between the Missouri and Ohio. For twenty years they were cut off from the world. But, in a land of peace and plenty, they built up the mission town of Kaskaskia, with a stone mill and chapel, wheat fields and herds of cattle. These were there when, in 1788, a fleet of big pirogues, or hollowed cypress log boats, armed with cannon and floating the lilies of France, came up the river with soldiers to build Fort Chartres, about sixty miles below the site of what is now St. Louis.

In some way rumors of fabulous wealth in the Illinois country had reached Paris. A company was chartered to develop the mines of gold, silver and precious stones it was supposed to possess. Fort Chartres was built below St. Louis, and command given to the proudest nobility of France. Colonists were sent out and slaves brought from the West Indies to work the mines, but nothing but lead was discovered, in the Ozarks of Missouri, and at Galena, Illinois.

Robert Cavelier, Sieur de la Salle

This fine picture of La Salle from the painting by Margry, brings out his character to a remarkable degree. Although his family were not nobles, they were wealthy and with great landed estates. You can see he belonged to the French aristocratic type—self-controlled, self-contained and with a calm exterior that hides great pride and ambition. His mind was always hungry for knowledge and achievement. He was very skillful in making other people see things as he saw them. It is said of him also that he was the first self-made man who ever walked on the land which is now occupied by the busy thoroughfares of Chicago—a city of self-made men. The principal financial street of Chicago is named after him, "La Salle" Street.

The soil, however, was rich, and soon the Illinois bottoms were golden with wheat fields. A dozen farming villages, like those on the lower St. Lawrence and above New Orleans, sprang up. The country sent wheat, furs, pork and lead to the Gulf and to the French West Indies, the garrison was kept in the fort and a new trade route over the Ohio was opened to Montreal.

There was trouble with the Chickasaw and Natchez Indians on the lower Mississippi, but by 1750 the Illinois bank was settled for fifty miles. France had taken root in three places in the New World, and connecting and defending the colonies in Canada, Illinois and Louisiana was a noble line of forts. Louisburg fronted the Ocean on Nova Scotia (Acadie), and Mobile the Gulf of Mexico. Between them were Quebec, Montreal, Frontenac, Niagara, Detroit, Presque Isle (now Erie City), Mackinac, Sault Ste. Marie, Green Bay, St. Joseph, and Fort Chartres below St. Louis.

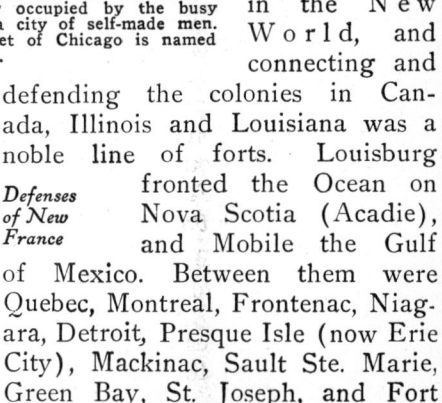

Defenses of New France

THE FRENCH IN AMERICA

The Struggle for a Continent

Then the French and Indian war broke out, first between New France in Canada and the colony of Virginia. It was really a struggle for the possession of the continent. Soon the war spread to France and England, involved all their colonies in America, and far off India. It was a world-wide contest between England and France for sea power and colonial dominion. In America the French stood on the defensive in their magnificent chain of forts. To British regulars, and New England and Virginia volunteers, was given the task of cutting through tangled forests, breasting wild floods and climbing mountains, and going on long voyages at sea to attack the enemy. No one believed that the French could ever be dislodged from their forts.

But the tide of fortune suddenly turned. Louisburg, Frontenac and Fort Duquesne (Pittsburgh) were taken. Quebec was left defenseless; Montreal was cut off from Illinois. By 1760 the British were in Detroit, Mackinac and Vincennes. In India, also, the courage and genius of a young clerk named Robert Clive, caused France to lose a fabulously rich empire. When the war was over England dictated the terms of peace. To Louisiana and Illinois the end came as a clap of thunder. Their forts had never been invested. Now, with a stroke of the pen the rich empire in the valley of the Mississippi was divided between England and Spain.

During all the nine years' war, but one event had, in any way, disturbed the French farmers, artisans, nobles, priests, lead mine operators and slaves, in the Mississippi valley. After the famous expulsion from Acadie (Nova Scotia) whose story *The Story of Evangeline* is told in Evangeline, heart-broken refugees, many separated from kindred and friends, found new homes in every French village from

The Spirit of La Salle Expressed in Stone
La Salle was a bold, determined man who had wider visions and bigger dreams than the other Frenchmen in America. This statue expresses the spirit of the explorer in its resolute, determined pose and eyes that seem to be gazing into the future. The pistol and sword tell of the dangerous work La Salle undertook—traversing a vast, trackless region where white men had never before set foot. La Salle's provisions and supplies were stolen and destroyed more than once in his attempts to reach the mouth of the Mississippi, so we see him here in suitable, durable clothing which would last the length of his journey. His coat is of leather, and probably his breeches are of leather too. The long, flaring-topped leggings that he wears were called "sherryvallies," and are also of leather. His pistol and sword are slipped in a wide leather belt or girdle, at just the right point to always be within easy reach of his right hand. This statue is in Lincoln Park, Chicago.

1479

New Orleans to Cahokia, Illinois, opposite the present site of St. Louis. In her search for her lover, Gabriel, Evangeline went up, "past the Ohio's mouth," westward into the wild Ozarks, up the Ohio and Wabash to Detroit and, after the war, around by water to the convent in Philadelphia.

How eloquent that story is of the entire possession by the French of the St. Lawrence and Mississippi valleys; how secure their hold on scores of tribes of Indians. Nowhere would that wandering damoiselle be in danger. In dozens of little chapels she told her beads, and in the graveyard sanctuaries in the shadow of the cross she

Sat by some nameless grave and thought that perhaps in its bosom, He was already at rest, and she longed to slumber beside him.

Priest and trader, coureur de bois and friendly Algonquin aided her in her search, watched over her weary footsteps on the wild trails, and carried her in canoes up and down hundreds of miles of waterways. At no later period of pioneer history in that region could a young girl have made such a journey in safety.

It was French people in Illinois who founded the new trading post at St. Louis. This was in Spanish territory on the west bank of the river; but it was settled by the French, named for the King of France, and an ex-commandant of Fort Chartres was made first governor of Upper Louisiana by the Spanish monarch. Later the country was receded to France, and in 1803 Louisiana was bought by the United States.

The French were thus in America nearly two centuries, furnishing the *Memories of the French* most heroic and romantic chapter in our history of exploration and colonization. They seem to have vanished, like a dream, but really they are still here. Along the St. Lawrence, in Canada, there are now 2,000,000 French-speaking people, living in their quaint, farm villages: "Such as the peasants of Normandy built in the reigns of the Henrys."

In New Orleans, along the lower Mississippi, in St. Louis, and in a few villages in Illinois, are thousands more, and French names are common around the Great Lakes. And on all the waterways traversed by their explorers, missionaries, voyagers and nobles, we find the names of French kings, saints, cities and heroes of the American wilderness.

THE FRENCH IN AMERICA
The Legend of the Kaskaskia Ball

Kaskaskia was a backwoods town in the Illinois country held by a few Creoles and Indians under the command of British officers. The British control of the northwest territory was a constant menace to the Americans during our War of Independence. So George Rogers Clark set out with his little force from Virginia, to drive them from the Illinois country in order to put a stop to the Indian outrages, which were encouraged by the British, as well as to gain the territory for the Americans.

The story goes that the gay Creoles of Kaskaskia were having a dance when Clark's little force came up. Everyone in the village, including the English officers and the guards, were said to be making merry when Colonel Clark walked into the rude log cabin that served for a ballroom, accompanied only by his guide and one or two others. He said nothing, but stood with folded arms looking upon the strange scene before him—handsome Creole beauties in ancient ball dresses belonging to their grandmothers in France, dancing with moccasined backwoodsmen to the tune of the lively fiddles scraped by a couple of old Frenchmen on a platform; swarthy Indians and trim English officers mingling with the French inhabitants; while the rude ballroom with its puncheon floor and rough walls resounded with the music and merriment.

Clark was unobserved for a few moments, so the tale runs, then an Indian saw the stern stranger and suspected who he was, for the people of Kaskaskia had been expecting an attack from the Americans, but since it had not come at once they had forgotten to watch for it. The picture shows the Indian in the background, uttering his war whoop which startles dancers and fiddlers alike. The English officer in the foreground looks very angry. The ladies, naturally, are terrified. Clark's posture is typical of the man—undaunted and determined. The story goes that he calmly bade the people go on with the dance, but to remember that they were now enjoying themselves under the flag of Virginia, not of Great Britain. Before the officers could make any resistance, Clark's men, who were waiting outside, rushed in, alarmed by the Indian's war whoop. The English, of course, were completely overpowered and captured.

The true story of the capture, however, you will find in Clark's Memoirs—how the Americans found the town unguarded and, guided by a friendly Frenchman whom they had captured, went straight to the commander's house and seized him as he was lying in bed, wholly unprepared for an attack. After that the garrison and people, who were at heart friendly to the Americans, surrendered without the firing of a shot.

But the romantic story of the ball serves its purpose in giving us a clearer idea, than any dry account could do, of the nature and customs of the people then living in the Illinois country.

Henry of Navarre

Now glory to the Lord of hosts, from whom all glories are!
And glory to our Sovereign Liege, King Henry of Navarre!
Now let there be the merry sound of music and of dance,
Through thy corn-fields green, and sunny vines, oh pleasant land of France!
And thou, Rochelle, our own Rochelle, proud city of the waters,
Again let rapture light the eyes of all thy mourning daughters.
As thou wert constant in our ills, be joyous in our joy,
For cold, and stiff, and still are they who wrought thy walls annoy.
Hurrah! hurrah! a single field hath turned the chance of war,
Hurrah! hurrah! for Ivry, and King Henry of Navarre.

Oh! how our hearts were beating, when at the dawn of day
We saw the army of the League drawn out in long array;
With all its priest-led citizens, and all its rebel peers,
And Appenzel's stout infantry, and Egmont's Flemish spears.
There rode the brood of false Lorraine, the curses of our land!
And dark Mayenne was in the midst, a truncheon in his hand!
And as we looked on them, we thought of Seine's empurpled flood,
And good Coligni's hoary hair all dabbled with his blood;
And we cried unto the living God, who rules the fate of war,
To fight for his own holy name, and Henry of Navarre.

The King is come to marshal us, in all his armor drest,
And he has bound a snow-white plume upon his gallant crest.
He looked upon his people, and a tear was in his eye;
He looked upon the traitors, and his glance was stern and high.
Right graciously he smiled on us, as rolled from wing to wing,
Down all our line, a deafening shout, "God save our Lord, the King!"
"And if my standard-bearer fall, as fall full well he may,
For never saw I promise yet of such a bloody fray,
Press where ye see my white plume shine, amidst the ranks of war,
And be your oriflamme to-day the helmet of Navarre."

Hurrah! the foes are moving. Hark to the mingled din
Of fife, and steed, and trump and drum, and roaring culverin!
The fiery Duke is pricking fast across Saint André's plain,
With all the hireling chivalry of Guelders and Almayne.
Now by the lips of those you love, fair gentlemen of France,
Charge for the Golden Lilies now—upon them with the lance!
A thousand spurs are striking deep, a thousand spears in rest,
A thousand knights are pressing close behind the snow-white crest;
And in they burst, and on they rushed, while, like a guiding star,
Amidst the thickest carnage blazed the helmet of Navarre.

Now, God be praised, the day is ours! Mayenne hath turned his rein.
D'Aumale hath cried for quarter. The Flemish Count is slain.
Their ranks are breaking like thin clouds before a Biscay gale;
The field is heaped with bleeding steeds, and flags, and cloven mail;
And then, we thought on vengeance, and all along our van,
"Remember St. Bartholomew," was passed from man to man;
But out spake gentle Henry, "No Frenchman is my foe;
Down, down with every foreigner, but let your brethren go."
Oh! was there ever such a knight, in friendship or in war,
As our Sovereign Lord, King Henry, the soldier of Navarre!

Ho! maidens of Vienna; Ho! matrons of Lucerne!
Weep, weep, and rend your hair for those who never shall return.
Ho! Philip, send for charity, thy Mexican pistoles,
That Antwerp monks may sing a mass for thy poor spearman's souls!
Ho! gallant nobles of the League, look that your arms be bright!
Ho! burghers of Saint Genevieve, keep watch and ward to-night!
For our God hath crushed the tyrant, our God hath raised the slave,
And mocked the counsel of the wise, and the valor of the brave.
Then glory to his holy name, from whom all glories are;
And glory to our Sovereign Lord, King Henry of Navarre!

LORD MACAULAY

STORIES OF AMERICAN HISTORY
THE ENGLISH IN AMERICA

The Homebuilders of the North Atlantic Seaboard

When the Puritans Lived in Their Ship

The Mayflower reached America in the fall of 1620, you remember, but Plymouth, the place decided upon for a permanent settlement, was not found until December 21st, and the Pilgrims did not have houses built on shore so that they could leave the Mayflower for good and all until March 31, 1621. During that long severe winter the Mayflower was home to the women and children who came on shore only during the daytime, while the men were very busy building shelters and defenses for their families.

Here we see a party of men leaving the ship for their work on the land. The Mayflower is encrusted and surrounded with ice, but safely anchored in the protecting harbor of Plymouth. Plymouth beach can be seen in the distance. The Pilgrims chose this place to anchor because the bay was full of crab and lobster and fish. If you have ever visited this bay you will not recognize it from the picture, for today the shores are crowded and busy with shipping and manufactures, not lonely and wooded as in the Pilgrims' time.

WE HAVE seen how the Spanish and French dared everything in the New World, explored far, won vast empires—and lost them. Behind them were no irresistible movements of people to sweep everything before them and possess the continent such as we find in the English colonies. These colonies spread along the North Atlantic seaboard from the Gulf of St. Lawrence to Florida. On this shore broke wave after wave of migration, not only from England but from every country of northern Europe. In reading the history of the Thirteen Colonies we find our interest centered, not in kings and their policies or in romantic adventurers, but in people, and how they dealt with their strange and terrifying experiences. It will help us to understand the later history of our country to know something of these colonists—their characters, origins, race traits and ideals, and how they

PICTURED KNOWLEDGE
Modest Homes of the Pilgrims

COPYRIGHT BY A.S BURBANK 1891. STORE HOUSE — P. BROWN — J. GOODMAN — W. BREWSTER — J. BILLINGTON — I. ALLERTON — F. COOKE — E. WINSLOW — GOV'R BRADFORD — OLD FORT
PLYMOUTH IN 1622

When you visit Plymouth, Massachusetts, today and walk up Leyden Street, you are going over the only street there was in the town at the time shown in this picture—1622. The house at the extreme left was built first. The food of the colonists was stored in this building and everybody ate and slept there while the other modest little houses were being built. Next to it in order are the houses of Brown, Goodman, Brewster, Billington, Allerton, Cooke and Winslow. Governor Bradford lived in the large house across the street. The stockade around it was made of upright, pointed logs and was a defense against the arrows of the Indians, though it wouldn't have been much protection against bullets. The houses were of rough hewn timber with roofs of thatch and windows of oiled paper. The chimneys of the fireplaces, as you see, ran up on the outside, and were of stones held in place with clay. On the hill can be seen the fort which at first was used as a meeting-house. At the mouth of the "very sweet brook" behind the houses, the shallop of the Mayflower is anchored.

were affected by their experiences and neighbors in America.

The Anglicizing of Many Peoples

We are apt to think of all the English colonists as Puritans. But there were few Puritans outside of New England, and even there, were many other sorts of people. Pennsylvania was settled by English Quakers; *Melting Pot of the Nations* Maryland by English Catholics; Virginia by English "gentlemen"; Georgia by poor debtors ransomed out of English prisons by a benevolent company. Then, New York and the Jersey shore of the Hudson were colonized by the Dutch; Delaware by the Swedes, and the Carolinas first of all by Huguenots—French Puritans. Pennsylvania, the Carolinas and Georgia, when still young colonies, had large migrations of Germans; and into every settlement, from Massachusetts to Virginia, after 1700, poured such numbers of Scotch-Irish that, in many places they outnumbered those of English birth. In the beginning, as it is today, the United States was a "melting pot" of nations, receiving people from many lands. Long before the Revolutionary War these various people had become blended into a new English-speaking nation, quite different from any in the Old World, and were consciously working toward a common destiny, a larger freedom than any of them had ever known.

THE ENGLISH IN AMERICA

They all figured in our history, giving us Colonial leaders, Indian fighters, Revolutionary patriots, statesmen, presidents and pioneers. The Adamses and Benjamin Franklin were of New England Puritan, Washington of Virginia "gentleman" stock. Jefferson, Madison, Monroe, Patrick Henry and Daniel Webster were Scotch-Irish; Van Buren and Roosevelt, New York Dutch. General Francis Marion was a Huguenot. William Penn was an English Quaker with a Dutch mother. Garfield's mother, that brave lady of the backwoods of Ohio, was the daughter of a Huguenot minister. "Dolly" Madison, the most beautiful and gracious of all the mistresses of the White House, was a Quaker; and one authority says that Priscilla Mullins, the heroine of the pretty story of "The Courtship of Miles Standish," was a French-speaking Belgian. The name sounds English but it may have been corrupted from the French Moulin. The Pilgrims, you know, lived in Holland eleven years before coming to America. And some of the men married Dutch and Belgian wives which they brought over in the Mayflower. All these people were as upright and independent as the Puritans, and were marked by the same courage, energy and determination. There was nothing in this wild land of privation and struggle to attract the vicious and weakling. Any but the stoutest hearts would have been daunted by the ten weeks' voyage of the Pilgrims across the stormy North Atlantic. In the pest-hole of a little wooden ship, half the brave company were infected with tuberculosis, and were soon laid away in the forlorn graveyard of Plymouth. And that experience was not unique. Fully half the first settlers at Jamestown, Virginia, died of malarial fever, and the colony was all but wiped out by famine and hostile Indians.

Yet ship after ship full of brave immigrants came to the bleak and sterile coast of New England, and

Rose Standish

This is Rose Standish, first wife of the famous military leader of Plymouth Colony. After her death Captain Standish married her sister, Barbara. The story of the Courtship of Miles Standish in Longfellow's poems is one of those pretty romances of history that have no foundation in fact.

PICTURED KNOWLEDGE
Where the Standishes Kept Their "Sunday Best"

Instead of the plain iron and leather affairs we use today to carry our clothes in when we go traveling, Rose Standish packed the family's best garments in this lovely, carved, oak chest when they came over here in the Mayflower. It is in the style known as "Jacobean." Jacobean furniture and architecture were common in England during the reign of James I, in the early part of the 17th century. This style was marked by paneling, geometric designs, and spindle or pillar decoration, all of which you see on this chest. The split spindles, which show that the chest was made in the latter part of the Jacobean period, divide the face of it into panels, which are ornamented with the geometric diamond-shaped design. You will notice by the grain of the wood that the cover is all in one piece. This and the two drawers at the bottom were also common in Jacobean chests. We may be sure that the casters have been added later—that Miles Standish never possessed such convenient little implements for moving his chest about.

to the low, hot, swampy tide-water belt of the South. Virginia had four thousand inhabitants when Plymouth was settled in 1620, and twenty thousand colonists were landed in Boston and Salem before 1640. All the colonies were settled and the earlier ones became populous, in the seventy-five years between 1607 and 1682.

The Steady Westward March

Unlike the Spanish and French, who returned to Europe oftener than they remained in America, these immigrants turned their backs definitely on the Old World. Wasting little time in exploration or treasure-seeking, they set about the sober business of building homes and getting their living from the soil, the forest and the sea. Settling on every good harbor and navigable stream, they held fast to every foot of ground won by hardship, toil and danger, and pushed steadily westward. It took them another hundred years to gain the crest of the mountains which walled them on the west from Maine to Georgia.

THE ENGLISH IN AMERICA
The Pewter Spoons and the Spoon Molds

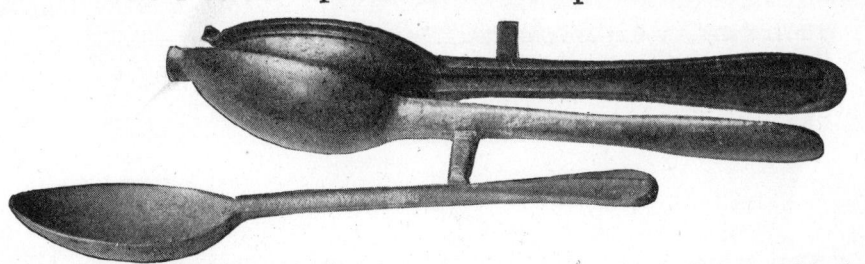

Pewter was a variable alloy of tin and lead or brass. It was used by the Romans, and in the Middle Ages, before china and glass became cheap, nearly all dishes and utensils were made from it. At first it was expensive and only the rich could afford it, but by the time of the American colonial period it was found in every kitchen. Yet by that time china and glass were beginning to be used by those who could afford them. Pewter utensils were made by pouring the molten metal into a mold like this spoon mold and pressing it into shape. Notice what a big bowl and straight handle this old pewter spoon has. Like all true antiques, real old pewter ware is rare and very valuable nowadays.

But, twenty years after the Revolution, the seaboard was crowded with three million people, and the surplus population was swarming through all the water gaps into the Mississippi Valley. And they soon bought Louisiana, and sent their explorers through old French and Spanish territory to their new boundary in the Rocky Mountains.

Most of the early colonists to what is now the Atlantic Coast of the United States, came for the same reason as the Pilgrims: for "freedom to worship God" in their own way. They differed widely in their creeds, but all had suffered persecution for their faith.

The Foundations of a Free Land

It was a turbulent time in religious history of Europe. Following the Renaissance, or "New Birth" of literature, art and science in Columbus' day, came the Reformation, when the countries of northern Europe and Switzerland separated from the Roman Catholic Church and set up Protestant churches of their own. In Catholic France there were a half million

A New Set of Spoons

When mother wanted a new set of spoons in the days of the Home Builders, getting them wasn't quite so simple a matter as it is today. Instead of going to a jewelry store, she sent Johnny into the woods, where he got just the right kind of wood for making wooden spoons. Then, as you see, she helped him make them. As you know, we use wooden spoons in the kitchen today. Ask your mother why.

Huguenots, and thousands of Scotch Presbyterians were colonized in North Ireland, a Catholic country. These were the Scotch-Irish, who

kings into exile. And when the Protestants split up into many sects and began to persecute each other, there was no security or peace for

Story of the Sugar Bowl, the Tea Party, and the Prince Who Didn't Know What to Do

If mother had owned that sugar bowl and those sugar tongs in the days of the Home Builders, it would have meant that you were pretty rich and could give tea parties. Only rich people could afford sugar in those days and loaf sugar was the most expensive of all. Those sugar tongs, you notice, are not like the sugar tongs we have today. They were made for cutting off sugar lumps from the sugar loaf.

The ladies of the Colonies used to give their tea parties in the big front room on the second floor and so it was referred to by fashionable people as the "tea room," while those who were not so fashionable called it "the parlor." When mother gave a tea party she presided at the table while the guests were scattered around the room and the servants took them tea, rusks and cake, and often fruit and wine.

Good manners required that the hostess should keep asking a guest to have more tea, or a helping of anything else, every time a cup or a plate was empty, and it was considered rude for a guest to refuse. This custom used to puzzle foreigners who were not familiar with it and a certain French prince who visited the United States shortly after the Revolution, tells in one of his letters he was invited to dine at the beautiful home of Robert Morris, where he was asked to have his tea cup refilled over and over again. When he had swallowed the twelfth cup, his neighbor, seeing that he was becoming more and more embarrassed, whispered to him that if he had had quite enough he should put his spoon across his cup, or else his hostess would be obliged to go on urging him to drink until the family supply of sugar and tea gave out, or the well went dry.

later emigrated to America in such numbers.

In Europe there were nearly two centuries of religious wars. The kings of Spain and France as "defenders of the faith" of Rome, made war on heretics in their own and other lands. Spain carried the war into her provinces of The Netherlands where dwelt the Dutch and Belgians, and threatened England. Then France took up the quarrel when England drove the Catholic Stuart

anyone. Puritans, Catholics, Church of England people, Scotch and Scotch-Irish Presbyterians, Quakers, and Baptists were each, in turn, driven from the British Isles. Moravians and Mennonites were exiled from Germany, and Huguenots from France. In all Europe there was only one small refuge for the persecuted of all sects. This was The Netherlands, or Dutch Republic. Through that little country, northern Europe, for a hundred and fifty

THE ENGLISH IN AMERICA

Dippers That Grew in the Garden

Manufactured articles were at a premium in the rough, new land and every family made as much of its household equipment as it could. Gourds have tough, woody fruit, suitable for dippers when they are hollowed out as you see them here. Some farms still have an old, open well with one of these queer, home-made dippers hanging above it—and oh, how good the cool, fresh water tastes from it on a hot summer day!

years, drained its best and bravest into the English colonies in America.

Learning Toleration from the Dutch

It was in Holland that the Pilgrims and many other colonists learned toleration of other peoples' opinions. As long as the little company of the Mayflower was in control in Plymouth, there was freedom of conscience for all Christian sects. So there was in Connecticut and

The Colonists and Their Spice Mills

During the Crusades, Europeans learned to like Eastern spices, and a lively spice trade sprang up between Europe and the Orient. The spices made their long journey across Asia by caravan and then across the Mediterranean on sailing vessels. The journey was so long that the spices were expensive and only the rich people could afford to use them in food, but they were considered very delicious and were in great demand. So we are not surprised to find these spice mills in the kitchen of a wealthy New England merchant, for by the time the English colonies in America were established, spice was being brought from the West Indies as well as around Cape of Good Hope and by the old caravan route from the East. Two of these old spice mills are metal "querns" similar to the stone hand mill for grinding flour, of which we show you a picture elsewhere. The upper part, corresponding to the upper stone of the quern, has projections for cutting and crushing the spice, as you see. The lower part is a true dish or bowl, instead of the flat, hollowed-out stone we see in the quern. The spice mill on the right is similar to our present day kitchen coffee mills.

PICTURED KNOWLEDGE
From the Outfit of the Night Watchman

Here is a hook and two of the kinds of "police whistles" used by night watchmen in colonial times. It was the duty of these night watchmen to go their rounds, all through the night, to call out the hour from time to time and to add the words, "All is well." But sometimes all wasn't well. There were burglars and street fights in those days just as there are today, and when the watchmen wanted help they called for it by swinging one of those rattles round and round. They made a clattering noise that everybody understood. The hook he carried to defend himself, if necessary, and also to lengthen his arm, so to speak, when he wanted to catch a man.

Rhode Island, Quaker Pennsylvania, Dutch New York and English Georgia. The Puritans of Boston and Salem, coming directly from England, denied this principle. Only members of their church were allowed to vote. They persecuted the Quakers and drove out everyone who differed from them. But, in time, the Puritans had to yield to the steady pressure of public opinion. In every colony were people who insisted on liberty of conscience. Old, worn-out notions of European monarchies, tyranny in any form, would not work in America.

The Puritans and Public Opinion

The people who came here were tired of being told what to believe and what to do. Besides, they were obliged to act for themselves. There were problems of existence to be solved at once, of which king and parliament could know nothing. The fullest liberty of action was needed if they were not to perish in the wilds of America. In every colony were people who knew just what to do in setting up an orderly, self-governing community, for they had studied the free institutions of The Netherlands. They had seen the seven Dutch states united into a strong republic, with the separate states and cities managing their own local affairs, and securing peace, justice, toleration and prosperity.

Dutch ideas worked like yeast in all the English colonies. The spirit of independence was in the cabin of

THE ENGLISH IN AMERICA

the Mayflower. Expecting to land in Virginia, the Pilgrims found themselves without authority on Cape Cod. But that did not trouble them. They drew up and signed a proper agreement by which they governed and defended themselves for the next seventy years. While the colony was small, laws were passed and questions decided in the Town Meeting. Later the New England colonies had Assemblies, to which each settlement sent delegates. But they still kept the town meetings for local questions.

The First Town Meetings

The colonists who went out from Boston to Rhode Island, at first managed their own affairs, and then secured a liberal charter from the king. The people who walked through the woods from Boston to the Connecticut Valley formed a republic of three settlements and adopted a constitution. All citizens were given the vote, and the monarch's name was not mentioned. The king signed this charter and then, advised that this was dangerous both in method and doc-

This is a Whole Flour Mill

This is one of the stone hand mills or querns used by the English colonists. Wheat was poured through the hole in the center of the top stone. Two handles were fitted into the holes and the top stone turned upon the lower. The stone was turned back and forth and not round and round. In this way two persons—two of the children, for example—could operate the mill together. The product of this mill was what we today call "whole wheat" flour. Hand mills like this are still in use in out-of-the-way places in Scotland and Ireland.

The Glassware in Colonial Homes

Glass was first made in the Orient and from there it was brought to Europe. For many years Venice led the world in the production of beautiful glass, and even today, in spite of our improved methods of manufacture, old Venetian glass is considered very choice. But England soon developed a thriving glass industry of her own, and English colonists in America were not content to import their glassware from England but set up glass works of their own. The glass in the picture was made in Massachusetts before the Revolution. Some of it is etched with steel or diamond instruments. It is thick, but clear and colorless. The variously shaped glasses were for different beverages—the smaller ones for the drinking of liquors which were taken in small quantities, the large engraved one for toddies. A toddy stirring rod is stuck in this toddy glass. The long iron rods were flip irons, for "flipping" glasses of liquor—that is, heating them by thrusting in the iron heated red hot in the fire.

trine, demanded that the document be surrendered. You know what happened. The paper was hidden in the hollow of an oak tree to be brought out and used again when the king's plan of uniting all the colonies down to Pennsylvania under a royal governor, had to be abandoned. The people of Boston put Governor Andros in jail and shipped him home because he abolished the Assemblies and levied what taxes he pleased. When Governor Andros was gone, Connecticut and Rhode Island resumed their charters.

Resisting the Charter Governors

Clashes with authority were frequent in every colony, and the office of a royal, proprietary, or company charter governor was seldom a pleasant one. A governor could veto measures and even dismiss Assemblies, but the legislatures could bring him to terms by refusing to vote him a salary. The Dutch of New York, under English rule, refused to pay taxes or elect officers until popular government was restored. South Carolina and Maryland both languished and grew turbulent under tyrannical rule, and were revived only by restoring a larger measure of liberty. In Virginia a serious rebellion against Governor Berkeley was led by Nathaniel Bacon. Pennsylvania had a tranquil history because it was founded on the most liberal principles of self-government. Although settled more than sixty years later than Massachusetts and Virginia, Pennsylvania rapidly caught up with them in population and prosperity, and before the Revolution Philadelphia was the largest city in America.

Now there was no conspiracy on the part of the separate colonies in this matter or in any other. Scattered along two thousand miles of seaboard there was, at first, little communication between them, and settled by widely differing people, who had quarreled bitterly in the Old World, they had, or thought they had, few interests in common. Each was isolated in a wilderness of woods and waters, and obliged to supply its own needs. But common experiences made them all more alike, and created sympathies. Practically all colonists were obliged to cultivate small farms which, for protection and for co-operation in many kinds of work, were cleared around a village of log houses, and a little stockaded fort. And, of course, there was always a church or two.

The Growth of Industries

All the grains and forage crops of Europe were grown, with the In-

A "Clock" That Counted the Skeins

In the days when every housewife spun the yarn which was later woven or knitted into clothing for the family, this device for measuring and keeping track of it was used. It was called a "clock" reel because the number of revolutions of the reel, as the skein was wound, were recorded by that hand pointing to numbers on the circular face.

THE ENGLISH IN AMERICA
Priscilla at Her Wheel

Do you remember how John Alden
"Heard, as he drew near the door, the musical voice of Priscilla
Singing the hundredth Psalm, the grand old Puritan anthem,
       *   *   *
Then, as he opened the door, he beheld the form of the maiden
Seated beside her wheel, and the carded wool like a snow-drift
Piled at her knee, her white hands feeding the ravenous spindle,
While with her foot she guided the wheel in its motion.
       *   *   *
She, the Puritan girl, in the solitude of the forest,
Making the humble house and the modest apparel of home-spun
Beautiful with her beauty, and rich with the wealth of her being!"
          Longfellow: The Courtship of Miles Standish.

dian plants of corn, potatoes, pumpkins and tobacco. There were soon gardens and orchards and domestic animals. Sheep were imported into New England and Pennsylvania very early; and flax was grown in the North and cotton and hemp in the South. It was not long anywhere before spinning wheel and loom were busy in every cabin. But on every frontier, men and boys long wore the Indian hunting suits of deerskins.

Water and wind mills ground the grain and sawed logs into timbers and lumber, but most of the manufacturing was carried on in the homes, as was also the case in the Old Country. Until long after the Revolution all the commoner cloths, even heavy sail-cloth, were woven on hand looms, dyed and made into garments by the women of each household. Even such mansions as Mount Vernon had its weaving room managed by the mistress. Soap was made of waste fats and lye leached from wood ashes; sea-water was evaporated for salt; stone and oyster shells were burned for lime. Every village had a cooper and a tanner, but barrel staves were split out of white oak in the forest, and boots

What Busy Homes Were These

PICTURED KNOWLEDGE
How They Printed the Calico Prints

Ages ago the Egyptians printed calico by means of carved wooden blocks like these. The practice was brought to Europe from India in the seventeenth century. Many of the designs used in America in the early days of its settlement came from France and were very artistic indeed. In printing the cloth, it was stretched over a padded table and marked with chalk to indicate where the print block was to be applied. The blocks shown in the picture were dipped in the dye, then pressed on the cloth. The print block was squared with the pattern already printed each time and tapped smartly with a small mallet to make sure that it left a firm clear impression on the cloth.

Making Nails by Hand

Whatever they didn't have in colonial days, people made for themselves, provided they needed it badly enough. Here you see a boy in a blacksmith shop, hammering out a nail. Nowadays nails are made from long rods which a machine chops up into proper lengths. They have their heads hammered on them, but this is done by machines that turn out nails at the rate of 1,000 per minute. The perfection of nail-making machinery is due largely to American invention and it was in colonial times when boys got so much "manual training" in the blacksmith shops and elsewhere that they developed the ingenuity that made us the great nation of inventors that we are. The first American patent for nail-making machinery, by the way, was taken out not so very long after the period when the blacksmith's apprentice used to shape them on the anvil.

THE ENGLISH IN AMERICA

In Great Grandmother's Kitchen

An American kitchen of 1750 looks quite different from a modern one, doesn't it? Instead of a gas jet or electric light, the 1750 kitchen was lighted by candles. The lantern on the mantel shelf is made of horn. The "flat irons" are brass shells into which the irons were thrust after having been heated in the coals. Above the flat irons are toasting irons for holding the bread before the fire. What a long handle that frying pan has! You see why, don't you? The blaze was so hot you didn't want to get any nearer to it than necessary. And, besides, frying things spit grease. At the right of the fireplace is a little chamber with a door to it. That is where mother made the spicy cookies and baked the bread. Leaning against the brick is a "peel," a sort of long, flat shovel for putting dishes into the oven and removing them. A bellows for blowing the fire hangs at the left of the fireplace.

In Mrs. Ward's Parlor

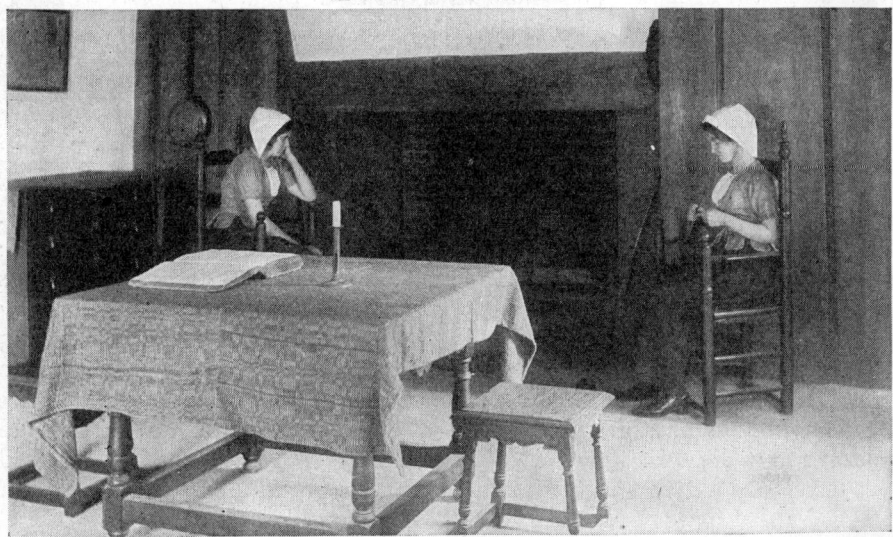

The parlor of the seventeenth century house is shown here exactly as it looked when John Ward lived in it, including the costumes of the two girls who are helping to bring the old scenes back to life. Notice the solid, substantial lines of the furniture, quite different from the slender Chippendale and Sheraton which became the vogue in the next century. The table cloth was called a "carpet" in 1684 and is made of hand-woven "woolsey." The open book is "The Whole Duty of Man," published in London in 1684.

PICTURED KNOWLEDGE
The Money of Our Forefathers

Perhaps you have heard the expression, "not worth a continental." It originated at the time when the paper money shown in this picture was in circulation. The Continental Congress issued this paper money and with it paid the soldiers, bought supplies, and met other indebtedness. Of course, pieces of paper issued by any government are not real money but simply promises to pay real money in gold or silver. Somewhat like promissory notes of a private individual. If the war failed, of course the Continental government would cease to exist and these promises would never be redeemed. As there were many times when it looked very much as if Great Britain would succeed in putting down her rebellious colonies, these promissory notes had very little value. The states also issued paper money. By 1779 when the four-shilling bill, which you see on the left, was issued by Massachusetts, it took twenty-eight of these bills to equal four shillings in coin. At that rate you would have needed a handful of them just to pay your street car fare down town. Those coins shown are made of silver and so are real money; that is to say, they have value in themselves.

and shoes for the family were cobbled on a bench in the chimney corner. All New England farmers had a small forge for hammering out nails and bolts from iron bars and they shod their own horses. No "Yankee," or Scotch-Irishman, or German bought anything he could contrive to make. In New England was developed a genius in the handicrafts that led to many useful inventions.

But these activities did not supply all needs. Every colony was obliged to find something to sell so that they could buy better clothing, furniture and building material abroad; and build churches, schools, roads and bridges. England was exactly like France and Spain in wanting from her colonies only the things which could not be grown or made at home; and to them she wished to sell her surplus manufactures and the luxuries of Europe and the East Indies. Virginia and Maryland found a profitable crop and a steady income in tobacco; the Carolinas in the naval stores of the pine woods—the pitch, tar, turpentine and resin

1496

In the Days of the Spinet

The spinet was one of the favorite musical instruments of the time in our history when men wore wigs and ladies dressed their hair very high. The girl in the picture is not a Colonial maiden but a girl of today. The spinet, as you can see, developed out of the harp and was the beginning of our pianos. The strings were picked with a quill or plectrum which was caused to rise and fall as the keys were struck. The strings referred to were not those which you see in the picture which are simply part of the ornamental design.

so much needed in those days of wooden ships. The Carolinas and Georgia grew rice, indigo, and cotton. In all the southern colonies men of birth, wealth and education bought large plantations on the banks of the navigable rivers, and found an outlet for their ability and energy in developing and managing their landed estates. And in the Hudson River Valley rich Dutch merchants and aristocratic Englishmen colonized large grants of land, or "manors." The Dutch were few in number, and did little farming, devoting their talents to the rich fur trade of the Hudson and Mohawk valleys. In Pennsylvania, the Germans cultivated large farms in the Delaware and Schuylkill valleys, and shipped fine cavalry horses to the English army.

How the Preacher Knew When to Stop

This pulpit glass stood at the right of the minister and told the clerk when the sermon had lasted for two hours. If the sermon was to be four hours long the clerk turned the glass over, but if two hours were all that the minister was to talk, the clerk rapped sharply three times and the minister finished his talk.

What the New Englanders Did

In New England, however, the climate was too severe, the soil too sterile to make farming on a large scale profitable. Living in villages, they cultivated what was needed at home, and some corn and peas to trade with the Indians for beaver skins. They also made wampum beads of shells, and wove woolen blankets. They built glass and salt works and iron furnaces to supply home needs.

The Family Coach in Penn's Day

This is William Penn's family coach. You may see it among the historic relics in Independence Hall, Philadelphia. It is not so luxurious as were many other coaches in this time, because Penn was a Quaker and did not believe in display.

THE ENGLISH IN AMERICA

Every man, beside his farming, engaged in cod-fishing, whaling in the Arctics, lumbering in the Maine woods, or ship-building. They sold rum, cod-fish, salt meats, whale oil, boards, barrel staves, shoes, straw, fur, and felt hats, all the way from Labrador to the West Indies, and in England and Holland; and they brought back cotton, rice, sugar, molasses, naval stores, indigo, tobacco, and the manufactures of Europe. They also brought Spanish silver dollars from Cuba and melted and re-coined them into pine-tree shillings and sixpences. Many of their ships they sold in London.

The growing trade of these bold New England sailors so alarmed the merchants of the mother country, that the English Parliament, in which the colonies had no representation, passed navigation acts. They required that all foreign goods for the colonies must pass through England, and no foreign vessel could trade with the colonies. This was so unjust that it led to smuggling of goods into and out of West Indian ports. And ships from New England sailed to Africa and engaged in the slave trade. Having to take many risks, to evade English laws and to escape capture and confiscation of cargoes by Barbary pirates and Spanish warships, the "old salts" of New England grew to be the most daring seamen and shrewdest traders on the ocean. Theirs were the naval victories in the wars with the French and their Indian allies.

The colonies of the North and South were settled by different breeds of men, in the first place. More peo-

Where Virginia Lawmakers Warmed Themselves

In Colonial days most houses and public buildings were heated by enormous fireplaces in which great logs were burned, letting half the smoke out into the room and half the heat up the chimney. Stoves were rare and very expensive. This stove stood in the Virginia House of Burgesses. It is very highly ornamented, like a modern base-burner. It is a Dutch stove and has a hollow fire box opening into the bridge arrangements on top. The fire rests on iron bars at the bottom, through which the draft enters. This kind of stoves often became red hot and the heated air, passing from them out into the room, was full of poisonous gases, the products of combustion and contact with the heated iron.

PICTURED KNOWLEDGE
An Old Thanksgiving Proclamation

BY THE HONORABLE

JONATHAN TRUMBULL, Esq;
Governor, Captain-General, and Commander in Chief of
the State of *Connecticut*, in *New-England*, in *America*:

A PROCLAMATION.

*A*MID the many private and public Distresses of a temporal Nature,—Arguments for Praise and Thanksgiving multiply and arise from almost every Quarter,—for it is of the LORD's Mercies that we are not utterly consumed, because His Compassions fail not.—And tho' he has caused Grief, yet He has had Compassion according to the Multitude of His Mercies:—He has not dealt with us according to our Sins, nor punished us according to our Iniquities :—His Interpositions in Behalf of a sinful and backsliding People are very obvious, and more than we can reckon up.

I HAVE therefore thought fit, by and with the Advice of the Council, and at the Desire of the Representatives, in General Court assembled, to appoint, and do hereby appoint THURSDAY the Fifth Day of December next, to be observed as a Day of Public THANKS-GIVING throughout this State ; directing and exhorting all Denominations and Orders of People, to present their Thank-Offering unto the Fountain of all our Mercies, and pay their Vows unto the MOST HIGH; who giveth Songs in the Night of their Affliction :---To bless and praise His Name for all the Bounties of His Providence, and the far richer Blessings of His Grace, in which we share.---In an especial Manner to ascribe Blessing and Praise, Honour and Thanksgiving unto our GOD, for the Enjoyment of the Means of Grace, Sabbath and Sanctuary Advantages :---For that Harmony & Stability which subsists in the public Councils of the United States :---For the Courage, Resolution, and Readiness of the People to stand forth in the Defence of their Rights, Liberties, and Privileges :---For every Instance of Protection and Success in their military Operations against their powerful Enemies :---For that Measure of Health enjoyed in the Country and Army :---For the Competency of the former, and plentiful Supply of the latter Harvest :---And for every Expression of his loving Kindness, and tender Mercy.---And at the same Time, to implore GOD's gracious Presence with the General Congress of the United States of America :---That he would give them Wisdom, Ability and Fidelity equal to the Trust reposed in them, and the Weight of public Business laid upon them :---That all our Assemblies, Conventions, and Councils may be directed, owned and blessed :---That HE would form our Generals, Officers, and Soldiery for their Department, and honor them as the Instruments of our Deliverance :---That HE would pour out HIS SPIRIT in plentiful Effusions upon HIS Churches and Ministers in this and all the States, and that the whole Land may be a Temple in which GOD is served and glorified ;---That Seminaries of Learning, and other inferior Schools of Instruction may be every where amongst us, succeeded :---That the People of this State in particular, may be blessed in all their temporal and spiritual Concerns :---That GOD would make us glad according to the Days wherein we have been afflicted, and the Time wherein we have seen Evil :---That his Work may appear unto his Servants, and his Glory unto Childrens Children ;---That the Beauty of the LORD our GOD may be upon us, and that HE would establish the Work of our Hands :---That HE would bring the Heathen into CHRIST's Sheep-fold ;---And fill the Universe with the Display of HIS glorious Perfections, in and through JESUS CHRIST our Lord and Saviour.

All servile Labour is forbidded on said Day.

Given under my Hand at the Council Chamber in New-Haven, the 25th Day of October, Anno Domini, 1776.

JON^TH TRUMBULL.

As you see by this proclamation issued by Governor Trumbull of Connecticut in 1776, Thanksgiving Day was not observed on the last Thursday in November at that time as it usually is today. Plymouth Colony celebrated the first Thanksgiving after the harvest in 1621 and Thanksgiving Days were appointed after this at different times in New England and New York. Congress recommended a Thanksgiving Day yearly during the Revolutionary War, but there was no national appointment of the festival, each State issuing its own proclamation. At first Thanksgiving was observed almost exclusively in New England.

ple of the leisure class, of high birth, wealth and social distinction had gone into the region below Pennsylvania. Into the northern colonies had poured college-bred professional men, skilled workmen, farmers, and merchants. Climate, soil, and industries, made all these

THE ENGLISH IN AMERICA
What Colonial Newspapers Were Like

Imagine reading in a newspaper of April 14th about what happened in London on the 20th of last November! In 1720 all the news from Europe was brought across the Atlantic in slow sailing vessels which sometimes took several months to make the voyage. Even the best and biggest newspapers in America came out only three times a week, and consisted of only four small pages. They were printed with blurry type on coarse, brown paper. There was not much news in any of them. A good deal of space was filled up with advertisements for runaway slaves and stray horses. Much space also was given to letters written from distant places to friends of the editor, who, by the way, usually printed his own paper as well as editing it. Instead of short editorials, such as we have today, there were long essays on politics and morals, by prominent men who signed a high-sounding Roman name to their articles. But news of the outside world was so scarce that people welcomed these meager sheets eagerly, even when they were many weeks old.

differences more marked. Slavery, perhaps, was the deciding factor. To be sure there were slaves in every colony—50,000 of them north of Maryland before the Revolution. But the Negro did not thrive in a cold climate, and could not be used profitably in the many complicated tasks of small farms and shops. The African laborer was used to the greatest advantage on the large plantations of the South, in cultivating single crops, such as tobacco, cotton and rice.

This slave labor made the South rich, and caused a scattering of the population. Men of wealth built up

PICTURED KNOWLEDGE
The Home of the Washingtons

This is the attractive home of the Washingtons at Mount Vernon as it appears today. It stands on a bluff overlooking the Potomac. It is entirely of wood, but the siding, you will notice, is of thick boards and is divided up so as to give it somewhat the appearance of stone work. Mount Vernon gets its name from Admiral Edward Vernon of the British Navy under whom Lawrence, George Washington's half-brother, served. Lawrence owned the house, but provided that at the death of his widow it should pass to George Washington. The house, or villa, as it originally stood, forms the middle portion of the present mansion house, George Washington having built an addition at each end. In 1860 the house, which was showing the effects of time and neglect, was purchased by the Mount Vernon Ladies' Association on behalf of the nation. The purchase price was $200,000, which included the buildings and 200 acres of the original estate.

The Garden at Mount Vernon

President and Mrs. Washington were people of exquisite taste and, as you see, even the part of the estate devoted to the raising of vegetables for the table was beautifully laid out and cared for. From each end of the mansion at Mount Vernon was a colonnade with a paved walk underneath it, leading through a beautiful lawn with shaded drives along which were trees planted by Franklin, Jefferson, Lafayette and other famous men who were connected with the Revolution.

THE ENGLISH IN AMERICA
In George Washington's Study

This is the study in Washington's home at Mount Vernon as it looks today. On the right you see the tripod, the three-legged stand for his surveying instrument, and near it a globe. Globes became very popular after Columbus discovered America and in 1507 a German mapmaker made a globe on which the map was printed in separate pieces or gores and pasted on the globe. You can plainly see the sections in this one.

The Bedroom of Washington

Here we are looking into the bedroom of Washington at Mt. Vernon. The chair near the window on the left is his mother's and one in which she used to sing him to sleep. The old round trunk is of the type that was used in Washington's day and for a good many years afterward.

large landed properties like the ancestral estates of Old England. Every river up to the falls was lined with plantations, each with its private wharf where vessels from London called for the staple crop and unloaded every luxury of living.

classics, sent their sons to English universities to be educated, and devoted their leisure to politics. With much property at stake and a keen sense of their personal worth, they were natural leaders in public life, both in peace and war. William and Mary College was founded in 1688, but with the population so scattered, primary schools were unknown. Every plantation with children had a governess and a tutor.

On the Front Porch at Mt. Vernon

Can you imagine any home more delightful than Mt. Vernon must have been when the Washingtons lived in it? This picture represents Washington conversing with Lafayette when the noble Frenchman visited the United States after the Revolution, and was the guest of the nation. Among the trees in the background you see a little summer house and beyond that, the waters of the Potomac. Seated with Mrs. Washington at the table is her daughter, Nellie Custis. That dear little girl leaning her head on grandmother's lap is Martha Parke Custis, and on the ground near the porch is her brother Jack. You see, boylike, he goes in for toy cannons while his little sister prefers the hoop. The two little dogs have evidently heard that toy cannon go off before and are quite interested, but they don't seem to be quite sure whether they had better wait and hear it "bark," or run away. In the household the children were known as "Jack and Patcy." Washington loved both them and their mother dearly as if they were children of his own blood. In the first invoice of goods shipped to him from London after he became their stepfather, he ordered "Ten shillings worth of toys, six little books for children beginning to read, and one fashionably dressed baby to cost ten shillings." The dressed baby was, of course, a doll. For their mother he bought a "Forte Piano," and later at a cost of $1,000, a very fine harpsichord, and one of his greatest delights was to have her play and sing to him. He was very systematic in everything he did and his ledger shows the cost of constant gifts he made to her. One of these items is, "The Wayworn Traveler," a song for Miss Custis.

The Southern Country Gentry Washington was a typical planter, and beautiful Mt. Vernon, his home on the Potomac, a typical plantation. These wealthy proprietors cultivated all the refinements of living, in their houses, dress and lavish entertainments. They rode and danced, read Shakespeare and other British

In the North everyone worked, and lived close together. The people crowded into farming villages which rapidly grew into towns and

At One of Mrs. Washington's Receptions

Here we are at a reception at the White House when Washington was President. Of course, we will meet here the most distinguished people in the land. As there are so many we will not try to get introductions to all of them, but one of "those present," whom I am sure you will want to know, is Master George Washington Parke Custis. He is that little boy, with the long hair, on the extreme right. He is the grandson of Mrs. Washington and the adopted son of the President. The lady who has her hand on his shoulder is a Mrs. Randolph, and the one who has turned to speak to him is Mrs. Winthrop. Both ladies were prominent in the society of the time. Assisting Mrs. Washington in receiving are Nellie Custis and Mrs. Robert Morris. (Mrs Morris, you remember, is the lady at whose house the foreign prince was so much embarrassed because he didn't know what to do when she kept urging him to have more tea.) Nellie is standing between Mrs. Morris and Mrs. Washington. Distinguished foreigners were also to be seen at receptions at the White House in those days, just as they are now. For instance, one of the heads you see in the background under the arch is Louis Philippe, who afterward became King of France and reigned for a short time before Napoleon took charge of things. Conversing with Washington, whom you will readily recognize, is the Duke of Kent, who fought on the side of the British during the Revolution. Possibly they are discussing incidents of their campaigns.

At the left of the raised platform on which Mrs. Washington is standing, is a man in a long gown. That is Jonathan Trumbull. He was Chief Justice of the Superior Court of Connecticut, and it is for this reason that he wears the gown. You notice that John Jay, who stands not far from the platform on the right, wears a similar gown. He was Chief Justice of the Supreme Court of the United States, an office to which Washington appointed him. Washington also thought very highly of the abilities of Jonathan Trumbull and the name "Brother Jonathan," as applied to the United States, is said to have originated from Washington's frequent remark when important matters were to be discussed, "Let us hear what Brother Jonathan has to say."

Looking at the picture, it is hardly necessary to add that those were the days of hoops. The ladies' dresses stood out for two feet on each side and were made of gorgeous brocades and taffetas. The gentlemen wore their hair done up in a cue and their hair was always white, no matter what the natural color may have been, because it was thickly powdered. Their coats had silver buttons engraved with the initials of their names.

The cuffs were loaded with lead; and for the same reason that we put "sinkers" on our fish lines—to make them hang straight.

Martha Washington and Little Maria's Nose

Here is a portion of a letter written by Martha Washington to a relative. It sounds very domestic and home-like, and is particularly interesting because it tells about two handkerchiefs that Mrs. Washington made for a little girl and which she sent along with the letter. This reference to the handkerchiefs occurs in the last paragraph which reads in part as follows:

"The President set out this day week on a tour to the eastward. Mr. Lear and Major Jackson attended him. My dear children have had very bad colds but thank God they are getting better. My love and good wishes attend you and all with you.—Kiss Maria. I send her two little handkerchiefs to wipe her nose."

cities. Life was simple and frugal, for no one was rich. Everyone was deeply religious and society was sober. Here was no horse-racing, card-playing, dancing, hunting country gentry as in Virginia. Husking and quilting bees, shooting matches, athletic sports and the militia "training day" furnished the social pleasures. Reading was confined to the Bible, Milton and books of sermons. Boys went to school. Massachusetts voted taxes to help support schools as early as 1640, and Harvard College was founded in 1638.

Life and Culture in the North

All the New England colonies nad their men of classical education. There were one hundred graduates of Cambridge and Oxford among the first generation in Boston. There were large private libraries in every northern colony, and distinguished scholars to use them. Yale, Dartmouth, Brown and Pennsylvania Universities, and King's College (Columbia) were all founded before the French and Indian War. Princeton was started by Scotch-

THE ENGLISH IN AMERICA

Irish graduates of Edinburgh and Dublin in a log cabin in 1746. Massachusetts gave us our first and best-loved names in American literature; but it was in Philadelphia that Benjamin Franklin found the ablest lawyers and doctors, and men to form societies for the discussion of science and philosophy.

days or two weeks, depending on the weather. There were stage-coach lines only between Boston, New York and Philadelphia. A post-office and mail routes had been established, and there were hand printing presses and small weekly newspapers in the larger towns. The English Licensing Act, under which no book, pamphlet or almanac could be printed or sold anywhere without permission from the authorities, expired in 1695, and there was now liberty of the press. Virginia had its first newspaper in 1732, the year George Washington was born. The *Boston News Letter* was founded in 1704, and boasted that its European news, received by sailing vessel, was only two months old. Just think of it!

A Pleasant Way to Travel

To go by stage coach used to be the quickest way to make a long journey, but it was so uncomfortable to be jolted about for several days and nights over the rough roads, that people with plenty of time liked to make their trips by water if they could. This is a flat bottomed canal packet with a dining room and bedrooms for passengers. It is pulled through the water by horses on the tow path at the side. See how the people on top seem to be enjoying the fine weather. The Erie Canal, opened in 1825 between Albany and Buffalo, N. Y., was the first important canal in the United States.

The Colonies in 1760

Now let us see what our country was like in 1760, a little over a century and a half after the first settlement. There were probably about 2,000,000 people, all east of the mountains, with the frontier settlements nowhere more than one hundred and fifty miles from the ocean. Massachusetts, Pennsylvania and Virginia were the most populous. Philadelphia had 16,000 people, Boston 20,000, New York 12,000. Charleston was the only city of any size in the South. Roads were few, bridges poor. Most travel was by water, in sailing sloops and schooners along the coast and up the rivers. Any voyage might take two

And yet, somehow, news traveled. Philadelphia was the meeting place for planters from the South, local *Beginning* men of science, and *of the* professional men and *Union Idea* merchants from New England. And there was one topic of conversation of unfailing interest

PICTURED KNOWLEDGE
Dancing Out the History Lesson

These two pictures show you how one of the stately colonial dances is reproduced in the school assembly room. If this is not one of the physical exercises in your school, show these pictures and the following directions to your teacher. Such exercises not only bring fresh color to your cheeks but add greatly to the feeling of life and reality in the history lesson.

Children enter in rows, girls at the right, holding skirts daintily with right hands, boys holding girls' left hands high with their right. Boys' left hands behind back.

Touch left heel forward, 1. Touch left toe backward, 2. Change step, or catch step, left, 3-4. Touch right heel forward, 1. Touch right toe backward, 2. Change step, right, 3-4. Drop hands and turn left about, grasp inside hands and repeat in opposite direction, 9-15 counts.

Part II. 16 Measures.

At end of Part I all turn left about and finish facing forward, ready for Part II. Same formation as in Part I. All step left sideward, 1. Step right foot over left, 2. Step left sideward, 3. Step right foot behind left, toes pointed downward, right knee turned outward and bend knees slightly. (This is the dip step), 4. Same thing right, 5-8. Repeat all, 9-16. Repeat Part I. 32 counts in all. Finish, partners facing.

Part III. 8 Measures, Picture Number 1.

Partners join right hands and hold high, girls' left hands holding skirts at side, boys' left behind back. All walk forward 4 steps, partners changing positions. On fourth count turn about and make a slight bow, 1-4. Join left hands and repeat, 5-8. Boys take girls' left hands in their right, still facing each other. Boys step sideward left, girls sideward right, all moving front, 1. Point step front (one foot crossing over the other, toes pointed). With opposite foot), 2. Boys step sideward right, girls sideward left, 3. Point step, 4. All turn about away from partners and make a low bow, girls holding skirts with both hands, boys with right hand across chest, left behind back, 5-8. (See the next Picture.) Repeat all, 16 counts. 32 counts in all.

Part IV. 8 Measures.

Partners face each other and join right hands. Boys walk backward, girls forward. 4 counts (on fourth count make slight dip step). Repeat in opposite direction, 4. Drop hands, all step sideward right and bow low, 1-2. Step to position, heels together, not changing position of hands, 3-4. Repeat to left, 5-6. Step to position, 7-8. Repeat the whole dance.

and importance to all—the Indian Wars. New Englanders on the sea and Virginians on the land, they had fought and died and won victories for seventy years. Involved in all of England's wars, they had defended her colonies unhelped, and had profited nothing from the endless strife, not even winning peace and security for themselves. Very slowly another principle of the Dutch Republic took root in the colonial mind: "United we stand, divided we fall."

It was the French and Indian Wars that knit the thirteen colonies into a compact nation of people standing shoulder to shoulder. That will make another story.

How First Graders Built a Pioneer Home

The pupils of the first grade in a Franklin, Indiana, school collected and arranged the material for this pioneer schoolhouse after studying pioneers and their primitive ways of living. The "logs" are dowel rods and the "ground" is a sand table. The forest in the background was sketched in charcoal on cardboard, by children in the upper grades. The rods were notched to fit each other and are held in place with clay. The chimney is of sticks stuck together with clay.

The Pilgrim Fathers

The breaking waves dashed high
  On a stern and rock-bound coast,
And the woods against a stormy sky
  Their giant branches tossed.

And the heavy night hung dark,
  The hills and water o'er,
When a band of exiles moored their bark
  On the wild New England shore.

Not as the conqueror comes,
  They, the true-hearted, came;
Not with the roll of the stirring drums,
  And the trumpet that sings of fame;

Not as the flying come,
  In silence and in fear—
They shook the depths of the desert gloom
  With their hymns of lofty cheer.

Amidst the storm they sang,
  And the stars heard, and the sea;
And the sounding aisles of the dim woods rang
  To the anthem of the free!

The ocean-eagle soared
  From his nest by the white waves' foam;
And the rocking pines of the forest roared—
  This was their welcome home!

There were men with hoary hair
  Amidst that pilgrim band;
Why had they come to wither there,
  Away from their childhood's land?

There was woman's fearless eye,
  Lit by her deep love's truth;
There was manhood's brow serenely high,
  And the fiery heart of youth.

What sought they thus afar?
  Bright jewels of the mine?
The wealth of seas, the spoils of war?—
  They sought a faith's pure shrine!

Ay, call it holy ground,
  The soil where first they trod,
They have left unstained what there they found—
  Freedom to worship God.

FELICIA HEMANS

The Story of Black Hawk

This giant work of art stands on a lofty promontory called "The Eagle's Nest," near Oregon, Illinois, and overlooks the picturesque valley of the Rock River. It is one of the best known works of Lorado Taft. It is known as the Black Hawk Statue, although the face is not a portrait of the famous chief but a composite of the features of the Fox, Sac, Sioux and Mohawk tribes. You notice that this giant wears no feathers, or Indian trappings. He expresses in grand simplicity the stern dignity of an Indian chief and his resentment at the wrongs inflicted upon his race by the white man. As grand chief of the Sacs and Foxes, Black Hawk vigorously opposed to a contract between his people and the United States in 1809 by which, for an annual allowance of only $1,000, they give up their rights to something like seven hundred square miles of territory along the Mississippi. In 1823 when, lead by Keokuk, a greater part of the Sacs and Foxes emigrated to a government reservation, Black Hawk and a few followers refused to go. He remained on the eastern side of the Mississippi and lived peaceably until the white man confiscated his possessions. With a few followers he then destroyed several white settlements but all were finally driven west of the Mississippi, and Black Hawk and his two sons were captured and imprisoned in Fortress Monroe.

STORIES OF AMERICAN HISTORY
THE INDIAN WARS

The Indian Wars and How They Helped to Bring on the Revolution

Sowing Wheat on the Graves

In the first winter in New England only the hardiest of the little band of Pilgrims survived. Quick consumption caused the death of many of them before they reached America, for alternating the foul air of the crowded Mayflower hold in stormy weather with the piercing cold of the northern Atlantic on clear days when they could go on deck, made them particularly susceptible, and the hard life in this country, with no suitable shelter, carried off a great many before the first, long, hard winter was over. Before the end of March nearly one-half of their number had died. They were buried near the sea, on Cole's Hill, and grain was sown above the graves so that the Indians couldn't find them and discover how small was the force of white people left.

The picture shows a Puritan sowing grain over a freshly-made grave as the funeral procession disappears over the hill. Notice how the man in the foreground is dressed. Even at the sad business of a funeral he wore his armor and carried his gun and sword, because the Indians' war whoop might be heard at any moment and it was best to be always prepared.

WHO does not know the thrilling and romantic story of how Captain John Smith was rescued from a cruel death by the Indian Princess Pocahontas? The lady did not marry the hero, who was, indeed, a grizzled veteran of wars in The Netherlands and with the Turks. In due time she was wedded to young John Rolfe in the church at Jamestown and went away to London, to be made much of by Queen and Court. Because of this marriage, Captain Smith was able to make a treaty of peace with Chief Powhatan, one that was kept for twenty years. Before that, and afterwards, the colonists of Virginia were constantly in danger of attack by the Indians.

The Story of Pocahontas

Beginning of the Wars

Many of the early uprisings were too small and brief to be called "wars." Both tribes and colonies were far apart and, with the exception of the Iroquois Nations of Western New York State, the Indians were not organized. Each attack was simply a separate, treacherous raid on a sleeping settlement, led by some warrior of local fame. But by and by, when the white people increased in number and began to crowd the Indians out of their best hunting grounds, the tribes joined forces to resist. Then the French in Canada took advantage of this feeling to organize and arm the Algonquin tribes of the St. Lawrence, and with their help to try to drive the English and Dutch out of America.

To understand these later wars and their very important consequences, we must go back to the early Indian uprisings. We are obliged now to admit that most of them could have been avoided. They were due to the unfriendly spirit of the English people of certain colonies toward their red neighbors. Every European people who came to America made its own terms with the Indians according to its disposition. The Spaniards killed or enslaved them. The French lived with their "wild brothers" and won their undying devotion. The English were unlike both Spanish and French, and those of different colonies differed widely from each other. All Englishmen felt their moral and social superiority to the semi-barbarians of the American forest, and the marriage of Pocahontas and John Rolfe was one of the very few unions of the two races. But the people of some colonies were friendly, and fair in their dealings with the Indians, and were met with friendship and faith. In other colonies contempt and

The English and the Indians

John Smith, Author, Explorer, Adventurer

Captain John Smith set out to see the world for himself when he was a very young man. He went first to fight in the Low Countries, in the Dutch wars against Spain. Leaving there he was robbed, by four adventurers, of everything he possessed. In those days many worthy and even noble gentlemen made a business of piracy, so when John Smith turned pirate and helped capture a Venetian ship whose cargo made him wealthy for awhile, he was not doing anything so very disreputable in the eyes of the world. According to his own story of his life, he next joined the Austrians in their battles with the Turks. There he was captured and sold as a slave to a lady who took pity on him and protected him from some of the hardships and sufferings which fell to the lot of Turkish slaves. Then he stole a horse and rode away into Russia with his slave's iron collar still about his neck. There he found some enemies of the hated Turks who gladly filed away his collar, the mark of his slavery, and he set out for home. He made his way through Germany, France, Spain and Morocco, back to England again, with many thrilling adventures along the way. In England he joined the Jamestown expedition and had much to do with making the first permanent English settlement in Virginia successful. John Smith has been accused of being a boaster, and of making himself the hero of hair-breadth adventures which he never experienced, but we must remember that in the age in which he lived, the habit of bragging was much more common than it is today and a modest man wasn't likely to get all the attention and respect he deserved. And John Smith's adventurous career was remarkable, even for those stirring days.

injustice bred hatred and revenge.

Friendship Between Indians and Englishmen

Had the Indians been so disposed, the Pilgrims could easily have been destroyed, for they were in the sorest straits of poverty and sickness. But Indians aided them, taught them how to plant and cook corn, to hunt and fish and make snow-shoes. And the people of Plymouth invited their red neighbors to share their first Thanksgiving feast. This was long remembered, for hospitality is an Indian virtue. Plymouth colony had no trouble until after the arrival of the Boston and Salem colonists.

In Rhode Island, Roger Williams bought his land, traded fairly and was unmolested by tribes which waged war against Massachusetts and Connecticut. William Penn and the Quakers of Pennsylvania made the famous treaty of peace that was "never sworn to and never broken" until all the colonies and all the tribes became involved in the French and Indian War of 1754. But the Delawares had already learned to trust white men by living as near neighbors to the fair-dealing Dutch and Swedes for a half century. The Dutch in the Hudson River Valley made a perpetual treaty of peace—the "Covenant of Corlear" with the Iroquois Nations, the most fierce and warlike of all eastern tribes.

Six of the thirteen colonies had no trouble whatever with Indians in their immediate neighborhood. Most of the early "Wars" were in New England and Virginia. Puritan and Cavalier alike felt nothing but disgust and contempt for the red man. They often cheated him in trade, and they thought that a charter from the King gave them a good title to the whole American wilderness. Indian rights to their forest homes and hunting grounds were ignored. Crowded back and reduced to poverty, many tribes were obliged to fight, or to submit and die miserably.

Raleigh's settlement on Roanoke Island was destroyed and only the good sense of Captain John Smith saved Jamestown. After the long peace, Virginia fought an endless succession of border wars back to

Princess Pocahontas in Her Court Dress

This shows Princess Pocahontas in her court dress as she appeared when she went to London and was presented to the Queen. Although it is painted in the stiff style of the time, you can see that she must have been a beautiful woman. The painting is now in possession of one of her descendants, Col. Frank S. Robertson, of Abingdon, Va. He kindly loaned it for reproduction for the benefit of readers of Pictured Knowledge. In his letter with regard to it, Colonel Robertson says: "This English painting of my distant grandmother, Pocahontas, my father believed to be the only authentic portrait of her extant, and he looked into the subject very thoroughly."

the crest of the Alleghenies. The Puritans in New England had no security until they had conquered the Pequots and Narragansetts, and looking forward with confidence to peace, began to push back the frontier.

Only eleven years later, however,

How Pocahontas Saved John Smith's Life

Captain John Smith was one of a party of Englishmen who set out to explore the country near their settlement. They were captured by the Indians and all murdered except John Smith. His cleverness and presence of mind saved him again, for he made the Indians afraid of him and they treated him with the superstitious respect accorded to their own medicine men. He was taken on a long march through the country to Powhatan, head chief of the Indians of that region. Captain Smith, in his diary written, like Caesar's Commentaries, in the third person, tells the story of how Pocahontas rescued him from death:

"A long consultation was held; but the conclusion was, two great stones were brought before Powhatan. Then as many as could, laid hands on Smith, dragged him to them, and thereon laid his head, being ready with their clubs to beat out his brains. Pocahontas, the king's daughter, when no entreaty could prevail, got Smith's head in her arms and laid her own upon his, to save him from death; whereat the Emperor was contented he should live to make his hatchets and her bells, beads and copper, for they thought him as well trained for all occupations as themselves."

The truth of this story has been doubted, especially since John Smith is known to have loved romance to such an extent that he sometimes exaggerated the romantic side of his adventures far beyond the actual facts in the case. But this story is credited by as great authority as John Fiske, who says that this event was not at all romantic from the Indians' point of view, but was an everyday occurrence. Smith had killed some Indian warriors and consequently, according to their custom, he must pay the blood-debt with his life or be adopted into the tribe. At first it was decided to kill him, but Pocahontas wanted him adopted because she had taken a little girl's fancy to the pale-faced stranger—she was only thirteen years old at the time, and though little Indian girls grow up more quickly than white girls, she was still a good deal of a spoiled child. When her father refused, she ran out and laid hold of him, as any spoiled girl will try to seize what she wants to possess. This time she was successful and Powhatan agreed that John Smith should be adopted as a member of the tribe. It was one of the Indians' customs to adopt a captive instead of killing him if some member of the tribe insisted on it. This picture is fairly authentic. The saving of Smith's life occurred in one end of an Indian long house, as shown here—one entrance to the house is at the left of the picture. Pocahontas is shown as older than thirteen, perhaps, and she is shown as warding the Indians away instead of protecting Smith as he describes, but the Indians are well represented, and the two stones are there, with John Smith's head upon them.

ended the career of the famous chief, "King Philip," in a swamp. By 1678 local tribes were wiped out or broken up, and New England, all the northern colonies, from New Hampshire to New Jersey, were attacked by French and Indians from Canada. This was a part of the

THE INDIAN WARS

first of the royal wars between England and France in the Old World and of their colonies in the New. In Europe they were known by different names, but in America simply as King William's, Queen Anne's and King George's wars. Beginning in 1689, they ran, with long intervals of peace to 1748. In 1754 they were followed by the French and Indian War which, starting in the colonies, spread to Europe. That war ended in the loss of her American colonies to France and, finally led to the Revolution and the independence of the English colonies.

This is the best time in American history to study the deep-lying and remote causes of all wars, their far-reaching effects, and their permanent influence on the characters and destinies of a people. These French and Indian royal wars had their roots in the past, in both Europe and America. France sought to force back upon the English people the Stuart kings whom they had driven into exile, and the two governments took opposite sides in the wars of Frederick the Great of Prussia upon Austria. Their rivalries were made all the keener by the rich prizes of North America and India to be won by the victor. None of the colonists, of any nation, had broken with their past. They were all loyal subjects of their kings, and thought it their duty to defend and to add to their monarch's possessions. So, although hundreds of miles of trackless forests, wild rivers and mountains, and stormy coasts lay between the settlements on

Family Feuds Among the Nations

The Wedding of Pocahontas

Pocahontas aided the English settlers in Virginia in many ways besides saving Captain John Smith's life. Her marriage with John Rolfe helped to keep the Indians under Chief Powhatan, her father, friendly to the English. She was baptized a Christian, assuming the name of Rebecca, and was then married in the church at Jamestown, April, 1614, with Governor Dale looking on. He is sitting at the left near the minister, with a group of soldiers behind him. The church is decked with vines and flowers and filled with a goodly company of spectators. Pocahontas is wearing a queer combination of English and Indian clothing—Indian moccasins, bracelets and peacock feathers in her hair, while her other garments were undoubtedly woven by some English housewife who perhaps gave them to Pocahontas for a wedding present. The picture shows the ceremony at the moment when Rolfe, with his right hand upraised, is taking the marriage oath, while Pocahontas demurely droops her head.

the St. Lawrence and the seaboard, English and French colonists fought valiantly in three long wars that were not their own. Peace was signed each time, in Europe, without consulting them, and no territory changed hands because of colonial victories.

with the desperation of despair. They hated and feared the English who were allied with the powerful Iroquois, and gladly joined in every war against them.

History sometimes turns on very small events. The Iroquois might not have made friends with the

Why John Smith Broke His Pistol

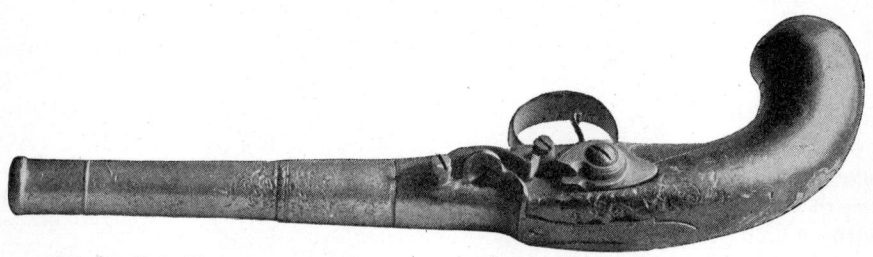

This deadly-looking weapon once belonged to Captain John Smith. You notice the hammer has been broken, and this is how it happened: Once when Captain Smith was captured by Indians, the Indians brought him his pistol and commanded him to fire it off. Firearms were new to them, of course, and John Smith knew very well that they wanted to learn how to shoot the pistol, and would then keep it to use against the colonists. The habit of quick thinking which had helped him out so often in the past came to his rescue this time and he fumbled with the lock of the pistol, breaking it as you see. Then, of course, it would not go off and he couldn't show the Indians how it worked.

Pistols had only been in use about forty years in Captain Smith's time, and they were long, heavy affairs, you see, quite different from the modern revolvers used in the army. Some of them were very beautifully carved and mounted with silver. The carving on the wooden butt of Smith's pistol is half obliterated by dents and scratches, and the iron barrel is badly scarred.

Fanning the Embers of Ancient Wars

Now as to the part played by the Indians in the mighty struggle for the continent, that lasted three-quarters of a century. When white men came to America, an ancient enmity already existed between the small but highly organized Iroquois Na-

The French and the Algonquins tions who occupied New York State between the Hudson River and Lake Erie, and the numerous but weak tribes of Algonquins who were scattered along the St. Lawrence from New Brunswick to Lake Superior. The Algonquins, all but conquered, were sadly in need of help when the French arrived at Quebec in 1609. They immediately collected around the French forts and, for the next hundred and sixty years, fought for their faithful friends and protectors

Dutch so readily, when they appeared on the Hudson, had they not previously had a little skirmish with the French. The French explorer, Champlain, with Algonquin guides, went south from the St. Lawrence, discovered Lake Champlain, and

A Little Battle with Large Results started across the narrow divide to the valley of the Hudson. There in the woods, near Ticonderoga, they met a band of Mohawk hunters. This was one of the Iroquois Nations, and the Algonquins were trespassers. In the fight which followed Champlain had an easy victory, for he killed a few Mohawks and scared the rest half to death with his guns. The Iroquois had never seen guns before. But the Algonquins fled. Knowing that all the Iroquois would soon be on the warpath they hurried

THE INDIAN WARS

Champlain back to Canada, to build forts and mount cannon at Quebec and Montreal.

Small as it was, that was one of the decisive battles of American history. When the Dutch soon after appeared at Albany, the Iroquois eagerly filled the holds of their vessels with beaver skins in return for guns with which to punish the Algonquins and their French allies. They succeeded in shutting the French up in their three fortified towns for thirty years, and in chasing the Algonquins to hiding places on the upper lakes. The Iroquois made a treaty of peace and friendship with the Dutch, and when New Netherland was captured by the British and named New York, this treaty was transferred to the English. King and colonists were very careful indeed to keep faith with the powerful Iroquois, and the Six Nations were allies of England until the end of the War of 1812.

This English alliance with the Iroquois no doubt decided the ownership of the continent. In colonial days the Hudson River Valley was never thickly peopled or strongly defended. If the French and their hordes of Algonquin warriors could have captured it, they would probably have split the English colonies, taken New England from the rear and then moved down on Virginia.

This was the plan of conquest of Count Frontenac, who was twice sent to Montreal as Governor of New France. A brilliant and daring leader, he sent Joliet, Marquette and La Salle to explore the Mississippi and lay claim to Louisiana. When King William's War broke out in 1689, his flying columns of French and Indians poured down the Connecticut River and Lake Champlain and ravaged the frontier from Maine to the Delaware. They burned Haverhill, Deerfield and Schenectady, but they were never able to break through

Why Young William Penn Doesn't Look Like a Quaker

William Penn doesn't look like a Quaker here, does he—in armor and a fine flowing neckcloth? But then he is quite young, you say, and perhaps this picture was painted before he turned Quaker. You are right, for this picture was painted when he was only twenty-two years old and is the only one we have of him made during his lifetime, though after his death several portraits of him were painted from the descriptions of him by people who knew him. This picture shows him in the costume of a Royalist army officer. We all know how he gave up the idea of being a statesman and courtier in order to preach the Quaker teachings, and how he finally led a band of the peace-loving, simple Quaker folk to a new home in America, but it was only after a struggle with his family that he accomplished it.

The Penns came from a fine old English family, prominent at court. Admiral Penn, William's father, intended his son to be a statesman, so when he came home from making war on the Dutch, and found William turning Quaker, he was very much displeased. He sent the young man to the court of the Duke of Ormond, viceroy of Ireland and a friend of his, in the hope that he would abandon his Quaker ideas, in the gay life there. Penn joined a local Royalist military organization and took a prominent part in the merry life about him for a time. It was then that this picture was painted.

The Plan of Count Frontenac

1517

PICTURED KNOWLEDGE
Penn's Treaty with the Indians

The picture was painted by Benjamin West. You know his story, don't you? He was a little Quaker boy and he first showed his talent by painting a picture of his baby sister smiling in her sleep. He was only seven then. His colors were made from berries, and his brush was made of hairs borrowed from the cat's tail.

In his painting of "The Death of Wolfe," he led the way toward the modern idea of accuracy in pictures of historic scenes by showing the figures in the uniforms they actually wore, instead of the classical draperies you see in the pictures of other artists of those days. Yet this picture of Penn's treaty is not accurate. For instance, Penn is represented as an elderly man, say of fifty or sixty, while in reality he was only thirty-eight at the time. And the conference took place soon after the Quakers landed. They had not yet had time to build the houses you see in the background. The Quaker movement was in its infancy at the time of this treaty, and the typical Quaker dress in which the artist clothes Penn and his followers was not introduced until thirty years later.

the wall of Iroquois warriors which stretched from Albany to Lake Erie.

In the three royal wars the northern colonies bore the brunt of the fighting. New York became the battleground on land, and New England sailors three times carried the British flag almost to Quebec. This was not fair, for the southern colonies were thus protected at no trouble or expense to themselves. Besides, had they all joined forces early they might have put an end to French and Indian attacks which, later, imperiled them all. One of the early Dutch governors of New York who had seen how, by uniting, the seven states of the Dutch Republic had driven out the armies

Failure to Learn from History

of Spain and won peace and independence, urged all the English colonies to unite, and prove the practical wisdom of the Dutch motto: "In union is strength." The New England colonies co-operated to put down the Pequots and Narragansetts, and they joined forces with New York in the royal wars. But the thirteen separate and widely differing colonial governments could not, at that time, be got to act together.

Threatened by a Common Peril

It was not until after the close of King George's War in 1748 that all were threatened by a common peril. Although no territory had changed hands, the French had, for a half

1518

THE INDIAN WARS
"The Apostle to the Indians"

John Eliot was a Puritan who came to this country because he couldn't preach what he believed in England. He was the man who began the work of converting the Indians to Christianity. In order to be able to preach to them, he spent a great deal of time acquiring their language, which, as it had never been written down, had to be learned verbally from the Indians themselves. And then, whenever he found a party of them who were willing to listen to him, he seized the opportunity of telling them about the gospel. Meeting these Indians in the depths of the woods—God's first temple—he began exhorting them with all the eloquence at his command. See how eager and earnest he looks as he tells the half-naked savages the message of the Scriptures. And what a contrast their lean, brown bodies and fierce eyes make to the gentle figure of the spiritual Puritan preacher. They are true Indians, you see, not Europeans with dark skins as some historical artists paint them.

This picture, by H. O. Walker, is a mural, or wall, painting in Memorial Hall, Boston State House. Its shape, square at the bottom and arched at the top, makes it just fit the space under an archway between two pillars. Many of the world's greatest pictures have been painted for this purpose, especially some of the work of the early Italian masters, which adorn the great medieval cathedrals.

century, been slowly gaining the advantage. In 1669 they had built a fort at Mobile on the Gulf of Mexico. Soon afterwards they were at New Orleans. Then, by fort-building, missions, trading posts, farming and lead-mining settlements, they pushed up the Mississippi almost to St. Louis. They held the upper lakes at Mackinac and Sault Ste. Marie; but, with northern Illinois and Wisconsin held by hostile Indians, communication between New France and Louisiana was over Lake Erie, the Wabash River and the lower Ohio. Their long chain of forts

Strategem of the French

1519

were placed on sites so well chosen that great cities stand on most of them today.

But this line of fortified waterways was a thousand miles back from the Atlantic seaboard, so no attention was paid to all this activity of the French in the heart of America. But it was a different matter altogether when the French decided to make a new route by leaving Lake Erie at Presque Isle (Erie City) and dropping down the Allegheny River to the headwaters of the Ohio. This brought them immediately behind Pennsylvania and Virginia. With no Iroquois warriors to bar the way, they would be able to attack the middle colonies from the rear. They had actually explored the Ohio Valley to the Miami River, taken formal possession of the country, and built forts at Presque Isle and on the Allegheny before the English colonies discovered what was going on.

Virginia was wild with anger and alarm. The Ohio Valley was included in her original sea-to-sea charter, and the Ohio Company, formed by Governor Dinwiddie, Lawrence Washington and other wealthy Virginia planters, had a further title to the land by purchase of the Iroquois Indians who had conquered the native tribes. Many sturdy Scotch-Irish settlers had pushed up the Potomac, and were eagerly waiting the word to pour over the mountains into the rich bottom lands of the Ohio's tributaries. Now, capitalists and colonists saw the French stealing a march on them, building forts, winning over tribes south of Lake Erie and preparing to shut in all the English colonies on the narrow seaboard. There were fully a million and a half of these colonists. Massachusetts, Connecticut, Carolina and Georgia were also concerned, for they too had sea-to-sea charters, and Quaker and German Pennsylvania saw with alarm, her long peace threatened from the rear.

The Threatened Wall on the West

The Puritan Maidens and the Indians

This picture shows a Puritan maiden teaching an Indian girl how to spin. If you wonder why they happen to be outdoors, with grass under their feet and trees behind them, the answer is that this is from a school pageant given in the suburbs of Boston to illustrate early New England history. The Puritan women, in these kindly relations with their darkskinned neighbors, really taught two lessons, one related to the household arts and the other human relationships; for if the men folks had been as thoughtful in their treatment of the Indians as the Puritan women were, the continual conflict between the white man and the red might have been avoided.

Sounding the Alarm

The call of all the colonies to unite in self-defense was first heard in 1754. The Iroquois Nations, ever on the watch for their English allies, sounded a warning. Benjamin Franklin, as editor of the *Philadelphia Gazette,* printed a crude cartoon of a snake cut in several pieces, with the motto: "Join or

Franklin's "Join or Die"

The First Bible Printed in America

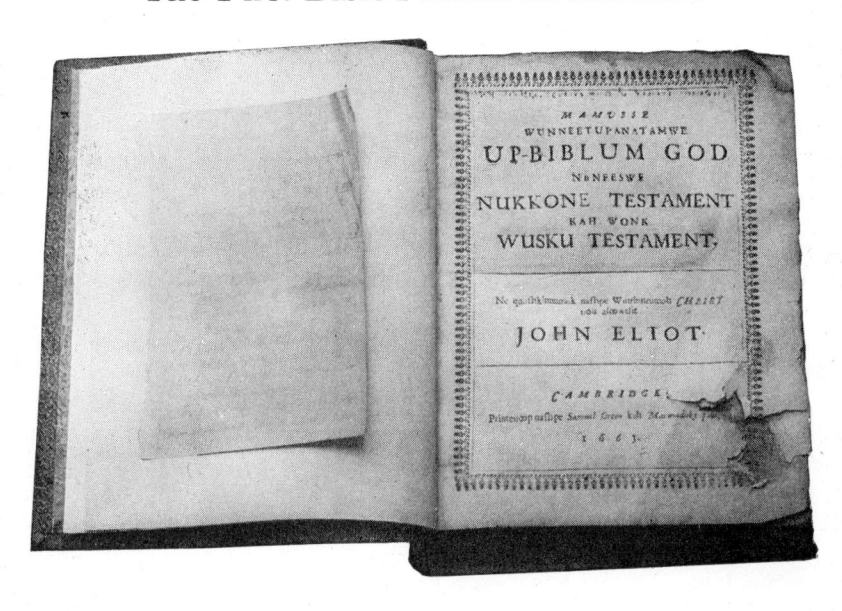

The first Bible published in this country was John Eliot's translation of the gospel into the Indian tongue. It took him over ten years to accomplish this task for the words of the Indian language had never been reduced to writing, so besides learning the language, John Eliot had to decide upon the letters which correctly expressed each sound. The title-page of this Bible is shown at the top. Literally translated, it reads, "The Whole Holy His-Bible, God, both Old Testament and Also New Testament. This turned by the-servant-of-Christ who is called John Eliot. Cambridge. Printed by Samuel Green and Marmaduke Johnson, 1663."

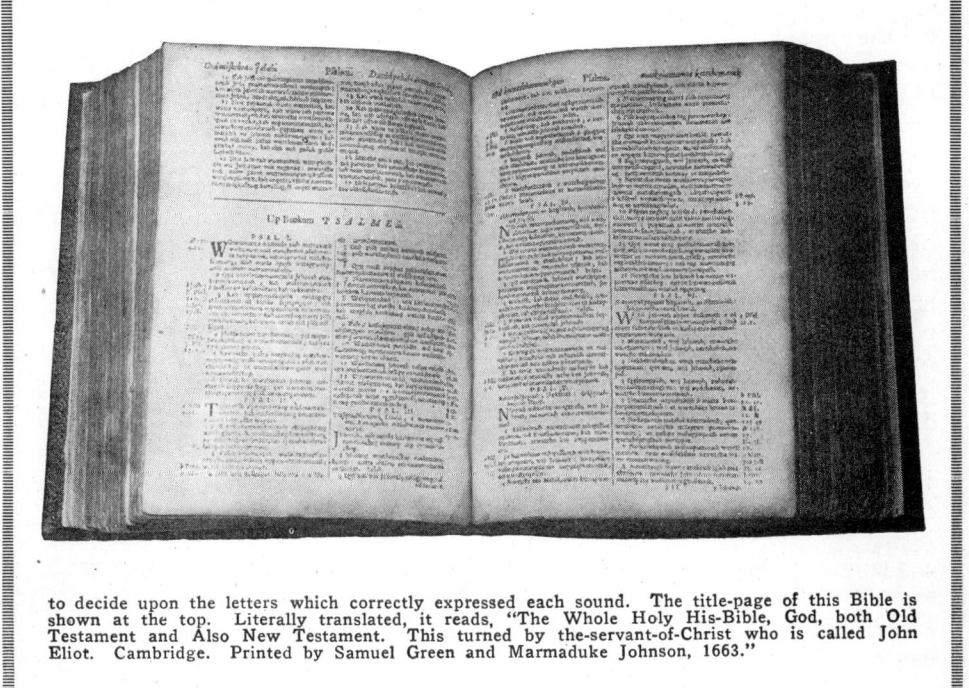

PICTURED KNOWLEDGE

die." The first colonial convention ever held in America was called to meet in Albany. Seven colonies and the Iroquois Nations were represented. Here the terms "Congress" and was chosen for this important and dangerous mission; but boys had to grow up early in those days of pressing needs and public duties. Since sixteen Washington had been in the

The Treaty with King Philip

This painting, the original of which hangs in Faneuil Hall, Boston, is by W. S. Savory, and commemorates a treaty made with the famous King Philip, chief Sachem of the Wampanoags, in what is known as "The Old Church" in Taunton, Mass., April 10, 1671. Treaties are usually made at the end of wars, but this treaty was made before King Philip's War began. Rumors had frequently reached the magistrates of Plymouth colony that Philip was meditating mischief. The men of Plymouth accordingly planned to attack him first, but as they could not get the other colonies to act with them, they decided to try persuasion, and so arranged a meeting with Philip at Taunton. The chief came with a number of his followers, said he was sorry for his past offenses, and signed the treaty in which he promised that his people should give up all fire-arms. It is now seen that this was a very unwise move on the part of the men of Plymouth, because it was an agreement that could not be enforced, and was a symptom of fear which had a bad effect on the Indians. At the end of three years from the day of the treaty, the Indians began a series of massacres which were a part of the horrible war that lasted until 1678.

"Continental Policy" were first used, no one dreaming of the stirring events to come that were to enlarge the meaning of those words.

Virginia failed to send a delegate. Perhaps she was too busy. Not waiting for "union," or for permission from London, this colony took matters into her own hands. Governor Dinwiddie sent George Washington with a letter to the commander of Fort Le Boeuf on the Allegheny, demanding that the French return to Canada.

It was a youth of twenty-one who

The Youth Named Washington

woods and mountains surveying wild land, living in the open, learning woodcraft and using Indians for guides. All the colonies had just such young men on their frontiers, of good birth and education, training in the colonial militia, used to hardships, resourceful and experienced in Indian fighting. At nineteen Washington was a major in the Virginia militia.

Many of the earliest colonial leaders, Raleigh, Captain John Smith, Miles Standish, Stuyvesant and Van

A BRIEF HISTORY OF THE VVARR

With the *INDIANS* in NEVV-ENGLAND,

(From *June* 24, 1675. when the first English-man was murdered by the Indians, to *August* 12. 1676. when *Philip*, alias *Metacomett*, the principal Author and Beginner of the Warr, was slain.) Wherein the Grounds, Beginning, and Progress of the Warr, is summarily expressed.

TOGETHER WITH A SERIOUS EXHORTATION to the Inhabitants of that Land,

By *INCREASE MATHER*, Teacher of a Church of Christ, in *Boston* in *New-England*.

Levit. 26.25. *I will bring a Sword upon you, that shall avenge the quarrel of the Covenant.*
Psal. 107.43. *Whoso is wise and will observe these things, even they shall understand the Loving-kindness of the Lord.*
Jer. 22.15. *Did not thy Father doe Judgment and Justice, and it was well with him?*

Segnius irritant animos demissa per aures,
Quàm quæ sunt oculis commissa fidelibus. *Horat.*
Lege Historiam ne fias Historia. *Cic.*

BOSTON, Printed and Sold by *John Foster* over against the Sign of the *Dove*. 1676.

This picture of the title page of Increase Mather's history of King Philip's War, tells its own story so well that little need be added. You will notice for yourself the peculiar spelling, the quaint type with its s's so much like the f's and the two V's used for a W in the larger letters, because the printing offices had a very small supply of types in those days.

Corlear, had served as officers in the army of the Dutch Republic, the wonder and admiration of Europe since its organization by Prince Maurice, and thousands of colonists of every nation had served there as private soldiers. The sons and grandsons of these first colonists never lost an opportunity to learn military tactics of any Dutch veteran who emigrated to America. Washington had Jacob Van Braam for a tutor. Of him he learned military engineering and strategy. And to these Old World scientific methods he added a knowledge of Indian fighting.

So it was as a commissioned officer, in the company of Christopher Gist, a famous frontiersman, that the young Virginian made the wild journey of three hundred miles, in mid-winter, to find the French in the wooded wilderness of northwestern Pennsylvania. He brought back the refusal of the French to withdraw, and a little later led a colonial force up the Potomac to build Fort Necessity.

The Most Famous of All Indians

PONTIAC.

This is the most famous Indian America ever produced and he deserves his fame, so far as talent is concerned, for it was Pontiac who organized and directed the largest and most powerful combination of Indians in history. It is always difficult to get a number of different nations to work together, even among civilized people, with rapid means of communication as we have them today. Think then what skill in persuading and managing men this red orator, warrior, and statesman must have had to bring about that great combination known as "Pontiac's Conspiracy." It was an achievement so great that an entire work, "The Conspiracy of Pontiac," by Francis Parkman, has been devoted to it.

The War and Its Results

Your school text book gives a very full account of the campaigns and battles of the long war that followed. The French remained in their forts and left it to colonials and British regulars to climb mountains, break through trackless forests ambushed by Indians, breast wild floods and navigate stormy coasts. In America the war ended with the fall of Quebec and Montreal, but, spreading to the Old World, and involving Spain as an ally of France, peace was not signed until 1763. And just as in the three royal wars that had gone before, the terms of peace were decided by kings in Europe, without consulting the interests of the colonists. Yet, with very little help colonial troops had won Canada and Florida for Great Britain, and they had still another Indian war to fight before they could win their way across the Appalachians.

From the Alleghenies back to the east bank of the Mississippi River, was also ceded to England, but this vast region was unconquered. From Mobile to Illinois no blow had been struck at any French fort. On orders from Paris the garrisons marched out, but French settlers, missionaries and fur traders remained in their villages, and from the Lakes to the Gulf the country swarmed with Algonquins and other tribes, who were unreconciled to this change of ownership and who burned to restore the country to their beloved friends, the French.

The Conspiracy of the Great Pontiac

Peace was no sooner signed than an Indian leader appeared in the person of Pontiac, Chief of the Ottawas, near Detroit. Convinced that the English, having driven out the French, intended next to exterminate the red men, Pontiac set about the gigantic task of organizing all the tribes west of the mountains. The most gifted of all forest statesmen, Pontiac had a well-thought-out plan, and an eloquence that gathered every tribe from the Lakes to the Gulf under his banner. He even won over the Natchez Indians, and the Senecas, one of the Iroquois Nations, who had always been enemies of the French.

He held the entire Mississippi Valley, and, within six months, had recaptured a number of the old French forts on the Great Lakes. The British garrisons and colonial troops got them back again and scattered the tribes, and Pontiac in the end was obliged to make a peace of unconditional submission (1765). Three years later he was brutally murdered by a drunken Indian.

England's Betrayal of Her Colonies

In 1763 the government in England issued a proclamation forbidding the colonists to settle in any of the territory from the crest of the Alleghenies to the Mississippi River. The purpose was to keep this vast region for the Indians, in order to increase the profitable fur trade and also to prevent the colonists from becoming too strong and independent.

Do you see what that meant?

A Famous Indian Orator

Here you meet Sagoyewatha, chief of the Wolf tribe of the Senecas. Beside being a warrior he was famous as an orator. During the Revolution his people were aroused by his eloquence to fight for the British, but in the war of 1812 they fought with the Americans and from that time forward he was a friend. He was known as Red Jacket because toward the close of the Revolution, a British officer gave him a richly-embroidered, scarlet jacket of which he was very proud. He was then a young man and probably cared more for fine clothes than he did at the age when this picture was made of him. You notice on his breast he has a large medal. This was given to him by President Washington on the conclusion of peace with the Six Nations to which the Seneca's belonged. The figures were those of a white man and Indian clasping hands and beneath it were the names, "George Washington" and "Red Jacket."

England had secured the interests of her traders at the expense and to the peril of her own large and growing colonies, which now numbered two million people. Virginia had begun the war, and all the colonies had fought for nine years in defense of their sea-to-sea charters granted by English kings, and to secure themselves against attack. They had paid their own expenses, voting taxes and maintaining colonial militia. They had helped defeat and drive out the French, won half the continent for England, and all but broken the power of the Algonquins. Now, by this proclamation, their rights were denied, and the Indians firmly entrenched in their rear. More effectually than before, they were shut in on the narrow seaboard, forbidden to colonize or trade beyond the mountains.

Baffled and angry, the colonies seethed with discontent. In union they had found strength, proved their worth and power, and gained a spirit of independence. With France gone they need never again be involved in the quarrels of European kings. Against the Indians they had always defended themselves, and would continue to do so. They had had no hand in making this proclamation and there was little disposition to submit to its unjust and even dangerous terms.

Black Hawk in American Dress

As a young man, Black Hawk was a fierce and sometimes cruel savage, in spite of the benevolent, kindly expression in his eyes as we see him here, an old man. He gained great influence over his people by his absolute honesty, his eloquence and great personal bravery. He was 5 feet 4 inches tall, had a full, rather large mouth, a high Roman nose, piercing, thoughtful eyes with very scanty eyebrows, and a high forehead which, as a young man, seemed higher still because he plucked out the hair almost to the top of his head, leaving only a scalp lock. This picture of him was painted when he was sent East as a captive to Fortress Monroe, and shows him in American dress and without the scalp lock. Notice the tatooing on his ear.

Further Acts of Injustice

Your history tells you how the English parliament next proceeded to pass trade laws for the colonies which seemed as tyrannous and blighting as those of Spain in Spanish America; to quarter an army of 10,000 British regulars on colonies that had no need of them, and, for the first time, to levy stamp duties and internal taxes for imperial purposes. All these measures were bitterly resented and defied, and some of them were so impossible of enforcement that they were revoked. Any one of these things, alone, could probably have been dealt with without revolution. Taken together they seemed a denial of those rights as Englishmen, for which their forefathers had fought from Magna Charta to the Bill of Rights.

Emigration had begun to flow westward even before the war, for Massachusetts, Virginia and eastern Pennsylvania were becoming crowded. Hardy English, German and Scotch-Irish emigrants had slowly fought their way to the mountain crest. Living the hard life of the frontier, remote from towns and courts, and obliged to rely upon themselves, they cared no more for a royal proclamation than for the bark of the timber wolf at their cabin doors in the wilderness. At the end of the war settlers began to pour down the Ohio into Kentucky, and through the Cumberland Gap into Tennessee. Wheeling, West Virginia, was founded in 1769, and in the same year Daniel Boone reached Kentucky. He soon had a fort at Boonesboro, and George Rogers Clark had another outpost at Harrodsburg. Every foot in the "dark and bloody ground" of Kentucky was won through horrid massacres, burnings, sieges and treacherous ambushes. And it became increasingly clear that the Indians were furnished arms at the British forts and trading posts at Detroit and Pittsburgh.

The Irresistible Westward Tide

The Iroquois Six Nations, too, long allies of the English colonists, were learning to look upon their white neighbors with contempt and suspicion, and to the British government for friendship. They had been confirmed in their ownership of western New York colony by treaty with England; their spokesman was the Indian agent, Sir William Johnson, and their trade was transferred from Albany to Fort Niagara. By treaties, taking over the immensely profitable fur trade of the interior built up by the French, and by payment in arms, the mother country won over all the Indians—Algonquins, Iroquois and Gulf tribes—in the eastern half of the United States. Thus, with incredible stupidity, and for her own temporary profit, she practically aided and abetted savage warfare against her own loyal colonists. Under an unintelligent king and a corrupt government in London, England had come to the same vicious view of her colonies as Spain, not as an empire, to be fostered and developed, but as an alien land and subject people, to be exploited.

England the Enemy of Her Colonies

But the people of the English colonies were not helpless and they did not propose to be submissive. It was in 1765, the year peace was signed with Pontiac and a British regiment marched across Illinois to Fort Chartres on the Mississippi, that Patrick Henry, voicing the resentment at England's latest acts of tyranny, raised the cry of revolution in the House of Burgesses of Virginia: "Taxation without representation is tyranny."

If You Had Been Otis What Would You Have Said?

The heavy duty laid by the English on all sugar and molasses imported from other than British possessions, worked a great hardship on the colonists. Think of trying to live without sugar and molasses! And people just couldn't afford them with the duty added.

As a result smuggling became common. To catch the smugglers, the customs officers took out search warrants. But here was the trouble: to secure the warrants it was necessary to state what goods they were searching for and the place to be searched. This gave the smugglers warning and they removed the goods. What the officers wanted was a general warrant, called a "writ of assistance," that would enable them to enter anybody's house or place of business at any time and examine any suspected goods. This sounds so reasonable, from the British standpoint, that we may well wonder what argument the colonists could offer against it. You could hardly expect to prevent violations of law if you first had to notify the violator so that he could hide all evidences of what he had been up to. But now, listen, and you will hear what a strong argument Otis is offering in this famous speech of his:

"This writ of assistance," he says, "is the worst instrument of arbitrary power, the most destructive of English liberty that was ever found in an English law book. By this writ, officers may enter our homes when they please, break locks, bars, and everything in their way; and whether they break, through malice or revenge, no man, no court, can inquire." To prove this he goes on to cite, among others, the instance of a judge who called a customs officer before him to answer a charge of swearing on the Sabbath day. As soon as the judge had finished talking, the customs officer said, "Now I will show you a little of *my* power. I command you to permit me to search your house for uncustomed goods"; and went on to search the house from garret to cellar.

Otis defends his conduct in resigning his position as Advocate General, in which he would have been obliged to appear as a lawyer for the English Government. "Let the consequences be what they will," he says, "I am determined to proceed. The only principles of public conduct that are worthy of a gentleman or a man are to sacrifice estate, ease, health, and even life to the sacred call of his country. I do not say that when brought to the test I shall be invincible. I pray God," he adds, "I may never be brought to the melancholy trial, but if ever I should, it will then be known how far I can reduce to practice, principles which I know to be founded in truth."

STORIES OF AMERICAN HISTORY
THE REVOLUTION

Leaders of the Revolution

"This writ of assistance," he says, "is the worst instrument of arbitrary power, the most destructive of English liberty that was ever found in an English law book. By this writ officers may enter our homes when they please, break locks, bars, and everything in their way; and whether they break, through malice or revenge, no man, no court, can inquire."

IF you have read the articles on our government you know how many men, working in well-organized departments, it takes to attend to the business of the United States even in times of peace. During war there is a great deal more to do. What do you think would happen if there were no central authority to direct the defense of the country—if each of the forty-eight states was a little nation in itself? They would be about as easy to conquer as it was to break the separated sticks of the bundle in the fable. "In union there is strength." You know that from the teamwork necessary to win a football game.

But that was exactly the situation in the English colonies during the Revolutionary War. Under the same conditions Napoleon conquered, one by one, the several hundred separate states and free cities of Germany. And yet, the Americans won that war. You think you know why. The colonies did unite and establish the Continental Congress to act for all. Yes, but that body of wise and patriotic men was simply advisory. It had no authority to vote taxes, coin or borrow money to carry on the war, and it had no power to compel any colony to furnish a single soldier or a single dollar. Each of the thirteen colonies de-

Days of the Ununited States

PICTURED KNOWLEDGE

An English Cartoon of the Tea Tax Tempest

This Revolutionary cartoon was published in 1783 in London. It is called "The Tea Tax Tempest or Old Time with His Magick Lan-Thorn." Father Time, leaning on the world, is throwing a picture on the screen and is described as saying to the spectators, "There you see the little Hot Spit Fire Teapot that has done all The Mischief. There you see the Old British Lion basking before the American Bon Fire (the Revolution), whilst the French Cock is blowing up a storm About his ears to Destroy him and his young Whelps. There you see Miss America grasping at the Cap of Liberty. There you see The British forces, beyoked and cramped, flying before the Congress Men. There you see the thirteen Stripes and Rattlesnake (another American emblem) exalted. There you see the Stamped Paper Helping to make the Pot Boil."

cided for itself just what it could and should do. Washington, as Commander-in-Chief of the army, had fourteen masters and was obliged to beg each of them for men and supplies.

We won that war chiefly through good luck. We had three advantages to offset this fundamental weakness. First, after 1778, England was also at war with France, and could not spare her best officers and enough troops to put down rebellion in her colonies. Second, we should not forget the timely help in soldiers, warships and money from France, without which there would have been no victory at Yorktown. But most important of all, perhaps, was the surprising number of men of very great ability and devoted patriotism who appeared and took the leadership. Wherever there was work to be done there was just the man to do it.

These leaders came from everywhere and in the nick of time—from the office, the plantation, the pulpit, *A Time of Great Leaders* the assembly hall, the counting house, the ship deck, the schoolroom of every colony. Dropping their private businesses and risking home, family, fortune, even life it-

King George and the "Rebels"

By the KING,
A PROCLAMATION,
For suppressing Rebellion and Sedition.

GEORGE R.

WHEREAS many of Our Subjects in divers Parts of Our Colonies and Plantations in *North America*, misled by dangerous and ill-designing Men, and forgetting the Allegiance which they owe to the Power that has protected and sustained them, after various disorderly Acts committed in Disturbance of the Publick Peace, to the Obstruction of lawful Commerce, and to the Oppression of Our loyal Subjects carrying on the same, have at length proceeded to an open and avowed Rebellion, by arraying themselves in hostile Manner to withstand the Execution of the Law, and traitorously preparing, ordering, and levying War against Us: And whereas there is Reason to apprehend that such Rebellion hath been much promoted and encouraged by the traitorous Correspondence, Counsels, and Comfort of divers wicked and desperate Persons within this Realm: To the End therefore that none of Our Subjects may neglect or violate their Duty through Ignorance thereof, or through any Doubt of the Protection which the Law will afford to their Loyalty and Zeal; We have thought fit, by and with the Advice of Our Privy Council, to issue this Our Royal Proclamation, hereby declaring that not only all Our Officers Civil and Military are obliged to exert their utmost Endeavours to suppress such Rebellion, and to bring the Traitors to Justice; but that all Our Subjects of this Realm and the Dominions thereunto belonging are bound by Law to be aiding and assisting in the Suppression of such Rebellion, and to disclose and make known all traitorous Conspiracies and Attempts against Us, Our Crown and Dignity; And We do accordingly strictly charge and command all Our Officers as well Civil as Military, and all other Our obedient and loyal Subjects, to use their utmost Endeavours to withstand and suppress such Rebellion, and to disclose and make known all Treasons and traitorous Conspiracies which they shall know to be against Us, Our Crown and Dignity; and for that Purpose, that they transmit to One of Our Principal Secretaries of State, or other proper Officer, due and full Information of all Persons who shall be found carrying on Correspondence with, or in any Manner or Degree aiding or abetting the Persons now in open Arms and Rebellion against Our Government within any of Our Colonies and Plantations in *North America*, in order to bring to condign Punishment the Authors, Perpetrators, and Abettors of such traitorous Designs.

Given at Our Court at St. *James's*, the Twenty-third Day of *August*, One thousand seven hundred and seventy-five, in the Fifteenth Year of Our Reign.

God save the King.

LONDON:
Printed by *Charles Eyre* and *William Strahan*, Printers to the King's most Excellent Majesty. 1775.

If you had been a small boy in the time of the Revolution, you would have seen proclamations like this with the royal coat-of-arms above them posted about in public places. As you see by the date at the bottom, it was issued on the 23rd of August. The colonies had not yet declared their independence, but the war which won their independence was already under way. The battle of Lexington had been fought in the previous May and the battle of Bunker Hill, in June. But the prospect of winning in the war against the most powerful empire in the world was more than doubtful, and the king hoped, as you see by the wording of this proclamation, to draw away from the colonists the support of all who were lukewarm in their resistance or selfish enough to consult their own safety in preference to the interests of their country.

PICTURED KNOWLEDGE

The Battle-Torn Flag and the Story of the Thirteen Stripes

This is the only one of the flags carried in the Revolution that has come down to us. It was the flag of the Third Maryland Regiment, and can be seen today in the flag room at the Capitol in Annapolis. The holes were made by bullets.

No one knows who designed our flag—one of the most striking and original in pattern of all the flags in the world—but it has been suggested that it was derived from the crest of the Washington family which consisted of red stars and bars on a white ground. When the Revolution began there were almost as many flags as there were colonies, and it was not until 1777 that Congress adopted the flag shown here as the national emblem. Then for forty years a new stripe as well as a new star was added for every state that came into the Union. But finally, when the flag showed twenty stripes and twenty stars, Congress decreed that we return to the original thirteen stripes, thus recognizing the fact that we began our life as a nation with thirteen states; but it was decided to keep on adding a new star for every new state. How many stars does our flag have now?

self, they gave every thought, every hour of time, every dollar, every talent they possessed to the sacred cause of human liberty. Your history tells you of the battles of the Revolution, so we will tell you of the heroic, devoted, and gifted men whose wise leadership won the war.

Patrick Henry, the Orator

BEFORE any great human conflict there is apt to appear an inspired public speaker to clarify the thought of the time and to inflame a whole people into action. Preceding the Civil War Lincoln put the moral issue of the day into burning speech. So, ten years before the Revolution, immediately after the passage of the Stamp Act by the British Parliament, Patrick Henry aroused the determined resistance of the colonies with his eloquence. His "Taxation without representation is tyranny," was based solidly on English principles, and was unanswerable.

The first one of the four American political orators of the first rank, classed with Lincoln, Webster and Clay, Patrick Henry was unknown outside Virginia before he made his first speech in the Virginia House of Burgesses. A young lawyer of Scotch parentage and classical education, he had failed at farming and storekeeping before winning success at the bar. He was only twenty-nine and had been a silent member of the House of Burgesses just nine days when he rose quietly to

Patrick Henry's Immortal Speech

THE REVOLUTION
Where the Revolution Began

The picture shows a group of the minute men at the Battle of Lexington, and from it you can judge how disorderly their formation was and how they were dressed—just as they came from work, with no attempt at a uniform. At the left of the picture, two men are loading their muskets which are the old-fashioned muzzle-loading kind, of course. And notice the powder horn which each man carries, slung over his shoulder.

offer a series of resolutions defining the rights of a colony, and to declare that the recent Stamp Act was a denial of English guarantees of liberty. Burning with indignation, as were many of his listeners, he cried: "Cæsar had his Brutus, Charles I his Cromwell, and George III——"

"Treason! Treason!" came from many parts of the hall. The speaker turned pale, but, leaning over his desk, he went on firmly to men on their feet and shocked to dead silence: "and George III may well profit by their example. If *this* be treason, make the most of it. Taxation without representation is tyranny."

A shout went up. This was a bold, brave man. He had put the secret thought of all into words, risking ruin in defense of the liberty of all. It would be base and cowardly to desert him. He inflamed not only Virginia but all the colonies to resistance, and that Stamp Act was repealed. For the next ten years of oppression, disorders and efforts to avoid war, Henry was the eloquent spokesman of the rights and the defiance of the colonies. His genius as an orator has been attested by every eminent man of the time. His power lay not only in his happy phrases and eloquent delivery, but in his sincerity. Like Lincoln, he said nothing that he did not passionately believe to be true. A profound thinker, a man of great executive ability and energy, and of spotless character, it has been said of him that his talents would have put him at the head of Rome in her days of glory.

For, behind his words was a man of solid deeds and sober service. In the midst of revolution he organized the colony of Virginia and served as its first governor for five years. He was a leader in the movement for independence, and, by sending George Rogers Clark to capture the British forts northwest of the Ohio, he helped to secure the Mississippi River as our western boundary. Sacrificing a private practice to public duty he was constantly in some drudging, ill-paid or unpaid, office for twenty-six years. He died comparatively poor, in 1791, two years after George Washington was inaugurated President of the United States.

Benjamin Franklin, the Diplomat

NONE of the colonies wanted war, or dreamed of separating from the mother country. For ten long years they tried to secure justice and keep the peace. To this service was devoted the most gifted and admired American ever sent to represent our country in European capitals. It is accepted by historians that, where Franklin failed, no one else could possibly have succeeded.

Born in Boston in 1706 of Puritan parents and intended for the pulpit, there was no money for his education, so he was apprenticed to the printing trade. An unruly boy, sarcastic, disputatious, vain and resenting control, he ended by running away from home. At seventeen he found himself in Philadelphia, with one dollar, a trade, plenty of self-confidence and a sudden conviction that he had very serious faults of character. He promptly turned over a new leaf, and was ever afterwards noted for his patience and good manners. By twenty-three he was the foremost journalist in the colonies. His weekly *Pennsylvania Gazette* still lives in *The Saturday Evening Post*. His wise and witty "Poor Richard's Almanac" was known in every frontier cabin. With incredible rapidity he accumulated wealth and learning. He studied the French, Spanish and Latin languages and literature, was deeply read in philosophy, and experi-

The Many-Sided Franklin

mented in science and invention. He kept the earliest weather records and made important discoveries in electricity.

Big and little things alike interested him. He organized police and fire departments, introduced street lighting and paving, built an academy of science, and collected books for a circulating library. A patriot of civil life, nothing was done without consulting Dr. Franklin. In 1757 he was sent to London by Pennsylvania to get more help for the colonies in the French and Indian War. He went again in 1764 when the first rumor of the intended Stamp Act reached America. A year later he was representing all the colonies. For the next ten years, with unfailing patience and urbanity, he presented the American view that the colonies were and must be self-governing. His wit and humor, his honesty, practical common sense, moral courage, very profound learning and open-mindedness made him famous. A self-educated man, he was given degrees by Oxford and Edinburgh Universities.

On the outbreak of the war he returned from England to help frame the Declaration of Independence. He gave the Continental Congress $20,000 out of his own pocket, and then went to Paris to win the friendship of France. There he represented only poor and struggling rebel col-

His Great Work in France

THE REVOLUTION
Franklin at the Court of France

Franklin was sent to France right after the signing of the Declaration of Independence and did a great deal in behalf of our new republic. France was especially sympathetic, because England was at that time her traditional enemy, and because liberty and republicanism were the topics of the day, at court and among the common people. (It was not long after our own Revolution, you remember, that the great French Revolution began, affecting every nation in Europe.) In the picture we see the great ladies of the French court vying with each other to do honor to the simple American citizen in his plain clothes, which are so different from those of the other men present. Notice how he is the center of interest for everyone in the room. The gorgeous hangings and furniture, the rich dresses with their huge skirts, and the elaborate powdered coiffures of both men and women are typical of the French court of Louis XVI.

Franklin's clothes were usually a somber brown, instead of the gaily colored, richly embroidered things that were fashionable. But so popular was this wise old man that others copied him. Gentlemen began to wear "Franklin" hats, and ladies had gloves, shoes, and dresses of "Franklin" brown.

onies, but prince and peasant and the world of learning were at his feet. He was the first great commoner representing a sovereign people. His simple dress became the fashion; his portrait was in palace and cottage; shopkeepers rushed to their doors to see him pass by. We are proud to think that, in mind, character, democratic manner and versatile genius he has become the typical American. In fifteen months he had signed the Treaty of Alliance, got warships and soldiers and an enormous loan of money on almost no security.

When, in 1785, he returned home he had spent nearly thirty years abroad in the service of America. Nearly eighty years of age, he begged for rest. But he helped frame the Constitution, and established the United States Postal Service. In 1790 he helped to form the first society to abolish slavery. This brings him into touch with Lincoln's work of seventy years later. Indeed, Franklin is the one man of early American history who projects himself into the present. Our every improvement would delight him. Were he living now men would "consult Dr. Franklin" in the fields of science, philosophy, literature, and public service. No one feared to go to him for he listened with deference to the humblest, and respected their opinions. This, no less than his wisdom, was the secret of his immense influence. Every vain, ar-

Franklin's Happy Hours in His Library

guing, bumptious boy who finds himself unpopular should read Franklin's autobiography and, as Franklin did, mend his manners.

This is one of the best portraits of Dr. Franklin ever taken. It is known as "The Thumb Portrait." You can see why. Dr. Franklin is here shown in his library looking over some manuscript. This attitude was very common with him when absorbed. The portrait was painted by David Martin in 1767 and is now owned by Henry William Biddle of Philadelphia.

His books were one of his chief sources of happiness throughout his long and useful life. It is said that he had the largest and best private collection in America. In the use of his library, he showed the same ingenuity as in other things. For instance he had a long artificial arm and hand for taking down and putting up books on high shelves. Under the seat of a reclining chair he had steps made, so that when he wanted to reach books on high shelves, he simply turned up the seat and climbed the steps. His great arm chair with rockers had a large fan over it with which he fanned himself and kept off the flies by a slight motion of his foot while reading. That was before the days of screens, remember.

In his last illness, when able to be out of bed, he passed nearly all his time in the library reading and writing. When the boys were playing and were very noisy in the lot in front of his room, he would open the window and call to them, "Boys, boys, can't you play without making so much noise? I am reading and it disturbs me very much." The servants in his family testify that he never used a harsh or hasty word to any one.

Washington, the Commander-in-Chief

FOR the highest military leadership the colonies had just one man—Washington. It is fortunate that they had the good sense to know it. Patriots there were, able officers and a few brilliant generals, but no one else worthy of such honor and confidence. Frederick the Great called Washington one of the greatest military geniuses that ever lived. And this was not because of the battles he won. General Gates won the decisive victory at Saratoga; Generals Marion and Greene cleared the South of British troops and drove them into the trap at Yorktown. Washington was defeated at Long Island and at Brandywine.

His genius lay in avoiding battle; in shutting the enemy up in Boston and New York; in escapes, surprise attacks, as at Trenton and Princeton, in strategy, engineering, swift decision, and in keeping an army together for eight long years ready for the finishing stroke at Yorktown.

Where Washington's Genius Lay

He not only had fourteen masters in the several colonies and the Continental Congress, but he had to contend with dissension, treason, failure of men and supplies and short and irregular terms of enlistment by which his armies were scarcely trained before they began to melt away. The record was crowned by the terrible winter at Valley Forge—the misery of his men; the delays of a fugitive Congress; the treachery and plots which encompassed him, the growing weariness of the long, slow, indecisive war. It is there, in the darkest hours, that we see him going into the woods to pray for help. He did all by sheer force and nobility of character. Like Lincoln, the man himself was infinitely greater than any and all the things recorded of him.

To understand him you should read the story of his mother and his boyhood in this book. As a boy his elder brother, Lawrence, got him an appointment as a middy in the British Navy, but his widowed mother refused to let him go to sea.

"But," insisted Lawrence, "George has it in him to be a great commander."

"He must first learn to command himself," she said, dryly. Like herself he had a hot, imperious temper.

You can learn there how this wise mother trained him in self-control. At twenty-one such was his reputation for trustworthiness and discretion that he was chosen to carry a message to the French on the Allegheny. And at the end of the war he was too confused to speak when the Virginia House of Burgesses voted thanks to him for distinguished military services. The Governor said:

His First Victory Over Himself

"Sit down, Colonel Washington. Your modesty equals your valor, and that is beyond question."

And beyond question, no other man was thought of, when the Revolution began, to command the army of 17,000 untrained, ill-equipped troops gathered at Boston. Still modest, he doubted his fitness for the task. But he did not hesitate an instant, although, one of the richest of planters; he risked his own and his wife's estates. And if the Revolution had failed, he would certainly have been executed, and probably along with him, Franklin and other leaders. He served without pay and spent $70,000, the income from Mt. Vernon, to meet his own expenses. He thought nothing of rewards or honors, but only of duty well done. In perfect patience he bided his time for the swift surprise march and blow at Yorktown.

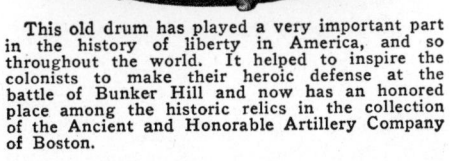

A Drum Beat Heard Around the World

This old drum has played a very important part in the history of liberty in America, and so throughout the world. It helped to inspire the colonists to make their heroic defense at the battle of Bunker Hill and now has an honored place among the historic relics in the collection of the Ancient and Honorable Artillery Company of Boston.

The King Who Refused a Crown

At the end of the war he was the court of last appeal in the six years' work of framing and adopting the Constitution. His canonization began long before his death. He could have made this country a monarchy and worn a crown. And in appearance he was every inch a king. Six feet two in height, his eyes were blue, his hair red-brown, his complexion ruddy, his aspect one of the greatest dignity and nobility. His manner was controlled, his speech brief and well-considered. Enormous weight was attached to his few words. His farewell address is one

Washington as He Was

This is the famous Stuart portrait of Washington, sometimes called the "Athenaeum Washington," because it originally belonged to the Boston Athenaeum. It is now in the Boston Museum of Fine Arts. Here is the same Washington, the same firm mouth and chin, the same imperious nose as in the bust by the Italian artist, but how different the expression! Here we have the man as he really was, the man who commanded himself as well as others; who was willing to sacrifice and suffer all for his country's sake in the long struggle of the war, to which we owe the fact that we have this great, free country; who won at last by the nobility of his character no less than by the strength of his intellect, and who, in his darkest hours, went into the woods to ask the help of God. "Like Lincoln, the man himself was infinitely greater than any and all things recorded of him."

Washington as He Might Have Been

This bust of Washington in the Metropolitan Museum of New York, to which we are indebted for the excellent reproduction, has a remarkable interest in the fact that it shows the great man, not as he was but as he might have been. It is the work of the Italian sculptor, Ceracchi, who came to this country during Washington's administration and made marble portraits of several of our famous men. Perhaps it was because the artist himself was of Roman blood that he unconsciously brought out in such a striking way, the sterner aspects of Washington's character. The classic toga, is, of course, a mere artistic convention, but the face is not that of a man who would sacrifice and endure all for the good of others, as Washington did. It is the face of a Roman conqueror; a military dictator, as Washington could easily have been, had not the noble character which went with his strong face, made him choose to be the Father of his Country.

None of the Roman tyrants who ruled the world with an iron hand ever had a more imperious will, and Frederick the Great, as this history story tells us, ranked him among the greatest of military leaders; but Washington chose to use all his strength of mind and will to serve and not to enslave his country.

PICTURED KNOWLEDGE
The First Salute to the Stars and Stripes

This picture was painted by the American artist, Edward Moran, and shows us the rolling, pitching Ranger, John Paul Jones's first ship, rigged for foul weather, being saluted by the guns of a French flagship.

Before John Paul Jones got the famous Bonhomme Richard from the French government, he had this little, badly equipped vessel, the Ranger, with which he scoured the seas and became the terror of the English. In February, 1788, he came upon a small squadron of the French fleet near the coast of France. The Ranger was gaily flying the stars and stripes which had just recently been adopted as the American national emblem. John Paul Jones sent a messenger to the commander of the French squadron, asking if he would return a salute from the American guns. (Saluting a ship means recognizing the flag it carries, you know. By most nations American fighting vessels were considered pirates and hence unworthy of recognition.) The French commander, of course, was friendly to the American cause as France was also at war with England. He replied that he would return John Paul Jones's salute, so the thirteen little guns of the Ranger fired their heaviest charge in greeting to the Frenchmen. The picture shows the big French flagship in the background at the left, answering with her heavier guns. At this moment John Paul Jones was remarking to his officers, "We hardly know what this means, gentlemen. I believe that we are at the christening of the greatest nation that was ever born into the world."

of the treasured utterances of history. The office of President was cut to the measure of his lofty character. That is why but one other man—Lincoln—has seemed quite to fill the place. John Richard Green, the English historian, has said of him: "Washington is the noblest figure that ever stood in the forefront of a nation's life."

The Father of the American Navy

AMONG the first men to offer their services in the Revolution was one of the naval geniuses of the world's history. As John Paul he had been born in the little port of Kirkbean, Scotland, twenty-eight years before, the son of a poor fisherman. At fourteen, tall, strong, and as skilled in handling a boat as any man, he shipped as a sailor in a vessel in the Virginia tobacco trade. Thus he came to America, and saw his elder brother William, who had been adopted by a distant kinsman and rich planter named Jones. Adoption was offered young John, but this he refused, for he loved the hard, adventurous life of the sea.

At seventeen he was a captain, and at twenty-five knew as much of seamanship as any admiral in His Majesty's navy. Besides he had educated himself, on shipboard, in languages, history, philosophy and polite literature, and in every port he had cultivated the society of leading men. Then, by the death of Mr. Jones, and of his brother, John Paul fell heir to the estate of three thousand acres of tobacco land on the Rappahannock, a mansion, hundreds of slaves, and the name of Jones. Virginia society welcomed him for his handsome person, fine mind and courtly manners. But the life of ease and social pleasure was very little to his liking. At the outbreak of the Revolution he put his estate in the hands of trustees and offered his services to the Continental Congress, to help build up a navy.

"A Scholar and a Gentleman"

It was he, chiefly, who induced each colony to build a warship, and to buy and outfit trading vessels. As lieutenant on one of eight cruisers soon assembled at Philadelphia, he raised the pine tree and rattlesnake flag. Then, in the first American man-of-war to put out to sea, he slipped down the Delaware and began his spectacular career of raiding British commerce. In the course of the war America lost twenty-four of its thirty naval vessels, but they sank or captured one hundred and two ships of the enemy, and no other commander was so bold or successful as John Paul Jones.

Crossing the Atlantic in the Ranger, and entering the Irish Sea, he destroyed ships, burned a seaport, and took an armed schooner as a prize to France. In the Bonhomme Richard he captured the Serapis in one of the most brilliant of naval victories. Lashing his sinking ship to the enemy he boarded it and then cut his own vessel loose. For this he was made a Chevalier of France. America could only vote him thanks and a gold medal. The young republic had no navy and no money to build one. The title of admiral would have been but an empty honor.

Epic Exploits of the Sea Fighter

Conscious of his genius, loving his hard-earned fame, he could be content with no other employment. For a time he served as an admiral in the Russian navy. But his heart was with people struggling for liberty. At the beginning of the French Revolution he hastened to Paris to offer his services. There he died in 1792, a week after being offered the command of the navy of the new French Republic. Only forty-five when he died, Napoleon deplored his untimely end, saying that, had he lived France would have had an admiral worthy to meet Nelson.

He did not end his days in poverty and neglect, as was so long believed, for he had sold his Virginia plantation for $50,000, and lived on the income of good investments. And he had, in Paris, his circle of devoted friends. His body was placed in a lead coffin to be shipped to America, but in the confused days of The Terror it was hurried into an unmarked grave. The coffin was found in 1905, and brought home in a United States warship. With all the honors of an admiral, John Paul Jones was laid away in the grounds of the Naval Academy at Annapolis. After a strange, adventurous, wandering life:

"Home is our sailor, home from the sea."

The Author of the Immortal Declaration

Among the spectators in the Virginia House of Burgesses, when Patrick Henry made his first fiery speech, was the twenty-year-old son of a planter, who was in Williamsburg, the capital, studying law. When an old man, and one risen to loftier fame than the orator of the Revolution, Thomas Jefferson loved to speak of that thrilling memory. He often said: "Patrick Henry was the greatest orator who ever lived."

Possibly that speech was the turning point in his own career. A few years later he was himself in the House of Burgesses, and had written a pamphlet on "The Rights of America" that made him known outside of Virginia. He entered the public service with the same tireless zeal that had won him the title of "the hardest student ever in William and Mary College." There he had often studied fifteen hours a day. On the very day that Washington took command of the army at Cambridge, Jefferson took his seat in the Continental Congress. Earnest, diligent, prompt, explicit, decisive in committee work, he very quickly became one of the leaders, although he was but thirty-two.

In person Jefferson, like Washington, was over six feet tall, and very erect. His features were delicate, his eyes a bright hazel, his hair auburn, his complexion ruddy. He had an air of distinction, but his manners were so simple and democratic that he was popular with all classes. In birth, fortune, intellect and social connections he was an aristocrat, but he was a lifelong apostle of democracy. His natural sympathies and his political principles were summed up in his immortal phrase: "All men are created free and equal." Even in the White House he would have no ceremony which smacked of kings and royal courts. "Jeffersonian simplicity" has become one of the small coins of speech.

Jefferson was one of a committee of five, which included Franklin and John Adams, to draft the Declaration of Independence, but such was his gift for putting things clearly and vigorously in writing, that he was left to work it out alone. Very few changes were made in his wording. It is, without doubt, the most noted and influential political document ever written. In its clear and fundamental treatment, in its eloquent declaration of the rights of man, it clarified, developed and united the thought and spirit of the colonists, dismembered an empire, destroyed age-old privileges, found-

Reading the Declaration

In our story of the origin of the great political parties is another portrait of Jefferson, painted when he was fifty-seven years old. Compare it with this statue which represents him as reading the Declaration of Independence. "In person, Jefferson, like Washington, was over six feet tall and very erect."

ed a new nation on principles of liberty and equality, and furnished a model for every people since who have struggled for the right of self-government.

Living until 1826, more than a quarter of a century after Washington and Franklin passed from the stage, Jefferson was long the most distinguished man in America, and known as "The Sage of Monticello." He succeeded Franklin as Minister to France, served in Washington's Cabinet, and was twice elected President. He purchased Louisiana and sent explorers overland to the Pacific. But all other services he counted as nothing beside the immortal Declaration. On the plain granite shaft which marks his resting place on his old estate at Monticello is cut the simple inscription:

THOMAS JEFFERSON
AUTHOR OF
THE DECLARATION OF
INDEPENDENCE.

Robert Morris, the Financier

SEVERAL times in the course of the Revolutionary War Washington's army almost went to pieces for lack of money to feed, clothe and pay the soldiers. The Continental Congress had no power to levy taxes, coin or borrow money. It did issue bills of credit to pay for supplies, loan office certificates, promissory notes and lottery tickets, all of which were so worthless that the phrase "not worth a Continental" still lives. France loaned us money on practically no security, and guaranteed a loan from Holland. Each colony issued its own money, chiefly paper notes, which had little or no value, and most of the colonies failed or were really unable to pay their share of the general expenses.

Money Matters in a Bad Way

The office of financial manager for the Continental Congress was entrusted to Robert Morris, of Philadelphia. An English immigrant boy of thirty years before, he had risen to wealth and influence in banking, and was one of the signers of the Declaration of Independence. And not a soldier in the field defended his country with greater zeal, or was willing to sacrifice more in the cause than this colonial financier. Often, in emergencies, he supplied Washington's army from his own pocket. On two occasions he saved the Revolution from failure by his timely help.

Every history tells you how, on Christmas night, 1777, Washington crossed the Delaware, and captured a thousand Hessians at Trenton. His army, starving and freezing and leaving their bloody footprints in the snow, had been hard to keep together in that terrible winter at Valley Forge. The time for which many had enlisted would expire on New Year's Day, but these men were anxious to remain in the ranks if they could be assured of supplies. In this extremity Washington appealed to Robert Morris. The banker, roused from his bed at dawn of a bitter New Year's morning, went from house to house begging money. Before noon he sent $50,000 to Washington, who, two days later, attacked Princeton, escaped a British trap, and camped for the winter on the hills of Morristown.

Gift That Saved a Nation

Again, in 1781, Robert Morris borrowed the enormous sum of

PICTURED KNOWLEDGE
Robert Morris, the Financier

This portrait of Robert Morris is one of the most famous of our historic pictures. It is the work of Peale. The original is in the Pennsylvania Academy of Fine Arts. It shows Morris seated in a richly upholstered leather chair, at a window overlooking the United States Treasury. As a matter of fact, his residence did not overlook the Treasury, but a picture of it is shown merely as a symbol to express the country's indebtedness to him for his management of the national finances during the Revolutionary period.

$1,400,000 on his own notes, to finance the march and siege of Yorktown. Had this sum not been repaid him, he would have been ruined in the day of victory for the country. After the war he was long prominent in private business and the public service, but he finally lost his fortune by speculating in western lands. Washington, Franklin and other powerful friends, who could have helped him, were dead, so he lay in prison for debt for four years, and died in poverty in 1806.

George Rogers Clark, the Frontier Fighter

DO you remember that at the close of the French and Indian and Pontiac's war, about 1769, Daniel Boone and other frontiersmen, crossed the mountains, and fought for a foothold in "the dark and bloody ground" of Kentucky and Tennessee?

The ablest of these men was George Rogers Clark, who built a fort at Harrodsburg. On hearing the news of Lexington, he organized

1544

THE REVOLUTION
The Good Fortune We Owe to this Chest

We owe a great deal to this old chest, for this was the savings bank of Robert Morris; and it was largely owing to the fact that he risked his personal fortune to pay the wages of the soldiers in the American Revolution, and to meet other expenses, that the cause of America and Liberty won the day. After having done all this, he finally lost his fortune and was even confined in prison for debt, according to the cruel laws of those times, during the last years of his life. This is something to remember when we are called upon to make sacrifices for our country and to perform services for the public good.

This chest you can see in the Historical Society of Pennsylvania. It is about three feet long and two feet high. Such chests were made by the carpenter and the locksmith. The iron clasps were fastened upward through those two eyes which, like all the other iron work, were wrought, and through these eyes were put heavy padlocks; so you see it would take almost as much time to open this old chest as it does the modern combination safe lock.

You will notice that they did not forget the ornamental part of the chest. Not only are the clasps ornamented, but in the squares between the bands on the front are pictures of birds and tulips. This was, perhaps, done by a Dutchman; you know Holland is the land of tulips.

Kentucky into a county of the new state of Virginia, and got himself elected to the Assembly. In the capital at Williamsburg, he met again an old friend and neighbor in Governor Patrick Henry. To him he unfolded an ambitious plan. Since the Indian War the old French forts northwest of the Ohio had been held by British garrisons, and there, too, were the trading posts at which Indians were being supplied with arms and incited to fall upon the undefended frontiers of the seaboard colonies. Clark proposed to capture these forts and break up this traffic. Governor Henry approved of his plan, but could give him little aid.

But Clark was determined. Gathering 180 backwoodsmen at Pittsburgh, he built boats and floated down the Ohio. At Corn Island, opposite Louisville, other "long knives," as the pioneers were called by the Indians, joined him. Leaving the boats at the mouth of the Ohio, the little force marched north across the wooded swamps and prairies to Kaskaskia, Illinois, the old French capital, where the British had built Fort Gage on the low bluff. This was taken by surprise attack. The French villagers welcomed the Ken-

The Surprise at Kaskaskia

PICTURED KNOWLEDGE

tuckians, for the French alliance had been announced. Lafayette was fighting with Washington, and loyalty to the American rebels meant loyalty to Old France.

the Mississippi River as the western boundary of the United States at the close of the war. Virginia made this pioneer soldier, who won and held for her all for which the colony

From the Doctor's Medicine Chest

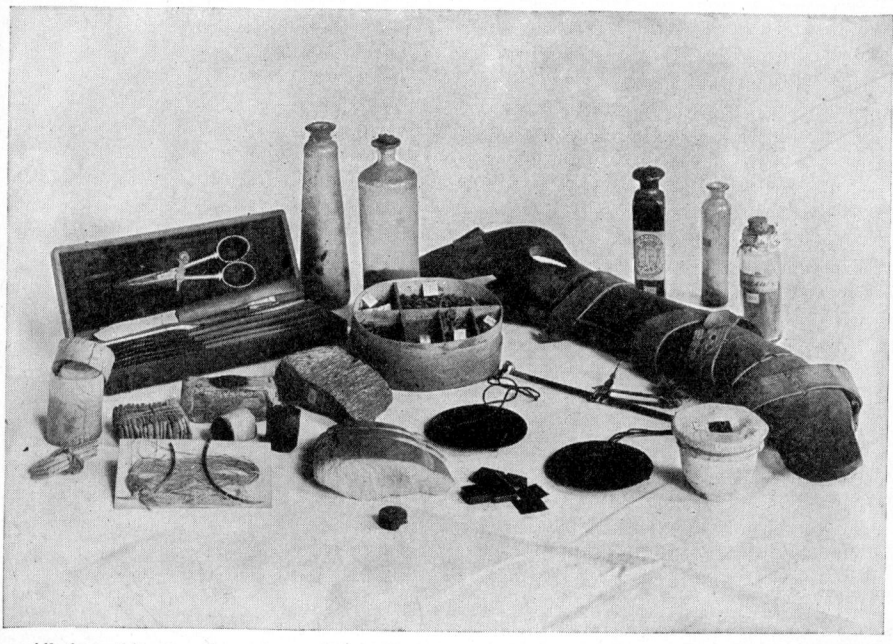

All these things are from the medicine chest of Dr. Solomon Drowne, a distinguished physician, who served his country in a professional capacity during the Revolutionary War. The long object on the right with straps around it, is a set of splints used in binding broken limbs. The little white jar contains healing ointment. To the left of it is a pair of scales for weighing medicine. In front of the scales you see the little square weights. The small round object to the left of the weights is a bone trepanned from the skull of a soldier of the Revolution. On the left is a case containing surgical instruments. The round box, with numerous compartments, to the left contained various kinds of bugs ground to powder in a mortar with a pestle, and used for plasters and other purposes.

There were no medical schools in those days, and young men who wanted to be doctors served as apprentices to established physicians. They ground the powders, mixed the pills, rode with the doctor on his rounds, and held the horses while he visited the patients and got a chance to ask him questions as they went from house to house. When not engaged in other duties, the young medical student swept the office, dusted the bottles and shelves, kept the skeletons properly wired, and answered the night bell.

The French now joined these pioneer forces, and, after a dreadful march across frozen swamps and streams in mid-winter, Clark captured Vincennes, Indiana. Civil rule was soon established by Virginia, which organized five big states of today into the County of Illinois. It was these daring adventures, perilous marches and brilliant military feats of Clark's which won

had fought in the long French and Indian War, a brigadier-general, and gave him 8,000 acres of land near the Ohio River in Indiana. That sounds magnificent, on paper, but the country was unsettled. As poor as any other backwoodsman of that early day, General Clark lived and died on his wild, ducal estate. But his name was written indelibly in our nation's history.

THE REVOLUTION
Nathan Hale, the Martyr-Patriot

ANY man who loves his country, and who serves it with unselfishness and zeal in any way that he can, whether in camp or court, legislative hall or counting house, is a patriot. But, best of all, the world understands and loves the self-sacrifice of the soldier. And when the soldier is a youth of brilliant promise, who goes voluntarily, on a secret and dangerous military mission, and suffers nobly the shameful death of a spy, his memory is held in special reverence. Such a hero was Nathan Hale.

He came of the best Puritan ancestry, of the family which gave us Dr. Edward Everett Hale, author of "The Man Without a Country." News of the battle of Lexington found him, a recent graduate from Yale, teaching school in the village of New London, Connecticut, to earn money to continue his studies for the ministry. He was much admired for his mental and moral gifts, his handsome person, and for his prowess in all clean, athletic sports. Fifty years afterwards his pupils described their twenty-year-old schoolmaster of that smiling April morning. His eyes were a clear, dark blue, his color ruddy with health, his bearing manly, his face lighted with fine intelligence. For any child or animal in trouble his sympathy was quick, his help generous and kind.

The town crier passed the school, ringing his bell and calling out the dreadful news of battle. As the people thronged into the streets, the schoolmaster stood up to his full six feet of beautiful and serious young manhood. In a voice described as low, sweet and musical, he said:

The Teacher and His Country

"School is dismissed. The time has come for men to fight, that you children may know the blessings of peace and liberty." In the town meeting he said: "Let us march at once, and never lay down our arms until we have won independence for our bleeding country."

As a lieutenant he joined Washington's forces at Cambridge. In the siege of Boston he rose to a captaincy in the famous Connecticut Rangers. It was certain that he would rise to the highest rank when the army followed the British to New York. There it was necessary for Washington to learn the size and disposition of General Howe's forces, and his plan of campaign. As this was information which only a man of superior intelligence could possibly get, he called for a volunteer from the younger officers. There was a painful moment of suspense, for the bravest shrink from the dangers of the spy. If caught he dies the death reserved for the lowest criminals, by hanging from the scaffold. Everyone's hat came off, including that of the Commander-in-Chief's, in grave salute, when Captain Nathan Hale stepped forward, head high, face pale, but quite resolute, and offered himself for this dangerous duty.

The Great Sacrifice

Discarding his uniform and disguising himself as a royalist schoolmaster, he boldly entered the British camp. He made observations, notes, and drawings of fortifications, and got away unsuspected. But, while waiting at a tavern on the shore for a boat that was to meet him, he was recognized by a royalist kinsman, betrayed and trapped on a British gunboat. Taken before General

Signing the Preliminary Treaty at Paris

Before the final treaty was signed which ended the Revolutionary War, preliminary articles were signed at Paris. England was represented by Richard Oswald, a British diplomat, and the colonies by John Adams, Henry Laurens, John Jay, and Benjamin Franklin. The preliminary treaty was signed on November 30, 1782, and the final treaty which was identical with the first, on September 3, 1783.

Howe, his papers were found, or a part of them, for it is known that he had managed to get much information to Washington. He was hanged at sunrise the next morning.

It was in an orchard, at Market Street and East Broadway, near where the statue of him stands today. He was denied a chaplain and a Bible, and his letters to his sister and to his betrothed—sweet Alice Ripley—were destroyed before his eyes, so that "the American rebels may never know they had a man who could die with such firmness." His open grave was at his feet. A royalist rabble jeered at him, as he faced the sun and breathed the odor of ripening apples, for it was late in September. A life of love, usefulness and high honors was closing for him at twenty-one. Yet, when asked if he had anything to say, he said: "I regret that I have but one life to lose for my country."

This legend is carved on the pedestal of the statue erected to him in New York City by the Sons of the Revolution. Children, many of them foreign immigrants, just learning to read, trace the letters and ask the corner policeman for the story. So he is still the schoolmaster, the inspiring teacher of patriotism. Another statue of him is in Hartford; and a granite memorial in Coventry, Connecticut, where he was born. And on the campus at Yale, where his name heads the list of honored graduates, rises the William Ordway Partridge statue in bronze. The face is uplifted, luminous with high re-

The Heroic Young School Master

This is the statue of Nathan Hale which stands in City Hall Park, New York City. As we look at the upright bearing and noble face of this young man of twenty-one, the words of the story of his heroism comes to us with particular force. He is here represented as he stood upon the scaffold, his feet tied together, his arms bound to his side. Below the laurel wreath which surrounds a brief statement of the circumstances of his death, are his last words: "I regret that I have but one life to lose for my country."

1549

solve, the foot advanced from the pedestal, as if eager to be off on some sacred duty. Every one looking at him, thinks: "Where is he going?" The sculptor answers: "To his death on the scaffold. This is the way an American patriot should be willing to die."

Warren's Address to the American Soldiers

Stand! The ground's your own, my braves!
Will ye give it up to slaves?
Will ye look for greener graves?
  Hope ye mercy still?
What's the mercy despots feel?
Hear it in that battle-peal!
Read it on your bristling steel!
  Ask it—ye who will.

Fear ye foes who kill for hire?
Will ye to your homes retire?
Look behind you! they're afire!
  And, before you, see
Who have done it!—From the vale
On they come! And will ye quail?—
Leaden rain and iron hail
  Let their welcome be!

In God of Battles trust!
Die we may,—and die we must;
But, O, where can dust to dust
  Be consigned so well,
As where Heaven its dews shall shed
On the martyred patriot's bed,
And the rocks shall raise their head
  Of his deeds to tell!

                      JOHN PIERPONT

STORIES OF AMERICAN HISTORY
EXPANSION PERIOD

The Making of a Great Nation

Daniel Boone and His Rifle

From boyhood Daniel Boone loved the woods, and no wonder, for all healthy boys love the woods and there were so many woods to love in those days! His moccasins as well as his shirt were usually of buckskin, although sometimes he made them of elk and in the winter of buffalo hide with the hair turned inward. His sandy hair was long and ragged, his cap was made of the fur of a wild cat, a raccoon, or an otter. In stories in which Boone figures as hero—and what boy doesn't know a lot of them—he is described as tall and angular with a "dark and piercing eye." As a matter of fact, he was not very tall,— about 5 feet 8 inches—he was heavy set, and his eyes were mild blue. Although he knew so much about the woods and the wild folks of the woods—the two legged and the four legged—he never learned much about spelling and for a long time there stood a tree in the forest on which was this autograph of the great frontiersman: "D. Boone cilled a Bar near this tree, year 1760."

AT the close of the Revolutionary War, the thirteen states formed from the old seaboard colonies, had won the region south of the Great Lakes, and the Ohio Valley clear to the Mississippi River. Spain owned Florida, the entire Gulf Coast, all the territory west of the Mississippi, then known as Louisiana, and claimed the eastern bank of the river up to Vicksburg. It was the middle of the century before, by purchase, treaty or war, with

PICTURED KNOWLEDGE

France, Spain, Mexico, and Great Britain, we straightened our northern and southern boundaries and secured the heart of the continent, of human daring and endurance is a century long, and every Middle and Far Western state furnishes a thrilling chapter. You should read your

A Fireplace without a House

This outdoor oven used by the American pioneers was you see a combination of the idea of the old-fashioned fireplace and the modern kitchen stove. Ovens like this were built outside the house. They were very convenient for boiling and baking in hot weather and you can see how much better it would be to do the washing outdoors than to do it in the kitchen. And these outdoor ovens had another advantage. They could be built before the log cabin was finished so that the whole family and the men neighbors who were helping with the building of the cabin could have better meals while the new home was going up.

from the Lakes to the Gulf and from ocean to ocean.

But in America people have never waited for formal treaties. Into every part of this vast country of forest, prairie, desert, mountain and distant coast, men from all the older, settled regions penetrated before we owned it. It was not soldiers, but heroic pioneers—pathfinders, Indian fighters, soil tillers, trail openers, gold seekers, cattle raisers, state makers and railroad builders who really explored, conquered, peopled and developed our land. This story

Romance in Your State's Story

own. Here we can tell you only of large movements of population, and name a few typical men and events of national importance.

Life on the Frontier

At least twenty years before the Revolution, men had pushed up the rivers of the Atlantic seaboard to the crest of the Alleghenies. Washington was in the mountains of Virginia by 1748, surveying wild land bought by wealthy planters. And wherever game became scarce and land dear, poor people moved westward. On

The Life of a Pioneer

1552

EXPANSION PERIOD

the frontier boys grew up strong, brave, inured to hardship and danger, and as skilled in hunting and the wood-crafts as Indians. With a hunting knife and a gun, the pioneer could sustain life; and with an ax, a plow, a horse or pair of oxen they could move their families, and soon have cabins and clearings in any wilderness.

Such a man was Daniel Boone, who, in 1769, broke through Cumberland Gap, the only pass through the mountains south of the Potomac, into the hunter's paradise of Kentucky and Tennessee. The news spread quickly and others followed. Dwellers in the rough mountain valleys had never seen such rolling meadows of bluegrass, laced with bright streams and shaded by enormous trees. The country was a wild park, teeming with game animals, but it had to be fought for, for it was the favorite hunting ground of many Algonquin and Gulf tribes. The white people were obliged, just as in New England and Virginia a century and a half before, to settle in villages around crude stockaded forts.

They lived in the rudest of log cabins. Floors were of split-logs; doors, tables and stools of hewn planks; beds of poles, laced with rawhide and spread with pine boughs, husks, and deerskins. Chimneys were of sticks plastered with clay. Often only corn, flax, and the Indian vegetables were grown. Domestic animals could not be kept, on account of timber wolves. The housewife had a few kettles, an out-

Daniel Boone at Eighty-Five

Chester Harding, the artist, made a trip to the Missouri frontier where Daniel Boone was living in 1819, to paint this portrait of the famous old man. Daniel Boone was then eighty-five and lived with one of his sons, mending broken rifles and powder horns, going on occasional hunting expeditions and recounting, for the delight of his neighbors, the adventures of his youth. Mr. Harding found him alone in a small cabin, part of an old blockhouse, cooking his dinner. He was lying on his bunk near the fire, with a long strip of venison wound around the ramrod of his gun which he was slowly turning before the brisk blaze.

Daniel Boone is described as about 5 feet 8 inches tall, very broad and powerful though lean, with blue eyes and a wide, thin-lipped mouth. People who saw him for the first time as an old man were surprised at the gentleness and simplicity of a man who had seen so much bloodshed, and who had played so large a part in the history of his country. When Mr. Harding asked him if he had ever been lost on any of his long journeys through the woods without a compass, he replied, "No, I can't say as I ever was lost, but I was bewildered once for three days." When his wife died in 1813 he made his coffin and kept it under his bed, with careful instructions to his children that he be buried in it and laid by his wife's side. He died while the convention to draw up a constitution for the new state of Missouri was in session. When the news reached them, the convention adjourned for the day and the delegates wore crepe on their arms for three weeks in respect to his memory. During his long life on the American frontier he had been first the subject of George II of England, then of George III, a citizen of the United States, the adopted son and citizen of a tribe of Shawnee Indians, the subject of Charles IV of Spain (when the Louisiana Territory belonged to Spain), then of Napoleon (when the territory was ceded to the French), and finally a citizen of the United States again after Jefferson made the Louisiana Purchase.

1553

PICTURED KNOWLEDGE

door oven, a trough or hollowed stump for pounding hominy. The dishes were wooden bowls and gourds. It was with the greatest difficulty that spinning wheels and

Boone, the Typical Frontiersman

Now Boone was no braver or more resourceful than hundreds of other men, and in military genius and public service he was not to be compared

The Growth of Our Country

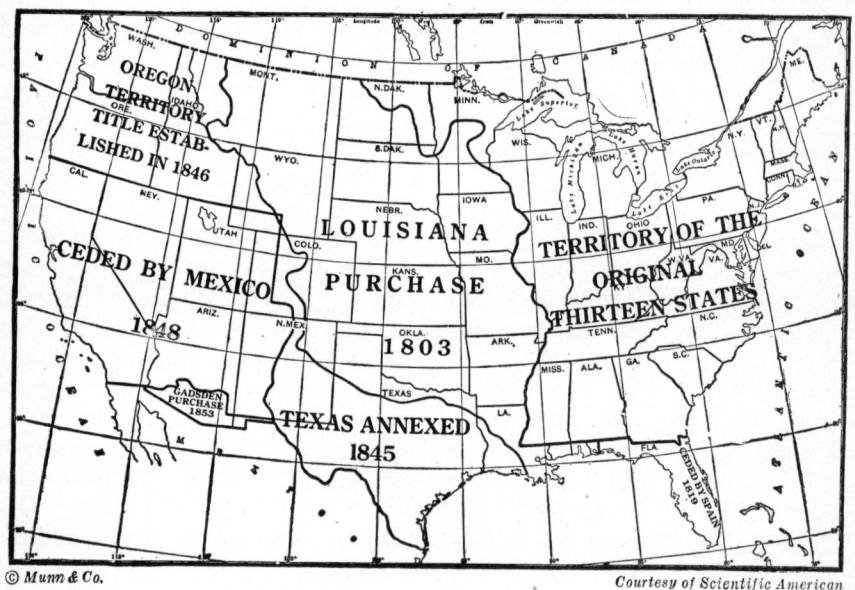

This map shows how the territory of the thirteen original states was expanded into the great United States of today. To the original thirteen states was added in 1803 the vast territory covered by the Louisiana Purchase. Then came the cession of Florida by Spain in 1819. Next, Texas was added in 1845, the title to Oregon territory was established in 1846, the territory indicated ceded by Mexico in 1848 and five years later came the Gadsden Purchase.

looms were brought over the mountains. Women, as well as men, had to know how to shoot, mold bullets and dress all kinds of game.

Much more than any colonists of old along the Atlantic, these backwoodsmen were beset by perils and privations. The Mississippi was closed to navigation until the United States bought Louisiana in 1803. Furs had to be carried on pack horses over the mountains, and very little beside the necessary guns and ammunition could be brought back. Travelers were often ambushed, so men journeyed in company, posted sentinels, and tied their food pouches and moccasins to their gun stocks.

with George Rogers Clark. His fame rests on the fact that in the midst of dangers in which most men made early and violent exits from the stage of life, he lived unharmed for more than eighty years. From the mountains to the Missouri, he blazed the way for three generations of settlers. A true backwoodsman, he was unhappy in towns. Whenever population got too thick he always moved west "for elbow room and game for his trusty rifle." Born on the frontier of Pennsylvania in 1735, three years after Washington—Lincoln was ten years old when Boone died at the age of eighty-six

The Fame of Daniel Boone

1554

EXPANSION PERIOD

—he was an intrepid hunter to the last, and he was visited by explorers, hunters, emigrants, and by artists, several of whom made long, wild journeys to paint his noble head. Wholly unlettered, he was a man of keen intelligence, unblemished character and the gentle manners of his Quaker ancestry. Next to Robinson Crusoe, Boone is the boys' hero. His romantic biography is more crowded with stirring adventure than any dime novel.

Kentucky and Tennessee grew so rapidly in population that they were admitted as states in 1792 and 1796, while the first white settlement was not made at Marietta, on the north bank of the Ohio, until 1788. To this point came a pilgrim band of Puritans from the seaport towns of New England. Officers of the Revolution secured a grant of land from Congress, and the government built a fort to protect them. They had money to finance the venture. So they crossed the mountains from Philadelphia in a train of good Connestoga wagons, whose boat-shaped bodies could be lifted from the wheels and poled across streams. In these they carried their families, household goods, tools, seeds and weapons. Military supplies, even small cannon, were sent up the Potomac. Among these emigrants were skilled workmen of every trade. Building the "Second Mayflower" at Fort Pitt, now Pittsburgh, they floated down the Ohio.

How Marietta Began

The Three Streams of Migration

Migration moved to this new region in three great streams, from Albany through central New York, across the mountains of Pennsylvania and up the valley of the Potomac. These are the routes followed by railroads of today—the New York Central, Pennsylvania Central and the Baltimore and Ohio. All the roads used by emigrants from the Atlantic to the Pacific were old Indian trails. The paths worn to deep ruts in the soil by moccasined feet and unshod ponies, were widened to wagon roads, and then graded for railroad beds. Rivers were bridged at ancient fords.

Standing as it did at the head waters of the Ohio, all roads met at Pittsburgh, which for quite half a century was the gateway to the West. By 1800 the town had 1,500 people, most of whom were engaged in boat building, ferrying and outfitting emigrants. Upon the high water of spring, a procession of flatboats moved down the flood to towns on both banks of the Ohio. These were not backwoodsmen. Hard times, following the Revolution, had ruined many of the oldest and best families in America, and they made a new start in the West, where land was cheap. Planters from the southern tidewater laid out new plantations in Kentucky and Tennessee. Into the region north of the Ohio were attracted eastern men of college education, professional training, and business experience, for public lands in the Northwest Territory had, for the first time in history, been set aside for the support of the public schools.

Settlers Who Weren't Woodsmen

Flatboats were peculiar to the waterways of the Middle West. Twelve feet wide and forty long, with high sides and partially roofed over, they could be steered down stream with a broad oar and tied to trees at night. Flour, pork and lumber were thus floated to New Orleans; and each

PICTURED KNOWLEDGE
"Prairie Schooners" Taking a Boat Ride

Here our artist shows how the "prairie schooners" looked when they were being carried down the Ohio River in one of those flat boats, the lumber in which was afterwards used in building houses. The "pilot" on the roof worked the rudder to steer it. When they came to a sharp bend or a shallow, one of the men would use a long pole to keep the boat from running aground.

carried two families, with all their goods, seeds, tools, weapons and domestic animals. And when a destination was reached, a boat was broken up and the planks used to build houses, stores and shops. Town after town sprang up along the Ohio, and up to the head of navigation on the tributary streams. Wherever canoes, rowed by Frenchmen—for Galliopolis was settled by refugees from the French Revolution—or pirogues poled by Kentucky Negroes, could go, carrying gunpowder and salt, the woodsman's ax and hunter's rifle were heard in the forested hills of Ohio.

This region, too, had to be fought for. The coming of white men had always meant the cutting down of forests, destruction of game and the crowding back of the Indians. The red tribes, alarmed by this invasion, attacked the boats, killed many people and burned clearings and settlements. They waged savage war for five years before they were beaten back, and the southeastern two-thirds of Ohio was secured for white settlers. There were a half million people in the three states west of the mountains when Ohio was admitted to the Union in 1803.

Five Years of War

A Year of Great Events

This was a historic year. It was the date of the Louisiana Purchase, and of the building of Fort Dearborn, at the mouth of the Chicago River. A site having been secured by treaty with the tribes of the Northwest, officers were ordered to proceed from the old garrison at Detroit. The officers and their families went around by sailing vessel,

EXPANSION PERIOD
Where Chicago was Born

This picture which is one of a series of paintings on the walls of the bank of the Central Trust Company of Illinois, in Chicago, may be said to be the birthplace of the great city. It was near this spot that Fort Dearborn stood, and the fort was the nucleus around which first the settlement and then the city grew. The dwelling you see is where John Kinzie, the first Chicago settler, lived.

The First Railroad Station in Chicago

What is now the Northwestern railroad system was begun in Chicago in 1849 with the building of ten miles of road across the swamp to the Desplaines River. On the return trip in November of that year, the first carload of wheat was brought to Chicago. There was then simply a shed for passengers at Kinzie and Halsted streets. The next year the city council granted permission to run the road east to Canal and then to Wells Street and the building you see here was put up. In the rear you see the schooners on the Chicago River near which this building stood. In course of time it was succeeded by a big brick station and this in turn by the magnificent structure, with its marble pillars, occupying a whole block and costing many millions of dollars, which takes care of the Chicago traffic on this great railroad system today.

1557

PICTURED KNOWLEDGE
How Clark Chose a Monument that Nature Built

When the Lewis and Clark Expedition reached this sandstone cliff on the Yellowstone River, Captain Clark named it Pompey's Pillar. Here is the account of it that appeared in the government's official story of the expedition.

"Captain Clark landed to examine a very remarkable rock situated in an extensive bottom on the right. . . It is nearly 400 paces in circumference, 200 feet high and accessible only from the northeast, the other sides being a perpendicular cliff of light-colored rock. The soil on top is five or six feet deep, of good quality and covered with short grass. The Indians have carved the figures of animals and other objects on the sides of the rock and on the top are raised two piles of stones. After enjoying the prospect from this rock, Captain Clark descended and continued his course."

The two piles of stone and the carved figures are gone now but the character and general appearance of the rock is unchanged.

the first one on Lake Michigan since La Salle's ill-fated *Griffin* of 1673. The company of soldiers, guided by French voyageurs, cut their way across southern Michigan and around the lake shore, through three hundred miles of woods, swamp, gullies of streams and billowing sand dunes. Long known as the Great Sauk Trail, then as the Detroit and Chicago Post Road, this is now the route of the Michigan Central railroad.

Thus was reopened, at Chicago, the old portage of the French explorers. The nearest posts were at Fort Wayne and Vincennes. Furs, the only commodity of the country, were sent to Mackinac, whence supplies came up from Detroit. Three hundred miles to the southwest lay the trading post of St. Louis, and the old French mission town, Kaskaskia.

St. Louis, settled in Spanish territory by the French in 1765, had one thousand people—French, Spanish, Indian and Negro—all engaged in the fur trade and river commerce, for it had always had an outlet through New Orleans. There was great excitement in the straggling frontier town in the spring of 1804. Louisiana Territory had been purchased from France the year before, and Meriwether Lewis, private secretary to President Jefferson, and Captain William Clark, brother of the famous George Rogers Clark, were sent to explore it. The extent, character and value of Louisiana were entirely unknown. No one knew the length, dangers or difficulties of that journey. Grave-faced people, who never expected to see these brave, adventurous men again, stood on the banks of the "Big

EXPANSION PERIOD

Muddy" and watched them embark in boats.

Altogether there were thirty, carefully chosen men: nine backwoodsmen from Kentucky, fourteen soldiers, two French Canadian voyageurs, an Indian interpreter, a hunter from the plains and a negro servant, besides the leaders. The party stopped for some days with Daniel Boone, who, at seventy years of age, was living on an estate of 8,000 acres in the Osage country. This had been given to him by Spain, on condition that he and his thirty children and grandchildren should keep the Indians of the district in order. His hunting trips ranged to Nebraska and Kansas. This veteran of the wilds, who had never feared anything, advised the explorers to turn back.

"White men," he said "cannot pass through the country of the savage Sioux." In fact, these Indians were not conquered until our centennial year of 1876, and that after the massacre of Custer's heroic little army.

Jefferson's Tribute to Meriwether Lewis

Meriwether Lewis was a handsome man, with clear, regular features and fine eyes. He is wearing a powdered wig here, with the pigtail looped up in the back—the same fashion that little girls sometimes adopt in the summertime when their braids feel hot on their necks. President Jefferson picked Meriwether Lewis to lead the important expedition into the newly bought Louisiana territory, because of his fitness for such a task. He said of him, in the preface to the first published account of the trip: "His courage was undaunted, his firmness and perseverance yielded to nothing but impossibilities. A rigid disciplinarian, yet tender as a father of those committed to his charge; honest, disinterested, liberal, with a sound understanding, and a scrupulous fidelity to truth."

None but such men, for Clark was of the same caliber, could have pushed through to the Pacific.

Guided by the "Bird Woman"

This was not cheering advice, but the intrepid explorers went on. As it happened, the Missouri turned far west of Sioux territory—instead of running through it, as Boone supposed—and, late in the autumn, Lewis and Clark reached a village of friendly Mandan Indians on the present site of Bismarck, North Dakota. They spent the winter there on the plains; and there they found a guide over the mountains in the person of a young Indian woman, who had been stolen from her home in the Shoshone Valley of Idaho by Sioux warriors, and then sold as a wife to Chabaneau, a French trapper. Light of foot, merry of heart, and with a singing voice which carried the old French chansons taught her by her affectionate husband, she was called the Bird Woman. Longing to see her old home, and knowing the trails, where to find food in the barrens and water in the lava desert, she begged

1559

PICTURED KNOWLEDGE
The Great Explorer's Autograph on the Rock

Captain Clark was the first white man to visit Pompey's Pillar, and his signature on it can be read today. In his notebook for July 25, 1806, he wrote, "I marked my name and the month and year on the rock." You can trace the work of foolish people who have scratched their names in the soft sandstone all around and even over the mark left by William Clark. The Northern Pacific Railroad passes near Pompey's Pillar so one of the officials had this grating put up to protect it.

the privilege of guiding the explorers.

She marched and rowed and swam streams with the men, caught fish, shot game, loaded canoes, set up tents, cooked, and kept the whole party in moccasins, and all the long, rough way she carried her papoose on her back. After passing the Great Falls of the Missouri, Bird Woman found the South Fork of the river. Then, straight as an arrow, she made for the Shoshone Trail, and found the tepees and grazing ponies of the Indian village in the valley. There new guides led the explorers to the Columbia, down which they paddled to the Pacific. They had been given up for dead when they returned to St. Louis late in 1806.

Their stories of vast, grassy plains, covered with herds of deer and buffalo, the lofty mountains, beautiful falls, and the fertile valleys, wooded slopes and mild climate of the coast, fired the imagination of the country. Such a party today would have had a geologist along, *The Plains Called a Desert* and would certainly have found gold and silver, to start a rush to the remotest boundaries of old Louisiana. But it was long before any attempt

EXPANSION PERIOD

was made to settle the Far West. Other and less favorable reports were brought in. In 1806-7 Zebulon Pike went west from St. Louis, and discovered Pike's Peak in Colorado. He and later frontiersmen gave dismal accounts of the plains from Texas to Canada. Perhaps they went in a dry season, when the prairies were burned brown, and deserted by herds and hunters. Certainly they caused this great grain and cattle country to be long marked on the maps: "The Great American Desert." It was thought by most people to be as barren and forbidding as the Sahara.

Then the Wave of Emigration

But, indeed, until after the War of 1812, when many Indian tribes were moved west of the Mississippi, the Middle West could make no further progress. After 1815 a new flood of people poured over the Ohio, thousands and tens of thousands, where there had been hundreds before.

All the old trails through the woods, widened to wagon roads, swarmed with travel. Land in Kentucky, laid out in great plantations, and tilled by slaves, as in Virginia, had become dear. So, many poor folks, like the Lincolns, crossed the Ohio into southern Indiana and Illinois where land was cheap.

Story of the Lincoln Family

The Lincoln family were typical emigrants from the South, at this period. Piling everything they possessed of any value on two pack-horses, they just "lit out fur Indianny," as Lincoln's cousin, Dennis Hanks, once said. A raft was built of logs lashed together, to cross the Ohio. "Abe toted a gun and kept it dry. He was only seven years old, but proud as a turkey cock" to be of use on that hard moving day.

Hardship and Sorrow

Camping in an open-faced pole shack for a year, the family lived

The Bird Woman and Her Papoose

Sacagawea, the Bird Woman of the Shoshone Valley, guided Lewis and Clark over the vast stretches of western wilderness. This statue of her was made by Leonard Crunelle for the Panama Pacific Exposition in San Francisco, and is now in the Art Institute, Chicago. See how the sculptor has shown Sacagawea standing straight and tall, ready to step lightly forward, with head high and brows slightly frowning in the effort to see something in the distance that has caught her sharp Indian eyes. Savages, you know, have much keener eyesight than we have, and they can follow a trail through the wilderness which we shouldn't be able to see at all. This papoose on his mother's back watched her pick out such a trail when he was too young to walk, and no doubt became very expert at it himself. And during all that long journey Sacagawea "marched, and rowed, and swam with the men, caught fish, shot game, loaded canoes, set up tents, cooked, and kept the whole party in moccasins."

1561

PICTURED KNOWLEDGE

The Pioneer Buffet Car

This shows the prairie schooner as fitted up by the more enterprising emigrants who went to California in the gold rush; a "buffet car" and "diner." When the emigrants went into camp, that curtain with the round hole in the center of it was rolled back, the end board lowered, the stove set on it and the pipe run through the roof as you see in the next picture. On the walls hang the kitchen utensils, including the big washpan. On one side is the home-made broom for keeping the floor swept, and in the forward part of the wagon are the beds which were occupied when the family stopped for the night.

rough, whipsawed boards of his mother's coffin. "The misery in that little, green log cabin in the woods" when Nancy Hanks Lincoln died! The little sister Sarah cried all winter, and, to console her, the boys found a baby coon for a pet. Abe studied Webster's spelling book, and wrote with charred wood on the wooden shovel. Books and schools were "sceercer than wild cats in that neck o' the woods."

Fourteen years later, in 1830, the whole family connection "lit out fur Illinois." This time they had ox wagons. It took them two weeks to cut through the

The Buffet Car in Camp

This picture shows one of the ways in which the stove was used when in camp. It was set on a platform at the rear of "Prairie Schooner" with the pipe sticking through a hole made for it in the canvas covering. On the ground is the traveling pantry. Little son is splitting wood to "keep the home fires burning" and mother is just putting something good in the oven —perhaps a cake. What do you say? Certainly it is too thick for a pie, although it may have been a game pie, to be sure.

like Indians, on game, fish, wild berries and pounded corn. The boys learned to trap rabbits, to find honey in the bee trees, to go on coon hunts, and to make moccasins of birch or slippery elm bark, with hickory soles tied on, and even a "little feller" could "drap corn fur pappy" among the stumps of the clearing. The new cabin was scarcely up before the mother died of milk sickness, for the one cow had been poisoned by weeds. The little nine year old boy whittled pegs for his father to put together the

1562

EXPANSION PERIOD

woods, raft across the Wabash, and pry wheels and even steers out of swamps with fence rails, "Abe crackin' a good-natured joke every time he cracked the whip." He helped put up the new cabin on the Sangamon, and split rails and fenced a clearing for corn. Then he "left home for good," at twenty-one.

Times were improving. The village of Salem, twenty miles above Springfield, in which he spent the next twenty years and studied law, was a northern outpost of the settled part of Illinois. But it had a mill, a tavern, all the crafts shops, stores supplied with goods by wagon freight from St. Louis, a good school house, and a school master who could teach Lincoln grammar and help him with surveying. In the state capital he found law books, and men willing to lend them to a poor, ambitious student. Star route mail carriers brought newspapers from the East and cities on the Ohio; and three hundred men of every nationality in the country, traded and voted in the town.

Advantages He Found in Salem

The Fortress on Wheels

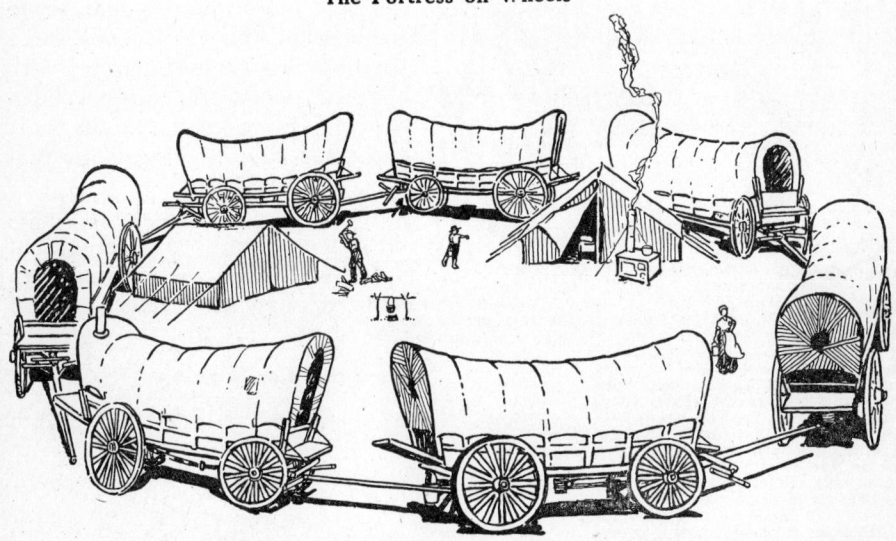

The versatile old prairie schooner might remind us of what Shakespeare said of man; in its time it played many parts. Here an emigrant train is made to play it's a fortress. All the wagons are arranged in a circle. At night the tongue of each wagon was attached to that in front so as to make it more difficult for hostile Indians in case of attack. This arrangement made a kind of fortified town, where the men could screen themselves and take aim at the approaching redskins.

Growth of the Middle West

The Middle West grew fast in population and power. With the admission of Missouri to the Union, in 1821, statehood crossed the Mississippi. In 1825 the Marquis de Lafayette went down the Ohio to St. Louis in a steamboat. In the thirties, Jackson, of Tennessee, was in the White House, and Henry Clay, of Kentucky, was shaping national policies in Congress with his oratory. It is hard to realize now that at this time, when the Ohio Valley was thickly peopled, and travel and trade had become easy and rapid, the region around the Great Lakes could not be settled at all until the Erie Canal was opened from Albany to Buffalo.

This 363-mile "ditch," completed in 1825, gave an all-water route from New York City to the head of Lake Michigan. This made New York instead of Philadelphia, the front door to America, and Chicago superseded Pittsburgh as the gateway to the West. Emigration moving out over Lake Erie, rapidly filled up northern Ohio and Indiana and southern Michigan, and then rolled like a flood over the prairies and hills behind Chicago and Milwaukee, when, after a short war, the last Indians were removed beyond the Mississippi.

The Day of Road Making and Canals

This was the beginning of a feverish era of canal digging and road making. Massachusetts opened a stage coach road from Boston to Albany. The government completed the Cumberland Road up the Potomac Valley to Wheeling. Pennsylvania began the most difficult task of all—a four hundred-mile highway over the mountains, that was part canal, part horsepower railroad. The West, not to be outdone, planned the National Road, to continue the Cumberland Road through the capitals of Ohio, Indiana and Illinois to the Mississippi. Every mile of this was crowded with travel, as fast as it was finished. There was a continuous procession of stage coaches, private carriages, men on horseback, families in caravans, mountains of freight on four-horse wagons, farm wagons loaded with produce, pedestrians with packs on their backs, droves of horses, cattle and sheep. All the world and his wife and children, goods and animals seemed to be moving west.

Lake Erie was connected with the Ohio and the Wabash with canals, and Lake Michigan with the Illinois River. Canal boats, pulled by horses

Kit Carson the "Gentleman" Frontiersman

Kit Carson was as famous in his day as Daniel Boone had been half a century before. This picture was made from an old daguerreotype of him and shows us the frontier guide and Indian fighter, not in the buckskins in which he won his fame, but as a correct gentleman in the fine garments of the latest fashion, for he was a man of the world as well as a frontiersman. We are told that Christopher Carson would have been a scholar had he not loved the wild frontier life so well. He spoke Spanish and was master of innumerable Indian dialects. That he had a kindly, intelligent, handsome face you can see here. The Assistant Surgeon of the United States Army who was with him when he died, has described him as a small man—only 5 feet 6 inches tall—weighing about 160 pounds. His eyes were dark gray and his hair, light brown streaked with gray. He had a large head and a high, broad forehead. His frame, though small, was broad and compact and he was very active.

He was called the "beau of the mountains," for his horse wore a silver-trimmed harness and he himself rode the wilderness trails in the dashing costume of a Mexican rancher. Kit Carson was more greatly feared and respected than any other single trapper in the West, and with one or two companions he could put to flight a party of Indians on the warpath more quickly than could a whole company of regulars.

EXPANSION PERIOD
On the Santa Fe Trail

Goods used to be carried like this on the backs of mules as well as in wagons over the Santa Fe Trail, which had so much to do with the development of our great West. The Santa Fe trail began in St. Louis, ran across Missouri and Arkansas, turned south to El Paso and then continued west by the Gila River to Los Angeles and San Francisco.

trotting on the tow path, made four miles an hour. Little Jimmie Garfield, and many another poor and ambitious boy of the backwoods, drove horses along the tow paths of these early canals. And every center of population was the starting point for stage coaches. In the middle thirties the Detroit-Chicago Post Road, three hundred miles long, was opened through woods, sloughs, gullies and sand dunes.

Many projected canals and turnpike roads were never finished. Before they could even be begun, the era of railroad building opened. Strap rails had, for years, been used for horse cars. On these roads locomotives that looked like fire engines were tried. It was long, however, before they could be used on steep grades, or before sufficient power was developed to pull heavy loads. And every road was stopped on the banks of such rivers as the Hudson, Delaware, Potomac, Ohio and Mississippi, which no one dreamed, as yet, of bridging. Everything had to be ferried over streams of any great width or depth. It was 1848 before the first ten miles of railroad were run out across the swamps west of Chicago. But the very first train found a cargo of wheat waiting at the Desplaines River. When this North Western Railroad was pushed out to Galena on the Mississippi, it was possible to ship lumber from the pineries of Michigan and Wisconsin to build houses for settlers on the prairies of Iowa.

Then Came the Railroads

Fremont and the "Wild West"

Up to the middle of the century the country west of eastern Kansas and the Missouri River was still a wilderness. It was not wholly unknown, however, nor entirely uninhabited. It had its hunters and trappers, and there were forts and trading posts at Omaha and Leaven-

PICTURED KNOWLEDGE

The Great March

This picture by E. H. Blashfield, called simply "Westward," hangs in the Iowa state capitol at Des Moines. western plains in the fashion you see represented here. The roadside was strewn with the bones of their out across the vast prairies, but the spirit of civilization, carrying books, free government and a knowledge work, hardship and suffering. See if you can find all these things and others represented in Blashfield's paint-

worth. In some strange way the old Spanish mission town, mining and ranching center of Santa Fe, had been kept alive for two and a half centuries. Hearing that it was ill-supplied from Mexico, the merchants of St. Louis reopened the Indian trail, now followed by the Santa Fe railroad, and shipped goods regularly by way of mule pack-train. This was in 1822. The Santa Fe Trail had been traveled thus for twenty years when General Fremont began his exploration of our western highlands, and won the name of "The Pathfinder." Taking Kit Carson for a guide, he tramped from Missouri to California and from the Columbia to the Rio Grande.

Going up the North Platte River, he found the South Pass through the Rockies. Thence by way of the Snake and Columbia Rivers he reached the northwest coast, by a shorter and easier route than that of Lewis and Clark forty years before. Pack trains were soon going over this Oregon Trail, to supply the fur-trading posts. Over this and the branching trail through Salt Lake, the present route of the Union Pacific Road, and the older Santa Fe Trail extended through Pueblo and Navajo villages, three thin streams of migration began to flow to Oregon and California. In southern California Fremont had found many old Spanish mission settle-

EXPANSION PERIOD to the Westward

Iowa was settled by emigrants from the East who marched the weary miles between their old homes and the oxen and horses that died on the way. They left the cornfields and settlements behind them when they set of agriculture went with them. They were strong, fearless and sturdy, and their women were used to rough ing.

ments, irrigated farms and sheep ranches. Emigrants from the East were growing wheat in the Sacramento Valley when the close of the Mexican War gave to the United States all the land north of the Rio Grande and back to the Pacific Ocean.

California and Its Gold

The Rush to the Land of Fortune With the discovery of gold in California in 1848, that trickling stream of travel became a torrent, which leaped across 1,500 miles of buffalo plains, jagged mountains, cactus-strewn desert, and towering glacier-capped ranges to the green valleys and pebble-bedded rivers of the coast.

People went by tens of thousands. Easterners took ship at some Atlantic seaport. In the Middle West steam boats carried gold-seekers to New Orleans. The voyage by sea was around Cape Horn or down to Panama. There, as in old Spanish treasure-fleet days, they crossed the fifty-mile-wide Isthmus by mule pack-train. But many proceeded to Chicago, which then had 20,000 people. There they bought the canvas-covered caravans called "Prairie Schooners," horses or oxen, flour, bacon, beans, blankets, clothing, guns, mining tools, and water barrels, for the two-thousand-mile overland journey. Eighty thousand men, some women and a few children passed through Chicago, bound for the gold fields, in the summer of 1849.

In the Geography articles you will find descriptions of the prairie, mountain, desert and coast country, over which passed this historic migration. Many people died on the way. Later comers found their bleaching bones, their broken wagons and the ashes of their camp fires along the trail. But many more did get through all the perils in safety, and mining camps quickly sprang up along the gravelly streams of California. Some found gold and grew rich quickly. Many more were disappointed.

Gold that Grew from the Soil

But very few went back East. They remained to grow golden wheat, golden oranges, to herd sheep and work the forests. The beautiful coast land had many other sources of wealth besides its precious minerals. California was admitted as a state in 1850, four years after Iowa and eleven years before Kansas.

But much of the travel for the next twenty years was by the primitive methods described. The Salt Lake Trail was extended to Sacramento, and the Santa Fe Trail to Los Angeles. Over these, pack-trains carried freight, and stage coaches carried passengers. Mail was by pony express, fleet riders covering a distance of two thousand miles in ten days. A telegraph line spanned the continent in 1861. And here and there, in every part of the highlands, groups of men appeared. Hunters became prospectors searching for gold. The precious metal was discovered, first in Colorado, then in Nevada and Utah, and silver in Montana, Arizona and many scattered places. Denver sprang up at the foot of the mountain wall, a halfway station for an immense freight business across the plains and central supply depot for the miners.

The Railroads to the Coast

All this development led to the building of the Union Pacific Railroad, a task of engineering, financing and endurance of men which still excites the wonder of the world. And while it was being pushed across mountain and desert, Eads was spanning the Mississippi with a steel-arch bridge, resting on piers, driven through a hundred-foot depth of river mud.

Fourteen years later, in 1883, the Northern Pacific Railroad was completed from Lake Superior to Puget Sound. It was built to reach the mines of the mountain and coast states. But that and the Southern Pacific, Santa Fe and Great Northern roads all opened up new corn and wheat country, and a ranching region at the base of the mountain wall, which stretched from Texas to Canada. The old "Great American Desert" disappeared from the maps.

What a historic march across the continent! Boone reached Kentucky in 1769. In 1869, exactly a hundred years later, the whistle of the locomotive answered the salute of steamers on San Francisco Bay. In the beginning of that century there were not more than 2,000,000 in the thirteen colonies along the Atlantic seaboard. At the end of it there were 40,000,000 between the two oceans, and one-third of these were west of the Alleghenies. In another story you will learn where all these brave, determined people came from.

Fremont, "The Pathfinder"

The mountains are put in the background of John G. Fremont's picture because he was a famous explorer of the Rockies; the cannon tells you that he saw service on many battlefields. He was a major-general in the United States army, as you can see by the two stars on his epaulettes. Fremont was a brave soldier and an unusually good explorer. He also knew how to write interesting descriptions of his expeditions, but he was too fiery and independent to submit to discipline easily, and he lacked the organizing ability necessary for managing campaigns such as were required of him in the Civil War. However, he held many honorable government positions and did his work creditably in them. He was twice nominated for the presidency. On account of his brilliant achievements as an explorer, he came to be known as "The Pathfinder," and received medals from the Royal Geographical Society of London and the Geographical Society of Berlin.

The Fatherland

Where is the true man's fatherland?
Is it where he by chance is born?
Doth not the yearning spirit scorn
In such scant borders to be spanned?
Oh yes! his fatherland must be
As the blue heaven, wide and free!

Is it alone where freedom is,
Where God is God and man is man?
Doth he not claim a broader span
For the soul's love of home than this?
Oh yes! his fatherland must be
As the blue heaven, wide and free!

Where'er a human heart doth wear
Joy's myrtle-wreath or sorrow's gyves,
Where'er a human spirit strives
After a life more true and fair,
There is the true man's birthplace grand,
His is the world-wide fatherland!

Where'er a single slave doth pine,
Where'er one man may help another—
Thank God for such a birthright, brother—
That spot of earth is thine and mine!
There is the true man's birthplace, grand,
His is a world-wide fatherland!

      JAMES RUSSELL LOWELL